Praise for *Job*

"Shields's commentary is highly readable and informed by careful scholarship on the text and its ancient Near Eastern contexts. His proposals for Job's interpretation for his contemporary Christian perspective are presented with nuance."

Rachelle Gilmour, Bromby Associate Professor of Old Testament, Trinity College, University of Divinity, Australia

"Martin Shields finds the perfect balance between providing helpful background on the ancient context, offering profound insights into the text, and giving wise counsel on how to understand this troubling book in the light of Scripture, and how to apply its wisdom to our lives today."

David T. Lamb, MacRae Professor of Old Testament, Missio Seminary

"They don't know everything about God's ways or the complexities of the universe. Not Job. Not his friends. Not Elihu. Accepting our limitations, according to Martin Shields's commentary on Job, is paramount to learning wisdom in the face of catastrophe and suffering. This study explores Job in its ancient and biblical contexts offering pointed and reliable interpretation. Shields's commentary will assist pastors, students, and Christian readers. It has already helped me with the most difficult passages of Job."

Gary Edward Schnittjer, Distinguished Professor of Old Testament, Cairn University

"Martin Shields remarkably combines rigorous scholarship with pastoral and practical sensitivity in this impressive volume that unpacks one of Scripture's most challenging books. He masterfully confronts questions concerning suffering, justice, and divine sovereignty, while tracing the biblical story's arc to its fulfillment in Christ."

David Emanuel, Associate Professor of Hebrew Bible and Hebrew Language, Westmont College

"Martin Shields provides the reader with an exegetically rich and theologically sensitive reading of this challenging book. Taking fully into account the ancient Near Eastern context of the book of Job, Shields demonstrates time and again the significance of Job for the twenty-first century."

W. Dennis Tucker, Professor of Christian Scripture, George W. Truett Theological Seminary, Baylor University

"This is an invaluable guide to the book of Job. With close attention to Hebrew text and ancient Near Eastern literature, Shields navigates reade through the complexities and questions inherent in the book. More than clarifying the logic of the text and the story of the book of Job, Shields illuminates its place within the story of God and its contributions to the life of faith. In the face of undeserved and inexplicable suffering, Shields leads readers to God and to God's governance of and involvement in finite human lives, each of which bring comfort."

> **Christopher Ansberry**, Associate Professor of Biblical and Theological Studies, Grove City College

"Rooted in thorough scholarly study, Shields's nuanced treatment balances Job's complexity with practical application, honoring its mystery within a theologically faithful exposition. With insight and grace, he reads Job's wisdom in the light of the Gospel in this accessible and compelling commentary."

> **Paul S. Evans**, Professor of Old Testament, McMaster Divinity College

"Martin Shields's commentary on Job is faithful, fresh, and fearless. He is unafraid to challenge assumptions about the book and brings a compelling new reading which is anchored in the text and its ancient context. He illuminates the pith and pathos of this passionate ancient work in a way which modern readers will find challenging, sensitive, and deeply rewarding. It is must-read for those wanting insight into Job and the problem of suffering."

> **George Athas**, Director of Research, Moore Theological College

"Martin Shields has produced an extremely useful commentary. He displays an obvious command of the comparative Ancient Near Eastern literature. His explanations of the text are careful, lucid, and do not shy away from honestly addressing the more troubling passages in the book. The connections to the New Testament, Christ, and contemporary Christian living are astutely drawn with a truly pastoral concern. Readers, teachers, and preachers will be well served by this contribution to the series."

> **Jerry Shepherd**, Emeritus Professor of Old Testament, Taylor Seminary

Praise for the Story of God Bible Commentary Series

"Getting a story is about more than merely enjoying it. It means hearing it, understanding it, and above all, being impacted by it. This commentary series hopes that its readers not only hear and understand the story but are impacted by it to live in as Christian a way as possible. The editors and contributors set that table very well and open up the biblical story in ways that move us to act with sensitivity and understanding. That makes hearing the story as these authors tell it well worth the time. Well done."

Darrell L. Bock
Dallas Theological Seminary

"The Story of God Bible Commentary series invites readers to probe how the message of the text relates to our situations today. Engagingly readable, it not only explores the biblical text but offers a range of applications and interesting illustrations."

Craig S. Keener
Asbury Theological Seminary

"I love The Story of God Bible Commentary series. It makes the text sing and helps us hear the story afresh."

John Ortberg
Former Pastor of Menlo Park Presbyterian Church

"In this promising new series of commentaries, believing biblical scholars bring not only their expertise but their own commitment to Jesus and insights into today's culture to the Scriptures. The result is a commentary series that is anchored in the text but lives and breathes in the world of today's church with its variegated pattern of socioeconomic, ethnic, and national diversity. Pastors, Bible study leaders, and Christians of all types who are looking for a substantive and practical guide through the Scriptures will find these volumes helpful."

Frank Thielman
Beeson Divinity School

"I'm a storyteller. Through writing and speaking I talk and teach about understanding the Story of God throughout Scripture and about letting God reveal more of his story as I live it out. Thus I am thrilled to have a commentary series based on the story of God—a commentary that helps me to Listen to the Story, that Explains the Story, and then encourages me to probe how to Live the Story. A perfect tool for helping every follower of Jesus to walk in the story that God is writing for them."

Judy Douglass
Director of Women's Resources, Cru

"The Bible is the story of God and his dealings with humanity from creation to new creation. The Bible is made up more of stories than of any other literary genre. Even the psalms, proverbs, prophecies, letters, and the Apocalypse make complete sense only when set in the context of the grand narrative of the entire Bible. This commentary series breaks new ground by taking all these observations seriously. It asks commentators to listen to the text, to explain the text, and to live the text. Some of the material in these sections overlaps with introduction, detailed textual analysis and application, respectively, but only some. The most riveting and valuable part of the commentaries are the stories that can appear in any of these sections, from any part of the globe and any part of church history, illustrating the text in any of these areas. Ideal for preaching and teaching."

Craig L. Blomberg
Denver Seminary

"Pastors and lay people will welcome this new series, which seeks to make the message of the Scriptures clear and to guide readers in appropriating biblical texts for life today."

Daniel I. Block
Wheaton College and Graduate School

"An extremely valuable and long overdue series that includes comment on the cultural context of the text, careful exegesis, and guidance on reading the whole Bible as a unity that testifies to Christ as our Savior and Lord."

Graeme Goldsworthy
author of *According to Plan*

JOB

The Story of God Bible Commentary

JOB

Martin A. Shields

Tremper Longman III & Scot McKnight
General Editors

ZONDERVAN ACADEMIC

ZONDERVAN ACADEMIC

Job

Published by Zondervan, 3950 Sparks Drive SE, Suite 101, Grand Rapids, MI 49546, USA. Zondervan is a registered trademark of The Zondervan Corporation, L.L.C., a wholly owned subsidiary of HarperCollins Christian Publishing, Inc.

Requests for information should be addressed to customercare@harpercollins.com.

Zondervan titles may be purchased in bulk for educational, business, fundraising, or sales promotional use. For information, please email SpecialMarkets@Zondervan.com.

Library of Congress Cataloging-in-Publication Data

Names: Shields, Martin A., 1965- author | Longman, Tremper, III editor | McKnight, Scot editor
Title: Job / Martin A. Shields ; Tremper Longman III & Scot McKnight, general editors.
Description: Grand Rapids, Michigan : Zondervan, [2025] | Series: The story of God Bible commentary | Includes index.
Identifiers: LCCN 2025012387 (print) | LCCN 2025012388 (ebook) | ISBN 9780310491064 hardcover | ISBN 9780310491071 ebook
Subjects: LCSH: Bible. Job--Commentaries.
Classification: LCC BS1415.53 .S54 2025 (print) | LCC BS1415.53 (ebook) |
DDC 223/.107--dc23/eng/20250613
LC record available at https://lccn.loc.gov/2025012387
LC ebook record available at https://lccn.loc.gov/2025012388

HarperCollins Publishers, Macken House, 39/40 Mayor Street Upper, Dublin 1, D01 C9W8, Ireland (https://www.harpercollins.com)

Cover design: Ron Huizinga
Cover image: Stockphoto.com
Interior typesetting: Kait Lamphere

Printed in the United States of America

25 26 27 28 29 LBC 5 4 3 2 1

For all who suffer but continue to wrestle with God.

Old Testament series

1 ▪ Genesis—*Tremper Longman III*
2 ▪ Exodus—*Christopher J. H. Wright*
3 ▪ Leviticus—*Jerry E. Shepherd*
4 ▪ Numbers—*Jay Sklar*
5 ▪ Deuteronomy—*Myrto Theocharous*
6 ▪ Joshua—*Lissa M. Wray Beal*
7 ▪ Judges—*Athena E. Gorospe*
8 ▪ Ruth/Esther—*Marion Ann Taylor*
9 ▪ 1–2 Samuel—*Paul S. Evans*
10 ▪ 1–2 Kings—*David T. Lamb*
11 ▪ 1–2 Chronicles—*Carol M. Kaminski*
12 ▪ Ezra/Nehemiah—*Douglas J. Green*
13 ▪ Job—*Martin A. Shields*
14 ▪ Psalms—*Yohanna Katanacho*
15 ▪ Proverbs—*Ryan P. O'Dowd*
16 ▪ Ecclesiastes/Song of Songs—*George Athas*
17 ▪ Isaiah—*Mark J. Boda*
18 ▪ Jeremiah/Lamentations—*Andrew G. Shead*
19 ▪ Ezekiel—*Havilah Dharamraj*
20 ▪ Daniel—*Wendy L. Widder*
21 ▪ Minor Prophets I—*Beth M. Stovell*
22 ▪ Minor Prophets II—*Beth M. Stovell*

New Testament series

1 ▪ Matthew—*Rodney Reeves*
2 ▪ Mark—*Timothy G. Gombis*
3 ▪ Luke—*Kindalee Pfremmer DeLong*
4 ▪ John—*Nicholas Perrin*
5 ▪ Acts—*Dean Pinter*
6 ▪ Romans—*Michael F. Bird*
7 ▪ 1 Corinthians—*Justin K. Hardin*
8 ▪ 2 Corinthians—*Judith A. Diehl*
9 ▪ Galatians—*Nijay K. Gupta*
10 ▪ Ephesians—*Mark D. Roberts*
11 ▪ Philippians—*Lynn H. Cohick*
12 ▪ Colossians/Philemon—*Esau McCaulley*
13 ▪ 1, 2 Thessalonians—*John Byron*
14 ▪ 1, 2 Timothy, Titus—*Marius Nel*
15 ▪ Hebrews—*Radu Gheorghita*
16 ▪ James—*Mariam J. Kamell*
17 ▪ 1 Peter—*Dennis R. Edwards*
18 ▪ 2 Peter, Jude—*Abson Joseph*
19 ▪ 1, 2, & 3 John—*Constantine R. Campbell*
20 ▪ Revelation—*Jonathan A. Moo*
21 ▪ Sermon on the Mount—*Scot McKnight*

Contents

Acknowledgments

Writing a commentary on any part of the Bible is neither a simple task nor a quick one. Perhaps surprisingly it is also not a lonely or solitary task but grows out of the contributions of many people. As is traditional and appropriate, I'd like to thank the people who have contributed to bringing this book to publication.

A few years ago, the Old Testament editor for The Story of God Bible Commentary Series, Tremper Longman, qualified a point he made about there being no great urgency to complete this commentary by adding that he would like me to have completed this work before he died. I was tempted then to ask about his health (which, I'm happy to report, was excellent). Nonetheless, I suspect there were times when I exercised his patience and left him wondering about just how long I might take! But aside from thanking Tremper for his patience—one might be tempted to say he has shown the patience of Job—I would also thank both Tremper and George Athas for their guidance, wisdom, and advice as this commentary grew. Their input has improved the final version of this commentary substantially.

Some years ago, I adapted my PhD dissertation on Qoheleth for publication as a book. While I was doing the initial copyediting, I discovered one place where I had quoted the Hebrew text of Ecclesiastes but had accidentally omitted the Hebrew word for "not" (which, as you may be aware, results in a quite different meaning for most sentences)! My error had not been noted by anyone who had read the dissertation to that point. This has made clear the importance of good editors in the production of books! And so, I am most appreciative to Katya Covrett, Lee Fields, and all those at Zondervan tasked with the burden of taking the text I have created and working it into the final form that has now found its way into your hands.

Another observation that I am sure many commentary writers can relate to is the way it can somewhat consume one's thinking. So, to everyone who has enjoyed years of me pointing out that Job's story has something to say to just about every circumstance in life, and so proving that it is possible to turn almost any conversation to Job, I thank you. Those conversations have helped me to come to a better understanding of Job as a whole and a better understanding of how it speaks to us today. Your suffering at my hands has borne fruit in this volume, so thank you all.

To my three sons Simon, Wesley, and Alec, my hope is that the lessons of Job help you as you live your lives and prepare for the future.

Finally, I wish to thank my wonderful wife, Wendy. She has not only encouraged me to get back to work on completing this book but also provided a welcome distraction at times when a break was needed. Your wisdom and love have gotten me back on track when I desperately needed it.

The Story of God Bible Commentary Series

Why another commentary series?

In the first place, no single commentary can exhaust the meaning of a biblical book. The Bible is unfathomably rich, and no single commentator can explore every aspect of its message.

In addition, good commentary not only explores what the text meant in the past but also its continuing significance. In other words, the Word of God may not change, but culture does. Think of what we have seen in the last twenty years. We now communicate predominantly through the internet and email. We read our news on iPads and computers. We carry smartphones in our pockets through which we can call our friends, check the weather forecast, make dinner reservations, and get an answer to virtually any question we might have.

Today we have more readable and accurate Bible versions in English than any generation in the past. Bible distribution in the present generation has been very successful; more people own more Bibles than previous generations. However, studies have shown that although people have better access to the Bible than ever before, people aren't reading the Bibles they own, and they struggle to understand what they do read.

The Story of God Bible Commentary hopes to help people, particularly clergy but also laypeople, read the Bible with understanding not only of its ancient meaning but also of its continuing significance for us today in the twenty-first century. After all, readers of the Bible change too. These cultural shifts, our own personal developments, and the progress in intellectual questions, as well as growth in biblical studies and theology and discoveries of new texts and new paradigms for understanding the contexts of the Bible—each of these elements work on an interpreter so that the person who reads the Bible today asks different questions from different angles.

Culture shifts, but the Word of God remains. That is why we as editors of The Story of God Bible Commentary, a commentary based on the New International Version 2011 (NIV 2011), are excited to participate in this new series of commentaries on the Bible. This series is designed to speak to this generation with the same Word of God. We are asking the authors to explain what the Bible says to the sorts of readers who pick up commentaries so they can understand not only what Scripture says but what it means for today. The Bible does not change, but relating it to our culture changes constantly and in differing ways in different contexts.

As editors of the Old Testament series, we recognize that Christians have a hard time knowing exactly how to relate to the Scriptures that were written before the coming of Christ. The world of the Old Testament is a strange one to those of us who live in the West in the twenty-first century. We read about strange customs, warfare in the name of God, sacrifices, laws of ritual purity, and more and wonder whether it is worth our while or even spiritually healthy to spend time reading this portion of Scripture that is chronologically, culturally, and—seemingly—theologically distant from us.

But it is precisely here that The Story of God Commentary Series Old Testament makes its most important contribution. The New Testament does not replace the Old Testament; the New Testament fulfills the Old Testament. We hear God's voice today in the Old Testament. In its pages he reveals himself to us and also his will for how we should live in a way that is pleasing to him.

Jesus himself often reminds us that the Old Testament maintains its importance to the lives of his disciples. Luke 24 describes Jesus's actions and teaching in the period between his resurrection and ascension. Strikingly, the focus of his teaching is on how his followers should read the Old Testament (here called "Moses and all the Prophets," "Scriptures," and "the law of Moses, the Prophets and Psalms"). To the two disciples on the road to Emmaus, he says:

> "How foolish you are, and how slow to believe all that the prophets have spoken! Did not the Messiah have to suffer these things and then enter his glory?" And beginning with Moses and all the Prophets, he explained to them what was said in all the Scriptures concerning himself. (Luke 24:25–27)

Then to a larger group of disciples he announces:

> "This is what I told you while I was still with you: Everything must be fulfilled that is written about me in the law of Moses, the Prophets and the Psalms." Then he opened their minds so they could understand the Scriptures. (Luke 24:44–45)

The Story of God Bible Commentary Series takes Jesus's words on this matter seriously. Indeed, it is the first series that has as one of its deliberate goals the identification of the trajectories (historical, typological, and theological) that land in Christ in the New Testament. Every commentary in the series will, in the first place, exposit the text in the context of its original reception. We will interpret it as we believe the original author intended his contemporary audience to read it. But then we will also read the text in the light of the death and resurrection of Jesus. No other commentary series does this important work consistently in every volume.

To achieve our purpose of expositing the Old Testament in its original setting and also from a New Testament perspective, each passage is examined from three angles.

Listen to the Story. We begin by listening to the text in order to hear the voice of God. We first read the passage under study. We then go on to consider the background to the passage by looking at any earlier Scripture passage that informs our understanding of the text. At this point too we will cite and discuss possible ancient Near Eastern literary connections. After all, the Bible was not written in a cultural vacuum, and an understanding of its broader ancient Near Eastern context will often enrich our reading.

Explain the Story. The authors are asked to explain each passage in light of the Bible's grand story. It is here that we will exposit the text in its original Old Testament context. This is not an academic series, so the footnotes will be limited to the kinds of books and articles to which typical Bible readers and preachers will have access. Authors are given the freedom to explain the text as they read it, though you will not be surprised to find occasional listings of other options for reading the text. The emphasis will be on providing an accessible explanation of the passage, particularly on those aspects of the text that are difficult for a modern reader to understand, with an emphasis on theological interpretation.

Live the Story. Reading the Bible is not just about discovering what it meant back then; the intent of The Story of God Bible Commentary is to probe how this text might be lived out today as that story continues to march on in the life of the church.

Here, in the spirit of Christ's words in Luke 24, we will suggest ways in which the Old Testament text anticipates the gospel. After all, as Augustine famously put it, "the New Testament is in the Old Testament concealed, the Old Testament is in the New Testament revealed." We believe that this section will be particularly important for our readers who are clergy who want to present Christ even when they are preaching from the Old Testament.

The Old Testament also provides teaching concerning how we should live today. However, the authors of this series are sensitive to the tremendous impact that Christ's coming has on how Christians appropriate the Old Testament into their lives today.

It is the hope and prayer of the editors and all the contributors that our work will encourage clergy to preach from the Old Testament and laypeople to study this wonderful, yet often strange, portion of God's Word to us today.

Tremper Longman III, general editor Old Testament
George Athas, Mark Boda, and Myrto Theocharous, editors

Abbreviations

ÄAT	Äegypten und Altes Tedstament
AB	Anchor Bible
ABR	*Australian Biblical Review*
AIL	Ancient Israel and Its Literature
ANEP	*The Ancient Near East in Pictures Relating to the Old Testament.* 2nd ed. Edited by James Pritchard. Princeton: Princeton University Press, 1969
ANET	*Ancient Near Eastern Texts Relating to the Old Testament.* Edited by James Pritchard. 3rd ed. Princeton: Princeton University Press, 1969
BA	*Biblical Archaeologist*
BASOR	*Bulletin of the American Schools of Oriental Research*
BCOTWP	Baker Commentary on the Old Testament Wisdom and Psalms
BDAG	Danker, Frederick W., Walter Bauer, William F. Arndt, and F. Wilbur Gingrich. *Greek-English Lexicon of the New Testament and Other Early Christian Literature.* 3rd ed. Chicago: University of Chicago Press, 2000 (Danker-Bauer-Arndt-Gingrich)
BeO	*Bibbia e oriente*
Bib	*Biblica*
BibleRec	*Journal of the Bible and Its Reception*
BZAW	Beihefte zur Zeitschrift für die alttestamentliche Wissenschaft
CBQ	*Catholic Biblical Quarterly*
CEB	Common English Bible
ConBOT	Coniectanea Biblica: Old Testament Series
COS	*The Context of Scripture.* Edited by William W. Hallo and K. Lawson Younger Jr. 4 vols. Leiden: Brill, 2003–2017
CSB	Christian Standard Bible
CTA	*Corpus des tablettes en cuneiforms à Ras Shamra-Ugarit de 1929 à 1939.* Edited by Andrée Herdner. Mission de Ras Shamra 10. Paris: Paul Guethner, 1963
DBSJ	*Detroit Biblical Seminary Journal*
DCH	*Dictionary of Classical Hebrew.* Edited by David J. A. Clines. 9 vols. Sheffield: Sheffield Phoenix, 1993–2014

EQ	*Encyclopedia of the Qur'ān*
ESV	English Standard Version
EvT	*Evangelische Theologie*
GNT	Good News Translation
FOTL	Forms of the Old Testament Literature
HACL	History, Archaeology, and Culture of the Levant
HALOT	*The Hebrew and Aramaic Lexicon of the Old Testament*. Ludwig Koehler, Walter Baumgartner, and Johann J. Stamm. Translated and edited under the supervision of Mervyn E. J. Richardson. 4 vols. Leiden: Brill, 1994–1999
HTR	*Harvard Theological Review*
HUCA	*Hebrew Union College Annual*
IBC	Interpretation: A Bible Commentary for Teaching and Preaching
ISBE	*The International Standard Bible Encyclopedia*. Edited by Geoffrey W. Bromiley. 4 vols. Grand Rapids: Eerdmans, 1979
JAOS	*Journal of the American Oriental Society*
JB	Jerusalem Bible
JBL	*Journal of Biblical Literature*
JESOT	*Journal for the Evangelical Study of the Old Testament*
JETS	*Journal of the Evangelical Theological Society*
JHebS	*Journal of Hebrew Scriptures*
JJS	*Journal of Jewish Studies*
JNES	*Journal of Near Eastern Studies*
JPS	Jewish Publication Society
JQR	*Jewish Quarterly Review*
JSOT	*Journal for the Study of the Old Testament*
JSOTSup	Journal for the Study of the Old Testament Supplement Series
JSS	*Journal of Semitic Studies*
KJV	King James Version
KTU	*Die keilalphabetischen Text aus Ugarit*. Edited by M. Dietrich, O. Lorentz, and J. Sanmartin. Münster: Ugarit-Verlag, 2013. 3rd enl. ed. of *KTU: The Cuneiform Texts from Ugarit, Ras Ibn Hani, and Other Places*. Edited by M. Dietrich, O. Lorentz, and J. Sanmartin. Münster: Ugarit-Verlag, 1995 (= *CTU*)
LEB	Lexham English Bible
LHBOTS	Library of Hebrew Bible/Old Testament Studies
NAC	New American Commentary
NASB	New American Standard Bible

NET	New English Translation Bible
NETS	*A New English Translation of the Septuagint.* Edited by Albert Pietersma and Benjamin G. Wright. New York: Oxford University Press, 2007
NIB	*The New Interpreter's Bible.* Edited by Leander E. Keck. 12 vols. Nashville: Abingdon, 1994–2004
NICOT	New International Commentary on the Old Testament
NIV	New International Version
NIVAC	NIV Application Commentary
NJB	New Jerusalem Bible
NJPS	*Tanakh: The Holy Scriptures: The New JPS Translation according to the Traditional Hebrew Text*
NKJV	New King James Version
NRSVue	New Revised Standard Version, updated edition
OBO	Orbis Biblicus et Orientalis
RC	*Religion Compass*
REBC	The Expositor's Bible Commentary. Revised edition. Edited by Tremper Longman III and David E Garland. 13 vols. Grand Rapids: Zondervan, 2010
RSV	Revised Standard Version
SAACT	State Archives of Assyria Cuneiform Texts
SBL	Society of Biblcal Literature
TJ	*Trinity Journal*
TOTC	Tyndale Old Testament Commentaries
TynBul	*Tyndale Bulletin*
VT	*Vetus Testamentum*
VTSup	Supplements to Vetus Testamentum
WBC	Word Biblical Commentary
WUNT	Wissenschaftliche Untersuchungen zum Neuen Testament
ZAW	*Zeitschrift für die alttestamentliche Wissenschaft*
ZIBBCOT	Zondervan Illustrated Bible Backgrounds Commentary (Old Testament)

Introduction

The Theme of the Book of Job

In 1873, the lawyer and devout Christian Horatio Spafford planned a trip for his family to England. Work prevented Horatio from joining his wife and four young daughters, who set out on the steamship *Ville du Havre* across the Atlantic toward their holiday destination. On November 22, 1873, their ship was struck by the Scottish ship *Loch Earn*. The damage to both vessels was extensive, and the *Ville du Havre* sank in only twelve minutes with the loss of 226 of the 313 people on board. Among the dead were all four of Spafford's daughters—only his wife, Anna, survived. Spafford would famously go on to pen the hymn, "It Is Well with My Soul," expressing his continued faith in spite of the tragedy. We admire such faith, but we, while believing in a sovereign God, are also led to ask why did this happen when God could easily have prevented it?

Stories of tragedies like this are not hard to find, and many are much closer to home. A few years ago, my friend Anne and her husband Will were minding their grandchildren when Will set out to walk the short distance to the shops to get some milk. Will would never return home—he was struck and killed by a car while crossing a local road. The driver of the car was at fault and charged by police. It is difficult to grasp the impact such a tragedy has on the lives of those most immediately affected by it. For Christians, tragedy is invariably a time to come together in shared grief to "mourn with those who mourn" (Rom 12:15; Sir 7:34 [NRSVue]) and to pray. But it can also be a time when hard questions are asked. If God is truly sovereign, why would he not simply have prevented the accident in the first place? Why allow—or even inflict—suffering of this magnitude on his people?

The biblical wisdom literature, particularly the books of Job and Ecclesiastes, provide some answers to questions like these. In some respects, the fact that the Bible deals with such questions is a sign that they have been asked by God's people throughout history. Ecclesiastes recognizes the problem and the teacher, known by the Hebrew title Qoheleth, acknowledges that things do not make sense—a human being cannot discern meaning in the most difficult events of their life. Job gets even more personal, with Job himself suffering in the worst way possible: losing his children, his possessions, his social standing, and his health. He cannot fathom why this has all happened to him. However, unlike the book of Ecclesiastes, God offers a specific answer to Job's questions—even if many find that answer (which comes in the form of many questions) perplexing or unsatisfying. As we shall see in what follows, God's questions of Job do ultimately have something very clear to say both to Job and to us. I would be so bold to suggest that the message of the book of Job functions to make faith in a senseless world—a world where pain and suffering do not seem to be distributed fairly on the guilty and innocent—possible. In short—and I am hesitant to give away the message of the book so early in the piece, but here it goes—, God's unanswerable questions make it clear to Job, and hopefully to the reader of the book of Job, that we live in a universe that is complex beyond our understanding and even beyond our imagining. In such a universe, should we really expect to understand all that happens, or should we trust the Creator who does understand and even orchestrate all that exists and all that happens?

Job in the Story of God

The book of Job raises a number of questions about God and what he is like, and some of the answers are not all that obvious. Beginning with the obvious, it is clear that God in the book of Job is the God of Israel whose name is Yahweh. It is important to acknowledge this at the outset, because most of the characters in Job are not Israelites and so this might be a little surprising (although it does lend support to the idea that the entire story is set in patriarchal times). More importantly, however, is the fact that although the book does not provide a comprehensive description of Yahweh and sometimes may describe him in ambiguous terms, the identification of God as Yahweh means that we, as the readers of Job, are expected to fill out the details and resolve any ambiguities by reference to information found elsewhere in the Bible. Job's God is the God of Abraham, Isaac, and Jacob. He is the God of Israel. He is the Creator of the heavens and the earth. He is the God we come to know through his dealings with the people of Israel in the Old Testament and who will be fully revealed as the Trinitarian God with the arrival of Jesus in the New Testament. Job's God is not an unknown God and not a God about whom we know nothing, thus allowing us only to make inferences from what we read in Job. No, we know this God, for we have met him in the story of Israel, the story of the church. This God is the God whose story spans all sixty-six books of the Old and New Testaments and the one whom we ultimately meet in the person of Jesus. As we read of God in Job, we know who Job is dealing with.

Beyond this, however, the book of Job does highlight some aspects of God's nature that are important both in the events of the book as well as in the way modern readers relate to God and understand the events of Job. For one, it is clear that God is absolutely sovereign. Even when the Satan[1] comes into Yahweh's presence to question Job's motives for his devotion to God, nothing happens without Yahweh's approval. Then, this is further reflected throughout the dialogues, which constitute the bulk of the book, where both Job and his friends work with the assumption that the Almighty stands behind the calamities that have befallen Job and his family. Finally, when Yahweh confronts Job, his words, which describe his vast wisdom, reveal that nothing in nature lies outside his control, even the great and terrifying Leviathan, even the stars of the heavens. God alone is in control of all that happens, and so Job is right to turn to God for answers to his predicament, for he alone knows the way to that most hidden wisdom (see Job 28).

For many readers, however, the book also raises some disturbing questions about God and his actions toward Job, questions that should not be dismissed. Job, it would seem, suffers terribly for the very fact that he is good and appears to suffer simply so that God can win a wager made at the beginning of the book with the Satan. If God knows the heart (1 Sam 16:7), why is it necessary to subject Job to such terrible suffering—and furthermore to do it twice? In short, as some have asked, does the book of Job portray Yahweh as a monster?

Quite a few readers have thought that this is the case. Roland Murphy, for example, wrote that "the scene in the heavenly court may be imaginative, but it raises a nagging question: what kind of a God is this who is willing to prove a point of honor by sorely afflicting a faithful servant? The scene presupposes an understanding of God that the modern reader may be loath to share."[2]

Yet, as we look closely at the book of Job, we will see that this assessment of God in Job is premature. If the message of Job is that we live in a universe of such unimaginable complexity that only God can fully grasp the past, present, future, and all that happens throughout the ages, then it only seems appropriate that we should not know all the answers. One thing that will become clear as we read through the opening chapters is that we are only getting a glimpse behind the scenes when we see into the heavenly court of chapters 1 and 2. There is more going on, and only God knows all of it. Job's suffering is not

---

1. Even though the translations of Job typically use "Satan" as a name, I use the designation "the Satan" because in the Hebrew of Job the noun *Satan* always has the article. See subsection The Satan below in the section The Characters of the introducion.

2. Roland E. Murphy, *The Tree of Life: An Exploration of Biblical Wisdom Literature*, 2nd ed. (Grand Rapids: Eerdmans, 1996), 36.

fully explained by the wager with the Satan. If we do not recognize this, then we fall victim to the same trap that Job's friends did, that is, we believe that we have sufficient information about the world and the way God operates in it to form an infallible judgment![3]

How does Job fit into the Bible's overall story? This has not always been an easy question to answer for Job and for the biblical wisdom literature in general. While the historical books clearly fit into an overarching story, the poetic books do not so obviously find a place within the story of God.

Early Christians tended to see in the character of Job a type of Jesus—the innocent who suffered. Although there are important differences between Job and Jesus, there is nonetheless some truth to this connection. Job may not necessarily have been sinless, but he was blameless (Job 1:5 records Job's being scrupulous about sacrifices to ensure that his children's sins were dealt with, and this implies that he was scrupulous about his own sins as well). What is made abundantly clear is that Job did not deserve the suffering he endured. In this, at least, he foreshadowed Jesus's own suffering.

We can, however, say more about Job's place in the Bible's story. The story of Job sets out to break the connection between suffering and sin—the idea that one who suffers is doing so because they do, in some way, deserve it in payment for something they have done to offend God. This idea, sometimes referred to as retributive justice, could be derived from such passages as Deuteronomy 28 (where it applies to the nation, not the individual), the prophets (who apply the blessings and curses of Deut 28 to the nation), and even the book of Proverbs (which in places makes such a connection between act and consequence).[4] The concept of a one-to-one correspondence between sin and suffering was—and is—so deeply ingrained that the author of Job repeats the argument numerous times through the cycles of speeches in order to debunk it comprehensively (the book of Job is perhaps the most repetitive in the Bible). Job's blamelessness is emphasized by both the narrator and God in the prologue and the epilogue. It is quite clear that Job's suffering was not the result of some sin he had committed. Yet this idea is so entrenched that it persisted to Jesus's day (e.g., Luke 13:1–5; John 9:1–3) and beyond, plaguing us to this day—how often do people ask, "What have I done to deserve this?"

This is not to say that there is no connection between sin and suffering but rather that we cannot assume such a link. Clearly, sometimes the connection is apparent to all: when someone gets into a car after drinking too much

3. For a more detailed discussion of this point, see Martin A. Shields, "Malevolent or Mysterious? God's Character in the Prologue of Job," *TynBul* 61.2 (2010): 255–70.

4. This, I would argue, is a misreading of Proverbs, precisely as is warned about in Prov 26:7!

alcohol and crashes into a telegraph pole, when someone is convicted after having defrauded their employer, when a marriage fails following adultery. Suffering can often be recognized to be the consequence of some specific sin. Yet sometimes it cannot, at least without a prophetic word from God. There are examples of such revelation in the pages of the Bible as well, such as when the prophet Nathan confronted David following his rape of Bathsheba and the murders that were associated with it (2 Sam 12).

Beyond such examples, there are the many instances where it is not clear that some specific sin has resulted in the pain we bear. Furthermore, there is no promise to be found within the pages of the Bible that we should each be given a full and frank explanation for the difficulties we face in our lives. To be sure, many can look back on their lives and see how God has worked through difficult times. *Yet there is no promise and no guarantee that we will be given such insight.*

Breaking this nexus between individual sin and suffering prepared Old Testament believers to accept the possibility that someone may suffer and yet be innocent. This was developed to its greatest end in the book of Isaiah's songs of the suffering servant. There Isaiah built upon this insight and again introduced something new: not only could an innocent person suffer, but they could suffer vicariously (e.g., Isa 53:4–12), that is, on behalf of others. When Jesus, the suffering servant, finally walked the earth, this story was completed. Jesus suffered, but he was himself blameless. He suffered for others, not for his own sins but to bear our iniquities.

What often gets overlooked, however, is that the book of Job is about more than just understanding suffering. It tells us about how God operates in the universe, about the universe itself, and about human finitude. Whenever we wonder what God could possibly be doing in our lives, in the lives of those around us, and in the world in general, Job's story provides us with some light—even if it does not give us specific answers. For when God finally speaks to Job, he does not give detailed specific information to answer Job's questions. Instead, he asks a series of unanswerable questions—questions that highlight just how little Job (and we) know about the complexities of the world in which we live.[5] God questions our understanding and expectations, our

5. While some of the questions asked of Job in chs. 38–41 might now be answered through the growth of human knowledge, the point of the chapters is to pose questions the readers understood but knew that they could not answer. (In other words, it would not have made the point as well to ask more modern unanswered questions such as, "Given an arbitrary compact gauge group, does a non-trivial quantum Yang-Mills theory with a finite mass gap exist?" If we do not understand the question, then the point itself is a little lost, for we do not even know if the question is meaningful.)

presuppositions and our wisdom. Do we really know enough to object to the way our lives pan out? Do we presume to tell God how to run the universe? Can we even begin to comprehend the scale of the complexity of overseeing the operation of a world with billions of people such that everything moves toward the ultimate goal that God has in mind?

In Job, God calls us to accept our limitations and to break free of them, to view the world from above. Whenever we find ourselves doubting God, the book of Job is here to remind us that we live in a complex world in a vastly complex universe and that God's sovereign governance of this universe is complex beyond our imagining, and certainly far beyond our comprehending. Once we have learned this and accepted it, we are left to trust in God's goodness along with Job and all who have suffered and remained faithful before us. There is no promise in Scripture that we will someday understand all that has transpired in our lives, only that "God works for the good of those who love him, who have been called according to his purpose" (Rom 8:28).

Job in the Ancient World

The various issues raised in Job—about innocent or underserved suffering and about the manner in which the gods governed the world of men and women—are not new and were not new when Job was written or even when his story was set. Suffering has always been a problem to be addressed for anyone who has believed in a higher power. As such, it is no surprise that the book of Job is not the only work from the ancient Near East to have delved into these things.

These other ancient texts help us to get a better understanding of the thought world from which the book of Job arose. For one thing, we note that the book itself is set in patriarchal times (see below under Date) before the people of Israel had occupied the promised land, indeed before they existed as a nation. Most of the human protagonists in the story are not Hebrews, and so the author has presented an account of part of Job's life that explicitly interacts with a broad intellectual tradition that is presented as encompassing the ancient Near East. So, as we look to the broader region, we do indeed find these issues addressed in ancient texts, and familiarizing ourselves with those texts provides further insights into the background worldview against which Job stands.

Scholars have identified a number of texts that delve into the problems associated with human suffering. While many of these texts do bear a superficial similarity to Job in terms of the issues raised, closer examination will reveal that Job stands alone in maintaining that the suffering protagonist is actually innocent of a sin that prompted the suffering. For the majority of the other stories, either the intent of the text is not to address suffering at all—it is merely an incidental part of the story—or else the sufferer ultimately proves to have committed some sin that warranted the suffering after all!

Perhaps the earliest example of such a text where the protagonist suffers but ultimately discovers that they had done something to warrant it is the Sumerian work known as "Man and His God," which probably dates from around the end of the third millennium BC. It relates the tale of a young man who is delivered following persistent prayer and lament, which includes a confession of sin. S. N. Kramer wrote of this as follows:

> The proper course for a Sumerian Job to pursue was not to argue and complain in face of seemingly unjustifiable misfortune, but to plead and wail, lament and confess, his inevitable sins and failings.
>
> But will the gods give heed to him, a lone and not very effective mortal, even if he prostrates and humbles himself in heartfelt prayer? Probably not, the Sumerian teachers would have answered.[6]

Its message is largely about persistent devotion to one's personal deity.[7] The Babylonian "Man and His God" is poorly preserved, but it, too, includes references in the sufferer's prayer to sins that may have inadvertently been committed.[8]

Another Babylonian text, known as "Ludlul Bēl Nēmeqi" (also known as "The Poem of the Righteous Sufferer" or "The Babylonian Job") appears on first blush to recount the tale of an innocent sufferer. Ultimately, however, the cause of his misfortune is announced to be his failure to fulfill his religious duties at Marduk's temple, and his misfortune is reversed when he redresses this failing.[9]

Other texts include "The Babylonian Theodicy," which takes the form of a dialogue between the sufferer and his friend. The sufferer decides that there is no benefit in serving the gods only to be rebuked by his friend. Of relevance to our understanding of Job is that the friend does make the point that the ways of the gods are beyond human understanding:

6. Samuel Noah Kramer, *The Sumerians: Their History, Culture, and Character* (Chicago: University of Chicago Press, 1963), 125–26.

7. See Nili Samet, "Mesopotamian Wisdom," in *The Wiley Blackwell Companion to Wisdom Literature*, ed. Samuel L. Adams and Matthew Goff (Hoboken, NJ: Wiley & Sons, 2020), 336.

8. "Dialogue Between a Man and His God," trans. Benjamin R. Foster (*COS* 1.151:485).

9. Alan Lenzi, *Suffering in Babylon: Ludlul Bēl Nēmeqi and the Scholars, Ancient and Modern*, OBO 300 (Leuven: Peeters, 2023).

> The strategy of a god is [as remote as] innermost heaven,
> The command of a goddess cannot be dr[awn out].
> . . .
> Divine purpose is as remote as innermost heaven,
> It is too difficult to understand, people cannot understand it.[10]

The Babylonian "Dialogue of Pessimism" is another dialogical text presenting a discussion taking place between a master and his sycophantic servant. Their interaction follows a repeated pattern wherein the master proposes a course of action that the servant wholeheartedly endorses only to have the master change his mind, after which the servant wholeheartedly supports the reversed decision. The pattern is reflected in the following extract:

> "Slave, oblige me again!" "Here, master! Here!"
> "Get a move on and get water for my hands and give it to me
> so that I can make a sacrifice to my personal god!"
> "Make a sacrifice, master, make a sacrifice!
> A man who makes a sacrifice to his personal god will be content.
> On trust he is making loan upon loan."
> "No way, slave. I will not make a sacrifice to my personal god."
> "Don't do it, master, don't do it.
> Can you teach your personal god to run after you like a dog?
> He'll just demand of you rites, a votive statue,
> and many other things."[11]

The dialogue concludes with a break in the pattern when the slave offers a response to the master that they both be put to death, to which the master suggests that the slave die first to go into the afterlife in advance of him. The slave finally disagrees, suggesting that the master would not last three days without him! The text's final apparently pessimistic tone and dialogical structure prompts some to make connections to Job, but in the end this text may be more a comedy than a serious piece about suffering, and so any parallel is unclear.

Moving to Egypt, the "Dispute Between a Man and his Ba" (*Ba* is the Egyptian word for "soul") has the main character contemplating suicide. The dialogue is internal—between the man and his soul—so perhaps reflecting

10. "The Babylonian Theodicy," trans. Benjamin R. Foster (*COS* 1.154:493–94).

11. "The Dialogue of Pessimism or the Obliging Slave," trans. Alasdair Livingstone (*COS* 1.155:496).

Qoheleth's self-deliberations in Ecclesiastes (in which the subject of death also plays a central role). Job, while desiring his own death (e.g., Job 6:8–10), does not contemplate ending his life himself.

"The Complaints of Khakheperrē-Sonb" records a man's self-deliberation about problems facing the empire, at one point concluding that "none is wise (enough) to recognize it."[12] The notion that comprehension of the nature of the problems faced is beyond the capacity of even the wise to understand reflects a similar recognition of the limits to human wisdom espoused by the book of Job.

Beyond texts relating specifically to innocent suffering, there are also Egyptian texts that reveal that the theological presuppositions held by Job and his friends—specifically the notion that justice in the world is implemented according to the idea of retribution where bad is punished and good is rewarded—were found in the ancient world. Some clear reflections of this appear in the "Instruction of Amenemope," which dates to the latter part of the second millennium BC. These teachings repeatedly show the dire consequences of exploiting the poor and innocent, together with the simple advice to "do the good and you will prosper."[13] For example:

> Don't use for yourself the might of god,
> As if there were no Fate and Destiny.
> Hand over property to its owners,
> Thus do you seek life for yourself;
> Don't raise your desire in their house,
> Or your bones belong to the execution-block.[14]

There are also echoes of Job's story in later ancient texts, in particular, the deuterocanonical book of Tobit. The parallels between Tobit and Job have long been recognized, but since it was written later than Job, it tells us more about Job's reception than its background or how its original audience would have understood it.[15]

---

12. "The Complaints of Khakheperrē-Sonb," trans. Nili Shupak (*COS* 1.44:106).

13. "Instruction of Amenemope," trans. Miriam Lichtheim (*COS* 1.47:119). Amenemope includes numerous similar exhortations to right behavior and avoidance of wicked, each with the note that the consequence of such behavior will be prosperity.

14. "Instruction of Amenemope," *COS* 1.47:120. The capitalization of "Fate" and "Destiny" occurs because the text uses the names of the Egyptian deities Shay (or Shai) and Renenutet (or Renenet) but translates them to convey their significance in the text.

15. For further discussion of the parallels see Jiseong James Kwon, "Meaning and Context in Job and Tobit," *JSOT* 43.4 (2019): 627–43.

Finally, the question of innocent suffering is universal, and that it is so is attested to by the existence of literature addressing the issue from outside the ancient Near Eastern setting in which Job originates. For example, the Hindu writing from India the "Legend of Harichandra" tells of an exceptional and virtuous king who is tested by the gods to determine whether he is corruptible. He experiences a series of calamities but remains faithful and is ultimately rewarded.[16] Again, the polytheistic background for this text produces a significantly different story, in which Harichandra ultimately learns the reason for his suffering (unlike Job). Nonetheless, it is similar to Job in that the sufferer is truly underserving of the calamities that befall him (at least in some versions of the legend).

These texts from the ancient world demonstrate a widespread concern with the experience of suffering, its causes, and finding relief from that suffering. Unlike Job, however, the suffering experienced is inevitably traced to some moral or religious failing on the part of the sufferer who, after making redress, is restored to well-being. At this point the book of Job departs from its ancient parallels and ventures into a more sophisticated answer to the problem of innocent suffering.

Job and Jesus

In the New Testament Jesus makes the claim that the Old Testament is about him (Luke 24:25–27, 44–49). If we are to take this seriously, then the obvious question we must next ask as we look at the book of Job is, How is this book connected to Jesus? We shall return to this question at various places throughout the commentary, but it is worth highlighting some points as we begin looking at this book.

There are numerous parallels between Job's life and character and the life and character of Jesus—but there are also significant differences. The Satan tests Job, seeking to demonstrate that his piety is entirely self-serving. Jesus was also tested by the devil (Matt 4:1–11; Luke 4:1–13). Job is both like and unlike us—he is a man, but the prologue goes to some lengths to highlight just how special he is (Yahweh notes in Job 1:8 that "there is no one on earth like him"). Similarly Jesus is both like and unlike us—he too is a man, but that which was said of Job could also be said of him: "This man was blameless

16. See D. Gnanaraj, "On the Suffering of the Righteous: Reflections on Job and an Indian Legend of Harichandra," *New Life Review* 2 (2013): 21–40. However, many scholars have erroneously overstated the parallels to Job, a point revealed in David Clines's research; see David J. A. Clines, "In Search of the Indian Job," in *Joban Papers*, Hebrew Bible Monographs 102 (Sheffield: Sheffield Phoenix, 2023), 218–38.

and upright; he feared God and shunned evil" (1:1), "he was the greatest man among all the people of the East" (1:3), "there is no one on earth like him; he is blameless and upright, a man who fears God and shuns evil" (1:8).

In spite of these clear similarities where Job is depicted as blameless and upright, Job is more like us than we might initially suspect. Blameless is not sinless (although the reverse would be true)—he even admits to being sinful (e.g., 7:21). Jesus was sinless and hence blameless, whereas Job had sinned (even if he lived a far better life than we could hope to) yet was blameless. This situation arose because God had provided a means by which sin could be dealt with. For Job, that was through making sacrifices that, when made trusting God's promise that faithful sacrifice would result in forgiveness, rendered Job blameless. Furthermore, we see just how scrupulous Job was in offering sacrifices for sin when necessary, going so far as to preemptively offer sacrifices on behalf of his children just in case they had sinned (1:5).

In this way Job was like us: he was dependent upon God's grace to be made blameless, and he had faith in God's promise that through the offering of appropriate sacrifices his blamelessness would be achieved. While we now know more about the mechanism of forgiveness and reconciliation, it is not through perfect understanding that we are forgiven and made blameless but by grace through faith. Job met these conditions as they were revealed at his time, and the onus is on us today to follow in his footsteps and trust in the one to whom the sacrificial system of Job's day pointed.

Beyond this, Job leads us toward Jesus through his suffering. Job's suffering was undeserved, as was that of Jesus. The story of Job makes the point that one who suffers need not invariably be guilty of some sin that prompted the suffering they experience. This paved the way for people in Jesus's day to understand that suffering was not a reliable indicator of guilt, for Job suffered terribly and was thought thus to be guilty of some egregious sin by his friends but was not actually guilty of an offence that had brought on his predicament.

Job's suffering, however, is also unlike that of Jesus. For one, Job does not choose to suffer, nor does he have any say in it. He does not understand the purpose of his suffering (and the purpose is never explained to him or fully to us, the readers of his story). Jesus, on the other hand, chooses to suffer and understands the purpose of his suffering. Job is an innocent sufferer—that much is made explicit by God and the narrator of the story in the prologue—but there is no hint to suggest that his suffering is vicarious, that it in any way benefits others. Jesus, however, suffers *for* us (see, e.g., 1 Pet 2:21). His suffering replaces our own; it makes us blameless before God and makes the way for us to have a relationship with God.

Job, then, is a step along the path that leads from the fall of humanity into sin and out of relationship with God to humanity's forgiveness and restoration to God. He shows us that innocent suffering is possible and paves the way (together with the Old Testament sacrificial system) for the next step: vicarious innocent suffering.

Through all of this, both Job and Jesus teach us something of how to approach suffering as well as how to approach the questions we face when we do not understand what is happening in our lives. We learn from them to look to God for the answers but, more so, not to expect answers to all our questions. We learn from Job that there is no point in attempting to conceal our hurt, confusion, anger, or any other feeling from God, and that we ought to be honest with God. No matter how much we might wish to hide our negative feelings, feeling them to be inappropriate or bad or even sinful, God sees through our attempts to conceal them. Yes, there is a danger that in our anger about the circumstances and events of our lives we may go too far and sin, but it is also true that you cannot hide your feelings from God, and all too often suppressing your feelings only makes things worse.

What Is the Book of Job?

To properly understand a piece of literature it is important to understand what type of literature it is or, more precisely, what literary genre it fits into. This encompasses broad categories—whether it is fiction or nonfiction, prose or poetry—as well as more specific matters. There are many genres of literature within the Bible. There are historical accounts, parables, love songs, prophetic oracles, wisdom sayings, and more. Working out what type of literature we are reading helps us determine how to understand what we are reading.

So, what can we say about the book of Job? A few things should be apparent. If Job was a historical figure, then we are probably not dealing with a historical account of his life in any modern sense of "history"—people have never spoken only in poetry to one another, as Job and his friends do. At the very least the story of Job is a stylized telling of his story, or it may even be something like an extended parable.

Could Job have been a piece of performance literature like a modern play? It is hard to rule the idea out. While the opening includes such dramatic events as fire falling from heaven and hordes of raiders, all these events appear offstage, and so there is no need for a large special-effects budget! The speeches of the characters are introduced, and there is even a possible intermission in the middle (Job 28). The suggestion that Job was a performance piece is certainly possible and intriguing but cannot be proven with any certainty without accounts of actual performances in the ancient world.[17]

What we can say is that this is a piece of wisdom writing. In Job 27:1; 29:1, Job's speech is described using the Hebrew word *mashal*, a term, commonly translated "proverb," which broadly describes wisdom sayings (and which is the basis of the Hebrew name for the book of Proverbs). This and the subject matter associate Job's words with wisdom in the Bible. To what extent we can refer to the wisdom literature of the Bible as a literary genre, however, is less clear—as the book of Job shows, wisdom literature (Proverbs, Job, and Ecclesiastes) incorporates an array of different literary forms. Nonetheless, the books are connected through their treatment of similar issues, their vocabulary, and their focus on providing advice and instruction to their audience. Job reads somewhat like an extended parable, a tale intended to instruct its audience (see also the comments below on Job 1:1). As such, the story's historicity does not ultimately bear on the message of the book.

Date

There are two date-related issues that must be addressed for any book in the Old Testament. The first is the obvious one: When was the book written? The second is perhaps less obvious but no less important: When was the narrative of the book *set*?

The book of Job makes no reference to external historical events or people that would readily allow us to determine a date for its composition. The author does not identify himself. In light of these considerations, scholars appeal to a couple of factors in an attempt to work out when it was written. First, some scholars try to analyze features of Job's Hebrew in order to attempt to work out where it fits with models of the chronological evolution of the Hebrew language.[18] Yet such attempts are fraught with difficulties: there are good indications that the Hebrew text could have been updated as it was transmitted, making it difficult to be certain that the features relied upon to date the text are accurate reflections of the original version of the text. On top

17. For some discussion of the possibility that Job was a performance piece, see Pauline Shelton, "Making a Drama Out of a Crisis? A Consideration of the Book of Job as a Drama," *JSOT* 24 (1999): 69–82.

18. For example, in 1974 Avi Hurvitz argued that the prose prologue and epilogue together reflected a postexilic date while the poetic sections were to be dated earlier (see Avi Hurvitz, "The Date of the Prose Tale of Job Linguistically Reconsidered," *HTR* 67 [1974]: 17–34). The problems with this argument have been highlighted by Ian Young, "Is the Prose Tale of Job in Late Biblical Hebrew," *VT* 59 (2009): 606–29.

of this, however, is the fact that most models of the evolution of the Hebrew language are inherently problematic, such that when texts supposed to derive from one period are analyzed they almost always contain features assigned by scholars to completely different periods.

Slightly stronger evidence for a later date for the composition of Job can be found in some textual considerations. Notably, the author employs euphemistic language about cursing God in Job 1–2, apparently in order to avoid explicitly associating the word "curse" with God. This does not appear to be a concern of other writers in the Old Testament. For example, in Exodus 22:28 (27 in Hebrew), there is a command not to curse (*qll*) God (cf. Lev 24:15). Associating God with negative terms such as "curse" is, however, a concern that is manifest in later texts and tradition where people avoided even speaking God's name (as reflected in some of the Dead Sea Scrolls). This would suggest (but not prove) a date for composition later in the Old Testament period.

The second feature of the book of Job often used in attempts to work out when it was written is the story itself. The argument goes that Job's story of profound innocent suffering must have arisen when the nation of Israel itself faced profound suffering, and the most obvious candidate for this is the exile. There are, however, a number of problems with making too much out of this assumption. For one, Job does not contain any clear indications that it is connected to such events. Second, if an author did require some impetus for writing this tale, why could it not have been prompted by profound personal suffering and loss? Why must it have been a national tragedy? Third, such an association would put Job in immediate conflict with the prophets, who insisted that the exile was prompted, at least in part, by the sinfulness of God's people. The book of Job insists that Job is not deserving of his suffering; the prophets insist that the people were deserving of theirs. Finally, even if Job's composition was prompted by an event of national suffering, why choose the exile as that tragedy and not some other event such as famine, war, or subjugation? Such events can be found throughout Israel's history as far back as the slavery in Egypt.

In the end, then, every attempt to determine a date for Job's composition leaves some uncertainty. Most scholars place its composition sometime between the seventh and second centuries BC, and in all likelihood it was written sometime after the suffering servant songs of Isaiah.[19] Job is also mentioned in Ezekiel 14, but that does not necessarily mean that the book of

19. The argument by Will Kynes is compelling on this point, see his "Job and Isaiah 40–55: Intertextualities in Dialogue," in *Reading Job Intertextually*, ed. Katharine Dell and Will Kynes, LHBOTS 574 (New York: Bloomsbury T&T Clark, 2013), 94–105.

Job was written before Ezekiel—it could just mean that the book of Job and Ezekiel both refer to an earlier tradition about the man Job. Beyond that little can be said, although our ignorance on this point would seem to have little bearing on our understanding of the meaning of the book.

More significant to understanding the meaning of the book is the question of when the story of Job is set. There is little doubt among scholars that the story is set in patriarchal times, and the indications of this can be quickly summarized. First, Job has a non-Israelite setting that is paralleled predominantly in biblical stories set before Israel was established. Second, Job's wealth is measured in animals and servants in a way found elsewhere primarily in the patriarchal narratives. Third, Job offers sacrifices without a priest, suggesting no formal priestly or cultic organization had yet been established. Fourth, Job lives well over 140 years, much like the patriarchs but unlike anyone later in history. Fifth, the land of Uz may refer to Genesis 10:23, so placing the tale in antiquity. Sixth, the unit of money used in Job 42:11 ("a piece of silver and a gold ring") is only elsewhere mentioned in times prior to the period of the judges (Gen 33:19; Josh 24:32). Seventh, the use of the term "Almighty" (Heb. *shadday*) to refer to God throughout Job has strong ties to patriarchal times (appearing in Genesis more frequently than any other book of the Bible except for Job). Finally, the phrase "he was the greatest man among all the people of the east" in Job 1:3 may play on a deliberate ambiguity in the Hebrew word translated "east" (*qedem*), which could also mean "in ancient times" (cf. Gen 2:8) so explicitly placing Job in patriarchal times.

Clearly there are pretty strong indicators that Job was set far back in history. The important question that arises from this, then, is why has the author gone to such lengths to make it clear that Job's story is so old? One simple reason might be that the story of Job was widely known before it had been written down, and so the author wanted to reflect that knowledge in the written version. This is unlikely to be the only reason, however, because if Job were already widely known, then this sort of information would already have been known, and the author would scarcely have needed to labor the point. So perhaps other considerations are important, and a couple of points could be relevant.

First, the author may have wanted readers to know that the lessons taught in the book were not new. If belief in God's retributive justice was widespread in the author's time (and that would seem to be true for pretty much any period in history), this story makes it clear that it should not be thought a new teaching that such assumptions were invalid (or, at least, not universally true). Rather, the tale explains that it had always been true that there were exceptions to the rule that suffering arose only as a consequence of some specific sin committed.

Second, the author may have wished to present the idea that underserved suffering was possible in the world throughout history to underpin more elaborate claims that it might even be possible for the suffering of an innocent to be vicarious in some way. This latter point is the argument made for the suffering servant of Isaiah and prepares God's people for the coming of the innocent Messiah Jesus, who would suffer vicariously for his people.

Authorship

There really is not a whole lot to say about the author of Job. The book makes no claim about its author. Uncertainty over the date of composition certainly complicates matters, and while speculation does exist (ancient Jewish tradition named Moses as the author), there is simply no firm ground upon which to build a case for any specific author known from history.[20] Most important, however, is the fact that the message of the book in no way depends upon us being able to identify the author, and so we shall spend no more space speculating on the topic.

The Text of Job

The story of Job we read in our Bibles is a translation of an original Hebrew text. The Hebrew of Job is widely regarded as among the most difficult of the Old Testament, and it presents numerous problems for translators. For one, much of the text is poetry, using obscure language and uncommon metaphors to express its message. More than this, however, are the indications that the text has not always been perfectly preserved, and so there are places where better sense can be made of the text by altering the forms of words found in it or by following suggestions found in early translations of Job. Consequently, there are a few places in this commentary where I will suggest that the Hebrew that we do have can be better understood by reading it slightly differently. On the whole, however, the meaning of the book of Job is not changed by these considerations.

Early translations of Job, such as the Greek translation read by many in the early church, represent some clear changes to the original story. The Greek, for example, presents a far more mellow Job who never gets quite as worked up as

---

20. Raik Heckl, "How Wisdom Texts Became Part of the Canon of the Hebrew Bible," in *Was There a Wisdom Tradition?: New Perspectives in Israelite Wisdom Studies*, ed. Mark Sneed, AIL 23 (Atlanta: SBL Press, 2015), 221–22; Shmuel Vargon, "The Date and Composition of the Book of Job in the Context of S. D. Luzzatto's Attitude to Biblical Criticism," *JQR* 91.3–4 (2001): 378–79.

the Hebrew Job. He is far more irenic. He does not get so fired up in his accusations against God; he is more patient and less agitated. Later stories about Job take this even further, all displaying a tendency to shy away from harsh language directed toward God. The words of Job in the Hebrew that we might find somewhat uncomfortable in their forthright attack on God are softened, so the later versions of Job's story sit far more comfortably with readers than does the Hebrew original. This trend reaches its apex with the Testament of Job, which was composed in the first century BC or AD, in which patience and perseverance are presented as the ultimate virtue. The story of Job's suffering that it contains, however, departs significantly from the biblical account, and so its value for understanding the Hebrew text is extremely limited.

Reading Job as Wisdom

Before turning to a detailed examination of the book of Job, we need to spend a few moments reflecting on how to read this book. Job is usually identified as one of the Bible's wisdom books, along with Proverbs and Ecclesiastes. These books share many common features and adopt similar means to communicate their messages to their audience. Understanding how they do this will help us to read each of the books, and fortunately the book of Proverbs begins with a simple statement of the purpose of that book and a guide to how to read it, and that information applies to understanding the wisdom of Job as well. The opening verses of Proverbs read:

> The proverbs of Solomon son of David, king of Israel:
>
> for gaining wisdom and instruction;
>   for understanding words of insight;
> for receiving instruction in prudent behavior,
>   doing what is right and just and fair;
> for giving prudence to those who are simple,
>   knowledge and discretion to the young—
> let the wise listen and add to their learning,
>   and let the discerning get guidance—
> for understanding proverbs and parables,
>   the sayings and riddles of the wise.
>
> The fear of the Lord is the beginning of knowledge,
>   but fools despise wisdom and instruction.

Proverbs opens with six verses explaining the intent of the contents of the work followed by a verse that describes the fundamental presupposition necessary for making sense of wisdom. From this, a couple of particularly salient points should be noted. First, verse 6 refers to "the sayings and riddles of the wise." This tells us that the teaching of the sages is not always straightforward; it can involve riddles. Surprisingly, riddles are mentioned nowhere else in biblical wisdom literature, but that should not lead us to think that everything we read in these books is straightforward or simple; we should expect to have to dig deeply, to think carefully, and not to jump to simple answers. After all, as Proverbs 26:7 says,

> Like the useless legs of one who is lame
>   is a proverb in the mouth of a fool.

That is, anyone can quote the wisdom literature, but one needs to be wise and must invest some careful thought and understanding shaped by fear of Yahweh to making true sense of the wisdom therein and applying it to one's life. We should not be surprised to find that Job is carefully crafted and demands some effort to understand its meaning.

The other important point to note comes from Proverbs 1:7: "The fear of the Lord is the beginning of knowledge." That is, to make true sense of the words before us requires that we begin with a faithful trusting relationship with their ultimate author. How does this make a difference? There are at least two obvious implications. First, when Job speaks of the Lord (1:6, 7; 12:9, etc.), that is, of Yahweh, he is speaking of the God of Abraham, Isaac, and Jacob. This is not some unknown character only encountered in the book of Job; this is Yahweh who is revealed throughout the Bible and ultimately in the person of Jesus of Nazareth, the Messiah. The book of Job does not provide a comprehensive picture of Yahweh, but it assumes that we know more than it reveals because we already know him and have encountered him elsewhere in history and in Scripture.

Second, where the tale of Job is ambiguous, this hermeneutical guide from Proverbs tells us that we ought to choose to resolve that ambiguity in light of what we know about Yahweh from the remainder of Scripture. Job is not to be read in isolation, and its meaning is not meant to be worked out in isolation either. While some of the characters we meet in the book are only found here in the Bible, Yahweh is not, and he is identified in Job specifically so we can recall all that we already know about him from the remainder of Scripture.

The upshot of these considerations works its way out most clearly in the opening chapters, which is when many are left wondering about Yahweh's character as a result of his behavior in allowing Job to be afflicted and his children and servants killed, apparently for no other reason than to win a wager with the Satan. If this behavior does not seem to accord with the way Yahweh behaves elsewhere in Scripture, then perhaps we have failed to look carefully enough at the story to find one of the "riddles of the wise" that the prologue to Proverbs mentions. This idea will be filled out more in the closing discussion of Job 1–2 below, so read on!

Suffering in the Bible

We cannot read the book of Job without being made acutely aware of the problem of suffering. If God loves us, why do we suffer? How do we make sense of this inescapable truth? The answer to this question is multifaceted and far from simple, and the Bible provides a number of answers in different places for different circumstances. Without going into great detail, the biblical authors provide at least the following explanations for human suffering:

1. Human sin in general (e.g., Gen 3; Rom 1; 8:22)
2. Individual sin (numerous places, particularly in the Old Testament)
3. Character building (Rom 5)
4. Discipline (Heb 12)
5. Preventative (Job 33—see discussion in the commentary)
6. Glorification of God (e.g., John 9:2–3)
7. "Completing" Christ's afflictions (Col 1:24)
8. Persecution (2 Tim 3:12)
9. Escaping evil (Isa 57:1–2)
10. Mystery (Job)

Job, then, does have something to say about suffering, but (despite the depth and length of the book) it does not say everything there is to say about suffering. Above all the other answers, however, it forces us to approach the subject with a degree of humility, for like so many aspects of life in this fallen sinful world, Job reminds us that we are human, and God is God. It also reminds us of just how limited our understanding of the world is. If all we learn from Job is to listen more and judge with more humility, we will have learned a lesson worth the time we have spent with this amazing account of the life of a man who suffered greatly.

An Overview of Job

One of the perils of using a commentary on any book of the Bible is that the detail obscures the overall plan and message of the text being studied. There may be a number of ways to mitigate this risk, but the one I have adopted herein is to present a summary overview of the story of the entire book in just a few paragraphs. It will be helpful to keep this in mind as you look at the detail section dealing with each passage in turn, for it will help you to read each section in the broader context of the book.

Before giving the summary, let us consider the structure of the book as a whole:

A	1–2	Prologue
B	3	Job's lament
C	4–14 15–21 22–27	Three speech cycles
D	28	Hymn to Wisdom
C′	29–31 (Job) 32–37 (Elihu) 38–41 (Yahweh)	Three speeches
B′	42:1–6	Job's comfort
A′	42:7–17	Epilogue

Although a far more detailed breakdown of the book's structure could be made, this version is more helpful since it gives a clear overview and shows where each part falls. It shows the clear chiastic structure of the book, with the Hymn to Wisdom of chapter 28 falling in the middle and thus being given a quite prominent place. As it turns out, the message of that hymn anticipates the message of the book as a whole: *there are some things only God knows.*

So, let us turn to an overview of the story of the book.

The opening of the book (chs. 1–2) introduces us to Job, the most upright and blameless man of his day, so much so that God boasts about him to the Satan. The Satan suggests that Job behaves purely for selfish reasons, as such behavior has resulted in his wealth and status. This prompts God to accept the Satan's challenge to test Job, and so all his possessions and children are destroyed. If Job does not curse God when he loses everything, he will have passed the test. And Job does not curse God.

Not to be outdone, the Satan returns for another try at Job, and God allows him to afflict Job with a horrible disease that affects his entire body. In spite of all of this, Job does not curse God as the Satan had predicted. This debate is won, and we do not hear from the Satan again in the book. Furthermore, there is no hint that what transpires from this point is related in any way to the debate between God and the Satan in the prologue—no one calls upon Job to curse God (despite claims to the contrary by some commentators).

The elephant in the room in the book of Job, then, is: Why is Job's affliction not removed by God once the wager has been won? Why is Job still covered in painful sores? Why are his fortunes not reversed? The point has been made; the argument won. Why does Job continue to suffer—indeed why is his suffering exacerbated by the long-winded arguments of his friends?

The pain of the loss of Job's children would not be erased by a restoration of his fortunes, so an estimate of the length of time through which Job's suffering endured cannot easily capture that aspect of the calamities that befell him. Beyond that, however, there are indications that the time between the onset of the disasters reported in chapter 1 through to his restoration in chapter 42 was months, if not years. One indicator is found in Job 7:3: "I have been allotted months of futility." Later Jewish tradition recorded in the Testament of Job 5:9 maintains that Job suffered for many years:

> In this way, I survived for seven years, sitting on a dung-hill outside of the city while being covered with a plague.[21]

In the end we cannot be certain, but it is likely that Job's suffering was not short-lived and endured well beyond the point where the original wager between Yahweh and the Satan had been decided.

Through all that time, Job engages in a longwinded debate with three friends who come to offer him support when they hear of the calamities that have befallen their friend (Job 3; 4–27). They, like Job, hold to the idea that God punishes the wicked and rewards the faithful. So, when terrible things happen to Job, they conclude that it must be a punishment for some sin he has committed that has offended God. As a result, they try to convince Job to repent from his sin and then God will restore him. Job, however, is confident

---

21. Testament of Job 5:9 (Pauly Hart and M. R. James, *Testament of Job: In Modern English and Original Translation* [Savannah, GA, 2021]). Some versions of the Testament of Job, however, mention forty-eight years (see Ian W. Scott, ed., "Testament of Job," in *The Online Critical Pseudepigrapha*, ed. Ken M. Penner, David M. Miller, and Ian W. Scott [Atlanta: Society of Biblical Literature, 2006], https://pseudepigrapha.org/docs/text/TJob, which uses a different numbering system and so records this passage as Testament of Job 21:1).

that he has done no wrong worthy of the afflictions that God has put on him. While he believes in the principle of retributive justice, he is perplexed and can only conclude that God has made a mistake or there is some other problem with God. And so, he vociferously defends himself against the accusations of his friends and seeks an opportunity to confront God to resolve his situation.

We might ask why the debates are as long and repetitive as they are. There are a couple of reasons worth considering. First, the logic of retributive justice, which both Job and his friends believe determines God's behavior, was (and is) deeply entrenched in the thinking of people about God. God punishes the wicked and rewards the good. This idea was common in Job's day, in Jesus's day, and in our day when we think, "What have I done to deserve this?" As such, it deserves a thorough analysis and rebuttal, which in part arrives in the long debates of the book. Second, however, is the rhetorical effect of the long debates. They help us to enter into Job's life, to experience his suffering, and to appreciate his perspective. We come to see the potency of his questions about God's goodness. We begin to share his uncertainty about whether God really has got everything under control. We learn to better empathize with Job in his circumstances.

Eventually these arguments end without resolution. At this point there is a break, and the narrator includes a poem about wisdom (ch. 28). It almost appears as an intermission in a play, yet this chapter is central to the book. This poem makes clear that there is some wisdom that is not available to anyone but God. There are some things human beings will never understand. This message is one we will encounter again at the end of the book when God does ultimately come to speak to Job.

Following the intermission we have three speeches (chs. 29–41). Unlike the first half of the book, these are not dialogues, in that the characters do not formally argue with each other. Rather, these speeches function to reiterate the problem presented in the book before providing the answer when God appears. So first we have Job, who essentially restates the case for his innocence (chs. 29–31). Second, we have a new, younger friend, Elihu, who makes the case that God is righteous without overly focusing on Job's guilt or innocence. Indeed, Elihu even offers another possible explanation for Job's suffering that lies outside the strict bounds of retribution (chs. 32–37; you will have to read through the commentary to get the details).

Finally, God appears (chs. 38–41). Surprisingly, he does not offer an explanation for Job's suffering. Instead, he asks questions about the natural world, questions that are clearly beyond Job's knowledge and so serve only to emphatically remind Job of how little he really knows in the scheme of things compared to God. The point is to remind Job (and us) that the universe in which we live is vastly complex beyond any hope of us ever understanding it, yet God knows it all intimately.

From this, Job comes to the realization that his complaints about how he has been treated by God ultimately arise from ignorance (42:1–6). The simplistic assumption that good is rewarded and evil punished fails to account for the reality of a complex world where so much is beyond our hope for understanding. In the end, Job realizes this, admits it, and finds some closure knowing that it is indeed possible that the calamities that befell him were not as a result of some sin he had committed but that God was also just and had not made a mistake (vv. 7–17).

The Characters

Almost all the characters we meet—aside from Job's wife—play a prominent part in the book. As such, it is helpful to provide a paragraph or two for each introducing them to us. Thus, in order of their appearance, here are the characters we shall meet through this tale.

Job

The first person we meet in the book is Job himself. While his age is not mentioned, he is the father of ten children, so he is likely to be of a similar age to the first three friends, and somewhat older than Elihu, who begins by stating that he deferred to his elders by allowing them to speak first (32:6). In 32:6, Elihu describes the friends as "old," using a rare Hebrew word (*yashish*) that appears only in Job and is used in parallel with the adjective "gray-haired" in Job 15:10. As such, Job and his three friends are at least in their late forties.

Yahweh/God

God appears only at the beginning and end of the book, although he is the topic of conversation throughout. In the opening two chapters God is referred to by the name Yahweh (1:6, etc.). This is significant because it signals to the reader that this God is the God of Abraham, Isaac, and Jacob. This is the God of Israel. Given that Job and his friends are not Israelites (indeed, the book is set before the nation of Israel existed), this is an important point to make. Using the divine name allows the audience of the story to place it within a broader setting: this is the God you know; this is Yahweh. The book of Job does not provide a comprehensive introduction to God because it expects the audience to already know him, to fill in the blanks from the remainder of the story of God.

Through the body of the book, where Job and his friends are talking, God is commonly referred to by the Hebrew *shadday*, "Almighty," appearing thirty-one times here out of forty-eight total appearances in the Old Testament. Most of the other instances occur in the patriarchal period described in the early chapters of the Bible, making its use quite fitting for characters living in those times.

The Satan

The Satan appears in the opening two chapters of the book, then retreats and never returns. Why do I write "*the* Satan"? There are a couple of reasons. First, the Hebrew text of Job always includes the article, indicating that this word functions more as a title than as a proper name from the author's perspective (and that of the original audience). Second, as a title we should be wary of importing too much of what we know from the New Testament of Satan into this character. While doubtless later authors held this character in their minds as they sought to explain more of who Satan is, it would be a mistake to impute all that later knowledge of Satan to this character in the book of Job.

This distinction can also be illustrated through other places in the Old Testament where the Hebrew term *satan* is used. One example is in Numbers 22:22, where the angel of Yahweh is described as operating as an adversary, a *satan*, to Balaam. So, rather than importing later ideas that would not yet have been familiar to the original story's audience, we should focus primarily on what we learn from the prologue about this character. Doing so allows us to understand the story in the way the author intended and the original audience would have.

The Hebrew word *satan* provides us with our first guide as to the function of this character. The term refers to an adversary, possibly even an "attacker" or "executioner." While it is sometimes suggested that the Satan functions simply as an accuser, the title itself points to a more aggressive role.[22] To fill out that role, however, we ought to look at what we are told about this character in the book of Job itself.

The prologue provides some insight into the job description for the Satan: he is said to roam the earth and, based on Yahweh's question (Job 1:8: "Have you considered my servant Job?"), observes the activities of human beings in some manner. A number of scholars have drawn parallels with individuals in the employ of kings in the ancient world who are variously described as

22. For more discussion see Ryan E. Stokes, "Satan, Yhwh's Executioner," *JBL* 133.2 (2014): 251–70.

"the eyes of the king" or "the ears of the king." There are accounts of such individuals from ancient Egypt and Greek accounts of such individuals in ancient Persia.[23] Their function was to secretly report dissent or disloyalty back to the king—a role that is to be found in many later systems of government throughout history. It is likely that the existence of such people would have been known to the original audience of the book of Job, and so there is a good chance that the role of the Satan as described in the prologue was meant to provoke the audience to think of such spies. As such, while the Satan of the prologue to Job could not have been understood by the work's original audience in the more comprehensive terms that he is in later history, the character would have nonetheless provoked a degree of trepidation in the minds of the audience. After all, secretly listening and watching for anyone to fall would inevitably provoke a degree of unease among those subject to such scrutiny.

Job's Wife

Although she only gets a single verse, it is worth noting both her appearance and a few things about this undervalued woman. In general, she gets a bad rap (see the commentary below). Amid that, however, it is important to acknowledge that Job's losses were shared by his wife—her home, her servants, and her children were all gone too. Furthermore, it seems that early interpreters of the book were aware of this, for the ancient translation of Job into Greek (which is arguably the version of Job people in New Testament times were most familiar with) both expanded upon and softened the Hebrew text's treatment of Job's wife. Rather than the six Hebrew words she speaks in the Hebrew text—"Are you still maintaining your integrity? Curse God and die!" (2:9)—in the Greek version we read the following:

> Then after a long time had passed, his wife said to him, "How long will you persist and say, [9a]'Look, I will hang on a little longer, while I wait for the hope of my deliverance?' [9b]For look, your legacy has vanished from the earth—sons and daughters, my womb's birth pangs and labors, for whom I wearied myself with hardships in vain. [9c]And you? You sit in the refuse of worms as you spend the night in the open air. [9d]As for me, I am one

23. Ancient Greek descriptions of the Persian Empire are found in Xenophon, *Cyropaedia*, 8.2.10; and Aristophanes, *Acharnians*, lines 90–95. For further discussion, see A. L. Oppenheim, "The Eyes of the Lord," *JAOS* 88.1 (1968): 173–80; John E. Hartley, *The Book of Job*, NICOT (Grand Rapids: Eerdmans, 1988), 71n7, who notes, "The Persian emperor had secret servants who toured the realm at random to discern the allegiance and behavior of the people and especially of various officials. These agents were called 'the eyes and ears of the king' (Herodotus). So in Job the Satan appears as the roving eye of the monarch to report on the loyalty of subjects."

> that wanders about and a hired servant—from place to place and house to house, waiting for when the sun will set, so I can rest from the distresses and griefs that now beset me. [9e]Now say some word to the Lord and die!" (NETS)

Aside from recognizing the equal travails of Job's wife, her advice to her husband appears less harsh. On that account, however, even the Hebrew text is not quite as blunt as most English translations, for the Hebrew uses the word for "bless" in place of "curse." This is a euphemism found throughout the prologue of Job, where the author avoids juxtaposing "curse" and "God," but it also leads to ambiguity, particularly in regard to the precise intent of Job's wife's words.

Eliphaz the Temanite, Bildad the Shuhite, and Zophar the Naamathite

We do not have much biographical information on these three older men who set out to help Job in his distress, aside from the important point that they, like Job, are not Israelites, and no specific connection is made between these characters and the lineage of Abraham, Isaac, and Jacob. Like many who are faced with someone who is suffering, they move from their initial empathy to offering a solution for Job. They arrive at the solution from their theology, which states that suffering is a sign of divine judgment and so an indication of sin in the life of the sufferer. Consequently, they advise Job to repent of his sin, turn his life around, and be restored. We, however, know that they are wrong, because we have been privy to some of the causes of Job's suffering in the prologue.

Although these three friends do, by and large, reiterate the same point—that Job's suffering arises out of some sin he has committed—they are not mere mirrors of one another. As we read through the book, this will become clear. For one, their responses to Job differ in their tone and assessment of Job as a person. David Clines has highlighted the differences, noting that Eliphaz regards Job as a righteous man undergoing discipline by God, Bildad holds out hope for Job turning back to God, as his sin had not yet resulted in his death (unlike his children), while Zophar has the most severe attitude to Job—yet even he holds out some hope that Job could yet be restored. In summary Clines notes that,

> Eliphaz argues from the piety of Job in order to offer consolation; Bildad argues from the contrast between the fates of Job and Job's children in order to offer warning; Zophar argues from the suffering of Job in order

> to denounce Job. Secondly . . . Eliphaz's intention is to encourage Job to patience and hope (5.8; 4.6); Bildad's intention is to urge Job to search his heart before God in order to ensure that he is not guilty of crimes such as those for which his children have died (8.5–6); Zophar's intention is to summon Job to repentance for sins that he clearly has already committed (11.6c).[24]

The three friends, therefore, agree in their theology but differ somewhat in their assessment of Job and their application of their theology to him. In the end, however, God will tell Job (and us) that they were wrong in their claims about God and the way he was working in Job's suffering.

Elihu

After everyone has had enough and the three friends have given up responding to Job, we hear from a young man named Elihu, who does not seem to have been present at the beginning of the discourse (he is not mentioned when the friends first arrive at the end of ch. 2) but has been around long enough presumably to hear some of the debate between Job and his friends. Nonetheless, Elihu is the most verbose of all the friends. Furthermore, he is the only one of Job's friends to address him by name. Reading his speech, particularly the extended introduction he gives himself, leaves the reader with the impression that Elihu is rather uncertain about entering into the debate. Like a student asking a question in the midst of a group of professors at a conference, Elihu recognizes his lack of formal qualification in taking up the discussion with Job. Nonetheless, Elihu is also overwhelmed with the sense that the older friends have missed something that he has seen. So, he enters into the fray and says his piece.

When he has finished speaking, he disappears. He is not included in the assessment of the friends' speeches given by Yahweh at the end of the book, so we are left wondering whether what he said was right or wrong. As it turns out, this is exactly where the author of the book of Job wants to leave us. For Elihu suggests that suffering may not only be a consequence of sin but that it could be there to prevent one's falling into sin (see commentary on Job 33:12–18).[25]

---

24. David J. A. Clines, "The Arguments of Job's Three Friends," in *Joban Papers*, Hebrew Bible Monographs 102 (Sheffield: Sheffield Phoenix, 2023), 55–56; see also Susanna Baldwin, "Miserable but Not Monochrome: The Distinctive Characteristics and Perspectives of Job's Three Comforters," *Themelios* 43.3 (2018): 359–75; Marvin H. Pope, *Job*, 3rd ed., AB 15 (New York: Doubleday, 1973), 36.

25. See also Martin A. Shields, "Was Elihu Right?," *JESOT* 3.2 (2014): 155–70.

The author of Job wants us to know that suffering is not only connected to sin, but the author also does not want us to replace one simplistic connection with another. And so, we are left knowing that there are other possible explanations for Job's suffering without ever being certain of the true reasons.

The epilogue to the book does mention other minor characters: Job's beautiful daughters Jemimah, Keziah, and Keren-Happuch. But they do not say anything, and the only other words in the book are those of the narrator.

Orientation to This Commentary

Job is one of the more repetitive books of the Bible. Aside from the repetition in chapters 1 and 2, where much of the first appearance of the Satan to accuse Job (Job 1:8–12) is repeated in the second appearance (Job 2:1–8) when the Satan enters the heavenly court to challenge God about Job, the three cycles of speeches—with Job and each of his older three friends responding—covers much the same ground through each cycle. Despite this, the dialogue does evince signs of progression through each cycle such that each argument is not identical, and the speeches are not simply restating the previous speech's assertions in different language.

In light of this, much of the background material relevant to all of the speeches is consolidated in the commentary's Listen to the Story sections for the opening speeches in chapters 3–14, while the remaining sections will focus on any material relevant only to the speech immediately under examination. As such, if your focus is on a speech in a later chapter, it would be worthwhile reviewing the background information at the opening section of the speeches in the above-mentioned chapters.

Resources for Teaching and Preaching

Alden, Robert L. *Job*. NAC 11. Nashville: B&H, 1993.

Alter, Robert. *The Art of Biblical Poetry*. Rev. and updated ed. New York: Basic Books, 2011.

Andersen, F. I. *Job*. TOTC. Downers Grove, IL: InterVarsity Press, 1976.

Annus, Amar, and Alan Lenzi. *Ludlul Bēl Nēmeqi: The Standard Babylonian Poem of the Righteous Sufferer*. SAACT 7. Winona Lake, IN: Eisenbrauns, 2010.

Ash, Christopher. *Job: The Wisdom of the Cross*. Preaching the Word. Wheaton, IL: Crossway, 2014.

Baldwin, Susanna. "Miserable but Not Monochrome: The Distinctive Characteristics and Perspectives of Job's Three Comforters." *Themelios* 43.3 (2018): 359–75.

Ben-Barak, Zafrira. "Inheritance by Daughters in the Ancient Near East." *JSS* 25.1 (1980): 22–33.

Ben-Yosef, Erez, Ron Shaar, Lisa Tauxe, and Hagai Ron. "A New Chronological Framework for Iron Age Copper Production at Timna (Israel)." *BASOR* 367 (2012): 31–71.

Beyerstein, Barry L. "Whence Cometh the Myth That We Only Use 10% of Our Brains?" Pages 3–24 in *Mind Myths: Exploring Popular Assumptions About the Mind and Brain*. Edited by Sergio Della Sala. Chichester, UK: Wiley, 1999.

Brown, William P. *Character in Crisis: A Fresh Approach to the Wisdom Literature of the Old Testament*. Grand Rapids: Eerdmans, 1996.

Budge, E. A. Wallis, and L. W. King, eds. *The Annals of the Kings of Assyria: The Cuneiform Texts with Translations and Transliterations from the Original Documents*. Vol. 1. London: Harrison & Sons, 1902.

Burns, John Barclay. "The Identity of Death's First-Born (Job XVIII 13)." *VT* 37.3 (1987): 362–64.

Burns, John Barclay. "The Mythological Background to Job 18,5–61." *BeO* 33.3 (1991): 129–40.

Carson, Don A. "Matthew." Pages 23–670 in *Matthew–Mark*. REBC 9. Rev. ed. Edited by Tremper Longman III and David E. Garland. Grand Rapids: Zondervan, 2010.

Cassuto, U. *The Goddess Anath*. Translated by Israel Abrahams. Jerusalem: Magnes, 1971.

Cheney, M. *Dust, Wind and Agony: Character, Speech and Genre in Job*. ConBOT. Stockholm: Almqvist & Wiksell, 1994.

Clines, David J. A. "The Arguments of Job's Three Friends." Pages 44–59 in *Joban Papers*. Hebrew Bible Monographs 102. Sheffield: Sheffield Phoenix, 2023.

Clines, David J. A. "Deconstructing the Book of Job." Pages 106–23 in *What Does Eve Do to Help? And Other Readerly Questions to the Old Testament*. JSOTSup 94. Sheffield: Sheffield Academic, 1990.

Clines, David J. A. *Job 1–20*. WBC 17. Dallas: Word, 1989.

Clines, David J. A. *Job 21–37*. WBC 18A. Nashville: Nelson, 2006.

Clines, David J. A. *Job 38–42*. WBC 18B. Nashville: Nelson, 2011.

Clines, David J. A. "One or Two Things You May Not Know About the Universe: The Cosmology of the Divine Speeches in Job." Pages 328–42 in *Joban Papers*. Hebrew Bible Monographs 102. Sheffield: Sheffield Phoenix, 2023.

Cohen, Yoram. *Wisdom from the Late Bronze Age*. Writings from the Ancient World 29. Atlanta: Society of Biblical Literature, 2013.

Cornelius, Izak. "Job." Pages 246–301 in *The Minor Prophets, Job, Psalms, Proverbs, Ecclesiastes, Song of Songs*. ZIBBCOT 5. Grand Rapids: Zondervan Academic, 2009.

Crenshaw, James L. *Old Testament Wisdom: An Introduction*. Atlanta: Westminster John Knox, 2010.

Declaissé-Walford, Nancy, Rolf A. Jacobson, and Beth Laneel Tanner. *The Book of Psalms*. NICOT. Grand Rapids: Eerdmans, 2014.

Dennett, Daniel. *Intuition Pumps and Other Tools for Thinking*. New York: Norton, 2013.

Dunham, Kyle C. "Ransomed from the Hand of Sheol: The Heavenly Destiny of Old Testament Saints in the Afterlife." *DBSJ* 26 (2021): 3–33.

Fox, Michael V. "Behemoth and Leviathan." *Bib* 93.2 (2012): 261–67.

Frayne, Douglas R., and Johanna H. Stuckey. *A Handbook of Gods and Goddesses of the Ancient Near East: Three Thousand Deities of Anatolia, Syria, Israel, Sumer, Babylonia, Assyria, and Elam*. University Park, PA: Eisenbrauns, 2021.

Frymer-Kensky, Tikva. "Patriarchal Family Relationships and Near Eastern Law." *BA* 44.4 (1981): 209–14.

George, Andrew. *The Babylonian Gilgamesh Epic: Introduction, Critical Edition and Cuneiform Texts*. 2 vols. Oxford: Oxford University Press, 2003.

Ginsberg, H. L. "Interpreting Ugaritic Texts." *JAOS* 70.3 (1950): 156–60.

Gnanaraj, D. "On the Suffering of the Righteous: Reflections on Job and an Indian Legend of Harichandra." *New Life Review* 2 (2013): 21–40.

Gordis, Robert. *The Book of Job: Commentary, New Translation, and Special Notes*. New York: Jewish Theological Seminary of America, 1978.

Gordon, Cyrus H. "Belt-Wrestling in the Bible World." *HUCA* 23.1 (1950): 131–36.

Greenberg, Moshe. "Job." Pages 283–304 in *The Literary Guide to the Bible*. Edited by Robert Alter and Frank Kermode. Cambridge: Harvard University Press, 1987.

Greenstein, Edward L. "The Poem on Wisdom in Job 28 in Its Conceptual and Literary Contexts." Pages 253–80 in *Job 28: Cognition in Context*. Edited by Ellen van Wolde. Biblical Interpretation 64. Leiden: Brill, 2003.

Griffiths, J. C. "The Idea of Posthumous Judgment in Israel and Egypt." Pages 186–204 in *Fontes atque pontes: Eine Festgabe für H. Brunner*. Edited by M. Görg. Wiesbaden: Harrassowitz, 1983.

Harding, James Edward. "The Book of Job as Metaprophecy." *Studies in Religion/Sciences Religieuses* 39.4 (2010): 523–47.

Hart, Pauly, and M. R. James. *Testament of Job: In Modern English and Original Translation*. Savannah, GA, 2021.

Hartley, John E. "From Lament to Oath: A Study of Progression in the Speeches of Job." Pages 79–100 in *Book of Job*. Edited by Willem A. M. Beuken. Leuven: Peeters, 1994.

Hartley, John E. *The Book of Job*. NICOT. Grand Rapids: Eerdmans, 1988.

Heckl, Raik. "How Wisdom Texts Became Part of the Canon of the Hebrew Bible." Pages 221–39 in *Was There a Wisdom Tradition?: New Prospects in Israelite Wisdom Studies*. AIL 23. Edited by Mark Sneed. Atlanta: SBL Press, 2015.

Heide, Martin, and Joris Peters. *Camels in the Biblical World*. HACL 10. University Park: Pennsylvania State University Press, 2021.

Hernández, Dominick S. "The Expression of Moral Judgments through Imagery in Job and Ancient Near Eastern Literature." Pages 150–63 in *Teaching Morality in Antiquity: Wisdom Texts, Oral Traditions, and Images*. Edited by T. M. Oshima and Susanne Kohlhaas. Orientalische Religionen in der Antike 29. Tübingen: Mohr Siebeck, 2018.

Horowitz, Wayne. *Mesopotamian Cosmic Geography*. Mesopotamian Civilizations 8. Winona Lake, IN: Eisenbrauns, 1998.

Hundley, Michael B. "Divine Presence in Ancient Near Eastern Temples." *RC* 9.7 (2015): 203–15.

Hurowitz, Victor Avigdor. "Is Ludlul Bēl Nēmeqi Wisdom Literature? A Review Article of: Annus, Amar and Alan Lenzi, Ludlul Bēl Nēmeqi: The Standard Babylonian Poem of the Righteous Sufferer." *JHebS* 11 (2011). https://doi.org/10.5508/jhs.2011.v11.r53, https://jhsonline.org/index.php/jhs/article/view/16488.

Hurvitz, Avi. "The Date of the Prose Tale of Job Linguistically Reconsidered." *HTR* 67 (1974): 17–34.

Irwin, William A. "Job's Redeemer." *JBL* 81.3 (1962): 217–29.

Janzen, J. Gerald. *Job*. IBC. Louisville: Westminster John Knox, 1985.

Johnson, Timothy Jay. *Now My Eye Sees You: Unveiling an Apocalyptic Job*. Sheffield: Sheffield Phoenix, 2013.

Johnston, Philip S. *The Shades of Sheol: Death and Afterlife in the Old Testament*. Downers Grove, IL: IVP Academic, 2002.

Joüon, Paul, and T. Muraoka. *A Grammar of Biblical Hebrew*. 2 vols. Rome: Pontifical Biblical Institute, 1993.

Kaiser, Walter C., Jr. "Exodus." Pages 333–561 in *Genesis–Leviticus*. REBC 1. Rev. ed. Edited by Tremper Longman III and David E. Garland. Grand Rapids: Zondervan, 2010.

Kidner, Derek. *The Wisdom of Proverbs, Job and Ecclesiastes: An Introduction to the Wisdom Literature*. Downers Grove, IL: InterVarsity Press, 1985.

Kline, Meredith G. "Trial by Ordeal." Pages 81–93 in *Through Christ's Word: A Festschrift for Dr. Philip E. Hughes*. Edited by W. Robert Godfrey and Jesse L. Boyd. Phillipsburg, NJ: P&R, 1985.

Koehler, Ludwig, Walter Baumgartner, and Johann J. Stamm, eds. *The Hebrew and Aramaic Lexicon of the Old Testament*. Translated by M. E. J. Richardson. 5 vols. Leiden: Brill, 2000.

Kramer, Samuel Noah. *The Sumerians: Their History, Culture, and Character*. Chicago: University of Chicago Press, 1963.

Krüger, Thomas. "Job Spoke the Truth About God (Job 42:7–8)." Pages 71–80 in *"When the Morning Stars Sang": Essays in Honor of Choon Leong Seow on the Occasion of His Sixty-Fifth Birthday*. Edited by Scott C. Jones and Christine Roy Yoder. BZAW 500. Berlin: de Gruyter, 2018.

Kwon, Jiseong James. "Meaning and Context in Job and Tobit." *JSOT* 43.4 (2019): 627–43.

Kynes, Will. "Job and Isaiah 40–55: Intertextualities in Dialogue." Pages 94–105 in *Reading Job Intertextually*. Edited by Katharine Dell and Will Kynes. LHBOTS 574. New York: Bloomsbury T&T Clark, 2013.

Lambert, W. G. *Babylonian Wisdom Literature*. Oxford: Clarendon, 1960.

Lenzi, Alan. *Suffering in Babylon: Ludlul Bēl Nēmeqi and the Scholars, Ancient and Modern*. OBO 300. Leuven: Peeters, 2023.

Long, V. Philips. "On the Coherence of the Third Dialogic Cycle in the Book of Job." Pages 113–25 in *Studies on the Text and Versions of the Hebrew Bible in Honour of Robert Gordon*. Edited by Geoffrey Khan and Diana Lipton. VTSup 149. Leiden: Brill, 2012.

Longman, Tremper. *Job*. BCOTWP. Grand Rapids: Baker Academic, 2012.

Luc, Alex. "Storm and the Message of Job." *JSOT* 23 (2000): 111–23.

Maisler, B. "Two Hebrew Ostraca from Tell Qasîle." *JNES* 10.4 (1951): 265–67.

Mann, Thomas W. *Divine Presence and Guidance in the Israelite Traditions: The Typology of Exaltation*. Baltimore: Johns Hopkins University Press, 1977.

Mendelsohn, I. "The Family in the Ancient Near East." *BA* 11.2 (1948): 24–40.

Millard, Alan R. "Daniel 1–6 and History." *EQ* 49.2 (1977): 67–73.

Murphy, Roland E. *The Tree of Life: An Exploration of Biblical Wisdom Literature*. 2nd ed. Grand Rapids: Eerdmans, 1996.

Murphy, Roland E. *Wisdom Literature: Job, Proverbs, Ruth, Canticles, Ecclesiastes, and Esther*. FOTL 13. Grand Rapids: Eerdmans, 1981.

Newsom, Carol A. "The Book of Job." Pages 317–637 in vol. 3 of *NIB*. Edited by Leander E. Keck. Nashville: Abingdon, 1996.

Niehaus, Jeffrey Jay. "Joshua and Ancient Near Eastern Warfare." *JETS* 31.1 (1988): 37–50.

Niehaus, Jeffrey Jay. *God at Sinai: Covenant and Theophany in the Bible and Ancient Near East*. Grand Rapids: Zondervan, 1995.

Oeming, Manfred. "'Ihr Habt Nicht Recht von Mir Geredet Wie Mein Knecht Hiob': Gottes Schlusswort als Schlüssel zur Interpretation des Hiobbuches und als kritische Anfrage an die modern Theologie." *EvT* 60 (2000): 103–16.

Oppenheim, A. L. "The Eyes of the Lord." *JAOS* 88.1 (1968): 173–80.

Ortlund, Eric. "The Identity of Leviathan and the Meaning of the Book of Job." *TJ* NS 34.1 (2013): 17–30.

Parpola, Simo. *Assyrian Prophecies*. Helsinki: Helsinki University Press, 1997.

Pope, Marvin H. *Job*. AB 15. 3rd ed. New York: Doubleday, 1973.

Pritchard, J. B. *Ancient Near Eastern Texts Relating to the Old Testament*. 3rd ed. with Supplement. Princeton: Princeton University, 1969.

Rollston, Christopher A. "An Ur-History of the New Testament Devil: The Celestial שׂטן (Śāṭān) in Zechariah and Job." Pages 1–16 in *Evil in Second Temple Judaism and Early Christianity*. Edited by Chris Keith and Loren T. Stuckenbruck. WUNT 2.417. Tübingen: Mohr Siebeck, 2016.

Samet, Nili. "Mesopotamian Wisdom." Pages 328–48 in *The Wiley Blackwell Companion to Wisdom Literature*. Edited by Samuel L. Adams and Matthew Goff. New York: Wiley & Sons, 2020.

Sarna, Nahum M. "The Mythological Background of Job 18." *JBL* 82.3 (1963): 315–18.

Savran, George. "Theophany as Type Scene." *Prooftexts* 23.2 (2003): 119–49.

Scott, Ian W., ed. "Testament of Job." In *The Online Critical Pseudepigrapha*. Edited by Ken M. Penner, David M. Miller, and Ian W. Scott. Atlanta: SBL Press, 2006. https://pseudepigrapha.org/docs/text/TJob.

Seow, Choon-Leong. *Job 1–21: Interpretation and Commentary*. Interpretations. Grand Rapids: Eerdmans, 2013.

Shead, Andrew G. "Burning Scripture with Passion: A Review of The Psalms (The Passion Translation)." *Themelios* 43.1 (2018): 58–71.

Shelton, Pauline. "Making a Drama Out of a Crisis? A Consideration of the Book of Job as a Drama." *JSOT* 24 (1999): 69–82.

Shields, Martin A. "Malevolent or Mysterious? God's Character in the Prologue of Job." *TynBul* 61.2 (2010): 255–70.

Shields, Martin A. *The End of Wisdom: A Reappraisal of the Historical and Canonical Function of Ecclesiastes*. Winona Lake, IN: Eisenbrauns, 2006.

Shields, Martin A. "The Ignorance of Job." *ABR* 68 (2020): 28–39.

Shields, Martin A. "Was Elihu Right?" *JESOT* 3.2 (2014): 155–70.

Shields, Martin A. "You Can't Get a Sage to Do a Prophet's Job: Overcoming Wisdom's Deficiency in the Book of Job." Pages 182–98 in *Riddles and Revelations: Explorations into the Relationship Between Wisdom and Prophecy in the Hebrew Bible*. Edited by Mark J. Boda, Russell L. Meek, and William R. Osborne. London: LHBOTS 634. T&T Clark, 2018.

Simpson, William Kelly, ed. *The Literature of Ancient Egypt: An Anthology of Stories, Instructions, Stelae, Autobiographies, and Poetry*. 3rd ed. New Haven: Yale University Press, 2003.

Skehan, Patrick W. "Strophic Patterns in the Book of Job." *CBQ* 23.2 (1961): 125–42.

Smick, Elmer B. "Job." Pages 675–921 in *1 Chronicles–Job*. REBC 4. Rev. ed. Edited by Tremper Longman III and David E Garland. Grand Rapids: Zondervan, 2010.

Smith, Mark S., and Wayne T. Pitard. *The Ugaritic Baal Cycle*. 2 vols. VTSup 114. Leiden: Brill, 2009:

Snaith, Norman H. *The Book of Job: Its Origin and Purpose*. London: SCM, 1968.

Sneed, Mark. "Is Biblical Studies Stuck in Antiquarianism? The Case of Behemoth and Leviathan." *BibleRec* 10.2 (2023): 221–44.

Stokes, Ryan E. "Satan, Yhwh's Executioner." *JBL* 133.2 (2014): 251–70.

Suriano, Matthew J. "Death, Disinheritance, and Job's Kinsman-Redeemer." *JBL* 129.1 (2010): 49–66.

Thompson, James A. *Jeremiah*. NICOT. Grand Rapids: Eerdmans, 1980.

Timmer, Daniel. "God's Speeches, Job's Responses, and the Problem of Coherence in the Book of Job: Sapiential Pedagogy Revisited." *CBQ* 71 (2009): 286–305.

Vargon, Shmuel. "The Date and Composition of the Book of Job in the Context of S. D. Luzzatto's Attitude to Biblical Criticism." *JQR* 91.3–4 (2001): 377–94.

Waltke, Bruce K., and M. O'Connor. *An Introduction to Biblical Hebrew Syntax*. Winona Lake, IN: Eisenbrauns, 1990.

Walton, John H. *Job*. NIVAC. Grand Rapids: Zondervan Academic, 2012.

Watson, Wilfred G. E. *Classical Hebrew Poetry: A Guide to Its Techniques*. JSOTSup 26. Sheffield: JSOT Press, 1984.

Weeks, Stuart. *An Introduction to the Study of Wisdom Literature*. T&T Clark Approaches to Biblical Studies. Edinburgh: T&T Clark, 2010.

Wharton, James A. *Job*. Westminster Bible Companion. Louisville: Westminster John Knox, 1999.

Wikander, Ola. "Job 3,8—Cosmological Snake-Charming and Leviathanic Panic in an Ancient Near Eastern Setting." *ZAW* 122 (2010): 265–71.

Wilson, Lindsay. *Job*. Two Horizons Old Testament Commentary. Grand Rapids: Eerdmans, 2015.

Wyatt, Nicholas. "The Expression Běkôr Māwet in Job XVIII 13 and Its Mythological Background." *VT* 40.2 (1990): 207–16.

Young, Ian. "Is the Prose Tale of Job in Late Biblical Hebrew." *VT* 59 (2009): 606–29.

Zammit, Andrea. "What Were the Powers of the Paterfamilias over His Children?" Unpublished paper. 1 January 2011. https://www.researchgate.net/publication/336085568_What_were_the_powers_of_the_Paterfamilias_over_his_children.

CHAPTER 1

Job 1–2

LISTEN to the Story

1:1In the land of Uz there lived a man whose name was Job. This man
was blameless and upright; he feared God and shunned evil. 2He had seven
sons and three daughters, 3and he owned seven thousand sheep, three
thousand camels, five hundred yoke of oxen and five hundred donkeys,
and had a large number of servants. He was the greatest man among all
the people of the East.

4His sons used to hold feasts in their homes on their birthdays, and they
would invite their three sisters to eat and drink with them. 5When a period
of feasting had run its course, Job would make arrangements for them to
be purified. Early in the morning he would sacrifice a burnt offering for
each of them, thinking, "Perhaps my children have sinned and cursed God
in their hearts." This was Job's regular custom.

6One day the angels came to present themselves before the LORD, and
Satan also came with them. 7The LORD said to Satan, "Where have you
come from?"

Satan answered the LORD, "From roaming throughout the earth, going back and forth on it."

8Then the LORD said to Satan, "Have you considered my servant Job?
There is no one on earth like him; he is blameless and upright, a man who
fears God and shuns evil."

9"Does Job fear God for nothing?" Satan replied. 10"Have you not
put a hedge around him and his household and everything he has? You
have blessed the work of his hands, so that his flocks and herds are spread
throughout the land. 11But now stretch out your hand and strike every-
thing he has, and he will surely curse you to your face."

12The LORD said to Satan, "Very well, then, everything he has is in your
power, but on the man himself do not lay a finger."

Then Satan went out from the presence of the LORD.

[13]One day when Job's sons and daughters were feasting and drinking wine at the oldest brother's house, [14]a messenger came to Job and said, "The oxen were plowing and the donkeys were grazing nearby, [15]and the Sabeans attacked and made off with them. They put the servants to the sword, and I am the only one who has escaped to tell you!"

[16]While he was still speaking, another messenger came and said, "The fire of God fell from the heavens and burned up the sheep and the servants, and I am the only one who has escaped to tell you!"

[17]While he was still speaking, another messenger came and said, "The Chaldeans formed three raiding parties and swept down on your camels and made off with them. They put the servants to the sword, and I am the only one who has escaped to tell you!"

[18]While he was still speaking, yet another messenger came and said, "Your sons and daughters were feasting and drinking wine at the oldest brother's house, [19]when suddenly a mighty wind swept in from the desert and struck the four corners of the house. It collapsed on them and they are dead, and I am the only one who has escaped to tell you!"

[20]At this, Job got up and tore his robe and shaved his head. Then he fell to the ground in worship [21]and said:

"Naked I came from my mother's womb,
 and naked I will depart.
The LORD gave and the LORD has taken away;
 may the name of the LORD be praised."

[22]In all this, Job did not sin by charging God with wrongdoing.

[2:1]On another day the angels came to present themselves before the LORD, and Satan also came with them to present himself before him. [2]And the LORD said to Satan, "Where have you come from?"

Satan answered the LORD, "From roaming throughout the earth, going back and forth on it."

[3]Then the LORD said to Satan, "Have you considered my servant Job? There is no one on earth like him; he is blameless and upright, a man who fears God and shuns evil. And he still maintains his integrity, though you incited me against him to ruin him without any reason."

[4]"Skin for skin!" Satan replied. "A man will give all he has for his own

life. [5]But now stretch out your hand and strike his flesh and bones, and he
will surely curse you to your face."
[6]The LORD said to Satan, "Very well, then, he is in your hands; but
you must spare his life."
[7]So Satan went out from the presence of the LORD and afflicted Job
with painful sores from the soles of his feet to the crown of his head. [8]Then
Job took a piece of broken pottery and scraped himself with it as he sat
among the ashes.
[9]His wife said to him, "Are you still maintaining your integrity? Curse
God and die!"
[10]He replied, "You are talking like a foolish woman. Shall we accept
good from God, and not trouble?"
In all this, Job did not sin in what he said.
[11]When Job's three friends, Eliphaz the Temanite, Bildad the Shuhite
and Zophar the Naamathite, heard about all the troubles that had come
upon him, they set out from their homes and met together by agreement to
go and sympathize with him and comfort him. [12]When they saw him from
a distance, they could hardly recognize him; they began to weep aloud, and
they tore their robes and sprinkled dust on their heads. [13]Then they sat on
the ground with him for seven days and seven nights. No one said a word
to him, because they saw how great his suffering was.

Listening to the Text in the Story: "The Poem of the Righteous Sufferer" (Babylonian; also known as "The Babylonian Job" or "Ludlul Bēl Nēmeqi"); "A Righteous Sufferer's Prayer to Nabu"

Why do bad things happen to good people? This is a question that is raised in the opening chapters of the book of Job. It was a question that troubled many in the ancient world just as it continues to trouble us today. We know that the wisdom of the ancient sages was shared far and wide, across national and cultural boundaries, and so it is probable that Job's author and first audience were at least vaguely familiar with some of the thoughts of foreign sages on this topic.

We know that the problem of suffering was examined across all ancient cultures from the ancient Near East. From late Bronze Age Ugarit (c. 1500–1200 BC) we have a poem about a righteous sufferer which, although only preserved in a damaged form, presents a tale of a man who finds himself suffering at the hands of the gods he worships and seeks to learn why.[1]

The Akkadian text "Ludlul Bēl Nēmeqi"[2] (the opening words, which are also translated to provide the English title: "I Will Praise the Lord of Wisdom") expands on the format of the shorter Ugaritic text and includes a vivid description of a person (named Šubši-mešrê-Šakkan) suffering and so is frequently cited as a parallel to Job. There are indeed some quite striking parallels to Job.[3] In the Akkadian "Ludlul Bēl Nēmeqi," the sufferer first loses all his material possessions and is then afflicted with all manner of diseases (which are assigned a supernatural origin).

In spite of these parallels, there are significant differences between Job and "Ludlul Bēl Nēmeqi." The latter is essentially a poem of praise of Marduk (who is the "Lord of wisdom" of the title) for delivering his servant and also incorporates magic and incantations. Perhaps most significantly, however, is the reason for Shubshi-meshre-Shakkan's suffering, which appears to be the direct result of some "sin" or act of neglect committed against Marduk, as suggested on tablet III, lines 58–61, which, although only partially preserved, do reveal enough to warrant such a conclusion:

> . . . my sin . . .
> . . . my iniquity . . .
> . . . my transgression . . .
> He caused the wind to carry off my acts of negligence.[4]

This is further clarified in another line associated with tablet III, which reads "let the one who was negligent of Esagil learn from my example."[5] In the end, Shubshi-meshre-Shakkan's suffering appears to fall under the notion of retributive justice. The work does not represent an exposé of the failure of the wisdom movement to account adequately for the suffering of the innocent as the book of Job does by presenting the sages and their arguments (from the mouths of Job's friends) and then having God state that they are wrong.

---

1. The tablet is designated RS 25.460 and known as "The Righteous Sufferer" or "A Hymn to Marduk." See Yoram Cohen, *Wisdom from the Late Bronze Age*, ed. Theodore J. Lewis, Writings from the Ancient World 29 (Atlanta: Society of Biblical Literature, 2013), 165–75.
2. A Babylonian text also known as "The Poem of the Righteous Sufferer" or "The Babylonian Job."
3. Direct parallels will be discussed in the relevant passages throughout the commentary.
4. Amar Annus and Alan Lenzi, *Ludlul Bēl Nēmeqi: The Standard Babylonian Poem of the Righteous Sufferer*, SAACT 7 (Winona Lake, IN: Eisenbrauns, 2010), 39.
5. Annus and Lenzi, *Ludlul Bēl Nēmeqi*, xxiv. "Esagil" was the name for the temple of Marduk in Babylon.

A closer thematic parallel for this Akkadian text would be one of the psalms of thanksgiving. W. G. Lambert suggests that it would be better described as a Babylonian *Pilgrim's Progress* than as a close parallel to the book of Job.[6]

In spite of the various similarities, the story of Job introduces some unique elements. The most significant is that Job's monotheism raises unique problems of theodicy.[7] Yahweh is not like the gods of the nations—there are no other deities upon which blame for suffering can be leveled! Furthermore, Yahweh has revealed himself through his law. He has made it clear how his people should live and promised them good if they were obedient. So when good, faithful people suffered, it raised questions about why they were suffering, questions that are more acute for worshipers of Yahweh than for those who believed in a diverse pantheon of gods whose behavior was not always entirely predictable or consistent.

One of the closest parallels to Job is found in the "Righteous Sufferer's Prayer to Nabû," an Akkadian prayer text in which a wealthy man who finds himself nearing death defends his righteousness and asks why Nabû his god has abandoned him, calling for Nabû to save his life. As a prayer, it presents the predicament of the speaker but does not find a resolution, and so it reflects the book of Job to the point where Yahweh speaks to Job. There are, of course, differences. Aside from the relative brevity of the prayer, there is little to indicate that the sufferer believes that his troubles have been inflicted on him by Nabû, whereas Job assumes that Yahweh stands behind his troubles from the very beginning. Nonetheless, the general theme of the prayer is remarkably close to that of Job.[8]

---

6. W. G. Lambert, *Babylonian Wisdom Literature* (Oxford: Clarendon, 1960), 27. Hurowitz says: "it should not be compared with Job or called a 'Poem of the Righteous Sufferer' as is often done. Both Job and Šubši-mešrê-Šakkan suffered immeasurably even while they considered themselves righteous and wondered why they were so afflicted, but this is the full extent of the similarity. In the end Job comes out blameless while Šubši-mešrê-Šakkan is found lacking. In a broken context he speaks of 'my sin . . . my iniquity . . . my transgression . . . my negligence' (arnī . . . initta . . . šertī . . . egâtīja; III 58–61), and in fact he was worshipping the wrong god. He may have been ignoring Marduk inadvertently or out of ignorance but that was enough." See Victor Avigdor Hurowitz, "Is Ludlul Bēl Nēmeqi Wisdom Literature? A Review Article of: Annus, Amar and Alan Lenzi, Ludlul Bēl Nēmeqi: The Standard Babylonian Poem of the Righteous Sufferer," *JHebS* 11 (2011), https://doi.org/10.5508/jhs.2011.v11.r53, https://jhsonline.org/index.php/jhs/article/view/16488.

7. Note that Simo Parpola argues that the Assyrians were essentially monotheists worshiping Ashur and that their other "deities" were instead aspects or attributes of Ashur; see Simo Parpola, *Assyrian Prophecies* (Helsinki: Helsinki University Press, 1997), xix–xx.

8. The text of the prayer, translated by Alan Lenzi, is available online at http://akkpm.org/P338383.html.

EXPLAIN the Story

The opening chapters of the book of Job set the scene for all that will take place in the remainder of the book. Here we meet Job and are told by both the narrator and God himself that Job was "blameless and upright; he feared God and shunned evil" (Job 1:1, 8). We are given a glimpse into God's royal court in heaven so that we may know that what befalls Job is not the result of his sin—in fact, quite the reverse! Job is such an exemplary person that his motives are questioned, and the disasters that befall him serve to show not his sinfulness but that his motives are pure.

Introducing Job (1:1–5)

The syntax of the opening words to the book of Job, "In the land of Uz there lived a man whose name was Job," finds its closest parallel in two places in the Bible: in Nathan's parable (2 Sam 12:1) and Joash's fable (2 Kgs 14:9).[9] This suggests that the story of Job is introduced as some form of parable. Since parables were staples of wisdom teachers in the ancient world, this is hardly surprising. The idea that Job's story, at least as it is presented here, is not a verbatim record of historical events should not be a surprise to us—after all, the bulk of the book presents the characters speaking entirely in poetry, and real people do not debate in poetry! This is not to say that there was no historical Job any more than the modern musical *Hamilton* undermines the historical existence of Alexander Hamilton. Rather, it means no more than that this version of his story is stylized by the author. The existence of this poetic account of Job's life neither proves nor disproves the existence of an historical Job.

Scholars are unsure about the precise location of Job's home Uz. Most conclude that it lies somewhere near Edom (see Jer 25:20). The precise location is, however, less important to the story than the fact that it indicates that this tale is not set in Israel. This, along with a number of other clues, indicates that this story is set in patriarchal times (see the introduction on Date). Why would the Bible include a story from outside Israel in patriarchal times? One possibility is that the author wanted the reader to know that what we learn in Job is not something new; it is something God's people ought to have known from the beginning, and the mistakes of Job's friends—mistakes repeated by

9. Hartley, *Book of Job*, 65n1, suggests 2 Sam 12:1 and Esth 2:5 as parallels and says "nor does it signal that the account is fictional." Clines, however, explains why Esth 2:5 is not a true parallel; see David J. A. Clines, *Job 1–20*, WBC 17 (Dallas: Word, 1989), 9.

many throughout history—should never have been made and should not now be made.

The remainder of these opening verses introduce us to Job himself. The name Job does not appear to be a Hebrew name—fitting with the non-Israelite setting of the work—but the name does appear in other literature from the ancient Near East. Precisely what his name means is unclear—it could mean "where is my father" (perhaps in reference to God as his father and hence an implicit appeal for divine help), or else it could be related to the Hebrew word for "hate" and hence mean something like "the hated one." Whatever its derivation, the text does not attribute any explicit significance to his name, so perhaps we ought not to place too much weight on it either.

We are told that Job is "blameless and upright." For modern readers this and the subsequent descriptions of Job raise the question of whether we are being told that Job was sinless, for the remainder of the Bible makes it quite clear that no human being is sinless (and for Job, see Job 7:21; 13:26; 14:16–17). This question, however, goes beyond what we are told. That Job is blameless and upright indicates that he is both forgiven for any sins he may have committed (and so not held to blame for them) and one who seeks to live out a godly life (and hence upright). This is possible for a sinful human being because God has made a way for anyone to be blameless. In the Old Testament this involved sacrifices, which pointed to the ultimate sacrifice of Jesus. What we do see later in this chapter is that Job is scrupulous in offering sacrifices for sins (Job 1:5). Consequently, Job is "blameless and upright," and assuredly we should not expect him to be punished for sins dealt with through sacrifices already made.

The final clause tells us that Job feared God and turned from evil. Fearing God is elsewhere in the Bible the mark of both the righteous and the wise (cf. Prov 1:7). While it is certainly true that "fear" should be understood more as an attitude of respect and awe, it is probable that it should retain some amount of actual fear in the face of God who is supremely powerful and ultimately determines the course of one's life. The response of Isaiah to his vision of God in Isaiah 6 provides a salient lesson: Isaiah was a faithful servant of Yahweh, yet that did not fully prepare him for his encounter with God, at which point he cries out, "Woe to me, I am ruined!" Fearing God is a natural outworking of knowing who he is!

The author is at pains to assure us of this point: Job has not done anything to warrant the terrible events that are to unfold. There is nothing in his life that demands God's wrath. What is about to be unleashed on him is in no way a punishment for sin. The author states it here but also records God stating it explicitly later in this and the next chapter (Job 1:8; 2:3). It is vital to understand and remember this, for much of the later dialogue between Job and his friends turns on this very point. Too many readers throughout history have forgotten this point and wound up, like Job's friends, blaming Job for the trouble that befalls him.

In verses 2–3 the author turns to describe the blessings Job enjoys: he has seven sons, and it should be recalled that seven conveyed notions of completeness. So, aside from having many sons, which Psalm 127:3 notes is itself a blessing, Job has just the right number. He also has three daughters, a number significant primarily because it gives him a total of ten children, and powers of ten seem here to be used to express the notion of abundant blessing (7 sons + 3 daughters = 10 children; 7,000 sheep + 3,000 camels = 10,000 animals; 500 yoke of oxen (where a "yoke" refers to a pair of oxen) + 500 female donkeys = 1,500 working animals).

A brief note about Job's camels may also be helpful. For quite a while scholars argued that camels were not domesticated until some time in the first millennium BC, and so the Bible's references to camels in more ancient settings were thought to be clearly anachronistic. More recent research has overturned this thinking, and it is now held that camels were domesticated at least early in the second millennium BC. In light of that, references to camels here and elsewhere in texts set in ancient times should no longer be assumed to be anachronistic.[10]

As would seem appropriate to Job's personal righteousness, we are told that he was wealthy. In the ancient world, wealth was often considered a sign of divine approval, and Job is presented as, in all ways, the perfect example of the upright and righteous man who feared God and shunned evil. This depiction of Job sets the stage for all that is to follow.

The final clause of verse 3 summarizes the point the author has made thus far: Job is the greatest of all the people of the east. The reference here to the "east" places this story in patriarchal times, as this is where the bulk of humanity is said to have lived before Abram began his westward journey to the promised land. The point is thus not that there were better people in the west but that Job was outstanding in his godliness in a world so ancient that even the author of the book of Job could think of it as "ancient."

The narrator next informs us in verses 4–5 that Job's sons would hold regular feasts. The frequency with which these events took place is not particularly

10. See, most recently, Martin Heide and Joris Peters, *Camels in the Biblical World*, HACL 10 (University Park: Pennsylvania State University Press, 2021).

clear (the NIV's "on their birthdays" is woodenly "each on his day," which could refer to their birthdays as the similar "his day" does for Job in Job 3:1, or simply to them taking scheduled turns to host a feast). It is clear, however, that these feasts would last for several days ("a period of feasting" in v. 5 is rendered woodenly "the days of the feast"). The point of the text is simply to state that Job's children participated in regular, elaborate celebrations and to record Job's response.

The word "curse" in verse 5 (and also later in 1:11; 2:5, 9) translates the Hebrew verb *brk*, meaning "bless." The author uses the word euphemistically, perhaps to avoid explicitly associating the verb "curse" with God, but perhaps also to catch the attention of the reader (see further below on 1:9–11). The book of Job is a wisdom text, and as such we ought to be prepared to think carefully about the way the story is told.

These verses serve two functions: they set the scene for verses 18–19 below and they illustrate Job's piety. Job is meticulous in ensuring that his children remain blameless to the extent that he offers sacrifices even when he is not certain that they have sinned. Job's attention to detail and scrupulous sacrifices assure us that he is worthy of the description "blameless and upright." The point is not that Job is actually sinless (see 7:21; 13:26; 14:16–17), but that his sin is dealt with in accordance with what God requires and that his piety and devotion to God ensure that he wholeheartedly seeks to live in accord with God's precepts—he was, as it were, the model citizen par excellence. Job here is also depicted as being acutely aware that to curse God is a most egregious sin, a point that becomes important as the Satan will later insist that Job would be willing to curse God given the right circumstances.

Behind the Scenes: God's Heavenly Court (1:6–12)

The second scene in the book of Job takes us into a heavenly setting that depicts a royal court where the king, Yahweh, is enthroned before his attendants and courtiers (cf. 1 Kgs 22:19–22; Dan 7:9–14). The author uses the name of God to make it clear to the reader that this non-Israelite from patriarchal times serves the God of Abraham, Isaac, and Jacob. We already know who this God is and what he is like. The story of Job connects to this history of the true God whom we know from his activities throughout history. The author begins with the presumption that we are already familiar with his character in his story. Furthermore, as a text about wisdom, our reading of this text is to be subject to the fundamental principle to be employed when interpreting wisdom, namely, that "the fear of Yahweh is the beginning of knowledge" (Prov 1:7, NIV modified). Overlooking these points leads some readers to infer the entirety of Yahweh's character from the very limited presentation of the prologue of Job. While it is unfashionable to speak of what an ancient author knew, it is hard to dispute the point that the author of Job expected the audience to know who Yahweh was and, when reading the text, to include that information as they sought to understand what was written. To exclude that information is to misread the book. But Job is not a standalone book; it is inextricably connected to the larger context of the remainder of the Old Testament.

Into this heavenly court come the "sons of God," a reference to angelic beings. Among them is one described by a specific title, "the Satan," who is most likely here counted as one of their number, although the word "also" (Hebrew *gam*) and Yahweh's first question in the next verse could give the impression that the Satan is not normally to be found here.[11] Although frequently taken as a name, the Hebrew term here is more likely a title describing the role this particular angelic being undertook. Unlike names in the Old Testament, the word is preceded by the definite article.[12] It is also worth noting that the Hebrew word *satan* appears elsewhere without reference to the Satan (for example, see Num 22:22 where the angel of Yahweh opposes Balaam).

The Hebrew word *satan* refers to an adversary or opponent of some form. Traditionally the Satan is Yahweh's adversary despite being clearly subordinate to him. The manner in which he will address Yahweh in the coming verses shows little of the deference that would seem appropriate before the divine king. In the end, the Satan's presence here is intriguing. The scene that unfolds is somewhat reminiscent of a judicial setting where Job's faith is on trial with the Satan filling the role of the prosecutor.

By the time of the New Testament, Satan was universally recognized as a supernatural being who opposed Jesus and sought to derail his mission. As the Satan here opposes Yahweh, it seems probable that, while we don't yet have a fully developed (or revealed) understanding of this figure, there is nonetheless some connection between the Satan in Job and Satan who stands in opposition to God in the New Testament.[13]

---

11. Note that Crenshaw argues that the Hebrew particle *gam* implies that the adversary is an intruder, see James L. Crenshaw, *Old Testament Wisdom: An Introduction* (Atlanta: John Knox, 2010), 92. Contrary to this is Christopher A. Rollston, "An Ur-History of the New Testament Devil: The Celestial שטן (*Śāṭān*) in Zechariah and Job," in *Evil in Second Temple Judaism and Early Christianity*, ed. Chris Keith and Loren T. Stuckenbruck, WUNT 2.417 (Tübingen: Mohr Siebeck, 2016), 1–16.

12. See Paul Joüon and T. Muraoka, *A Grammar of Biblical Hebrew* 2 vols. (Rome: Pontifical Biblical Institute, 1993) §137b.

13. Clines says, "Although [Satan in later Jewish and Christian theology] is clearly derived from [the Satan in Job], it would be best to ignore the later development of the figure when establishing the nature and role of 'the Satan' in Job" (Clines, *Job 1–20*, 19).

Yahweh initiates the dialogue in verse 7 with a question for the Satan: "Where have you come from?" Doubtless Job's readers have always been aware that such a question was not necessary for an omniscient God, but we as readers are not blessed with all knowledge, and so the storyteller uses this opening dialogue to provide us with critical information.

The Satan's answer raises some questions. He says that he had been "roaming throughout the earth, going back and forth on it." David Clines suggests that the first verb, translated "roaming," refers to travels that are purposeful, but this may not be an inherent quality of the verb so much as a consequence of the contexts in which it is found. Nonetheless, the response of the Satan lets us know that he has been traversing the world of humans. Whether he was actively looking for something or someone is not clear, although in light of the subsequent discussion it has been plausibly suggested that part of the Satan's job description may have been to assess the piety and faithfulness of human beings. This makes sense of Yahweh bringing Job to the Satan's attention in the next verse.

God identifies Job as his servant (1:8). Although servant language is used frequently throughout the Bible, there are only a very few individuals explicitly described by God as his servant: most frequently Moses (Josh 1:1, 13, etc.) but also Abraham (Gen 26:24), Joshua (Josh 24:29; Judg 2:8), Isaiah (Isa 20:3), Eliakim son of Hilkiah (Isa 22:20), the servant of Yahweh in Isaiah (Isa 42:19; 43:10), Zerubbabel (Hag 2:23), and David (1 Chr 17:4).[14] At the very least, then, this draws attention to Job as special. And this point is made quite explicit: "There is no one on earth like him" (Job 2:3).

This highlights an element of this story that is worth emphasizing: Job is not representative of everyone. We cannot automatically identify with Job when we suffer because both the narrator of Job's story and God himself highlight Job's uniqueness—there is no one like him. Already this warns us that Job's story may not function as a theodicy, since Job is a special case.

The remainder of verse 8 presents God's reason for recognizing Job's uniqueness: "he is blameless and upright, a man who fears God and shuns evil." This reiterates what the narrator had told us in verse 1—the point is not that Job is sinless or that he has never sinned, as had been made apparent through the account of Job's habitual actions back in verse 4–5.

The Satan's answer (1:9–11) implies that he is aware of Job but argues that his upright life is motivated by self-interest. Job is as Yahweh has described

14. This list includes only individuals explicitly identified by God as his servant, not those described by others as servants of God, nor groups identified as servants.

him simply because of the benefits the relationship affords him: he is protected from harm ("Have you not put a hedge around him") and has had his endeavors in all areas aided by divine intervention ("you have blessed the work of his hands"). The Satan proposes that Job's true motives can easily be revealed through a simple test: take away the blessings he has been given and then "he will surely curse you to your face."

This last phrase is key in what follows, where the measure of Job's response will be found in his spoken response to Yahweh. The Hebrew text (and the Old Greek translation of it) literally read "bless you to your face," but scholars almost universally agree that the author has used "bless" here as a euphemism for "curse" in order to avoid actually writing the words for "curse" together with God's name (the same thing happens in 1 Kgs 21:10, 13). The other way to read it would be with "bless" used sarcastically, but the result is the same. The Satan is establishing the means by which his argument will be proven, and in each of the two tests of Job it is in Job's ultimate vocal responses (Job 1:20–22; 2:10) that we shall be able to assess the truth or falsity of the Satan's claims.

The scene that takes place in the heavenly court ends in verse 12 with Yahweh granting the Satan permission to strike Job's possessions (including his children). This response, however, immediately prompts the question: Why does God allow the test to proceed? Surely God could simply assert that he knows the heart of Job and knows that his devotion is not ultimately motivated by selfish concerns.

The initial answer to this question lies in the fact that Job is not a historical account but a wisdom tale—it is designed to teach the audience something. At that level, the story seeks to address a deeply ingrained belief that individual human suffering is the direct consequence of individual sin. That this belief is deeply ingrained is apparent from the number of times it appears throughout the Bible, raising its head explicitly in the Gospels when Jesus addresses the question (e.g., Luke 13:1–5; John 9:1–3). All too frequently today we still ask what we have done to deserve difficult times when they befall us. This warrants more than brief rebuttal. The point needs to be made clearly and repeatedly, and this is what the author of Job does for us.

Yet herein lies a further clue to something more that is happening in Job, something that is not immediately apparent on the surface of the story. One of the main points of the book of Job is that governing history is a complex task beyond the scope of human understanding. If we, the audience of the book, were to understand everything about Job's suffering, we would be in danger of failing to appreciate this major point of the book. Consequently, there are a number of clues throughout the book that point to the fact that more lies behind Job's suffering than merely this test prompted by the Satan's claims. Job's suffering will demonstrate that God truly does know his servant, but it will also serve some other purpose—a purpose we can only speculate upon.[15] In this way we, like Job, must come to the realization that we live in a vastly complex universe and should not expect to comprehend all that God is doing. We must, in the end, trust that God works in all things for the good of those who believe.

Job's First Test (1:13–19)

The scene is set for the unfolding tragedies that are inflicted upon Job. Verse 13 begins with the same words, "One day," that introduce verse 6 (cf. 1 Sam 1:4; 14:1; 2 Kgs 4:8, 11, 18) and, rather than identify a specific feast, simply inform us that Job's actions happened on the occasion of one of the feasts. The reference to the feast day envelopes the reporting of the disasters with the feasting of Job's children mentioned at the beginning and end of the reports.

That the events are reported to Job by messengers makes it clear that Job is not physically present to witness any of these events. This serves a couple of purposes: it allows the reports to be delivered in rapid succession so that neither the audience nor Job has any real time to process the significance of the events as they are reported. It may also have allowed this account of Job to have been a performance, like a play, wherein the complex depictions of disasters are replaced by simple reports of them.

Each of the reports to Job follows the same pattern: something happened and only the reporting messenger escaped with his life. The rapidity of the reports is underlined by the conjunctive phrase "while he was still speaking." Each disaster is reported by a single survivor, described as a "messenger"—the same word (Hebrew *mal'ak*) elsewhere in the Old Testament is used to refer to angels (e.g., Gen 48:16; Exod 23:20; etc.). Here, however, it is clear that these individuals are human, for they are each the sole survivor from among Job's servants.

Four disasters are reported to Job, of which two are attributed to people and two to divine causes. The first is the attack of the Sabeans resulting in the loss of Job's oxen and donkeys. The designation here for this group is also used of the Queen of Sheba who visits Solomon (1 Kgs 10), a place identified with modern-day Yemen. However, the identification here is not unproblematic—the description of these Sabeans as a marauding band prompts many to question a simple identification of these attackers with Sheba. In the end,

15. Shields, "Malevolent or Mysterious?," 255–70.

the precise identification of the Sabeans is of little import to the story that unfolds. Perhaps the one point that can reasonably be made is that the attack would seem so surprising that its unexpected nature reflects something of the supernatural manipulation going on behind the scenes.

The second disaster is described as "a fire of God." The same expression appears elsewhere in 2 Kings 1:12 to describe fire called down by Elijah, which consumes fifty soldiers (a similar but not identical expression is found in 1 Kgs 18:38). This description is in keeping with the biblical understanding that God is sovereign, so that even though we know that these disasters befall Job at the Satan's behest, ultimately they do so only because God has permitted them.[16]

The third disaster arrives at the hand of the Chaldeans. While this term is used to refer to members of the Neo-Babylonian Empire of the mid-first millennium BC, the account here does not appear consistent with an imperial force. Rather, the use of the term here designates a more ancient nomadic group to which Assyrian annals make reference.[17] The description of their attack on three fronts reflects a known military strategy (see Judg 7:16; 9:43; 1 Sam 11:11; 13:17) that establishes both their number and experience in carrying out such attacks. Job's camels were taken and servants stood no chance against them, as all bar one were slaughtered.

The final and greatest disaster is the loss of Job's children. While not explicitly ascribed to a supernatural source, the description of a wind that strikes four corners of a house together with such force that it destroys the building and kills all the occupants clearly points to a supernatural origin.

At the completion of seven brief verses, all Job's possessions and all of his family—bar his wife—are gone. The relentless, unremitting reporting of the disasters to Job leaves us reeling. The Satan has executed his task with overwhelming efficiency, allowing neither Job nor the audience to recover or even to respond. There was no other way to take all that Job had that could have struck him harder and tested him more, and so all eyes are now on Job to see whether he will bear out the Satan's claim or remain faithful to God.

Job's Response to His Losses (1:20–22)

Job's immediate response is presented in actions not words: he tore his robe and shaved his head. Both acts reflect traditional expressions of mourning in

16. It may also be that the Hebrew word *'elohim* here functions as a superlative with the meaning "an intense fire"; see D. Winton Thomas, "A Consideration of Some Unusual Ways of Expressing the Superlative in Hebrew," VT 3.3 (1953): 209–24.

17. See Clines, *Job 1–20*, 32–33; Alan R. Millard, "Daniel 1–6 and History," *EQ* 49.2 (1977): 69–71.

the Bible. For tearing one's robe see, for example, Genesis 37:29; Joshua 7:6. Although tearing one's robe could be a quick response, shaving one's head (see Isa 15:2; 22:12; Jer 7:29; etc.) would not have been. That the act itself was proscribed by the Law (see Deut 14:1) reminds us that this story is set outside of Israel and before the time of Moses. Job's deliberate and slow actions reflect thought and intention—Job's response is not rash but derives from thoughtful and faithful reflection of what he has experienced in light of his relationship with God.

Job's final physical act, falling to the ground to worship, preempts his spoken response. The words that describe Job's act here—falling to the ground and worshiping—are repeated identically in 2 Samuel 1:2, and similar expressions are found in Joshua 5:14; 1 Samuel 20:41; 2 Samuel 14:4, 22; 2 Kings 4:37. Surprisingly it is only Job's act that is directed toward God—the term translated "worship" in this verse more generally refers to bowing down before a person of greater import as an act of obeisance. This makes it clear that Job's response here is not an involuntary response to his pain (as could well be expected in the circumstances) but a deliberate act aimed toward God in recognition of his status.

Job's reply, when it finally comes in verse 21, is brief but powerfully emotive. His words are echoed later by the apostle Paul in 1 Timothy 6:7 and are a recognition that all that we have in this world comes ultimately from God, and there is nothing we can hold on to and take with us (a point also noted by the Teacher in Eccl 5:15). Both Job and the narrator of the story recognize that nothing in this universe that happens does so apart from God's sovereign rule, and so Job attributes his loss to Yahweh rather than the Satan or the various human agents described in the narrative.

The most significant words in these verses are the last: "may the name of the LORD be praised" (Job 1:21). The Satan had predicted that Job would curse Yahweh, but Job's words vindicate both Yahweh and Job: he does not curse, but instead he blesses (Hebrew *brk*; the word translated "be praised" in the NIV is often elsewhere translated as "bless"). The challenge appears to be over. Job's faith has been shown to not be self-serving and has stood up to the most devastating losses. To emphasize this point the narrator offers his own conclusion: "In all this, Job did not sin by charging God with wrongdoing" (1:22), and this will be reflected in Yahweh's own words to the Satan in Job 2:3.

The Satan's Second Challenge and Test (2:1–6)

The opening scene of Job 2 is strikingly familiar, more or less a verbatim repeat of Job 1:6–8. Yahweh explicitly notes that the Satan's claim that Job's faith was self-serving has been shown to be false. Rather than concede defeat, however, the Satan proceeds to argue that the test needs to be extended.

The meaning of the Satan's initial response—"skin for skin"—is itself not entirely clear. It is probably a colloquial or proverbial phrase familiar to the original audience, although it appears nowhere else in the Bible. Its meaning is clear from the context: Job is still preserving his own interests in order to remain healthy. Deprive him of his health and he will then certainly curse God and so prove that his faithfulness was merely self-serving.

The Satan's wording here is also enlightening: it is Yahweh who is to "stretch out your hand and . . . he will surely curse [*brk*] you to your face" (Job 2:5) Throughout the prologue it is clear that the ultimate responsibility for Job's fate lies in Yahweh's hands and that the Satan has no independent power to do anything to Job. Even though the Satan is the instrument of affliction, Yahweh, the Satan, and even Job himself (see 2:10) all recognize that it is ultimately entirely contingent upon Yahweh's sanction. The notion of divine sovereignty is never questioned in the book of Job. So once again, God allows the Satan to further test Job to prove this point. In chapter 1 the Satan was prevented from harming Job himself. This limitation is removed but replaced with another preventing him from taking Job's life.

In this context, the prohibition against taking Job's life appears to be a merciful constraint, but Job will not come to see it this way, for by the time we reach 6:8–10, Job will be longing for God to allow him to die.

Job's Second Test (2:7–8)

The Satan's actions are described more succinctly than in the previous chapter, requiring only one verse. While there is no indication of the timeframe for Job's affliction, the terse description gives the impression that the onset is rapid. Many readers have wondered what precise malady afflicted Job, but the text simply describes symptoms: "painful sores from the soles of his feet to the crown of his head" (2:7).

The remainder of the book does provide some further light on Job's symptoms and the effects of this disease. The very first is that Job presumably finds some relief from scraping the sores with a broken piece of pottery (2:8; whether this is physical or psychological relief is not made clear). David Clines summarizes some of the other references to Job's disease as including

> the repeated eruption of pustules (7:5) and blackening and peeling off of the skin (30:30) are the most definite signs in the poem of a skin disease, and correspond to the itching purulence mentioned here. Other symptoms

> are more general: emaciation (19:20), fever (30:30b), nightmares (7:14) and sleeplessness (7:4), weeping (16:16).[18]

In addition to these, the reference to strangling in Job 7:15 may suggest that his illness also manifested itself in breathing difficulties.

Perhaps the most helpful detail lies in the fact that the precise phrase, "painful sores" (Hebrew *shekhin raʿ*), together with a reference to the extent of the sores, appears as one of the curses for disobeying the covenant in Deuteronomy 28:35 in language strongly reminiscent of Job's affliction:

> The LORD will afflict your knees and legs with painful boils that cannot be cured, spreading from the soles of your feet to the top of your head.

This strong linguistic connection may well have been deliberate, such that Job's author wants to note that, while disobedience to the covenant may result in this malady, suffering from such extensive painful boils is itself not proof that one has either broken the covenant or (in Job's case) committed some sin that would result in this condition. On the other hand, the association would have also helped the audience appreciate the perspective of Job's friends. Their claim that Job was suffering as a consequence of disobedience was clearly not entirely irrational but rather a conclusion that appears a reasonable application of the covenant with which they (i.e., the audience) were familiar—and perhaps just the sort of reasoning they would themselves be tempted to apply when they encountered anyone suffering in this way. The stage is set so that such thinking will be appropriately nuanced in the minds of the audience as Job's story unfolds, if not in the minds of Job's friends.

While we know that Job's condition will not prove to be terminal (Job 2:6), Job did not know this. Job was faced with the very real possibility that the condition was incurable (cf. Deut 28:35), such that Job now faces the expectation that he will live the remainder of his life in this condition. His response needs to be seen in the light of this possibility to understand its full impact.

The final note in this verse indicates that Job is sitting among the ashes. Ashes are often associated with mourning (e.g., 2 Sam 13:19; Esth 4:3; Ps 102:9; Isa 61:3; Jer 6:26; Ezek 27:30), so this is an appropriate place for Job to sit—aside from the fact that, having lost everything, he has nowhere else to sit.

---

18. Clines, *Job 1–20*, 49.

Job's Second Response (2:9–10)

Thus far Job has not spoken in response to his new affliction. Until he does speak, the outcome of the challenge the Satan has put to Yahweh cannot be decided. This situation is resolved with just a few words from Job's wife. The first thing to note is that she begins by acknowledging that Job's integrity stands—thus far he has done nothing to warrant condemnation. While her advice—"Curse God and die!"—aligns her with the Satan by encouraging Job to curse God, it seems that she offers this advice in response to the suffering Job as a possible way of escape, probably thinking that death is better than living in this condition, and that cursing God would result in Job's death (cf. 1 Sam 3:13).

Job's wife woodenly says, "bless [*brk*] God and die" and, while most readers recognize here another example of the euphemistic use of "bless" in place of "curse," some have made alternate suggestions that are more charitable toward Job's wife. Nonetheless, Job's response makes it clear that we should understand her use of "bless" in the same way as the Satan's.

It is also apparent that Job's wife expects that, were he to curse God, he would die as a result. The alternative—that she is suggesting that Job should curse God and then take his own life—makes little sense. (Why then curse God? Why not simply tell Job to end his life?). Either way she is essentially encouraging Job to commit suicide and thereby to end his misery, but Job has no hesitation in rejecting her suggestion (although in the next chapter Job will come close to contemplating this again).

Another example of a wife speaking to her husband like this is found in the Hittite story "Appu and His Two Sons":

> Appu's wife questioned their servants: "He has never had success before. You don't think he has now had success, do you?" The woman went and lay down with Appu with her clothes on. Appu awoke from his sleep, and his wife questioned him: "You have never had success before. Have you now had success?" When Appu heard this, he replied: "You are a woman and think like one. You know nothing at all."[19]

Job's wife's comment demands a response from Job, and so it is forthcoming. He begins with a rebuke to his wife. Notably he does not say she is foolish, just that she is speaking as one of "the foolish women" would. He recognizes that her response may have arisen under duress, and we as readers ought to recognize that, to a large part, she too has shared in Job's suffering.

---

19. "Appu and His Two Sons," trans. Harry A. Hoffnew Jr. (*COS* 1.58:153).

Who are these "foolish women" to whom Job refers? The writer seems to identify them as a specific group through the use of the definite article, "the foolish women," but the precise identity of the group is not spelled out. David Clines suggests that this should be understood to refer to lower-class or common women as opposed to the higher class among whom Job and his wife would normally mix.[20] While this may be the case, there is only enough information to be certain that "the foolish women" were those who were not God-fearing (as Job was) and who offered advice without reference to any relationship with the living God (cf. Ps 14:1).

Job proceeds to elaborate on why his wife has spoken foolishly by offering an explanation of his thinking: "Shall we accept good from God, and not trouble?" (Job 2:10). His response makes it clear that he continues to recognize that, behind all that happens, is God. The Satan may have been the instrument through which his affliction arrived, but nothing would have happened to him if God had not allowed it. Job recognizes this, and neither the narrator nor God himself demur.

While the word translated "trouble" here has a broad range of meanings, including "evil," that is, in a moral sense, here it seems to refer to anything bad. The book opens by noting that Job turns away from trouble (1:1, 8; 2:3 where the NIV translates the same word with "evil") but also describes the boils that afflict Job with the same word in 2:7 (where the NIV translates it by "painful").

As in chapter 1, the narrator notes Job's faithful response: "In all this, Job did not sin in what he said." Job has been vindicated in his own words and in the words of the narrator. The concluding words to this comment, that Job "did not sin in what he said" may give the impression that the narrator is leaving open the possibility that Job did sin in some other way, but the emphasis is actually a response to the Satan's challenge, which anticipated Job's fall from grace through a verbal response as stated in verse 5: "he will surely curse you to your face."

The first challenge resulted in Job losing all of his possessions; the second results in affliction to his entire body. There is no room in either case for the Satan to return to argue that the testing was not complete. And while we might almost expect the Satan to return to issue another challenge, he does not. The point has been made, the claims of the Satan have been decisively disproven, and Yahweh's faith in his servant has been justified. Job is not a servant of Yahweh merely for the benefits he reaps from the relationship.

If the Satan doesn't return for a third round, we might wonder why Job's

20. Clines, *Job 1–20*, 53–54.

suffering continues. That is a good question worth pondering that we shall return to in the Live the Story section below.

The Arrival of Job's Friends (2:11–13)

The prose prologue closes with the introduction of Job's three friends. While this account follows in quick succession to all that has preceded it, there is likely some delay—news of Job's predicament would have taken time to reach the friends, and then they would have to make arrangements to meet up and visit Job.

It is not entirely clear where the friends are coming from. Teman, Eliphaz's home, is referred to elsewhere (e.g., Gen 36:34; Amos 1:12; Obad 9; etc.) and was an important town in Edom. Neither Shuah nor Naamah are easily identifiable, but it seems likely that these, too, were to be found in Edom. Their names are also not typically Israelite and seem to also be connected to Edom. The name Eliphaz appears in Genesis 36 as the father of Teman and eldest son of Esau, which further strengthens the connection with Edom. While various suggestions for the meanings of their names have been made, they do not appear to have any significant relevance to the story that unfolds.

The aim of the friends, to comfort Job in his affliction, begins something of a theme in the book. To comfort is an appropriate response in situations like Job's, and the friends' aim is noble. We shall learn, however, that they fail to fulfill their task, providing no real comfort to Job (cf. Job 16:2; 21:34) despite Job's need and desire for comfort. Ultimately, it is only at the end, following God's words to him, that Job will finally be comforted and be able to begin to rebuild his life (see comments on Job 42:6).

When they do eventually arrive and see Job, he is unrecognizable and so we, as readers, realize just how significant Job's transformation has been as a result of his affliction. Their response is to tear their robes and sprinkle dust on their heads. This echoes Job's own response to the first set of tragedies reported in Job 1:20 but adds to it what is most likely another mourning rite, that of throwing dust over one's head (cf. Josh 7:6; 1 Sam 4:12; Lam 2:10; etc.). After this they sit with Job, in silence, for seven days.

Seven days seems to be a typical period of mourning in the Old Testament (e.g., Gen 50:10; 1 Sam 31:13), but this may also be a simple reference to the fullness of time. Silence (or, more precisely, not speaking, as they may well have continued their weeping) itself is a common response to tragedy in the ancient world—probably both an empathic response as well as an expression of shock at his state. One such example is found in tablet III of the "Poem of the Righteous Sufferer":

Heavy was his hand upon me, I could not bear it!
Dread of him was oppressive, it [me].
His fierce [pun]ishment [ ], the deluge,
His stride was . . . , it . . . [ ].
[Ha]rsh, severe illness does not . . . [ ] my person,
I lost sight of [aler]tness, [ ] make my mind stray.
I gro[an] day and night alike,
Dreaming and waking [I am] equally wretched.
A remarkable young man of extraordinary physique,
Magnificent in body, clothed in new garments,
Because I was only half awake, his features lacked form.
He was clad in splendor, robed in dread—
He came in upon me, he stood over me.
[When I saw him, my] flesh grew numb.
[ ] "The Lady(?) has sent [me],
[ ]."
[ ] I tried to tell [my people],
"[ ] sent [for me]."
They were silent and did not [speak],
They heard me [in silence and did not answer].[21]

In tablet III of "The Great Cairo Hymn of Praise to Amun-Re," the netherworld is referred to as the "Land of Silence" and elsewhere Osiris, the Egyptian god of the dead, is referred to by the epithet of "Lord of Silence."[22] These backgrounds suggest that the response of Job's friends is more profound than merely not knowing what to say to him. They see him as being as good as dead.

LIVE the Story

Should We Identify with Job?

Job suffers greatly. He loses everything he owns. He loses his children. He loses his health. Suffering and loss are central to the story of Job. We all suffer too, and this shared human experience and a desire to find some application for the story of Job in our lives prompts us to ask how Job's suffering informs our own suffering.

21. "Poem of the Righteous Sufferer," trans. Benjamin R. Foster (*COS* 1.153:489–90).
22. "The Great Cairo Hymn of Praise to Amun-Re," trans. Robert K. Ritner (*COS* 1.25:39, 100).

The first thing to note, however, is that in some important respects we are not like Job. Job is singled out by the narrator and by God as being "the greatest man among all the people of the East." He was blameless and upright, feared God, and turned away from evil. He was exceptional and unlike anyone in his generation. Job was confident that he had not done anything to warrant the trouble that befell him. None of us can truly make that claim. None of us are likely to be singled out by God as unparalleled examples of godliness. And so, when difficult times come upon us, we cannot be certain that they are not some form of discipline, or punishment for a sin we have committed, or persecution for our faith, or something else altogether. We cannot be certain unless God reveals to us the reason for our suffering.

Furthermore, as readers of the book of Job, we are privy to a series of events taking place in heaven, where we discover that, at least in part, Job's suffering is a result of his exceptional piety and goodness. There is no way that any similar debate has taken place in heaven over our status, so at one level we cannot be suffering for the same reason that Job suffers.

These considerations all lead to the conclusion that we cannot identify with Job. But perhaps in this we are premature. For in some ways we are like Job. While Job was confident he did not deserve the suffering that had come upon him, he did not know—and he never found out—why he suffered. When we suffer we rarely discover why bad things are happening, at best only imagining vague generalizations or unsubstantiated suppositions as the rationale for the suffering. In this way we are like Job. We often share his ignorance surrounding the real reason behind our suffering.

And, like Job, we are right to look for a reason for the suffering. If we subscribe to the same worldview as Job—at least in so far as that worldview is founded upon the conviction that there is a sovereign Creator who is responsible not only for the formation of the universe but also for its ongoing sustenance—then the things that take place in our lives are not random or meaningless. There is a purpose, as Paul makes clear in Romans 8:28, "in all things God works for the good of those who love him." That is, not merely in *some* things but in *all* things. And if we believe that and the many other passages in the Bible that make it clear that God oversees even the most apparently insignificant events of this world, then the only logical conclusion is that there is a reason for our suffering, and there was a reason for Job's suffering.

And furthermore, as will become clear in the discussion below, Job's troubles are not solely the result of the wager between God and the Satan—something else is going on. So in the end Job suffers for unknown reasons just as we do. So in this, too, we are like Job.

So the answer is we are both unlike and like Job. There are lessons to be learned for each of us, but they are not going to be about why we suffer. The one foundational lesson about suffering that we must learn from Job is that, without specific divine revelation, we cannot know precisely why we are suffering. We cannot simply view our personal suffering as the inevitable outworking of some personal sin. It may be that it is, but it may also be that it isn't. The idea that our own troubles are penalties for our own sins is pervasive throughout human history. Jesus encountered it in his day (see Luke 13:1–5; John 9:1–3). The story of Job, however, warns us that this connection is not certain—some suffering in the world and in our lives does not arise from our own personal sinfulness.

Job and Jesus

If there are some ways that we are like Job, then there are also ways in which Job, the innocent man who suffered, both resembles Jesus and differs from him. Most obviously is that very point that this man Job did not suffer as he did for his own sins. While there is no doubt, reflecting on the consistent teaching of Scripture, that Job was a sinner and so needed to be saved from the consequences of his sin, the book of Job makes it very, very clear that the suffering of Job that it records is not the result of his sin—the point is made by both the narrator of the story and by God himself in the prologue. That is why we have the background we read in the prologue: this man was blameless and upright and feared God. His suffering came about, at one level, in response to the Satan's claim that Job was only pious out of self-interest—there was no true devotion to Yahweh, there was no love for God, just love for self that sought to manipulate God into blessing him. In light of this, God agreed to allow Job to be tested to prove his true motives—even though, of course, God knew Job's heart all along. But had the tale here ended with a simple assertion by God, then neither Job nor we would have learned the lessons the book teaches.

So it is clear that this suffering wise man, Job, did not suffer for his own sins. Such circumstances ought to immediately remind us of Jesus, the greater one who also suffered although innocent. Job establishes a precedent within the Bible for innocent suffering. His story makes it clear that it is possible for an innocent person to suffer and for that suffering not to be the invariable consequence of one's individual transgressions. The story of Job taught that the idea of an innocent person suffering was viable and prepared God's people, a people who—like almost all religious people through history—held strongly to the notion that God dispenses justice and that suffering was an instrument of that justice, for the idea that it was indeed possible for an innocent person to suffer.

This, in turn, allowed for a vital step in the preparation God was making for the coming of his Messiah. For his Messiah would not only be one who was innocent but suffered. No, he would be an innocent who suffered *vicariously*—who suffered in place of others—and who suffered *voluntarily*. And this idea, that the Messiah would ultimately be a king who served others by suffering in their place, was an idea that would also be revealed to God's people in the course of time. This next step in the story of salvation would be revealed in Isaiah, well before the arrival of the one to whom the words pointed:

> [4]Surely he took up our pain
> and bore our suffering,
> yet we considered him punished by God,
> stricken by him, and afflicted.
> [5]But he was pierced for our transgressions,
> he was crushed for our iniquities;
> the punishment that brought us peace was on him,
> and by his wounds we are healed.
> [6]We all, like sheep, have gone astray,
> each of us has turned to our own way;
> and the LORD has laid on him
> the iniquity of us all. (Isa 53:4–6)

Thus the suffering innocent Job pointed to the suffering innocent servant who would die to save his people from the wrath of God. As we listen to Job's story it is thus appropriate to ponder the innocent one who would come after Job and give thanks for the story of God we journey through as we read Scripture, and our place in it.

Who Is (the) Satan in Job's Life and Ours?

In these chapters of the book we are introduced to a character designated *the Satan*. While most scholars do not read back into Job what we know of Satan from the New Testament, we should not think that this character in Job does not inform later understanding of Satan. As a result, when we read about Satan in the New Testament, it is appropriate to acknowledge some link back to the prologue to the book of Job.

So, in Luke 22:31–34 we find Jesus warning Simon Peter that he will face trials at the hand of Satan:

> "Simon, Simon, Satan has asked to sift all of you as wheat. But I have prayed for you, Simon, that your faith may not fail. And when you have turned back, strengthen your brothers."
>
> But he replied, "Lord, I am ready to go with you to prison and to death."
>
> Jesus answered, "I tell you, Peter, before the rooster crows today, you will deny three times that you know me."

In this passage we hear that Satan continues to act in accordance with the way the Satan of Job's prologue behaves—testing the faithfulness of God's servants. While this establishes a pattern of behavior for Satan, it cannot be warrant for claiming that all difficult times in our lives are the direct result of us being "sifted as wheat." The book of Job makes that point: most of the time we simply do not have the data required to determine precisely why a particular event—whether it be suffering or anything else—takes place in our lives. Without specific divine revelation we cannot definitively know why we are suffering in any particular instance.[23]

Beyond this, when thinking about difficult circumstances in our own lives, we ought to remember that Satan's activities are completely circumscribed by God's sovereignty. As in Job, Satan is constrained by God and can only act as God allows. Although many focus on Satan—and it is right to recognize that supernatural forces are at work in the world—God's people ought to be wary of overly focusing on Satan and his activity in the world and in our lives. When we remember the opening chapters of Job and the limits imposed on the Satan there, and when we remember that Job appropriately looks to God for answers and nowhere else, we ought also to focus on God as the one who has the power over all that happens in our lives.

What Is God up to in Job 1–2?

Many people—from renowned biblical scholars to the writers of the satirical animated TV show *South Park*—have been troubled by God's behavior in the opening chapters of the book of Job.[24] For example, Roland Murphy stated that "it raises a nagging question: what kind of a God is this who is willing to prove a point of honor by sorely afflicting a faithful servant."[25]

---

23. For discussion of the ancient Near Eastern background to the character of the Satan, refer to the subsection on the Satan in the Characters section in the introduction.

24. The story of Job is recounted (after a fashion) in series 5, episode 6, of *South Park* in an episode entitled "Cartmanland."

25. Murphy, *Tree of Life*, 36.

A cursory reading of the opening chapters might well lead us to question God's character, but it is important to look a little deeper to understand the full scope of the events as they unfold. Superficially, concluding that Yahweh behaves in a dubious manner appears to be quite reasonable. At this point, however, it is important to understand something of the literary genre we call wisdom literature and the implicit consequences of this form of literature have for understanding the text as we read it. Wisdom literature is subtle, and its true meaning is not necessarily going to become apparent without doing a little more work. After all, Proverbs 26:7 notes that

> Like the useless legs of one who is lame
> is a proverb in the mouth of a fool.

This proverb makes it clear that anyone—even a fool—can quote a proverb (i.e., a wisdom saying), but that does not make one wise. Wisdom derives not from memorizing wise sayings but rather from understanding them and knowing when to heed the warning and when to ignore it (see Prov 26:4–5 where the true wise person will use wisdom to determine when it is appropriate to answer the fool and when to keep silent). Applied to Job, it becomes clear that anyone can read the words of the book, but only the wise will understand the true meaning.

Furthermore, the sages, as we are told by Proverbs 1:6, taught using "riddles." Their teaching was not always straightforward; understanding it involved the application of intellect and an approach shaped by the reader's fear of God (Prov 1:7). Reading wisdom literature without the appropriate presuppositions results in a misreading of the text. It is, to adapt the words of Proverbs 26, to read as a fool!

How does all of this shape our understanding of what is taking place in the book of Job? There are a few considerations. First, perhaps here we have encountered an example of the riddles of the wise. The problem is that this apparent behavior of Yahweh—causing an innocent man to suffer just to win a bet with the Satan—does not fit well with what we know of him from the remainder of Scripture. In light of the demand that the beginning of wisdom is to be found in the fear of Yahweh, this ought to give us pause. We need to proceed with caution and look carefully before jumping to any conclusions.

Sometimes when watching a TV show or movie, my wife asks if I think that there is likely to be another twist in the plot. At that point I check how much time remains until the end of the show. If there are only a couple of minutes left, I assume nothing new will happen; but if there is still half an hour left, I conclude that something else will happen before the end. In the book of Job we have already learned that suffering is not necessarily the consequence of sin—a lesson that will be reinforced through the remainder of the book. However, we ought also to realize that this is unlikely to be the sum total of the book's message, for there are yet forty chapters that lie before us.

So clearly, we should dig deeper into this riddle. There may be multiple paths we could take, but perhaps the most profitable is to note that those who see a problem with Yahweh's behavior here do so based on the single assumption that the prologue reveals to us the full reason for Job's suffering. Hence the question we need to ask is whether the account of the exchange between Yahweh and the Satan does indeed provide a complete explanation for all that happens to Job. The answer to this must be "No," for a number of reasons. First, Job's suffering does not cease at the point when Yahweh's case has been proven. Although there were two separate days on which the Satan came into Yahweh's presence to make accusations against Job, there is no third day. The Satan does not return to claim that God needs to adjust again the challenge with the claim that if only God would allow Job's suffering to continue for a few months, then the Satan's point will be proven. No, the challenge was over in Job 2:10. Yahweh's faith in Job has been vindicated, and the Satan's allegations have been shown to be without merit.

Why, then, does Job remain destitute and diseased? That he does so remain suggests that more is going on than merely that which was explicitly described in the opening chapters.

Strengthening this observation is the fact that nothing that takes place in the remainder of the book is presented as an attempt to encourage Job to curse God and so fulfill the Satan's goal. The friends, as we shall see, repeatedly insist that Job ought to repent, but repenting—even unnecessary repenting—is hardly tantamount to cursing God. In addition, when Yahweh eventually does appear to answer Job, all that he has to say is designed to highlight Job's ignorance and hence show that he is unqualified to question the way that Yahweh is running the universe. Job remains ignorant of the reasons for his suffering—even more than we as the readers of his story (who were at least given part of the answer in the prologue). The book of Job repeatedly insists that some of God's ways remain beyond human understanding (see Job 28; 38–42), so it makes good sense to acknowledge that the author has deliberately written a tale in which the reader shares in Job's ignorance and thus (hopefully) shares in his realization that the universe is incredibly complex beyond human understanding.[26] After all, the reason Job's story is recorded for us is so that we will learn the lessons that Job learned!

The point of all of this is that any judgment made about God's character based solely on the events recounted in the prologue is premature. The design of the book and the nature of wisdom (see Reading Job as Wisdom in the introduction) imply that there is more going on and that Job's suffering persists for reasons never revealed either to Job or to us. The one point that is made perfectly clear, however, is that Job did not suffer as a consequence of some sin he had overlooked. That is ruled out so that when the debate begins in Job 4, we should realize that the friends do not understand any more than we do, despite the certainty with which they speak and despite even their claims to special revelation (see 4:12–21).

26. For a more detailed discussion of this point, see Shields, "Malevolent or Mysterious?," 255–70.

CHAPTER 2

Job 3

Job's Initial Lament

LISTEN to the Story

1After this, Job opened his mouth and cursed the day of his birth.
2He said:

3"May the day of my birth perish,
and the night that said, 'A boy is conceived!'
4That day—may it turn to darkness;
may God above not care about it;
may no light shine on it.
5May gloom and utter darkness claim it once more;
may a cloud settle over it;
may blackness overwhelm it.
6That night—may thick darkness seize it;
may it not be included among the days of the year
nor be entered in any of the months.
7May that night be barren;
may no shout of joy be heard in it.
8May those who curse days curse that day,
those who are ready to rouse Leviathan.
9May its morning stars become dark;
may it wait for daylight in vain
and not see the first rays of dawn,
10for it did not shut the doors of the womb on me
to hide trouble from my eyes.

11"Why did I not perish at birth,
and die as I came from the womb?
12Why were there knees to receive me

and breasts that I might be nursed?
13For now I would be lying down in peace;
I would be asleep and at rest
14with kings and rulers of the earth,
who built for themselves places now lying in ruins,
15with princes who had gold,
who filled their houses with silver.
16Or why was I not hidden away in the ground like a stillborn child,
like an infant who never saw the light of day?
17There the wicked cease from turmoil,
and there the weary are at rest.
18Captives also enjoy their ease;
they no longer hear the slave driver's shout.
19The small and the great are there,
and the slaves are freed from their owners.
20"Why is light given to those in misery,
and life to the bitter of soul,
21to those who long for death that does not come,
who search for it more than for hidden treasure,
22who are filled with gladness
and rejoice when they reach the grave?
23Why is life given to a man
whose way is hidden,
whom God has hedged in?
24For sighing has become my daily food;
my groans pour out like water.
25What I feared has come upon me;
what I dreaded has happened to me.
26I have no peace, no quietness;
I have no rest, but only turmoil."

Listening to the Text in the Story: "Bilgames and the Netherworld"; Theognis, *Elegies* 1; Sophocles, *Oedipus at Colonus*

Job 3 records a lament or, more correctly, a complaint by Job that is an emotionally raw expression of his response to his losses and suffering. Much of what he says transcends his historical and cultural context, but some of it also reflects his world and his understanding of that world. One particular aspect of that is his reflection on where he would be had he died at birth in verses 13–15. These words reflect some common ancient Near Eastern ideas, and some ancient texts help give us some idea of what Job's notions about postmortem existence may have been like. Throughout the ancient Near East there was widespread acceptance of some form of continued existence after death, although the precise nature of that varied both from place to place and through time. Mesopotamian thought, for example, reflects a mixed picture, with some in the afterlife enjoying a pleasant enough existence while others endured ongoing suffering.

The Sumerian tale of "Bilgames and the Netherworld" recounts a situation where a piece of sporting equipment is lost down a hole that leads to the netherworld. Bilgames (who is known as Gilgemesh in later Babylonian texts) accepts his friend Enkidu's offer to descend and retrieve the item. When Enkidu eventually returns (after experiencing some problems getting back) he reports on conditions in the netherword as he is questioned:

> "Did you see the man with one son?" "I saw him." "How does he fare?"
> "For the peg set in his wall bitterly he laments."
> "Did you see the man with two sons? I saw him." "How does he fare?"
> "Seated on two bricks he eats a bread-round."
> "Did you see the man with three sons?" "I saw him." "How does he fare?"
> "He drinks water from the waterskin (slung) on the saddle."
> "Did you see the man with four sons?" "I saw him." "How does he fare?"
> "Like a man with a team of four donkeys his heart rejoices."
> "Did you see the man with five sons?" "I saw him." "How does he fare?"
> "Like a fine scribe his hand is deft and he enters the palace with ease."
> "Did you see the man with six sons?" "I saw him." "How does he fare?"
> "Like a man with plough in harness his heart is content."
> "Did you see the man with seven sons?" "I saw him." "How does he fare?"

"Among the junior deities he sits on a throne and listens to the proceedings."[1]

The account continues by detailing the lot of people who had died in various circumstances. For most their postmortem existence is dismal. One exception is the stillborn baby:

r 1 "Did you see the little stillborn babies, who knew not names of their own?" "I saw them." "How do they fare?"
r 2 "They play amid syrup and ghee at tables of silver and gold."[2]

Although these ideas are not reflected in biblical view of the afterlife, we must remember that Job, set in patriarchal times outside of Israel, has a more limited understanding of these things than we who live after the incarnation do. Job was a product of his times, and with more complete revelation on this topic limited to a time after his life and even after his story was written, his limited understanding likely reflected the general understanding of his time. And if these ideas were at all shared by Job, then it makes sense of his desire to have died at birth so that his postmortem existence would have escaped the suffering he was enduring.

David Clines notes a number of other parallels to Job's desires here from ancient literature:

> 2 Bar 10:6 "Blessed is he who was not born, or he, who having been born, has died" (Charles, 2:485 . . .); 4 Ezra 7.116 "Better had it been that the earth had not produced Adam, or else, having once produced him, (for thee) to have restrained him from sinning" (Charles, 2:591); Ecclus 30:17 "Better death than a wretched life, and everlasting rest than chronic illness" (JB); Theognis, *Elegies* 1.425–28 "Best of all for mortals is never to have been born, but for those who have been born to die as soon as possible"; Sophocles, *Oedipus at Colonus*, 1224–27 "Not to be born at all / Is best, for best that can befall, / Next best, when born, with least delay / To trace the backward way" (F. Storr, Loeb edition); Menander, *The Double Deceiver* (frag. 125K) "Whom the gods love dies young."[3]

1. "Bilgames and the Netherworld" in Andrew George, *The Babylonian Gilgamesh Epic: Introduction, Critical Edition and Cuneiform Texts*, 2 vols. (Oxford: Oxford University Press, 2003), 2:774.
2. George, *Babylonian Gilgamesh Epic*, 2:776.
3. Clines, *Job 1–20*, 89–90. A similar sentiment can be found in Isa 57:1–2.

As to the genre of Job's opening poem here in chapter 3, we find a number of similar poems throughout the Old Testament. Psalm 88, for example, is a lament somewhat reminiscent of Job's laments in this and the coming chapters.

Formally this chapter of Job has been identified as a complaint rather than a strict lament, the complaint including lament but going beyond it. As such we also find, in Job's words, a curse (on the day of his birth).[4] The poetic lament serves to highlight the depth of feeling Job expresses in these words. The magnitude of this can be seen in the contrast between the description of the siege of Jerusalem in the books of Kings with the words "the famine in the city had become so severe that there was no food for the people to eat" (2 Kgs 25:3) with the horrors described in Lamentations depicting the same situation (e.g., Lam 5:11–12). The lament poem was employed to provide a graphic depiction of the magnitude of pain experienced by the poet and as a means to draw the reader into that world of pain. Here Job gives full expression to the horrors of his existence.

Many other biblical parallels could be cited. Harding, for example, notes a parallel between Job's lament over his birth (Job 3:3–10) and Jeremiah's seventh lament (Jer 20:14–18):[5]

> 14Cursed be the day I was born!
> May the day my mother bore me not be blessed!
> 15Cursed be the man who brought my father the news,
> who made him very glad, saying,
> "A child is born to you—a son!"
> 16May that man be like the towns
> the Lord overthrew without pity.
> May he hear wailing in the morning,
> a battle cry at noon.
> 17For he did not kill me in the womb,
> with my mother as my grave,
> her womb enlarged forever.
> 18Why did I ever come out of the womb
> to see trouble and sorrow
> and to end my days in shame?

4. See Clines, *Job 1–20*, 76–77.

5. James Edward Harding, "The Book of Job as Metaprophecy," *Studies in Religion / Sciences Religieuses* 39.4 (2010): 526.

It is important, however, to note the unique elements in Job's complaint. Timmer notes that:

> The form-critical differences between Job's lament and those in the Psalter show this clearly: Job omits the typical affirmation of trust and vow to praise, and his initial addresses to God lack any mention of God's character, reputation, and past actions on Job's behalf. Rather, "Job grounds his search for a resolution to his anguish in his own innocence more than in God's mercy."[6]

Timmer suggests that this is what upsets Job's friends and prompts their response. We ought to be able to discern the basis for the friends' objections in Eliphaz's initial response in chapter 4, which we shall come to soon.

EXPLAIN the Story

When Nonexistence Is Better (3:1–10)

Seven days after his friends arrive, Job finally speaks. This entire speech is characterized by the writer as a curse of the day of Job's birth (woodenly translated, "he cursed his day," but what follows makes it clear this is a reference to the day of his birth). This is the first time in the book the word "curse" (Hebrew *qll*) has actually appeared. Previously the verb woodenly translated "bless" (*brk*, NIV "curse") had been used either euphemistically or sarcastically (1:11; 2:5, 9). The difference here is that the object of the curse is not God, or even another person (such as his parents); it is the day of Job's birth. Thus, even when Job is said to curse, he does not curse God, and so the Satan's claims remain false. Furthermore, Job's curse here is clearly powerless and merely rhetorical; the day of his birth has already taken place, and nothing can change that. This should thus be understood for what it is: a deep cry of anguish and pain.

The first part of Job's complaint focuses specifically on the day of his birth. Job is not alone in the Bible in expressing the sentiments recorded here, as the speaker of Ecclesiastes makes a similar point (Eccl 4:1–3) and, even more so as noted above, so does the prophet Jeremiah (Jer 20:14–18). Job's unique

6. Daniel Timmer, "God's Speeches, Job's Responses, and the Problem of Coherence in the Book of Job: Sapiential Pedagogy Revisited," *CBQ* 71 (2009): 290. At the end Timmer is quoting from John E. Hartley, "From Lament to Oath: A Study of Progression in the Speeches of Job," in *Book of Job*, ed. Willem A. M. Beuken (Leuven: Peeters, 1994), 89–91.

perspective has him wishing the day of his birth had never existed, that it be expunged from the calendar, that it never had happened. Job seems to concur with Qoheleth (the teacher of Ecclesiastes) that it would be better to never have existed than to suffer as he is now suffering.

Darkness and light play a key part in Job's language through Job 3:1–10. He calls for the day to be dark and the night to be darker still, as if a shroud were placed over it all. We shall see throughout the poetic sections of Job that many synonymous terms are used, and here we have several terms for the concept of darkness to express emphatically Job's disdain for the day of his birth. The ideas Job uses here are reminiscent of the creation in Genesis 1, so that it is almost as if, by calling for both the day and night to be dark, he asks that the day of his birth never to have been created. Job inverts the language of the creation. Instead of saying "let there be light" (Gen 1:3), he says, "Of that day [i.e., the day of his birth], let there be darkness" (Job 3:4).

In verse 7 Job extends the language of progeniture to day and night itself—as if night gives birth to day. Job wishes regarding the scheduled time of his birth that such a day may never itself have been born, that there never would have been a shout of celebration at its arrival in the same way that the birth of a child is heralded with such cries. In using this language Job finds another way to curse the day of his birth.

Verse 8 introduces the existence of people who curse a day (NIV "days"; the Hebrew is singular and indefinite). Precisely who Job has in mind is not clear, but there are examples of individuals called upon to curse (e.g., Balaam in Num 22–24), and Job calls upon such people to curse the day of his birth. The NIV offers an alternate reading in a footnote that would have the verse read, "May those who curse the sea curse that day." This reflects the suggestion of some scholars that "day" (*yom*) should be understood as "sea" (*yam*), which was also the name of a Canaanite deity Yam (as was Leviathan who is mentioned in the next part of the verse). The two—Yam and Leviathan—are known to be connected in an incantation recorded in a later Jewish magical text.[7] Clines has noted that the major problem with this is that since the sea generally represents chaos and darkness, cursing it would have the opposite effect to that which Job seeks here! Hence the best understanding of this verse is that Job is calling on others to join with him in cursing the day of his birth.[8]

7. See Choon-Leong Seow, *Job 1–21: Interpretation and Commentary*, Illuminations (Grand Rapids: Eerdmans, 2013), 349. For more on the alternate reading see Ola Wikander, "Job 3,8—Cosmological Snake-Charming and Leviathanic Panic in an Ancient Near Eastern Setting," *ZAW* 122 (2010): 265–71.

8. Clines, *Job 1–20*, 86.

The second half of Job 3:8 contains the first reference to Leviathan in the book of Job (see later in Job 41:1). There are four more references to Leviathan elsewhere in the Old Testament (Pss 74:14; 104:26; Isa 27:1). If these are all references to the same creature, then Psalm 74:14 tells us that it had multiple heads, an idea found elsewhere in the ancient world for this creature. The Ugaritic Baal Cycle (also known as "The Baʿlu Myth") includes the following reference:

> When you smite Lôtan [Leviathan], the fleeing serpent,
> finish off the twisting serpent,
> the close-coiling one with seven heads.[9]

Precisely how Job 3:8b is connected to verse 8a is not entirely clear. It may further identify those who "curse days" from the first clause, such that this one group of people who curse days are also those who would rouse the monster Leviathan to wreak havoc and destruction on the world or, more specifically, to swallow the sun or moon in accordance with the belief of some cultures that an eclipse was the result of a celestial dragon swallowing either of them.[10] In that case, the means by which these people would curse the day would be by rousing Leviathan to darken it.

Whatever the precise details, the gist of Job's words is that he wishes to enlist the aid of those more powerful than he is to curse the day of his birth. He wishes it thoroughly erased from history, such that he would never have come into existence.

In verse 9 Job asks that the "morning stars" that preempt the dawn (probably a reference to the planets Mercury and Venus) be darkened so that without them to herald the dawn, the day would never begin. The final phrase, "the first rays of dawn," renders a slightly obscure Hebrew phrase that speaks of something like the "eyes/eyelids/eyelashes of dawn," which likely refers either to the first signs of the day (hence the NIV translation "first rays") or else the final stars visible before dawn breaks. Either way, Job wishes for both the night and day of his birth to be completely darkened, to have never taken place.

Job concludes the first part of his lament with a reminder of the reason he wishes the day of his birth to have never happened: because it allowed him to be born and so to live and endure the trouble he now experiences. In keeping with the impersonal nature of the entire poem thus far, Job refers to

---

9. "The Baʿlu Myth," trans. Dennis Pardee (*COS* 1.86:264); note especially Isa 27:1.
10. See Seow, *Job 1–21*, 352.

"my womb" (or "my belly") rather than his mother's womb, but the meaning is much the same. Job has cursed the day of his birth since, had it never happened, he would have been spared the trouble that has come upon him.

When Dying at Birth Is Better (3:11–19)

The second stanza of this opening poem moves from Job's wishing he had never existed to his wishing he had died at birth (clearly either option would have spared Job the suffering he is now experiencing). Job expresses his desire in rhetorical questions that expect no answer. They instead reveal his recognition of just how much better his lot would be had his life ended at the moment he was born. These sentiments are not unique to Job, being reflected in a number of texts preserved from the ancient world. In the Second Temple Jewish wisdom text known as Sirach we read the words:

> Better death than a bitter life,
> and eternal repose than chronic sickness.[11]

As the book unfolds Job, feeling the futility and hopelessness of his situation, will return to these sentiments (see Job 10:18–22).

In 3:13–15 Job explains just why he considers that perishing at birth would be better than his present existence. He envisages death as a peaceful slumber, lying down with the great rulers of the earth. It is not clear whether Job anticipated some form of conscious existence for the dead, but it would not be surprising if he did, for such was common throughout the ancient Near East at the time. In Mesopotamian thought, the netherworld where the dead resided (the equivalent of Sheol in Hebrew thought) was not necessarily a place of rest. One's lot in the afterlife was determined to largely by the circumstances of one's death and the nature of one's life. That Job specifically refers to rulers of the earth here may indicate that he expected that dying at birth should have qualified him to share the afterlife with such people rather than suffer through further torment in Sheol (refer to the section Listen to the Story above for more background detail on this topic).

It would be unwise to make too much of this, for the text does not provide us with sufficient detail about Job's understanding of the nature of postmortem existence. At best we can say that the life Job lived prior to his losses in chapter 1 was clearly preferable to whatever Job may have believed about the

11. Sirach 30:17 (NETS). Clines, *Job 1–20*, 90, cites some ancient Greek examples that express the same sentiment.

afterlife, but his present circumstances were clearly far worse than anything he anticipated about the future.

In 3:16–19 Job continues his explanation as to why he believes he would have been better of dying at birth by noting that everything stops for those who have died—the wicked stop their aggression (NIV, "their turmoil"; the Hebrew word expresses agitation of some form, including "rage" in Hab 3:2; Dan 3:13 [Aramaic]). Those who are physically exhausted (NIV, "weary"; the Hebrew is woodenly, "weariness of strength") rest when dead. The reference to "captives" in verse 18 does not indicate those who have been imprisoned for a crime, as is made clear in the second line. These individuals are those who were under the control of a tyrannical oppressor of some form (hence NIV's "slave driver").

Job ultimately expresses his belief that death is the great equalizer—the expression "the small and the great" encompasses everyone between the extremes. Qoheleth, the voice who speaks in the book of Ecclesiastes, works with similar assumptions about death as Job appears to have here (e.g., Eccl 9:3).

Job 3:20–22 moves on to ask why it is that he must continue living when he yearns so desperately for an end. Yet Job does not countenance suicide as a solution to his suffering. The reason for this is not immediately clear—there are examples of suicide in the Bible, and not all are condemned (most obviously the case of Samson, cf. Judg 16:28–30). From a narrative perspective, however, had Job actively ended his life, his story would have had little didactic function and so would make no sense. Yet Job's emotional state at this time has him longing for death, and here he laments his continued life.

Job 3:20 unites "light" and "life." This association was found in 3:16 and the equation occurs elsewhere (cf. 18:5–6; 33:30), particularly in John's Gospel (e.g., John 8:12). Yet Job yearns for darkness, not light. The second line of Job 3:21 expands matters, for Job now speaks in the plural, recognizing his own suffering and loss to be of one with others who find themselves in similar circumstances. Job is not alone in longing for release from the troubles of this life.

Jesus inverts the imagery used by Job here by declaring that those who walk in darkness are those who live in this world but are alienated from God (John 8:12). From this perspective it is not darkness Job needs but light, for at this stage of his story he is ignorant of his own ignorance—a condition that will not be remedied until Yahweh speaks toward the end of the book. When that light is shed on Job's present circumstances, he will finally find the comfort he so desperately needs.

In Job 3:23–26 Job's words return the focus to himself by moving the reference to a singular rather than the plural of the preceding lines and then back to the first-person singular in verse 24. Verse 23 depicts the lot of a man whose future is hidden and whose way forward in life is lost and no longer clear. The reference is, of course, to Job himself. From this he complains that God has hedged him in, that is, given him no means to escape his suffering and grief. His words recall the Satan's argument that Yahweh had put a hedge around Job to protect him when that was supposedly the sole factor driving Job's faithfulness (1:10). Later, in 19:8, Job will again complain that God has barred his way (there using a different word) as he presents a longer list of complaints against God.

If food and water are the essentials for life, Job's life has come to the point where he feeds on his own suffering and groaning (3:24). Continuing this imagery, Job's groans pour forth like water being poured out. The word translated "groans" elsewhere refers to the roaring of lions (cf. Job 4:10; Isa 5:29; Ezek 19:7; Zech 11:3), and so translating it "groans" probably understates the intensity of Job's feelings at this point.

In Job 3:25 Job reveals finally that what has befallen him now had previously been a deep fear of his. The first phrase, "What I feared has come upon me," in Hebrew includes repetition: "I feared a fearful thing," emphasizing the dreadful nature of both what worried him earlier in his life and what has now befallen him. The prologue had made it clear that Job feared God, but did it mean that he lived his life in a constant state of anxiety about just how precarious his situation was, and thus was his piety driven by this anxiety?

The first point to note is that the term for "fear" (various forms from the root *yr'*) in the prologue (and elsewhere, where "fear of God" is referred to through most of the Bible) uses terminology (forms from the root *pkhd*) different from that which we read here. (For more on the nature of the fear of God, see above on Job 1:1.) Unlike "fear [*yr'*] of God," which is commended throughout the Bible,[12] Job here expresses something terrifying and dreadful, something to be avoided without any consideration of the effort involved. The emphatic language here is clear: this situation was one to be avoided at all costs.

The second point to note is that we are at a stage in Job's story where he has much to learn about both suffering and the ways in which God rules the universe. He may well have lived such an upright life as he did in order to maintain favor with God and so avoid the consequences of sin. Job, just like his three friends, held to the notion that God ruled the universe following a fairly simple rule of retributive justice, as represented in the notion of "an

---

12. The primary exception to this is found where the speaker of Ecclesiastes refers to the fear of God (e.g., Eccl 3:14).

eye for an eye and a tooth for a tooth" (Matt 5:38; cf. Exod 21:23–25; Lev 24:19–20). If Job had lived in this way, the events of the prologue make it clear that this was not his sole motivation—he did not "curse God to his face" when his circumstances changed. Job's response reflected that of someone with a personal relationship with his Creator, not that of someone who treated God as a machine to be manipulated. That left Job holding on to his integrity but still facing the paradox thrown up by his belief in God's justice while he faced the suffering he was now enduring. It is only through the suffering, debates, and finally the words of God that this paradox facing Job will ultimately be resolved.

So, Job's worst fears have been realized in his present situation, and even his devotion to God has not spared him these consequences—indeed, as we have seen in the prologue, it has actually prompted them! The remainder of the book records Job's journey to better understanding the ways of God and his own relationship with God.

The final words of Job's lament are profoundly poignant. Each line of the poem to this point consists of clauses of four or more words. Here that suddenly changes, disrupting the rhythm of the poem and closing Job's complaint with a series of clauses, each of which is just two words in the Hebrew, and for the first three clauses the first word is merely "no." Attempting to reflect this rhythm in an English translation might result in something like this:

> No peace.
>   No quiet.
>   No rest.
>   Only turmoil.

It is as if Job has run out of words to express his response to his pain. The breathless brevity of these words highlights his desperation.

Some of these qualities Job lacks here were ones he previously expressed a desire to attain through death: quiet in v. 13; rest in verses 13 and 17; and escape from turmoil in v. 17. The things he longs for are denied him, and for now he has run out of words through which to express his anguish, pain, and lament.

LIVE the Story

Being Honest About How We Feel

When my children were young, I noted that, among them and their friends, when they hurt themselves, the severity of that injury was often proportional to the length of time that transpired between acquiring the injury and the beginning of the screaming or crying. The worse the injury, the longer it seemed that the child took to draw in breath to let out a cry. If this is any sort of measure of the depth of suffering someone is enduring, then it is appropriately reflective that Job has spent seven days breathing in, preparing to let out his anguish. That time in silence really reflects the depths of Job's pain. Finally, Job's silence is over.

Job does not address God in his opening words. The closest he comes is in verses 3 and 23, but even there God is not addressed directly. He does not assign blame for his circumstances; he does not even look for an explanation for his circumstances. His lament here is not far removed from his response to his wife in Job 2:10. He is not looking for answers. Those will come later and, in part, follow provocation from his friends.

What we hear from Job in this chapter is a raw expression of his emotions. We should not expect a perfectly rational response any more than we should expect it of anyone we know who is experiencing profound suffering. Nonetheless, there are a few important points to note about Job's words here. For one, whereas some might expect that Job would completely despair of life to the point of contemplating the taking of his own life, he stops short of that option.[13] This observation may prompt us to think that there is some inherent taboo against taking one's own life that is restraining Job—and that may well reflect something of the thought world in the ancient Near East which has influenced Job (refer to the Listen to the Story above).

Is there an appropriate way to respond to overwhelming disaster and the grief that is associated with it? Thus far in Job we have seen two responses: the terse, pious response of Job in chapters 1 and 2, and this deeply felt response of chapter 3. So far, the response from the friends to Job's grief has been silence; they have put into practice the wisdom of Paul in Romans 12:15. It would seem, however, that the words of Job here have pushed them to speak. So far, however (and in light of Paul's advice), their response has perhaps been the best they could make.

The important point, in terms of responses to suffering, is that Job is not

---

13. There are at least six examples of suicide in the Old Testament: Abimelech son of Gideon (Judg 9:54); Samson (Jud 16:25–31); Saul (1 Sam 31:3–4; 1 Chr 10:3–4); Saul's servant (1 Sam 31:5; 1 Chr 10:5); Ahithophel (2 Sam 17:23); and Zimri (1 Kgs 16:18–19).

If you are struggling with some of the feelings and thoughts that Job here struggled with, please talk to someone about how you are feeling. If you have lost someone to suicide, or are helping someone who has, there are good resources available to help. One example is Albert Y. Hsu, *Grieving a Suicide: A Loved One's Search for Comfort, Answers, and Hope*, rev. and exp. ed. (Downers Grove, IL: InterVarsity Press, 2017).

taken to task by God for his response to his suffering. While the friends do challenge him, they are ultimately chastised by God for their words (see Job 42:7). Furthermore, as we read their words in the coming chapters it will become painfully clear that there certainly are inappropriate responses to the suffering of others. What can we say about Job's responses?

We often feel uncomfortable with really opening up about our feelings to God, perhaps because of an inherent notion that it is not appropriate to admit to despair when there are so many calls to be joyful, or to anxiety when we are told not to worry, or to anger when we are told not to be angry. And yet the Bible, particularly the Old Testament, is filled with people pouring out their hearts to God—or even just pouring out their hearts to anyone who will listen, as Job has done in this chapter. He does not sanitize his feelings for his audience, and as we move through the book, we shall continue to see that Job does not conceal his feelings from God.

What should we learn from Job in this regard? There are several lessons. First, be honest with God. Why present a facade when God sees the heart and knows your thoughts? God already knows how we feel, and so there is no point in pretending we feel otherwise in the hope that God won't notice. Out of everyone you know, the one person you do not have to worry about opening up to is God, because he already knows how you feel and what you think. Job, the psalmists, Jeremiah, and many of the other prophets all show us that being up front with God is the right thing to do. Moreover, sometimes we will only really acknowledge our feelings by expressing them. Sometimes we are not really concealing our feelings from God or from others so much as we are concealing them from ourselves. While Job is not here directly addressing God (there will be plenty of that to come), he is not holding back in expressing his feelings, and these words set the backdrop for what will come.

Having made the point that we ought to be honest with God, we also ought to note that this does not give us carte blanche to say absolutely anything to or about God and think that it is not sinful. Sometimes we think or say things that do require subsequent repentance, but Jesus teaches that the line is crossed whether it happens entirely in our minds or out in the open. Job was himself aware of such limits—hence his refusal to "curse God and die" in the previous chapter, and similarly the Satan's claim that Job would curse God was a claim that Job would cross a line if the blessings he enjoyed were removed. Yet he did not cross that line, and we ought also to beware of cursing God.

Second, many people seem to shy away from extreme feelings believing that the feelings themselves are inappropriate or even sinful for faithful Christians. Yet when we analyze Job's complaint and lament here in chapter 3, it is not at all clear what he has said that is wrong or sinful. He has been clear about how he feels—and we will hear more from him on this topic as the book unfolds—but in his honesty he has not, at least to this point, sinned (whether he does later is disputed by readers, so we shall return to consider this question at various points through the book).

Third, we need to remember Job's place in the story of God. As that story unfolds from Genesis to Revelation, things do change, with the most dramatic change taking place at the resurrection. The Bible has many laments and complaints—perhaps most prominently in Jeremiah, Lamentations, and a number of psalms. Similar sentiments are expressed by Jesus at Gethsemane when he prays in anguish to the Father. However, after Jesus we find little evidence of this sort of response to God. Now, in part, that is probably a result of the type of literature that makes up the remainder of the New Testament—didactic epistles are probably not the place we would expect to find laments. Yet there is also a transformation in attitudes to suffering in general in the New Testament after Jesus's resurrection and the giving of the Spirit. Renewed hope transforms lament. That is not to say that there is no place for lament or complaint in the life of the post-Pentecost believer, but it is to say that we have a new perspective, or at least a clearer perspective, on what God is doing and where history, and our lives, are going. Paul's assurance that the trouble we have now is almost worth nothing compared to what is in store for us in the new heavens and earth (Rom 8:18) provides a perspective that we have of which Job could only catch the briefest of glimpse.

CHAPTER 3

Job 4–5

Eliphaz's First Words

LISTEN to the Story

4:1 Then Eliphaz the Temanite replied:

2 "If someone ventures a word with you, will you be
impatient?
But who can keep from speaking?
3 Think how you have instructed many,
how you have strengthened feeble hands.
4 Your words have supported those who stumbled;
you have strengthened faltering knees.
5 But now trouble comes to you, and you are discouraged;
it strikes you, and you are dismayed.
6 Should not your piety be your confidence
and your blameless ways your hope?

7 "Consider now: Who, being innocent, has ever perished?
Where were the upright ever destroyed?
8 As I have observed, those who plow evil
and those who sow trouble reap it.
9 At the breath of God they perish;
at the blast of his anger they are no more.
10 The lions may roar and growl,
yet the teeth of the great lions are broken.
11 The lion perishes for lack of prey,
and the cubs of the lioness are scattered.

12 "A word was secretly brought to me,
my ears caught a whisper of it.

[13]Amid disquieting dreams in the night,
when deep sleep falls on people,
[14]fear and trembling seized me
and made all my bones shake.
[15]A spirit glided past my face,
and the hair on my body stood on end.
[16]It stopped,
but I could not tell what it was.
A form stood before my eyes,
and I heard a hushed voice:
[17]'Can a mortal be more righteous than God?
Can even a strong man be more pure than his Maker?
[18]If God places no trust in his servants,
if he charges his angels with error,
[19]how much more those who live in houses of clay,
whose foundations are in the dust,
who are crushed more readily than a moth!
[20]Between dawn and dusk they are broken to pieces;
unnoticed, they perish forever.
[21]Are not the cords of their tent pulled up,
so that they die without wisdom?'

[5:1]"Call if you will, but who will answer you?
To which of the holy ones will you turn?
[2]Resentment kills a fool,
and envy slays the simple.
[3]I myself have seen a fool taking root,
but suddenly his house was cursed.
[4]His children are far from safety,
crushed in court without a defender.
[5]The hungry consume his harvest,
taking it even from among thorns,
and the thirsty pant after his wealth.
[6]For hardship does not spring from the soil,
nor does trouble sprout from the ground.
[7]Yet man is born to trouble
as surely as sparks fly upward.

8"But if I were you, I would appeal to God;
I would lay my cause before him.
9He performs wonders that cannot be fathomed,
miracles that cannot be counted.
10He provides rain for the earth;
he sends water on the countryside.
11The lowly he sets on high,
and those who mourn are lifted to safety.
12He thwarts the plans of the crafty,
so that their hands achieve no success.
13He catches the wise in their craftiness,
and the schemes of the wily are swept away.
14Darkness comes upon them in the daytime;
at noon they grope as in the night.
15He saves the needy from the sword in their mouth;
he saves them from the clutches of the powerful.
16So the poor have hope,
and injustice shuts its mouth.

17"Blessed is the one whom God corrects;
so do not despise the discipline of the Almighty.
18For he wounds, but he also binds up;
he injures, but his hands also heal.
19From six calamities he will rescue you;
in seven no harm will touch you.
20In famine he will deliver you from death,
and in battle from the stroke of the sword.
21You will be protected from the lash of the tongue,
and need not fear when destruction comes.
22You will laugh at destruction and famine,
and need not fear the wild animals.
23For you will have a covenant with the stones of the field,
and the wild animals will be at peace with you.
24You will know that your tent is secure;
you will take stock of your property and find nothing missing.
25You will know that your children will be many,
and your descendants like the grass of the earth.

[26]You will come to the grave in full vigor,
like sheaves gathered in season.
[27]"We have examined this, and it is true.
So hear it and apply it to yourself."

Listening to the Text in the Story: "Man and His God" (Sumerian); "Epic of Kirta" (Ugaritic)

Eliphaz speaks in response to Job's complaint of chapter 3, finally breaking the silence of the friends. Unfortunately, he breaks the silence in words that fail to appreciate the pain inherent in Job's words, instead seeking to provide a theologically reasoned explanation for Job's pain. The theology that underpins his response—and indeed underpins the thinking of the other two friends we will hear from in the first half of this book—was not new, even at the time the book of Job is set. The idea that a person's life circumstances reflected either divine approval or divine condemnation can be found throughout the world and, of particular relevance for our study of Job, in the ancient Near Eastern world in which Job's story is set.

For example, in the Sumerian work "Man and His God," we find the sufferer lamenting his suffering much as Job does:

> Tears, lament, anguish and
> depression are lodged within me,
> Suffering overwhelms me
> like a weeping child.

But following this is a recognition that all people are sinful and thus that repentance is the appropriate response to suffering:

> Never has a sinless child
> been born to its mother,
> A mortal(?) has never been perfect(?),
> a sinless man has never existed from old' . . .
> My god, . . . after you will have
> let my eyes recognize my sins,
> I shall recount at the city(?) gate
> those of them that have been forgotten,

and those of them which are visible(?);
I, the young man, shall publicly
declare my sins before you![1]

The simple logic that identifies suffering as a consequence of sin is virtually universal in the ancient world. It is also apparent in the thinking of people in New Testament times. So, for example, John 9:2 and Luke 13:2–3 reflect this belief that bad circumstances in life were the consequences of personal or familial sin of some form. The idea can be bolstered by a rather selective reading of Proverbs and other biblical material and forms the basis for much of the logic underpinning the arguments of Job's older friends. (We shall later see that Elihu, Job's fourth and younger friend, has a slightly more nuanced approach than the older friends.)

What is perhaps not quite so obvious is that Job also held to this, as is apparent from his own response to his suffering. If suffering is a consequence of sin, then suffering apart from sin is underserved and unjust. Had Job not believed this, then he would have had quite a different perspective on his suffering, but as it was, he felt he had been treated unjustly. What is more, if the presupposition was true—that suffering was always the consequence of personal sin—then he would have been right. To a large extent, the repetition we find in Job wherein Job protests his innocence and the injustice of his situation followed by the friends' insistence that he must have sinned, serves to emphatically rebut this deeply ingrained belief about the causes of suffering.

Another aspect of Eliphaz's speech that may be elucidated by the ancient Near Eastern background appears in Job 5:7 where Eliphaz speaks the following words: "Yet man is born to trouble as surely as sparks fly upward." What is not immediately apparent here is that the Hebrew term translated "sparks" in the NIV is closely associated with the name of a Canaanite deity Rašap (woodenly reading "the sons of Rašap"). *HALOT* includes the following comments on this deity:

> Derivations evoke the sinister features which are the essence of this deity, who was worshipped throughout the Near East. Rašap was actually identified with the Babylonian god Nergal and can similarly be regarded as a god of the underworld, a god of plagues, and a god of war.[2]

1. "Man and His God," trans. Jacob Klein (*COS* 1.179:574).
2. " רֶשֶׁף I," *HALOT* 1297, §2.

A reference to such a deity would not be surprising in the book of Job, which includes a number of allusions or direct references to mythological creatures and demons from the ancient Near East (Leviathan being the most prominent example). Precisely who or what the "sons of Rašap" refers to is debated, although an interesting possible parallel is found in the Ugaritic work "Epic of Kirta" when the loss of Kirta's family is described. There we read a description of the loss of Kirta's wives followed by that of the remainder of his family. In particular, when referring to his fifth and sixth wives, the "Epic of Kirta" reads:

> A third spouse died in good health,
> a fourth in illness;
> A fifth Rašap gathered in,
> a sixth the lad(s) of Yammu,
> the seventh of them fell by the sword.[3]

Aside from the reference to Rašap (who, as the god or king of the underworld, takes people in death), the next line's reference to "lad(s) of Yammu" is reminiscent of the phrase "the sons of Rašap" from Eliphaz. Beyond this, the account of Kirta's loss of family lends it a thematic connection to Job's own losses, even if the precise details differ.

In the end the connection is not conclusive, but the sense found in the NIV and other English versions would seem to convey the intent of Eliphaz's reference here, even if it overlooks something of the depth of meaning in the metaphor.

EXPLAIN the Story

Trying to Help in an Unhelpful Way (4:1–6)

Job has poured his heart out to his three friends who, up to this point, have sat in silence with him for several days and then sat and heard Job's words. How do they then respond? Eliphaz gets the ball rolling, establishing the pattern where each friend will take their turn responding to Job. As we shall see, their aim is to be helpful—they wish both to reassure Job and to help him out of his predicament by pointing to what it is that they believe has caused his problems and how he may solve his problems. Yet for all their wisdom and words, we shall see they are wrong because their presuppositions are wrong.

3. "The Kirta Epic," trans. Dennis Pardee (*COS* 1.102:333).

Eliphaz tentatively begins his reply to Job (and it is worth noting that Job had not explicitly sought a reply; that Eliphaz felt a reply necessary is perhaps the first sign of his inability to truly understand the purpose of Job's complaint and lament in ch. 3) by wondering whether Job would be willing or able to hear him at all. Yet Eliphaz feels that, as a friend, he is compelled to reply. It would be ungenerous to assume at this stage that Eliphaz has anything other than Job's best interests at heart, and as he speaks, we shall see that his aim is to help Job find both the cause of his predicament and a way to escape it.

In verses 3–4 Eliphaz reminds Job that he had previously helped those in need, the implication here being that Job should now accept the help of his friends. He uses four images to present this idea. First, he mentions Job's instruction of others (the Hebrew word *ysr* has connections to wisdom instruction in the appropriate way to live rather than to mere intellectual instruction, cf. Deut 4:36; Prov 31:1). Second, he alludes to how Job has strengthened those with "weak hands," a reference not merely to physical weakness but to loss of courage (cf. Isa 13:7; 35:3; Heb 12:12). Third, he states that Job's words have helped those who stumbled to stand. Fourth, Eliphaz mentions that Job has strengthened weak knees (cf. Heb 12:12).

The four images really point to the one idea: Job has himself sought to help those who were weak or suffering or in need. He should not condemn his friends for seeking to do the same for him now. This is a plea for Job to listen to Eliphaz, for he believes that his words may help now.

Eliphaz reveals in Job 4:5 that he sees in Job's complaint and lament of chapter 3 a failure by Job to reflect on his circumstances objectively, as he had been able to in those situations where he had provided support to others. Instead, he is discouraged and dismayed. "Dismayed" here translates a word [*bhl*] that conveys intensity—an alternate that better reflects the tone would be to say that Eliphaz describes Job's response as one of horror or even terror.

Eliphaz is right (up to a point) in noting this, for it would be astonishing to think that anyone could endure the losses and suffering that Job had and yet retain perfect objectivity. That Eliphaz implies that Job should do so reflects poorly on Eliphaz's capacity to show empathy to Job.

In order to attempt to move Job to a more objective assessment of his situation, in verse 6 Eliphaz stresses that Job should trust in his "piety" (as the NIV here translates; in 1:1 it is translated "fear," a shorthand for "fear of God") and his blameless ways (also 1:1). Precisely what Eliphaz means here is not apparent until he expands in the following verses but, in short, his point is that once Job has sorted out his sin, then his piety and blameless life will allow him to be quickly restored.

Questioning Job's Innocence (4:7–11)

In verses 7–9 Eliphaz shows his hand, revealing what he believes lies behind Job's predicament. The truly innocent and upright are not destroyed and do not perish. In short, Job cannot be innocent. The imagery of sowing and reaping in verse 8 is found elsewhere in the Bible (cf. Gal 6:7; Rev 14:7–20) and is clear enough, particularly in an agrarian society. Actions have consequences, and Job is reaping the consequence of some action he had previously sowed.

Eliphaz, in verses 10–11, makes multiple references to lions, and in so doing uses five different Hebrew words. It would be folly to try and read too much into this lexical variety. Rather, it reflects a common feature of Hebrew poetry, which employs sometimes obscure and diverse terms to convey ideas in a more interesting manner.

The relevance of the discussion of lions is also not immediately clear, but a little background helps. In various places of the Bible, evildoers are associated in some way with lions (cf. Pss 7:2; 10:9; 17:12; 22:13, 21; Isa 5:29; Jer 4:7; and ultimately 1 Pet 5:8). This suggests that a reader of the text at the time it was written would have likely inferred that the references here to lions are essentially references to the wicked. As such, despite its ferocious roar, a lion with broken teeth is destined to starve, as it can no longer feed itself or its cubs, which will then be scattered. In Psalm 58:6 it is God who is called on to shatter the teeth of the lion, and it is probably the implication here that God is responsible for the fate of the lion as representative of the wicked. Again, actions have consequences in the simplistic view of retribution espoused here by Eliphaz, and God brings judgment on those actions.

Eliphaz Appeals to Spiritual Experience (4:12–21)

Eliphaz moves to bolster his argument by appealing to a vision he claims to have had. An appeal to a vision carries an implicit claim to authority. No longer is Eliphaz suggesting that he relies solely upon his own wisdom as a basis for advising Job; now he claims supernatural knowledge, a spiritual insight that conveys information to which he himself could not otherwise have been privy.

Verses 12–16 set the scene for Eliphaz's vision. This message was received in the depths of the night when people are deep asleep. It is not clear whether Eliphaz was himself asleep when he experienced this vision or was simply relating the time he experienced it (the NIV's "amid disquieting dreams in the night" is more literally "in troubling thoughts from night visions," as the Hebrew text does not have an unambiguous reference to dreams).[4]

4. See Clines, *Job 1–20*, 129.

The language ("secretly," "to me," "whisper") together with its timing all point to the very personal and targeted nature of this message. That it was not merely a random dream is highlighted by the fear the incident induced in Eliphaz (v. 14) and his physical response to the presence of a spirit (v. 15). The fear was not a response to the message the spirit brought (for he relates the response before the message, and the message itself is not one that would induce fear) but to the presence of the spirit itself.

Furthermore, Eliphaz's experience was not merely visual. The essence of the experience was conveyed to him through words. Although it may be inferred through the use of such language as "whisper" (v. 12) and "hushed voice" (v. 16) that the message was not conveyed in a clear manner, such that Eliphaz may have misheard it, this language more likely serves to highlight the overall impression that this message was delivered to Eliphaz in private, for his ears alone, and no other person had received it. Perhaps only now, in his encounter with Job, does he recognize the relevance of the words he heard from the spirit that night.

Almost all translations (including the NIV) and commentators understand the rhetorical questions posed by Eliphaz in verse 17 not to be expressing the idea that anyone is claiming that human righteousness and purity could surpass that of God (which would be a natural way to read the Hebrew) but instead to be pointing to the claims being made in the presence of God. For example, the NASB reads "Can a man be just before God?" This, it is argued, is more theologically cogent than the alternative, yet it is a more unusual reading of the Hebrew preposition *min* where other expressions are far more commonly used to express the idea conveyed by "before." A third way to read this would be to understand the preposition *min* in a privative sense as "Can a human be righteous *without* God?" This does not make much sense in the context, however, and all things considered the NIV is probably the best understanding of the Hebrew here.

This leads us to see in this spirit's words a more nuanced idea than simple comparison. The rhetorical question proposed by this spirit—"Can a mortal be more righteous than God?," implicitly comparing Job's righteousness with that of God—is not suggesting that any mortal could even attain to God's standard of righteousness, let alone surpass it (as if that were a thing!). Rather, the implication is that by insisting on his innocence, Job is placing himself above God!

The remainder of the message from the spirit is a reversal of the comparison of verse 17, highlighting the insignificance of human beings before God. The parallelism of verse 18 makes it clear that the servants referred to are angelic beings. While it might seem surprising that this spirit claims God does not trust angelic beings (while Eliphaz is trusting an angelic being giving him this message) let alone any human, it is also important not to place too much stock in what is said here. For one, Eliphaz's claims are ultimately not borne out—God tells us that what he says to Job about him is not right (Job 42:7), and so getting sidetracked by a discussion of why God does not trust angelic beings or humans is largely pointless. Eliphaz is arguing a point that is simply untrue in Job's case, even if it *might* be true that God does not completely trust angels, let alone humans. If that truly is the case, then it should be established from other passages, not this one!

The essence of the message conveyed by this spirit is simple: even the most upright and righteous person still has flaws. The reason Eliphaz makes this point is also clear: Job's losses are clearly the result of some such flaw, and so there is some sin he must atone for in order to be restored to his former health and wealth.

Yet the mere claim to a spiritual experience, as Eliphaz has made here, does not automatically mean that it is true. As such, we might be tempted to suggest that this vision is of demonic origin, and so it misleads Eliphaz by proposing an untruth about Job and God, for we know from Yahweh's words to Job at the end of the book that Job's friends did not speak truthfully about God or the causes for Job's suffering. Yet such a claim goes beyond what we are told. The words the spirit conveyed to Eliphaz are not themselves problematical (although perhaps their timing is). It is true that all human beings are flawed; none is without sin, even Job. Where Eliphaz has gone wrong is to then conclude that the causes for Job's suffering must be found in some sin he has committed. Nothing this spirit is reported to have said to Eliphaz makes such a connection, but the fact that these words were given to Eliphaz at a point where he was soon to encounter Job does suggest a somewhat nefarious motivation in their delivery. Nonetheless, it is in making this connection of Job's suffering to a sin that Eliphaz makes his mistake. We know from the prologue that Job scrupulously offered sacrifice to deal with sin, and we know that both the narrator and God himself have declared that Job is not deserving of punishment for some sin he has committed. As such it is not clear that the source of Eliphaz's vision is demonic, only that he has misappropriated the message he received and misapplied it to Job.

Don't Be Stubborn, Don't Be a Fool (5:1–7)

Having recounted the message from the spirit, Eliphaz advances his argument with Job by making it clear to Job that he has no one on his side. The first line rules out any human support, and the second line's reference to "holy ones" likely ups the ante by claiming that there will be no backing coming from supernatural sources either (the term "holy ones" can refer to people, as in Lev 11:44; Num 15:40, or to angelic beings, as in Zech 14:5).

The most generous way to read Eliphaz's words in verses 2–7, which begin with what appears to be a proverb, is to understand him to be warning Job against foolish behavior as opposed to him actually calling Job a fool. However, whichever way it is taken, it is difficult not to read this as a strong rebuke to Job.

"Resentment" (NIV) translates a term that elsewhere refers to anger, and so we have Eliphaz here warning Job against anger and jealousy, both of which spell disaster for the fool (indeed, Eliphaz goes so far as to say they "kill" the fool). Job will pick up this term as he begins his response in 6:2, making it clear that he understands Eliphaz to be targeting him directly here.

Verses 3–5 reflect on the fate of the fool's children whose lives are imperiled by the father's folly. The fool "taking root" appears to imply something like "becoming entrenched," that is, settling in for the long haul. This fool is not going anywhere (unlike the angry or jealous fool of verse 2). The suggestion here is that this fool's folly has long-lasting, ongoing implications for both himself and his descendants.

The NIV's "but suddenly his house was cursed" assigns no source to the curse, but the Hebrew text here has the verb in the first person, more literally reading "so I immediately cursed his farm." The repeated first-person verbs here and the emphatic use of a first-person pronoun give the impression that Eliphaz is very much speaking from personal experience. Eliphaz doesn't offer an explicit rationale for his cursing of the fool in this example, and it is not clear whether the problems he describes for the children of the fool and the fool's harvest in the subsequent verses are a result of Eliphaz's curse or the folly of the fool. Presumably, though, he recognizes the danger in the continued presence of the fool to be such that drastic action should be taken to eradicate the danger, hence his need to quickly curse the property of that fool. This attitude may well explain why he felt the need to jump in and respond to Job with such vigor!

The NIV helpfully situates verse 4 within a legal context, which is the modern equivalent of the town gate to which the Hebrew here refers. The fool's children are vulnerable to legal attack and have no one to defend them. Eliphaz will later use the same term to describe God who, he states, will rescue those who appeal to him (v. 8) from multiple calamities (v. 19). Job himself will pick this up in 10:7, yet there he will accuse God of failing to deliver or rescue him.

The theme of the vulnerability of the fool's children continues in verse 5, which suggests that the provisions made by the fool for his children are instead lost to others (even if they really are hungry and thirsty, although the terms are perhaps metaphorical in light of the connection between "thirst" and "wealth" here). Verse 6 clarifies the point: the source of this family's troubles is not the weather or the soil in which the crops grow, it is the folly of the landowner.[5]

The conclusion to this section presents an aphorism that generalizes the ideas of the preceding verses. The usual understanding of the first clause is that trouble is the lot of human beings—it is to be expected. This, however, does not quite sit easily with the preceding example, where it is the fool who causes the trouble he and his family endure. An attractive alternative is to change the vowels attached to the Hebrew word here (in the Hebrew text the vowels are marked by small dots and dashes around the consonants added around the ninth century AD) and read the clause as "for human beings give birth to trouble." This fits with Eliphaz's preceding argument, wherein the folly of the fool has resulted in calamity. It also better fits the presuppositions of both Job and his friends at this stage of the book.

The second half of this verse suggests that what has been described is inherently human. Just as it is inevitable for the sparks in a fire to fly upward, so it is inevitable that human beings in their folly will cause trouble for themselves (and, in light of the preceding material, for their progeny).

One might wonder what point Eliphaz is making in all of this. It would be a mistake to think that he is labeling Job a fool (at least explicitly at this stage of the dialogues), for he has not immediately cursed Job, as he stated he had done in a situation where a fool had taken root. Yet it is also hard to believe he is not thinking that Job has started to exhibit foolish behavior and so is in great danger, and to some extent Job's travails are a consequence of some foolishness on his part.

Eliphaz's Advice to Job: Turn to God (5:8–16)

The remainder of Eliphaz's speech is laden with irony, a rhetorical feature that will recur throughout the remainder of the book from all speakers. Eliphaz, it would seem, is setting the tone for pretty much all that will follow,

5. Some, such as Christopher Ash, *Job: The Wisdom of the Cross*, Preaching the Word (Wheaton, IL: Crossway, 2014), 109; Pope, *Job*, 42, suggest that the Hebrew word "not" in this verse should be read differently to mean "assuredly," essentially inverting the meaning. While the meaning may suit some readers, it is quite unlikely and such a change is not reflected in any of the ancient versions (the LXX, Vulgate, targums).

particularly for the interactions of Job and his three older friends in the first half of the book.

The introduction to the final sections of Eliphaz's initial speech sees him turn to offering advice to Job, and that advice is to seek God (the Hebrew term sometimes carries the idea of seeking in prayer, cf. Gen 25:22; Exod 18:15) so that he may present his case to him. It is perhaps worthy of note that Eliphaz does not actually pray here but rather indicates to Job what he would be doing in his situation.

The remainder of this stanza (Job 5:9–16) is effectively a poem of praise of God, describing and praising his virtues. Significantly for the case he is presenting to Job, Eliphaz makes note that God does indeed reward those who are lowly or mourning (v. 11) while cutting down the crafty (this word *'arom* is the same used to describe the serpent in the garden in Gen 3:1). Eliphaz essentially states the traditional doctrine of retributive justice and, while not explicitly stating where Job stands on the spectrum of good to evil or wise to foolish, the implication is clear: Job is the ultimate cause of his own calamities and he needs to repent, return to God, and be healed. At this point we, as readers, should clearly understand that Eliphaz is wrong, but we will be reminded of his error at the end of the book.

The statement that God "performs wonders that cannot be fathomed" (v. 9) may initially appear to undermine Eliphaz's own argument here, for it could be read as suggesting that God's ways are beyond human understanding (which is precisely the point of the divine speeches at the end of the book and precisely what Job admits to having learned in Job 42:1–6). However, the Hebrew here woodenly reads, "a doer of great things and without a search." The parallel second line of the verse makes it clear that Eliphaz is specifically thinking of God doing miraculous deeds. The language used here is used elsewhere of just such acts (e.g., Exod 3:20 referring to the miracles that led to the exodus; Josh 3:5 in reference to the events around the conquest of the land) and, as a description of God, is hardly in dispute (Job will essentially repeat this in Job 9:10). So Eliphaz is not suggesting to Job that his predicament could be the result of something other than his own sin. Instead, he is pointing to the fact that God has the power to restore Job, if only he would appeal to him.

Eliphaz continues describing the nature of God in verse 10. Aside from miraculous deeds, God also maintains the mundane by watering the land. In short, God provides for all the needs of his creation. More specifically, as David Clines points out, in a dry climate such as Palestine, rain transforms the land. Eliphaz is pointing Job to the God who can change the fortunes of the land and, as becomes clear in the next verse, those of people just as easily.

From the physical world, Eliphaz turns to the moral world and how God treats people (v. 11). The sentiments here are echoed by Jesus in the Sermon on the Mount: the lowly and those who mourn are raised up and comforted by God (cf. Matt 5:3–4). God reverses the fortunes of people, a point Eliphaz continues to make in the subsequent verses, yet with more focus on bringing down those who are haughty.

From those whom God would raise up, Eliphaz turns to those God brings low in verses 12–14. Whether it was Eliphaz's intent to target Job directly here or not, it is difficult not to come away from these words without the feeling that the way in which they broadly mirror the events of Job's life—falling from great height to lowest depth—exposes his thinking. Job had it all; now he has nothing. God gave and God took away. Everyone agrees on that, but in Eliphaz's thinking that only happens to the shrewd (v. 12), the wise, and the cunning (v. 13), terms commonly associated with wisdom through the Bible.

Eliphaz's use of this wisdom language to describe those whom God brings low reflects a recurrent theme throughout the Old Testament representing the shady side of human wisdom and even the sinful abuse of divinely given wisdom. The serpent in the garden was "crafty" (a word that is sometimes used positively, e.g., Prov 12:16) and Solomon, in all his wisdom, wound up abandoning God. The book of Ecclesiastes is largely about the failure of human wisdom to achieve its goals.[6] Indeed, the one clear citation of Job in the New Testament is of these very words (Job 5:13a, "He catches the wise in their craftiness") by Paul in 1 Corinthians 3:19, where he contrasts human and divine wisdom. The consistent witness of the Bible is that true wisdom is to be found in obedience to God (e.g., Deut 4:6) while trusting in our own wisdom leads nowhere (e.g., Prov 3:5).

So Eliphaz is entirely correct in what he says here. But where his assertions fall down is in their relevance to Job, for we know that Job's downfall has not been the result of anything Eliphaz has pointed to in his speech thus far.

Eliphaz closes this stanza with the assurance that those who have fallen on hard times, who are themselves powerless to escape, can find hope in God, who saves from the tongue (the "sword in their mouth," see Jas 3:3–12) and also from the power of the oppressor.

"Poor" in Job 5:16 encompasses more than merely those who are financially impoverished. It includes the idea of powerlessness and so those without the ability to turn their own lives around. Those in such a position should,

6. See Martin A. Shields, *The End of Wisdom: A Reappraisal of the Historical and Canonical Function of Ecclesiastes* (Winona Lake, IN: Eisenbrauns, 2006).

as Eliphaz said in verse 8, appeal to God for help, and he will help them. He will save them and protect them from further injustice: "injustice shuts its mouth." Eliphaz's message of this entire stanza is simple: "Job, you should reach out to God and he will reverse your fortunes."

God Is Clearly Disciplining You (5:17–26)

The final stanza of Eliphaz's speech clarifies his preceding comments by making explicit the idea that Job's predicament has come about because he is being disciplined by God. Yet Job, says Eliphaz, should be encouraged by this. Indeed, he is blessed to find himself in a situation where he is experiencing God's discipline. The idea itself is, once again, entirely biblical and a common theme in the wisdom literature (e.g., Prov 3:11; 12:1; Heb 12:5–11). Yet the problems in blindly applying this idea to Job are manifold. For one, it is entirely lacking in compassion. Job has lost all of his children, not just a few possessions. Another problem is that while it is true that divine discipline is for our betterment, we know that Job is not being disciplined. Eliphaz has been too hasty to make the general principle apply to the specific circumstances of Job, and he has done so out of ignorance.

Beginning with a faulty premise, then, Eliphaz proceeds to expound the reasons to be grateful for being disciplined by God.

For the first time in the book of Job God is referred to by the name or title *shadday*, "Almighty" (v. 17). The name is used thirty-one times in Job and only seventeen times in the remainder of the Old Testament (mostly in Genesis and Exodus). Although it is usually translated "Almighty," the meaning is not entirely certain. The term itself is most likely derived from a word referring to mountains, and it seems to point to the ascendency of God above all others. In the end, the translation "Almighty" (reflected in the Greek and Latin translations of Job) most likely captures the essence of the meaning of the word.

As far as Eliphaz is concerned, God's discipline can be followed by restoration. The one whom the Almighty wounds for disciplinary purposes can also be bound up with bandages and made well; the one whom he injures he also heals. This reflects God's nature as revealed elsewhere (e.g., Deut 32:39).

In Job 5:19–22 Eliphaz uses a common idiom that invokes sequential numbers (v. 19, "six . . . seven . . . "; cf. Prov 6:16–19 but elsewhere different values are used, e.g., "three . . . four . . . " in Prov 30:15–16, 18–19, 21–23; Amos 1:3–13; 2:1–6; "seven . . . eight . . . " in Eccl 11:2).[7] The use of seven as

7. For more information on this form, see Wilfred G. E. Watson, *Classical Hebrew Poetry: A Guide to Its Techniques*, JSOTSup 26 (Sheffield: JSOT Press, 1984), 144–49.

the greater number here may imply completeness, suggesting not specifically seven calamities but rather a "complete" number of calamities, the point being that the disciplinary acts are themselves never to be thought of as an end but rather as a means to achieve an end. Nonetheless, Eliphaz proceeds to list five or six (depending on whether Job 5:22a refers to one or two calamities) in order to complete the illustration. The calamities listed here (famine, battle, harsh speech, destruction, famine [a different Hebrew word from the one at the beginning of the list], and wild animals) do not readily correlate with the afflictions that have befallen Job in the prologue and so presumably are used merely for illustrative purposes (or perhaps because they fitted the poetry of the speech more readily than more immediately relevant alternative words).

Verse 23 breaks from the flow of the preceding, beginning with an explanatory "for." It is not immediately clear to the modern reader what a covenant with the stones of the field refers to, but stones were a clear danger to the fertility of a field (cf. Matt 13:5), such that there are examples where stones were scattered across fields by armies (cf. 2 Kgs 3:19, 25) in order to render them useless for agriculture. As such, the reference to a covenant with the stones of the field is a poetic means to provide assurance that one's fields will remain fertile. This, then, explains why Job would be able to laugh at famine (Job 5:22).

The wild animals (Hebrew "beasts of the field") is clearly a reference to dangerous wild animals that threaten livestock (see Lev 26:22). Eliphaz suggests that they will live at peace with a restored Job, so explaining why Job would not be afraid of them (Job 5:22).

Eliphaz builds on these assurances in verse 24, indicating to Job why he can be confident of his future if only he would recognize God's discipline in the calamities that have befallen him. The reference to Job's "tent" here is a poetic way to refer to his abode (the ancient Greek translation simply uses the word for "house"), and Eliphaz insists that the result of Job's reconciliation with God will be a secure home (the Hebrew word used for "secure" in the NIV is *shalom*, "peace, prosperity, complete, whole,"[8] and gives a broad sense of wellbeing and stability) and estate (the NIV's "property" translates a term [*naweh*] that often refers to the pastures in which cattle graze but here is used in parallel with "tent" to more broadly refer to the entirety of Job's future property).

Verses 25–26 advance the focus to a more distant future, assuring Job of the well-being of his progeny using agricultural imagery ("children" is woodenly

8. See "שָׁלוֹם," *HALOT*, 1506–10; "שָׁלוֹם," *DCH* 7:365–70.

rendered "seed"; "descendants" is woodenly rendered "sprouts, shoots," which are likened to the grass of the land or earth). The same parallelism used here is also found in Job 21:8; Isaiah 44:3; 48:19. The point is that the future of Job's line will be assured well beyond his own life, a sure sign of blessing in the Old Testament (cf. Job 42:12–17; Ps 128:6; Prov 17:6). And Job's life will not end prematurely. The Hebrew word in Job 5:26, "full vigor" (*kelakh*), only appears elsewhere in 30:2, where it seems to refer to strength, but the parallel line here implies that Job's life will end at the right time, just as grain is harvested at the right time. Eliphaz's point, though, is that Job's life will both be long and healthy, should he only return to God.

Aside from the fact that Eliphaz has completely misunderstood the fundamental cause of Job's suffering in calling Job to repentance, he demonstrates a clear lack of compassion and empathy with Job, who has only recently lost all of his children. Given Eliphaz's false premise that some action of Job's has alienated him from God and resulted in his losses, Job cannot share Eliphaz's confidence that reconciliation with God will achieve anything. He has lost everything without straying from devotion to Yahweh, contrary to what Eliphaz has assumed.

Eliphaz concludes his words to Job with an affirmation of his confidence in their truth by including the other friends—and probably the collective wisdom of the wise—in his argument by using the plural "we." His final sentence is worded strongly and emphatically, using imperatives as if to command Job on how to respond: listen to this (the Hebrew verb for "listen" often includes the sense "obey") and know it for yourself. There is no doubt in Eliphaz's mind that Job is guilty, but there is hope for him if he pleads with God.

LIVE the Story

Responding to Difficult News

Perhaps the first thing to note about Eliphaz's opening words to Job is that he does not respond to a question Job has asked. Job has not invited this response; he has not asked for an explanation for his suffering from his friends or even up to this point from God. Rather, he has poured out his pain in words for all to hear. Eliphaz chooses to respond and chooses how to respond. In itself this should be a warning to us in pastoral situations against too quickly offering answers to questions which have not been asked.

On the other hand, it would be easy to dismiss the words of Eliphaz and his friends. After all, we all know that in the end God himself will declare that they have not spoken correctly about God (Job 42:7). However, in some ways God's assessment is a bit of a surprise, for if we were to read through the friends' words to Job and about God without having first read the prologue, much of what they say sounds largely correct. It would not be out of place to hear many of these words in a contemporary sermon: suffering is inevitable in a sinful world, and no one is without sin, so do not be surprised if you suffer. How often are we called upon to repent? How often do we share in confession of our sins? There is certainly nothing unusual in any of these words for the modern churchgoer!

Of course, even if we were to dismiss everything they say, there would be some lessons in what not to do and say to be found among the friends' words. And yet dismissing everything said by the friends would also prove to be premature. God does not say that everything they said was wrong and, as in any debate, each speaker's words are a mixture of the good, the bad, and the ugly.

Furthermore, Eliphaz is not answering simply out of a desire to correct Job's theology. In Eliphaz's view, Job's predicament is the result of sin and can be remedied through repentance. Eliphaz's motives, at this point in the story at least, are essentially good. And we can understand that if he was right and Job could be restored through repentance, then that would certainly be rather good advice to offer. Yet even if Eliphaz were correct, he fails to recognize that Job is not ready to hear the words he has to say, and certainly not ready to accept them. Again, there are lessons for those in situations when caring for someone who is in any sort of difficult situation. Be patient, be kind, and if your words are to be words of correction, do not rush in but wait until the person is ready to hear what you have to say. And, most importantly, make sure you have listened long enough and hard enough to know that you are not making a mistake and leaping to unfounded conclusions. For here begins the lengthy attempts of Job's friends to mistakenly chastise him and correct him, a process that ultimately does far more harm to Job than it does help him.

Eliphaz's response is an important lesson in listening. Instead of listening to Job's pain, empathizing with him, and comforting him, Eliphaz responds to what he imagines Job needs by explaining what he believes Job's problem to be and how Job ought to go about fixing it. Yet people in all circumstances, including through suffering, do not always respond in a way that those who are not in their circumstances might expect, and the only way to meet that person where they are and help them is to begin by listening to them. The danger is assuming we know what people need—whether they are suffering or facing difficulties in life—and rush to meet the need we have identified rather than the need they have expressed. And while it is certainly true that there is a place for helping someone if we see a solution, we need to be careful—very careful—that any solution we identify is actually a solution. Eliphaz presumes much and offers his analysis without truly understanding or knowing the problem or its solution. That much has been made clear to us already in the opening chapters of the book but will be confirmed by God's words in chapter 42.

Doubtless Eliphaz responds because he believed in the righteousness and justice of Yahweh, a belief that is a fundamental tenet of Old Testament faith and that informs the idea that suffering was a punishment for sin. The idea, of course, is not without merit or without support from Scripture. Yet Eliphaz was wrong, and although he claimed to have arrived at this conclusion about Job's circumstances at least in part from a message proffered to him by a spirit, we know he was wrong. This ought to serve as a warning to us all should we ever be faced with similar circumstances.

An appropriate response to Eliphaz can be found in Proverbs 26:7:

> Like the useless legs of one who is lame
> is a proverb in the mouth of a fool.[9]

Quoting wise words does not make one wise. The teaching of Proverbs is that it takes wisdom to use wisdom well, and while Eliphaz likes to think of himself as wise, we as readers should know enough to see the folly of his words.

Illegitimate Appeals to Authority

Beyond this, and apparently to bolster the authority of his words, Eliphaz makes an appeal to some type of spiritual experience, some spiritual revelation that was given to him as he slept (Job 4:12–17). He feels he has some sort of divine warrant for reaching the conclusions about Job's situation that he has. Eliphaz, of course, is not alone. Many people throughout history have claimed to have had a message from God or the spiritual realm. On the basis of that message, some have gone and started new religions or broken away from orthodox Christianity to start a new sect or cult.

While such experiences carry a lot of emotional force, they are very difficult to verify. Paul encountered just such a challenge when he came up against the "super-apostles" (2 Cor 12:11) who similarly made appeal to their experience in order to grant themselves authority as described and challenged by Paul in 2 Corinthians 11–12. The Bible does offer a few tests for prophetic words,

9. The Hebrew word translated "proverb" here (*mashal*) can refer to extended wisdom discourse and is used to describe Job's speeches in Job 27:1; 29:1, so it should not be thought to refer in this quotation only to brief aphorisms of the type found commonly in the book of Proverbs.

but ultimately the test is to see whether the message conflicts with or contradicts God's authoritative revelation in the Bible itself. Some such messages cannot be tested in this way. When the prophet Agabus comes and warns the apostle Paul about what awaits him if he journeys on to Jerusalem in Acts 21, there is no way to verify the authority or veracity of his message from the Bible. On the other hand, of course, it is this sort of message that cannot form the basis for any serious doctrinal error or prompt someone to start their own cult, sect, or even religion. The revelations that are employed to do these things invariably contradict Scripture.

Examples of appeals to revelations abound in history. The founder of the Church of Jesus Christ of Latter-day Saints, Joseph Smith, claimed visionary experiences.[10] The author of The Passion Translation, Brian Simmons, after claiming to have experienced a series of other visionary and spiritual experiences, claimed to have had Jesus visit him in his room to commission him to produce his version of the Bible.[11]

Over and again throughout church history there have been those who claim authority based on their experiences, yet over and again God warns us not to judge others by such claims but by their fruit and by how they correspond to what God has said to us through his Word. In short, if you hear someone playing up their spiritual experiences—whether it be a vision, a dream, a miracle, or anything else—then be careful that you grant their words no additional weight because of these claims. The people of God have been warned against such practices since at least the words of Moses in Deuteronomy:

> If a prophet, or one who foretells by dreams, appears among you and announces to you a sign or wonder, and if the sign or wonder spoken of takes place, and the prophet says, "Let us follow other gods" (gods you have not known) "and let us worship them," you must not listen to the words of that prophet or dreamer. The Lord your God is testing you to find out whether you love him with all your heart and with all your soul. (Deut 13:1–3)

10. See https://history.churchofjesuschrist.org/content/the-first-vision?lang=eng. The result of these visions, however, was a new religion, which is clearly contrary to the Bible.

11. The claim was made by Simmons on Sid Roth's *It's Supernatural* show from February 15, 2015 (see https://sidroth.org/television/tv-archives/brian-simmons/). Yet the result, The Passion Translation (see https://www.thepassiontranslation.com/), has been widely condemned as heretical and blatantly adding to the text of the Bible. See Andrew G. Shead, "Burning Scripture with Passion: A Review of The Psalms (The Passion Translation)," *Themelios* 43.1 (2018): 58–71.

Authority does not come from anything I claim about myself or my experiences. Rather, *authority ought to come from how my words and actions stack up against Scripture.* Those who make claims based on their spiritual experiences—even if those experiences were true, if they refer to things that really took place—should not be trusted. Their words and their claims must be measured against Scripture and only against Scripture. Any other measure is liable to mislead and transport those who listen down a path to destruction.

Does a claim to revelation that stands at odds with Scripture then mean that the person relating such revelation is invariably making it up or lying? Certainly not. The Bible acknowledges the possibility that prophets can be deceived by lying spirits (1 Kgs 22:22–23; 1Tim 4:1; see also Deut 13:1–5). There are supernatural beings that can lead people astray, and a mere claim to a spiritual experience is clearly not sufficient basis for initiating a new belief. What this then means is that sincere, devout people can truly claim experiences that really did take place and had a profound impact on their lives, but experiences that ultimately lead them away from the living God and not to him.

Eliphaz is here an example of such a one who is sincere and yet misleads, and through his vision ultimately threatens to mislead Job, who, we know, has nothing of which he must repent. Fortunately, Job has the wisdom, we shall see, to remain steadfast in the face of Eliphaz's claims to a special prophetic experience. Job, as the coming speech will reveal, maintains his innocence.

CHAPTER 4

Job 6–7

Job's First Reply to Eliphaz

LISTEN to the Story

6:1 Then Job replied:

2 "If only my anguish could be weighed
and all my misery be placed on the scales!
3 It would surely outweigh the sand of the seas—
no wonder my words have been impetuous.
4 The arrows of the Almighty are in me,
my spirit drinks in their poison;
God's terrors are marshaled against me.
5 Does a wild donkey bray when it has grass,
or an ox bellow when it has fodder?
6 Is tasteless food eaten without salt,
or is there flavor in the sap of the mallow?
7 I refuse to touch it;
such food makes me ill.

8 "Oh, that I might have my request,
that God would grant what I hope for,
9 that God would be willing to crush me,
to let loose his hand and cut off my life!
10 Then I would still have this consolation—
my joy in unrelenting pain—
that I had not denied the words of the Holy One.

11 "What strength do I have, that I should still hope?
What prospects, that I should be patient?
12 Do I have the strength of stone?

Is my flesh bronze?
13Do I have any power to help myself,
now that success has been driven from me?

14"Anyone who withholds kindness from a friend
forsakes the fear of the Almighty.
15But my brothers are as undependable as intermittent streams,
as the streams that overflow
16when darkened by thawing ice
and swollen with melting snow,
17but that stop flowing in the dry season,
and in the heat vanish from their channels.
18Caravans turn aside from their routes;
they go off into the wasteland and perish.
19The caravans of Tema look for water,
the traveling merchants of Sheba look in hope.
20They are distressed, because they had been confident;
they arrive there, only to be disappointed.
21Now you too have proved to be of no help;
you see something dreadful and are afraid.
22Have I ever said, 'Give something on my behalf,
pay a ransom for me from your wealth,
23deliver me from the hand of the enemy,
rescue me from the clutches of the ruthless'?

24"Teach me, and I will be quiet;
show me where I have been wrong.
25How painful are honest words!
But what do your arguments prove?
26Do you mean to correct what I say,
and treat my desperate words as wind?
27You would even cast lots for the fatherless
and barter away your friend.

28"But now be so kind as to look at me.
Would I lie to your face?
29Relent, do not be unjust;

reconsider, for my integrity is at stake.
30Is there any wickedness on my lips?
Can my mouth not discern malice?

7:1"Do not mortals have hard service on earth?
Are not their days like those of hired laborers?
2Like a slave longing for the evening shadows,
or a hired laborer waiting to be paid,
3so I have been allotted months of futility,
and nights of misery have been assigned to me.
4When I lie down I think, 'How long before I get up?'
The night drags on, and I toss and turn until dawn.
5My body is clothed with worms and scabs,
my skin is broken and festering.

6"My days are swifter than a weaver's shuttle,
and they come to an end without hope.
7Remember, O God, that my life is but a breath;
my eyes will never see happiness again.
8The eye that now sees me will see me no longer;
you will look for me, but I will be no more.
9As a cloud vanishes and is gone,
so one who goes down to the grave does not return.
10He will never come to his house again;
his place will know him no more.

11"Therefore I will not keep silent;
I will speak out in the anguish of my spirit,
I will complain in the bitterness of my soul.
12Am I the sea, or the monster of the deep,
that you put me under guard?
13When I think my bed will comfort me
and my couch will ease my complaint,
14even then you frighten me with dreams
and terrify me with visions,
15so that I prefer strangling and death,
rather than this body of mine.

16I despise my life; I would not live forever.
  Let me alone; my days have no meaning.

17"What is mankind that you make so much of them,
  that you give them so much attention,
18that you examine them every morning
  and test them every moment?
19Will you never look away from me,
  or let me alone even for an instant?
20If I have sinned, what have I done to you,
  you who see everything we do?
Why have you made me your target?
  Have I become a burden to you?
21Why do you not pardon my offenses
  and forgive my sins?
For I will soon lie down in the dust;
  you will search for me, but I will be no more."

Listening to the Text in the Story: "The Baʿlu Myth" (Ugaritic)

Job's speech here introduces the first reference to Sheol, the place of the dead or the underworld (Job 7:9, translated in the NIV with "the grave"), although the concept has already been mentioned earlier in the book (see 3:13–15). Exactly what Job and his friends thought about Sheol can only be gleaned by collating the details revealed throughout the book (Sheol is mentioned in 7:9; 11:8; 14:13; 17:13, 16; 21:13; 24:19; 26:6). From these verses we know that for Job and his friends Sheol was thought to be a place deep under the earth—the opposite of the heavens above (11:8; 17:16), a realm of darkness (17:13), a place where wicked people, in particular, appear to go (21:13; 24:19), and yet a place that lies bare before God (26:6).

There is some debate about Job's comprehension of an afterlife and whether Sheol is the destination of all people or only the wicked.[1] Whatever the case, it is clear from Job's general attitude throughout the book that he expects that

1. See, for example, Kyle C. Dunham, "Ransomed from the Hand of Sheol: The Heavenly Destiny of Old Testament Saints in the Afterlife," *DBSJ* 26 (2021): 3–33.

his existence after death is unlikely to be as good (at least in general) as this life. He wants answers before he dies; he wants to see God now.

He also mentions the sea and the sea monster (7:12). The probable background here is ancient Near Eastern mythology, specifically the Ugaritic Baal myths. There we find mention of the sea monster (or "sea dragon") Tannin together with Yam (the sea deity). In one particular passage (*CTA* 3.3.34–37), the deity Anath recounts which of Baal's enemies she has already dispatched:

> What enemy has arisen against Baʿlu,
> (what) adversary against Cloud-Rider?
> I have smitten ʾIlu's beloved, Yammu,
> have finished off the great god Naharu.
> I have bound the dragon's jaws, have destroyed it,
> have smitten the twisting serpent,
> the close-coiled one with seven heads.[2]

Here, "dragon" is the Ugaritic word *tnn*, equivalent to the Hebrew *tannin* (NIV "monster") found in Job 7:12 and elsewhere (see Pss 74:13; 148:7; Jer 51:34; NIV "monster," "sea creatures," and "serpent," respectively). The point of this parallel is not to suggest that the author of Job is directly appealing to the Ugaritic "Baʿlu Myth" or that this text should specifically be in mind when reading Job, but rather that Job here references the thought world of the ancient audience, which shared some knowledge of these creatures. For the reader of Job in ancient times, these creatures represented the fiercest opponents to Yahweh, far exceeding human beings in terms of their threat to order in the universe.

As such, the references to these mythological monsters throughout Job usually appear in contexts where an appeal is made to a creature whose strength or power is beyond all others. In Job 7:12 it comes at a point where Job feels that God's treatment of him would be appropriate if he were such a being rather than a mere man, a point he makes to highlight the perceived disproportionality of God's treatment of him, no matter what he might have done. And given his avowed innocence, this highlights for us Job's true perception of his own situation.

2. "The Baʿlu Myth," (*COS* 1.86:252). In this translation "smitten" means "struck down" and has no association with causing one to fall in love with another!

EXPLAIN the Story

Job Justifies His Complaint (6:1–13)

The book of Job consistently notes when the speaker changes, but the language here makes it clear that the subsequent words of Job are—at least in part—a direct response to Eliphaz's words, just as Job 4:1 made it clear that Eliphaz's words were a response to Job's lament of chapter 3.

Job begins his response seeking to explain why he spoke as he did: the emotional magnitude of what has befallen him has prompted it. The Hebrew noun translated "anguish" (*ka'aś*) in 6:2 of the NIV occurs only in Job (although it is generally connected to a similar and more common verb *k's*, which has a final letter different from that of the noun mentioned above) and is variously understood as "grief, vexation, anger, irritation, provocation."[3] Job's use here is in direct response to Eliphaz, who had used the same term in 5:2 where it was one of the causes of the fool's death. Rightly or wrongly, Job has understood Eliphaz's words there to be in direct reference to himself. Even if Eliphaz were intending to issue some sort of vague, general warning, Job's response reveals the real danger that such language is very easily taken as a personal attack. Job's friends' lack of tact and empathy will be on display repeatedly through this debate, and Job only suffers more because of it.

The final clause of verse 3 makes Job's point: it is the magnitude of what has happened that has elicited the words he previously spoke. If they appear unseemly to Eliphaz and his friends, it is only because they have not grasped the weight—greater than the sands of the sea, perhaps the weightiest physical object Job could imagine—of all that has come upon him.

In verse 4 Job expands on what he has already said by laying blame for his predicament on God. He has already done this (Job 2:10), but his language now is more emotive and vivid. Arrows are a weapon elsewhere said to be used by God (see Deut 32:23, 42; Pss 7:13; 38:2; 77:17; Zech 9:14). These poisonous arrows (note the next line) are now sticking into Job, infecting his spirit. The final line of the verse increases the scope of Job's torment, for not only is he currently pierced by God's poisonous arrows, he also faces unspecified terrors of God in the way one might face an advancing army. Job's use of military imagery here establishes that he has come to think that God sees him as his enemy who has declared war on him.

In verse 5 Job also further elaborates on his explanation for the way he has

3. *DCH* 4:449.

spoken that he started in verse 3. Here he inverts his previous claim, noting that a donkey or an ox, when it has all that it needs, will not complain. For Job, those who are silent, or who do not complain, do so only because they have nothing to complain about. Eliphaz should have expected some sort of complaint from Job rather than objecting to it!

The reference to beasts finding satisfaction in food in verses 6–7 prompts Job to turn to explain his situation in terms of food: there are some foods that are simply not palatable. The first example is tasteless, bland food for which Job insists salt is necessary to make it appetizing. The parallel line in verse 6, "sap of the mallow," presents some translational difficulties (some translations [e.g., NASB, NET, KJV] refer to the "white of an egg" here; see below). The first part of the phrase, "sap" (Hebrew *berir*), refers to "spittle" in 1 Samuel 21:13, the only other place the word is used. The other word in the phrase, "mallow" (*khallamut*), occurs only here in the Bible. One ancient tradition understood this to be a reference to the flavorlessness of the white of an egg, but it is perhaps more likely a reference to slimy liquid of some form of melon (hence the NIV's "sap of the mallow"). Either way, the point is clear: some foods are inherently unpalatable (I am sure we all have memories of meals from our youth that we felt were like this, especially those who have tried the Australian "delicacy" of Vegemite!).

In verse 7 Job explains his revulsion for unpalatable food, stating that he avoids such food as it makes him ill. He has advanced his argument, quickly switching from the way in which food soothes the savage beast (to mangle a famous expression) to something in his present experience that is akin to unpalatable food. But what is it? It seems unlikely that his losses and afflictions could readily be described as flavorless and insipid, so it is more likely that he is referring to the words of Eliphaz he has just heard.

Having offered some justification for the manner in which he spoke in chapter 3, Job turns his thoughts back to those words of complaint and lament and builds upon them in verses 8–9. For the first time he gives voice to his desire that God would let him die now (rather than at birth). In 3:16 he had wished that he had never been born—clearly not an entirely realistic expectation—but now he expresses a more viable "hope" that God would end his life. Job's request here reminds the reader that God had previously barred the Satan from taking Job's life (Job 2:6). At that time it appeared to be a merciful restraint, but that is no longer Job's understanding of things.

This raises a difficult question: Is God unnecessarily prolonging Job's suffering, and if he is, why? The answer—particularly to the why part of this question—is not immediately forthcoming but shall come to light in part of the larger teaching of the book of Job, which shall only fully emerge when we come to the end of the book.

In contemplating the end of his life at God's hand, Job notes one point of comfort: he has remained faithful to God. The last phrase of verse 10 in Hebrew has Job insisting that he has not "concealed" or "hidden" the words of the Holy One. The expression is best understood to be a claim to have faithfully adhered to the statutes of God. We are reminded that the Satan had insisted that Job would betray his faith in God under the pain of the torture he faced, but that he had not. Even now, beyond the point where the Satan had conceded defeat and Yahweh had claimed victory in chapter 2, Job insists upon his continued faithfulness to God.

Why would Job hope for death rather than for an end to his suffering and then a long life? He explains his thinking in verses 11–13. Essentially Job tells us that he is exhausted; he has had enough. He is not made of stone and bronze but flesh, and he has reached the end of his resources. He announces that he has no ability to help himself, and so the only way out that he can see is for his life to come to an end.

Job's Disappointment with His Friends (6:14–23)

Job's admission that he does not have the strength to help himself turns his thoughts to his friends who stand before him and the hope that they may have provided help, for the next stanza in verses 14–23 moves to lament their failure to provide any help.

The Hebrew of the opening verse is difficult, as is reflected in differences in various translations (cf., e.g., NASB, NLT, NET), but the essence of the verse is to suggest that one who withholds kindness from a friend also forsakes the fear of the Almighty (the unusual Hebrew word *merea'* for "friend" here should be read as a preposition [*me-* from *min*] attached to the more common word for "friend" [*rea'*]).

Job initially likens his friends (whom he calls "brothers" here) to unreliable streams that periodically dry up and stop flowing. The NIV's "undependable" (v. 15) renders a Hebrew verb (*bgd*) that elsewhere refers to treachery (Prov 2:22; 11:3, 6; 13:2, 15; 21:18; etc.), highlighting the fact that Job is not merely concerned with the flow of the stream but with the betrayal of promise the thirsty person feels when they arrive at the stream expecting water only to find none. So, too, Job had expected kindness and aid from his friends but has found they offer neither.

From here Job elaborates on the impact of these unreliable streams on groups of travelers ("caravans" referring to a group of people traveling together rather than mobile accommodation) in Job 6:18–20. These travelers, expecting water to be available away from the road in known places, depart from the well-trodden trade routes to obtain water. Yet when they find them empty, they perish. The two places named—Tema (Jer 25:23; Isa 21:14) and Sheba (Ezek 27:22; 38:13; and Solomon was visited by this city's queen in 1 Kgs 10)—were well-known trade cities in Arabia. Job 6:20 highlights both their confidence in finding these streams flowing as well as their devastation at finding them empty.

Job finally makes the connection between the devastating circumstances faced by the thirsty travelers and his own encounter with his friends in verse 21. The Hebrew here is terser than most English translations indicate; Job simply says, "You are now [this]."[4] Sometimes fewer words make the point more clearly.

The usual understanding of the second line of the verse suggests that Job attributes his friends' inability to help him to their fear of his situation. There are a number of reasons Job may believe them to be afraid; they see his skin condition and fear catching it. They see his predicament, which they attribute to divine judgment, and might see themselves as possibly being caught up in his misfortune. However, following the suggestion made in footnote 4 below, Job may actually be highlighting the lack of any real foundation for his friends' response. Either way, Job's expectations of help, like the travelers hoping for water, have been dashed.

The close of this stanza (vv. 22–23) addresses some of the fears his friends may have harbored. Job offers a series of rhetorical questions making the point that he has never asked anything of his friends. He has placed no demands on them. To illustrate this, he denies having asked for his friends to offer gifts (or bribes!) on his behalf. The second denial—perhaps related to the first—makes the point that he has never called on them to put themselves in danger on his behalf.

Job's point is that he has not called on them to suffer or sacrifice for him. All he has asked for is their compassion and empathy (Job 6:14). They have nothing to fear, but Job finds they have nothing to offer except painful and misguided words of condemnation.

---

4. Scholars struggle with the Hebrew here, but the most natural way to read it (I would argue) is to divide the verse before the particle *lo'*, which normally appears at the beginning of a verse. The verse as a whole would then read, "You are now [this]; you have not seen a terror but you are afraid." If this is correct, the second half of the verse serves to highlight the lack of justification for Job's friends' response to him—they have no grounds to fear and yet they do. Read this way, the remainder of the stanza has Job provide reasons why the friends have no basis for their fear.

Job Calls on His Friends to Change Their Tack (6:24–30)

As if Job's lot were not difficult enough, he is faced with friends whose advice is hurtful and unhelpful. This puts Job in the difficult position of having to rebuke them while he also attempts to get them to understand what he is going through. That he does this in this stanza is an indication of his desire for them to help him, to accompany him on his journey through his suffering, and if they must offer advice, to offer at least correct and relevant advice.

Job begins this challenge in verse 24 by insisting that they should offer him some real instruction (the command "teach" is plural here) and, if they were to do that, he would listen. Up to this point in the discourse, Eliphaz has insinuated that Job is suffering for some sin but has not said what that sin is. Now Job pushes his friends to make clear what sin he has committed. It is not good enough simply to imply he has sinned in the face of his own denials and his own insistence on his innocence. Now is the time to explain exactly what he has done wrong. If they can do this, he will be silent. While the friends do not immediately respond to this ultimatum from Job, they will eventually postulate all manner of sin from Job (e.g., Job 22:4–9), sin of such magnitude that he cannot be silent as he promises here, for the accusations will be so heinous and false that silence would risk being taken as an admission of guilt.

Job's reference, in verses 25–27, to the pain that honest words can inflict acknowledges the possible impact of the honest correction he has called for from his friends in verse 24 but also describes the impact of his own words on his friends to this point (and in what follows). Indeed, what Job says next would almost certainly inflict pain on Eliphaz. Job implies that, to this point, Eliphaz's arguments have been futile, ignoring Job's own "desperate words" and treating them as empty.

Job's accusation of verse 26 asks the friends if their plan is simply to argue with him and, given the objection to his tone (which Job has been defending as reflecting his state of desperation), he is probably asking if their intention is simply to contend with the way he is speaking rather than actually explain what he has done wrong. The second half of the verse is somewhat terser than most English translations present it, saying no more than "the words of a despairing man to the wind." The friends are offended by Job's words; they are not hearing him or his need. They have cast his words to the wind, disregarding his plea for help and his request for honest instruction.

In an attempt to drive home the severity of their treatment of him, in verse 27 Job suggests that their response is akin to them treating an orphan badly. The Hebrew text does not explicitly mention "lots." It simply has the verb meaning "to cast down" (cf. the same abbreviated form in 1 Sam 14:42 for the full expression in 1 Chr 24:31; 25:8; 26:13, etc. that do include the noun "lots" with "cast"). Perhaps a better understanding here is that Job is suggesting that his friends' behavior is akin to casting out or abandoning an orphan (wording not found in the Old Testament but found in John 14:18; 2 Thess 2:17) who has come into their care. Orphans are frequently mentioned in the Bible as the object of God's care (e.g., Exod 22:22; Deut 10:18), and Job will refer to them again when critiquing his friends' treatment of him (Job 24:3).

Job brings the point home by drawing a parallel between the reference to the orphan and himself as their friend. Not only would they cast out the orphan, but they would also sell out their friend. From Job's perspective they have sold him out by neither showing him where he is wrong nor standing with him because he is not wrong.

Job ends this section of his response in verses 28–30 with an appeal to his friends (he continues to use plural references) to turn from their path and recognize that he still has his integrity. The initial appeal by Job for them to look at him is a sincere call for them to see that he is speaking truthfully. It is a request that they deal with him, not some abstract theoretical scenario derived from their presupposed understanding of the nature of suffering that insists that, regardless of whoever it is standing before them, the presence of suffering in his life invariably means he must be at fault. It is a plea for them to recognize that they are not just talking to some random person but to their friend whom they know and whom they know to be upright and blameless.

As such, Job calls on them to turn from the path they have taken. Verse 29 twice repeats the plea to turn. Job's words here are a little less direct than the NIV makes them out to be—a more wooden rendering of the Hebrew is "let there be no falsehood" (NET).[5] In repeating his call for his friends to repent, he further insists that his righteousness still stands (see the NIV note). To this he adds that he has not said anything wrong, repeating the reference to falsehood with a rhetorical question making the point that he has spoken only the truth.

The final line of verse 30 is best understood to underline the previous points. With this rhetorical question Job asks whether his mouth is incapable of differentiating between good and evil words. Job insists that he can and so tries to remind his friends to address him in person.

---

5. This is clear because the Hebrew switches from third-person plural to feminine singular here ("let her not be"). The second half of v. 29 offers an alternate reading that switches back to plural for the word "reconsider."

Suffering Without Hope of Respite (7:1–10)

Perhaps hoping that his friends have understood his appeal made through chapter 6, the focus of Job's response now turns back to lamenting his own suffering. Verses 1–2 reflect on the common lot of all people to endure hard labor throughout their lives. The "hard service" of verse 1 translates a term (*tsaba'*) frequently associated with military service in the Old Testament, and while the second line's "hired laborers" (*sakir*) is also used of military service (see Jer 46:21), it usually refers to a day worker who has no certainty of employment and who receives a relatively meager wage (cf. Matt 20:1–12). The point here is that the human lot is to toil throughout life (cf. Eccl 5:15).

That toil produces a longing for rest, as that of a slave longing for evening when the labors of the day are ended or the hired laborer who yearns for the wages paid out at the end of the day. This desire for rest from toil is also expressed in the proverb of Ecclesiastes 4:9 and underpins the hope expressed throughout the Bible of entering into God's rest (e.g., Gen 2:1–3; Heb 4:1–11).

Yet, the longing of the laborer or slave is not shared by Job. For him there has been no rest, day or night. The reference to "months of futility" may be a clue as to just how long Job has been enduring his suffering—certainly we should not imagine that the time has been brief. Nevertheless, all this time has achieved nothing in Job's eyes and unlike the toil of the slave or laborer, he has no rest at night. The difficulty Job has in finding rest at night is attributed, at least in part, to the illness that has struck him, some of the symptoms that he describes in more lurid detail in verse 5. The "worms" that "clothe" his body could well be maggots (cf. Job 25:6; Isa 14:11), revealing the severity of his skin disease.

Job's condition leads him to reflect on the likely brevity of his life in verses 6–10. Each day is the same as the last, and they pass by more rapidly "than a weaver's shuttle." Job's only expectation of the future would seem to be that he will soon die. A "weaver's shuttle" is the mechanism a weaver uses to pass the thread across the loom between the strands of the fabric being made. It was designed to move as rapidly as possible, especially in the hands of an experienced, competent weaver.

The Hebrew of verse 6 includes a wordplay lost in English. The word for "hope" (*tiqwah*) can also mean "cord, thread" (see Josh 2:18, 21). As such, this clause could either record Job asserting that his days pass rapidly and end without hope (as the NIV) or else have him continuing the weaving metaphor: "They are complete when the thread is finished." Once the thread is exhausted, the cloth is cut from the loom—perhaps representing the end of Job's life.

The NIV's reading is the more probable, although the choice of language is clearly influenced by the metaphor being used, and there is a chance that the verse is deliberately ambiguous, hinting at both meanings.[6]

Verse 7 begins with the imperative "remember." The verb is singular, not plural, and so indicates that the focus of Job's address has shifted from his friends to God himself (the NIV makes this explicit by adding "O God" into the verse). This shift is increasingly apparent as Job's words continue.

The call for God to remember is elsewhere a call to God for justice and action (e.g., Gen 8:1; Jer 15:15). Job underscores the urgency in his call for God to remember by affirming the brevity of his life and that, if left in his hopeless situation, he will never again see anything good. If God hesitates, then Job will be gone; it will be too late. His fate, once his life has ended, cannot be changed (Job 7:9).

This is the first time in the book of Job that Sheol has been mentioned (translated as "the grave" in the NIV). In Greek versions of the Old Testament and in the New Testament, Sheol is known as Hades, which in Greek refers to the abode of the dead.[7] The descent and ascent language used by Job here reflects the standard cosmology of the ancient world, which located the place of the dead below the human realm, hence the common designation as the underworld. The nature of existence in Sheol is explored only a little in the Old Testament, yet it is clear that in Job's mind that Sheol is an undesirable place from which there will be no escape (see more on Sheol in the discussion above on Job 3:13–15).

It is clear at this point that Job's worldview differs from that of New Testament believers, but we ought not to be either surprised or troubled by this. God's revelation has been progressive, and more has been shown to us than had been revealed to Job or the book's original audience. Job's fears and hopes were reflective of what he knew of God's creation. Indeed, Job will learn more by the time his troubles are over in chapter 42 than he knows here. Yet, the fullness of God's revelation to us would not come until Jesus the Messiah many years after Job's time.

Verses 6–10 make it clear that Job believes that his life is essentially over, that there is no hope for his future, and that death is near. If God is to intervene, then he must remember Job now.

---

6. The opening verb on the second line of verse 6 is plural, so it would seem to explicitly refer back to the plural "days" at the start of the verse. As such the reference of this part of the verse seems better understood as the days of Job's life rather than the weaving of the cloth.

7. See "ᾅδης," BDAG 19, §1.

Job Wishes That God Would Leave Him Alone (7:11–21)

Job believes that his circumstances warrant forthright speech, and so he announces (to God more than to his friends) that he will not hold back. Although Job's words arise from his extreme circumstances and are filled with passion, it would be a mistake to write them off because of this. Emotion does not inevitably negate truth.

After this warning that he will speak frankly, he asks whether he is the sea, or "the monster of the deep." The sea was, in Old Testament thought, a place of darkness and evil, of opposition to God. The same is true of "the monster of the deep." The Hebrew word here is *tannin*, a monster from the Ugaritic Baal myths (see Listen to the Story above in this Chapter). Job's point here is that he feels as though God is treating him as if he were one of these supreme enemies rather than the inconsequential human he is (cf. Job 7:7–9) and that the disasters that have fallen upon him are entirely out of proportion to his status in creation. Job's reference to this monster should make us rethink his reference at the start of verse 12 to "the sea," however, for in the ancient world the Hebrew term for "sea" (*yam*, cf. Ps 74:13) was also the name of the Ugaritic deity associated with the sea, an understanding that better parallels the reference to "the monster of the deep" and also makes better sense of Job's complaint that God is dealing with him out of all proportion.

Job's next complaint is that even those places where he should find comfort—the bed or couch where he seeks rest—are not places of refuge or escape from his troubles, for even there God afflicts him with nightmares so terrible that any comfort is lost. Comfort is a theme that runs through the book, with Job looking for comfort and finding none until the very end of the book (see below on Job 42:6).

Job's reference to strangling here prompts some to suggest that whatever ailed him, one of its symptoms may have included breathing difficulties (see above on Job 2:1–6). Whether that is the case or not, it is clear that Job would prefer death to continuing to live the way he is. The magnitude of Job's choice here is clear. It is not as though he seeks death because it is positive, only that it is the only escape he can see from his present suffering. Verse 16 reinforces this point. Job despises his life and does not wish to live forever, for an eternal existence in such painful circumstances is clearly intolerable.

The second half of verse 16 is perhaps the most dramatic and shocking of the entire speech. "Let me alone." The words are direct and directed to God. Job is fully aware that his suffering ultimately tracks back to the hand of God, and for him God has proven to be no source of comfort. While the psalmist (Ps 22:1) and ultimately the Messiah (Mark 15:34) portray their suffering as signs of abandonment by God, Job's circumstances are different. And we know that Job is right in seeing God as the ultimate source of his troubles, for we have been told this is true in the opening chapters of the book. In Job's mind he needs rescuing, but since God is the source of his troubles, his only rescue is if God leaves him alone!

Job offers one reason for his desire to be left alone by God: his days are without meaning. The Hebrew here is the same term used by the Teacher (Qoheleth) in Ecclesiastes to describe all of life in his repeated refrain, "everything is meaningless" (Eccl 1:2 etc.). The image here completes the picture Job has painted to show that there is nothing left for him in life; he is merely biding his time until life ends.

The final verses in Job's response to Eliphaz expand upon his desire to be left alone by God (Job 7:17–21). Following Job's inversion of the sentiments of Psalm 22:1 comes a similar inversion of Psalm 8:4: "What is mankind that you are mindful of them?" While the psalmist expresses wonder that Yahweh should be concerned with seemingly insignificant human beings, Job is troubled by the attention, for that attention brings constant testing. So incessantly does Job feel Yahweh's unwelcome gaze upon him and testing of him that he does not even have time to "swallow his spittle" (the wooden rendering of the NIV's idiomatic rendering "even for an instant" in 7:19).

Job's questioning turns to seek the justification for the way God has treated him by posing a hypothetical question, essentially asking what it is that he has done that has so offended God to prompt him to rain down such horrors on him? This, in turn, prompts Job to ask God about his sin. The Hebrew text of verse 20 has a number of difficulties. First, it lacks any word corresponding to "if" in the NIV, prompting some to translate this as "I have sinned." Yet it is likely that this should be understood as a question, for that is clearly the implication of the second clause asking that God disclose to Job what it is he has done that has prompted God to target him.

The intent of 7:20–21 appears to be to continue to question the proportionality of God's treatment of Job. Even if there is some sin he has committed, could it be so egregious as to warrant the response it has? Job simply cannot understand it and is unable to identify any such sin, and we who have read the opening chapters are aware that there is no such sin in Job's life, for both the narrator and God made that clear. Furthermore, even if there were some sin in Job's life that deserved this severe treatment, why has that not been forgiven? (Presumably Job thinks of his scrupulous offering of sacrifices mentioned in the prologue.) What Job does not yet realize is that his confusion arises largely because he still thinks according to the overly simplistic scheme that identifies personal loss or gain as retribution or reward and permits no other reasons for suffering and loss in this world.

The final point of Job's speech is to reiterate his belief that his life will soon be over. If he cannot escape God's incessant scrutiny and testing now, it will not be long before he will escape it through death. He offers no further thoughts on this argument; it is merely reflective of his state of mind, which sees the end coming and no longer holds onto any possible hope of relief.

LIVE the Story

Speaking the Truth with Love

It is difficult not to see Job's first response to his friends and its shift toward holding God accountable and upholding his own integrity as being provoked by Eliphaz's previous claims about the basis for Job's suffering and his suggestions for how he could remedy his situation.

It might be argued that we should seek to interpret the words of Job's friends generously, to see in them an attempt to help Job, and to view those words—such as Eliphaz's words back in Job 5:2, which referred to the behavior of fools—as not being a direct description of Job but more of a warning about where he could potentially find himself, if he were to continue down the path he has started. We might even be right about their intentions. They may be well-meaning. They may be designed to pull Job back from the brink. They may have his best interests at heart. Yet, even if all of this is true about the motives behind their words, to judge the friends' words by these measures is inappropriate, for it fails to treat the suffering of Job appropriately. Their words ought not to be measured against their intentions but against their effect on Job. They misunderstand Job's needs. They completely fail to show empathy to Job and so they devalue his suffering. As such, they do not heal but hurt. They make things worse, with the result that Job now feels not only as though God is his enemy but also his friends have abandoned him as well. The consequence of this thought process for Job is felt in this response to Eliphaz and only grows more and more through the remainder of the speeches. In the end, it is only going to be remedied when God appears and questions Job in the final chapters of the book.

There is a clear warning for us all here. Be quick to listen and slow to speak (Jas 1:19). Seek first to understand the point of view of the other person before assuming we understand it and launching into an attempt to fix things. Yes, speak the truth, but speak the truth in love (Eph 4:15). And make sure that what you think is true is actually true and not merely a conclusion you have reached based on a limited perspective into the life of the person you are speaking to. Eliphaz made these two mistakes: he did not speak truth to Job with love or kindness, and what he thought was true was not the truth. Let us not make these same mistakes!

Longing for Life to End

Job has now come to long for his life to end and specifically for God to end his life (Job 6:8–10; 7:15–16). If any modern reader has not shared that experience at some point in their life in the face of their own circumstances, then they have been blessed not yet to have had to endure suffering so profound as to prompt such a response. From their responses, we would have to suppose that Job's friends have not found themselves enduring such suffering. Yet, it is important to note that there is no point in the book where God condemns Job for this response to his suffering, and we ought not ourselves feel guilty for harboring such feelings at particularly difficult times in our lives.

Yet, this desire of Job's is nonetheless matched by a continued faith in God. His friends do not see it; they see him as being angry with God, accusing God, and condemning God. What they do not grasp, what they do not understand, is that despite being angry, accusing, and even condemning, Job never abandons God. These emotions expose in Job a profound depth of faith that reveals his own awareness that God is sovereignly in control of all that is happening. What Job lacks, as we shall see, is understanding. Once he is allowed to glimpse that when he hears God's words to him in chapters 38–41, all that has happened and is happening to him will be understood in a different light. The terrible loss will not be erased, the suffering will not even be explained, but the change in Job's outlook that grows from a better understanding of God's world will prove to be liberating for Job.

The real question that has been faced by Job's friends at this point—and might face us as we speak with people expressing the desire that Job had for his life to end—is, How do we respond? The first thing would be to understand and not condemn. However, if any person is expressing desire to end their life, they should be provided with experienced professional help. There is never any shame in seeking help either for yourself or for others.

There is another aspect to all of this that provides us with a different perspective. We do not occupy the same place in God's story that Job did. Living after the death, resurrection, and ascension of the Lord Jesus, our perspective should have undergone a transformation from Job's to Paul's. We have moved from a point where little had been revealed to a point in time where God has spoken through his Son (Heb 1:1–2) and made complete God's revelation (John 1:18). From our point in God's story, things look very different than they did for Job and his friends. From our perspective, we should stand with Paul when he can say that "to live is Christ and to die is gain" (Phil 1:21).

We also see that God does not grant Job's request of his opening speech (the somewhat unrealistic expectation that he never be born) or this speech—he is not allowed to die; he is forced to endure. In a world where many countries are legalizing euthanasia, it is widely recognized that there are circumstances in which quality of life overrides length of life. After all, when a treasured pet is suffering with no hope of that suffering being alleviated, it is routine to euthanize the pet. It is the kind thing to do. Would that not really apply to Job in this context, or to any of God's people facing a life without hope of relief from suffering aside from death? Ought this consideration not be even more appropriate for those whose relationship with God through the Lord Jesus promises an eternal life after death devoid of the suffering and pain of the present world?

This is no easy question to answer, and easy answers ought to be avoided. The place to start answering this here is with Job's situation itself. This situation thrusts the mystery of divine providence to the forefront, as repeatedly happens throughout this book. To Job there appears to be no rhyme or reason for his suffering. Yet, in the midst of the most terrible suffering, defending one's virtue is not always the easiest path to take. In his pain, Job only longs for it to be ended, to find some comfort in it all, and at this point he is ready for his life to end to make it so. In all this, however, Job's recognition that God is sovereign remains unshaken, and so he acknowledges that it is ultimately up to God to end his life, and it is not for him to take such action himself. This is not to say that Job (or the writer of the book of Job, or even God himself) would find suicide or euthanasia to be an unforgivable response to the predicament, but were the story to end at this point or indeed at any point prior to chapter 42 with Job's death, whether at his own hand or at God's, then there would have been no reason to record this story. To learn his lesson, and for us to learn ours, Job's life must indeed continue through his terrible sufferings for another thirty-four chapters.

And here is a beginning of an answer to the question about whether euthanasia is acceptable. There are, of course, a number of ethical concerns associated with it: Was every alternative really explored? Was pressure bought to bear on the sufferer or their medical aids to choose that option? Was there no palliative option that could be offered? But beyond these, when human beings choose to end a life, it presumes that God has no further work to do through that person's life. If Job's life had ended at this point, then neither his friends nor we who read his story millennia later would have learned from him, not to mention the fact that Job actually did have many years of good life that followed his time of suffering according to chapter 42.

We do need to remember, when thinking about this vexing issue, that situations in life are rarely clearcut. There are many shades of grey, and that is certainly true as a person approaches their final days. Some treatments that benefit the sufferer may also hasten death. Yet even that is not a certainty. Unalleviated pain may itself also hasten death, and we can never be completely certain how a person's body will respond to either treatment or lack of treatment in these circumstances. The unknowns then may leave us with a decision about which there is no clear answer. And sometimes the decision we make may prove in hindsight to have not been the best or right one. We do not know everything; we can only work with the information we have and trust in the mercy of God. And perhaps it is worth saying once more that our salvation does not depend on getting such terrible and difficult decisions completely right. This is not the unforgivable sin.

What I have argued to this point further assumes that the life in question is that of someone who has a saving relationship with Jesus. For others, for those who do not know or trust Jesus as Lord, then the situation is clearer. The choices they make now matter. What if their belief that death will be a release from their suffering is not true? If that is the case—and Jesus warns that it is the case for many (e.g., Matt 25:41, 46)—then hastening death can in no way be seen to be merciful.

CHAPTER 5

Job 8

Bildad's First Words

LISTEN to the Story

1Then Bildad the Shuhite replied:

2"How long will you say such things?
Your words are a blustering wind.
3Does God pervert justice?
Does the Almighty pervert what is right?
4When your children sinned against him,
he gave them over to the penalty of their sin.
5But if you will seek God earnestly
and plead with the Almighty,
6if you are pure and upright,
even now he will rouse himself on your behalf
and restore you to your prosperous state.
7Your beginnings will seem humble,
so prosperous will your future be.

8"Ask the former generation
and find out what their ancestors learned,
9for we were born only yesterday and know nothing,
and our days on earth are but a shadow.
10Will they not instruct you and tell you?
Will they not bring forth words from their
understanding?
11Can papyrus grow tall where there is no marsh?
Can reeds thrive without water?
12While still growing and uncut,
they wither more quickly than grass.

[13]Such is the destiny of all who forget God;
so perishes the hope of the godless.
[14]What they trust in is fragile;
what they rely on is a spider's web.
[15]They lean on the web, but it gives way;
they cling to it, but it does not hold.
[16]They are like a well-watered plant in the sunshine,
spreading its shoots over the garden;
[17]it entwines its roots around a pile of rocks
and looks for a place among the stones.
[18]But when it is torn from its spot,
that place disowns it and says, 'I never saw you.'
[19]Surely its life withers away,
and from the soil other plants grow.

[20]"Surely God does not reject one who is blameless
or strengthen the hands of evildoers.
[21]He will yet fill your mouth with laughter
and your lips with shouts of joy.
[22]Your enemies will be clothed in shame,
and the tents of the wicked will be no more."

Listening to the Text in the Story: "The Babylonian Theodicy"; "Man and His God" (Sumerian)

Whereas Eliphaz had appealed to a spiritual experience to lend authority to his claims about Job's circumstances, Bildad appeals to sages of the past to achieve the same end (vv. 8–10). When we consider the near universality of the concept of retributive justice throughout writings from the ancient world, it would appear that his argument would have carried some weight. The book of Job is swimming against the tide in claiming anything other than the notion that suffering was a divinely ordained consequence of sin. Since Job is set at the time of the patriarchs, the best examples of such assertions comes from extrabiblical literature.

For example, in "The Babylonian Theodicy," perhaps the text from the ancient Near East that is most like the book of Job, we find the logic of retributive justice clearly assumed by the friend speaking with the sufferer:

Unless you serve the will of a god, what will be your profit?
He who bears a god's yoke shall never want for food, though it may
be meager.
Seek after the favorable breeze of the gods,
What you lost for a year you will recoup in a moment.[1]

The fact that the sufferer in the Sumerian text "Man and His God" is restored once he has confessed his sins and pled for mercy again reflects the inherent notion that suffering arises out of sin. The problem for this sufferer is not so much his innocence but his ignorance of the particular offense. Hence, early on he expresses his expectation that his offence will be made clear to him at some point:

Never has a sinless child
been born to its mother,
A mortal(?) has never been perfect(?),
a sinless man has never existed from old' . . .
My god, . . . after you will have
let my eyes recognize my sins,
I shall recount at the city(?) gate
those of them that have been forgotten,
and those of them which are visible(?);
I, the young man, shall publicly
declare my sins before you![2]

Bildad's appeal to the sages of old in support of his argument is clearly reflected in these ancient texts which themselves simply reflect the wider thinking of the ancient (and, in many cases, the modern) world. In the end, however, we shall see that neither Eliphaz's appeal to a vision nor Bildad's appeal to the wisdom of past sages is any guarantee that their claims are true, and we should be reminded that such appeals to authority offer no guarantee that the claims are right or true.

EXPLAIN the Story

God's Justice Is Seen in His Retribution (8:1–7)

Bildad takes his turn and begins his first response to Job. Stylistically he begins his speech with a series of questions or conditional clauses. Nothing he says

1. "The Babylonian Theodicy," trans. Benjamin R. Foster (*COS* 1.154:1:494).
2. "Man and His God," trans. Jacob Klein (*COS* 1.179:574).

from verses 2–6 is framed as a plain statement, to the extent that he even hides assertions in the form of conditional comments (vv. 3–4). He is unmoved by Job's attempt to defend what he has said and how he has said it, immediately claiming that Job's words are a "blustering wind" and calling on Job to cease his protestations. The adjective translated "blustering" by the NIV does not refer to a breeze but rather a strong wind. As such, it is likely that Bildad is also warning that Job's words are dangerous just like the strong wind in Job 1:19 (although a different word is used there, it is hard to miss the parallel).

For Bildad, the fundamental flaw in Job's argument is that he has implied that God has not acted justly in his treatment of Job and his family. The rhetorical questions of verse 3 are to be answered in the negative, and even Job knows that God does not pervert justice (although he cannot fathom how that can still be true in his situation). Bildad is reminding Job of this fundamental knowledge about God that they all share.

In order to illustrate his point, Bildad points Job to his children in verses 4–7. Following the previous rhetorical questions about God's justice, he presents an assertion about Job's children in the unusual form of a condition. Verse 4 woodenly begins "if [*'im*] your children sinned against him" (although the NIV has "when" here, most English translations [e.g., ESV, NASB, NRSVue, NET] more closely render the Hebrew and begin with "if"). In framing this as a condition, however, Bildad is being disingenuous, for the outcome he points to as a consequence of the supposed sin of Job's children has indeed eventuated. In essence, Bildad is stating that God's justice is apparent, in that Job's children were punished for their sin (which explains the NIV's choice of "when" at the beginning of verse 4). At no point does Bildad suggest what that sin may have been, for their deaths are sufficient indication to him (and to the other friends) that the children must have sinned. The reasoning is circular but so deeply entrenched in their thinking that it need not be justified. No supporting argument is offered, and Job's questioning of the logic has simply been dismissed as empty words.

In contrast to his children, Job is still alive. Bildad understands this to be an indication that there remains hope for Job, and so he presents a course of action by which he believes Job can be redeemed. Bildad believes that Job must seek God and plead with him to be restored. If Job is now found to be "pure and upright" (v. 6), that is, if he has ceased whatever sinful behavior had led to his fall, then God will restore him to his former position. Indeed, so wonderful is God that Job's former glory will, according to Bildad, pale into insignificance beside the prosperity God has planned for him.

These verses need to be read carefully. Bildad is not affirming what we already know from the prologue that Job is blameless and upright. Rather, he assumes that Job has sinned, just not as seriously as his children, for the appropriate penalty for their sin was death. He calls on Job to plead with God, live a pure and upright life, and then he will be restored. This is the logic shared by the friends but which we know is fundamentally wrong when applied to Job.

Bildad Appeals to the Wisdom of His Forebears (8:8–22)

While Eliphaz appealed to a revelation from a spirit to strengthen his argument against Job (4:12–21), Bildad instead looks to the accumulated wisdom of former generations, taking the point Job has just made about the brevity of our lives (7:7, 16) and using it to his own advantage. In essence, Bildad appeals to tradition, implying that his wisdom has stood the test of time and is the result of long reflection by many generations, and so it ought to be heeded. He sees Job as rejecting or ignoring this wisdom in his stubborn refusal to acknowledge some sin that has resulted in his present suffering.

Bildad moves to explain the wisdom that Job should learn from his ancestors, beginning with a rhetorical question concerning whether papyrus or reeds could grow without water. Papyrus and reeds do indeed require water to survive and grow, and without it they perish rapidly (vv. 11–12). To whom do the papyrus and reeds refer? Verse 13 makes clear whom Bildad is talking about: the godless. Such people cut themselves off from the source of life and so are destined to die.

The Hebrew of the first clause of verse 14 is difficult, but the NIV's rendering is probably the best way to understand the text, which is largely elucidated by the parallelism with the second half of the verse. The fragility of the spider's web is apparent, and Bildad spells out the analogy for Job: just as it does not take much for a human being to destroy any spider's web, so also those who trust in something other than God trust in something that is fragile and unreliable. That something will let them down. Reading these words in the context of Bildad's speech to Job it seems that he wishes to make clear that this understanding of Job's situation that he presents is built on the wisdom of many generations and that to reject it is to put oneself in peril!

Bildad turns to a different botanical metaphor to further describe the situation of the godless in verses 16–19. Somewhat reminiscent of Jesus's parable of the seed scattered on different types of ground (Matt 13:3–9), Bildad speaks of a plant that grows up on rocky ground. While it is well watered and the sun shines on it, it grows well. But it has no firm foundation and is readily uprooted and the ground upon which it grew shows no sign that it was ever there. Those who place their trust in something other than God may similarly appear to do well for a while, but their inevitable fate is to be cut off and to wither away.

The Hebrew of verse 19 is again difficult, woodenly rendered, "Indeed, this is the joy of its way," which may be ironic, or else the word for "joy" here (*masos*, which is not the usual Hebrew word for joy but does occur some sixteen times in the Hebrew Bible[3]) may be associated with another term meaning "dissolve" and thus refers to the dissolution of the life of the godless. This latter notion best fits the context and reflects the way the verse has long been understood (if I may appeal to the wisdom of our own forebears!). This verse then reflects the inevitable end of the godless that Bildad warns Job about.

Once again, the words of Job's friends ring true in general terms and find adequate support elsewhere in the Bible. Bildad is right: the fate of those who trust in something other than God is destruction; their hope is futile. Bildad's mistake is in thinking that this applies to Job, for we know that in Job's case it does not! If we are to learn the lesson of those generations that preceded us, then we must learn the warning of this book that simple application of an unbending belief in retributive justice is not invariably right. We are in no position to reach such firm conclusions about the causes of suffering in the world around us, particularly in the lives of individual men and women. The repeated lesson of this book is that we live in a universe that is far beyond our comprehension—both physically and morally—and there are situations where we simply do not have enough information to be able to make sound judgments.

Bildad draws his speech to a close with a clear statement about the nature of God: he does not reject those who are blameless (8:20; this word, *tam*, was used to describe Job in 1:1, 8; 2:3) and he does not protect the wicked. The final two verses of Bildad's speech express his hope that Job will be restored. He has laid out the path to restoration for Job: if Job will only plead with God (8:5–7), then he will be restored and filled with joy.

LIVE the Story

False Appeals to Authority

Good debaters will attempt to bolster their arguments with all manner of claims, some of which are valid and compelling, but some of them should not

3. Wordcounts vary, depending on how scholars identify the word (see, e.g., "I מָשׂוֹשׂ" and "II מָשׂוֹשׂ," *HALOT* 640).

withstand close inspection. We have already seen Eliphaz's opening tactic: an appeal to a spiritual experience. Such appeals are not uncommon—Paul faced the "super" apostles who made their own claims to such experiences (2 Cor 10), and in the modern world false teachers frequently report similar experiences to bolster their own claims. Bildad has found a different, and equally compelling yet equally hollow, way to substantiate his argument (which is essentially the same argument as that of Eliphaz and Zophar—Job's suffering is a consequence of his sin). Bildad has appealed to commonly accepted wisdom, wisdom that has supposedly stood the test of time and that has originated with the great minds of the past.

It is not hard to find similar examples of exactly this strategy being employed in the modern world. It is sometimes asserted that Einstein, for example, claimed that human beings use only 10 percent of their brain power. Now Einstein was a rather smart person who was renowned for—at least apparently—using quite a lot of his brain. So, the claim starts to sound like it should be taken seriously. However, Einstein was a physicist, not a neuroscientist. If he actually made this claim (and just because someone asserts this to be true on the internet does not mean it actually is a true claim), and if he were not simply making a rude comment about someone, then he was speaking way outside of his area of expertise, and research indicates that the statement itself is simply not correct.[4] So while anyone attempting to argue that we use only a small fraction of our potential based on this claimed observation by Einstein may sound somewhat convincing, the claim will simply not stand close scrutiny. The appeal is spurious because it is made to a false authority!

Nonetheless, such arguments can be influential. The wisdom of the ages is considered wisdom for a reason—it has stood the test of time, and it is believed to originate with people who were thoughtful and had considerable lived experience. We see this in Ecclesiastes where the Teacher explains the detailed process he used to investigate the meaning of existence (see, in particular, the great experiment of Eccl 2:1–23). We also do find this in the book of Job where the author has presented us with an account of a man who lived in ancient times, in the days of the patriarchs. While Bildad makes a vague appeal to the wisdom of his forebears, the story of Job itself is presented as both reflecting ancient wisdom and, ultimately, the wisdom of God which will be revealed when God finally appears toward the end of the book. Yet while the author does present an ancient tale that presents human wisdom,

4. See, for example, Barry L. Beyerstein, "Whence Cometh the Myth That We Only Use 10% of Our Brains?," in *Mind Myths: Exploring Popular Assumptions About the Mind and Brain*, ed. Sergio Della Sala (Hoboken, NJ: Wiley & Sons, 1999), 3–24.

that ancient wisdom is ultimately refuted by the ancient wisdom of God, and so the lessons of the book of Job carry an authority not simply bound up in the uncertain credentials of Bildad's unidentified forebears; they carry the authority of God himself.

Not only does God's wisdom invalidate human wisdom, in particular Bildad's appeal to the wisdom of his human forebears, it does so in surprising ways. The wisdom of Job's friends reflects the conventional wisdom of their time, it made sense, it was, to their minds, logical. And yet it was wrong, as the prologue has established and as God makes clear at the end of the book. Despite our confidence in our abilities, human logic is not infallible. The way of wisdom that the book of Job points us down leads us to the cross, for that is the ultimate manifestation of God's wisdom, as the apostle Paul notes:

> For since in the wisdom of God the world through its wisdom did not know him, God was pleased through the foolishness of what was preached to save those who believe. Jews demand signs and Greeks look for wisdom, but we preach Christ crucified: a stumbling block to Jews and foolishness to Gentiles, but to those whom God has called, both Jews and Greeks, Christ the power of God and the wisdom of God. For the foolishness of God is wiser than human wisdom, and the weakness of God is stronger than human strength. (1 Cor 1:21–25)

Bildad's problem is ultimately that he places way too much stock in human wisdom and fails to leave room for God's wisdom. He, like the Greeks of Paul's day, invested too heavily in the power of human logic and left too little room for divine freedom. To Eliphaz, Bildad, Zophar, and even Job at this point, the true wisdom of God revealed in the cross would have seemed foolish. Not only would innocent suffering make no sense (as revealed in their inability to accept that Job could be suffering and blameless), but vicarious innocent suffering, as took place on the cross, would have been even more nonsensical. Only as we proceed through the book of Job to ultimately learn the true nature of God's ways as revealed at the end can we come to appreciate the wisdom of the cross.

Aside from this, the friends of Job present arguments that, taken alone, might well sound convincing. They sound orthodox; they agree with other things we do know from elsewhere in the Bible. Yes, suffering *can be* the consequence of sin; it can be used as a disciplinary measure by God. They are so close to being right! And this is the snare of false teaching and false teachers. They are often close; they can present arguments that do lean on things found in the Bible. Of course, if they were not close, if they did not refer to some parts of the Bible (generally out of context or misapplied to the modern world), then few would be caught in their snares. For this reason, we must be on our guard against false teachers who make spurious appeals to the Bible in an attempt to justify their teachings.

How do we best guard against such false teachers? The answer to that question is simple and yet difficult. It is difficult because it involves time and effort, but it is simple because it is relatively easy to articulate the solution: be thoroughly grounded in the Scriptures (see Acts 2:42; 17:11). False teachers inevitably focus on parts of Scripture that will support their particular claims but lack an understanding of the whole counsel of God, of the whole story of God from Genesis to Revelation, an understanding built through fellowship with the church (to safeguard against novel understandings produced by our own individual biases). Since it is clear that God is working toward a goal through all of history, there should not be parts of Scripture that are simply ejected. Rather, "all Scripture is God-breathed and [remains] useful for teaching, rebuking, correcting, and training in righteousness" (2 Tim 3:16).

CHAPTER 6

Job 9–10

Job's First Reply to Bildad

LISTEN to the Story

9:1Then Job replied:

2"Indeed, I know that this is true.
But how can mere mortals prove their innocence
before God?
3Though they wished to dispute with him,
they could not answer him one time out of a thousand.
4His wisdom is profound, his power is vast.
Who has resisted him and come out unscathed?
5He moves mountains without their knowing it
and overturns them in his anger.
6He shakes the earth from its place
and makes its pillars tremble.
7He speaks to the sun and it does not shine;
he seals off the light of the stars.
8He alone stretches out the heavens
and treads on the waves of the sea.
9He is the Maker of the Bear and Orion,
the Pleiades and the constellations of the south.
10He performs wonders that cannot be fathomed,
miracles that cannot be counted.
11 When he passes me, I cannot see him;
when he goes by, I cannot perceive him.
12If he snatches away, who can stop him?
Who can say to him, 'What are you doing?'
13God does not restrain his anger;
even the cohorts of Rahab cowered at his feet.

[14]"How then can I dispute with him?
How can I find words to argue with him?
[15]Though I were innocent, I could not answer him;
I could only plead with my Judge for mercy.
[16]Even if I summoned him and he responded,
I do not believe he would give me a hearing.
[17]He would crush me with a storm
and multiply my wounds for no reason.
[18]He would not let me catch my breath
but would overwhelm me with misery.
[19]If it is a matter of strength, he is mighty!
And if it is a matter of justice, who can challenge him?
[20]Even if I were innocent, my mouth would condemn me;
if I were blameless, it would pronounce me guilty.

[21]"Although I am blameless,
I have no concern for myself;
I despise my own life.
[22]It is all the same; that is why I say,
'He destroys both the blameless and the wicked.'
[23]When a scourge brings sudden death,
he mocks the despair of the innocent.
[24]When a land falls into the hands of the wicked,
he blindfolds its judges.
If it is not he, then who is it?

[25]"My days are swifter than a runner;
they fly away without a glimpse of joy.
[26]They skim past like boats of papyrus,
like eagles swooping down on their prey.
[27]If I say, 'I will forget my complaint,
I will change my expression, and smile,'
[28]I still dread all my sufferings,
for I know you will not hold me innocent.
[29]Since I am already found guilty,
why should I struggle in vain?
[30]Even if I washed myself with soap

and my hands with cleansing powder,
31 you would plunge me into a slime pit
so that even my clothes would detest me.

32 "He is not a mere mortal like me that I might answer him,
that we might confront each other in court.
33 If only there were someone to mediate between us,
someone to bring us together,
34 someone to remove God's rod from me,
so that his terror would frighten me no more.
35 Then I would speak up without fear of him,
but as it now stands with me, I cannot.

10:1 "I loathe my very life;
therefore I will give free rein to my complaint
and speak out in the bitterness of my soul.
2 I say to God: Do not declare me guilty,
but tell me what charges you have against me.
3 Does it please you to oppress me,
to spurn the work of your hands,
while you smile on the plans of the wicked?
4 Do you have eyes of flesh?
Do you see as a mortal sees?
5 Are your days like those of a mortal
or your years like those of a strong man,
6 that you must search out my faults
and probe after my sin—
7 though you know that I am not guilty
and that no one can rescue me from your hand?

8 "Your hands shaped me and made me.
Will you now turn and destroy me?
9 Remember that you molded me like clay.
Will you now turn me to dust again?
10 Did you not pour me out like milk
and curdle me like cheese,
11 clothe me with skin and flesh

and knit me together with bones and sinews?
12You gave me life and showed me kindness,
and in your providence watched over my spirit.

13"But this is what you concealed in your heart,
and I know that this was in your mind:
14If I sinned, you would be watching me
and would not let my offense go unpunished.
15If I am guilty—woe to me!
Even if I am innocent, I cannot lift my head,
for I am full of shame
and drowned in my affliction.
16If I hold my head high, you stalk me like a lion
and again display your awesome power against me.
17You bring new witnesses against me
and increase your anger toward me;
your forces come against me wave upon wave.

18"Why then did you bring me out of the womb?
I wish I had died before any eye saw me.
19If only I had never come into being,
or had been carried straight from the womb to the grave!
20Are not my few days almost over?
Turn away from me so I can have a moment's joy
21before I go to the place of no return,
to the land of gloom and utter darkness,
22to the land of deepest night,
of utter darkness and disorder,
where even the light is like darkness."

Listening to the Text in the Story: "Enūma Elish" (= "Epic of Creation"); "Gilgamesh"; "The Descent of Ishtar to the Netherworld"; "Nergal and Ereshkiga"

Many scholars have noted a parallel between Rahab (Job 9:13; see the note below on the distinction between this name and that of the prostitute Rahab in Jericho in Josh 2) and Tiamat in the Mesopotamian story of creation, "Enūma

Elish."[1] Tiamat was the primeval sea monster in Mesopotamian mythology, and she was escorted into battle by "her helpers, those who accompany her."[2] That the Rahab mentioned here by Job is also a sea monster is established in other passages where it is mentioned (Job 26:12; Ps 89:10; Isa 59:1; Sir 43:25).

The passage from "Enūma Elish" that gives an account of Tiamat reads:

> Tiamat and Marduk, sage of the gods, drew close for battle,
> They locked in single combat, joining for the fray.
> The Lord spread out his net, encircled her,
> The ill wind he had held behind him he released in her face.
> Tiamat opened her mouth to swallow,
> He thrust in the ill wind so she could not close her lips.
> The raging winds bloated her belly,
> Her insides were stopped up, she gaped her mouth wide.
> He shot off the arrow, it broke open her belly,
> It cut to her innards, it pierced the heart.
> He subdued her and snuffed out her life,
> He flung down her carcass, he took his stand upon it.
> After the vanguard had slain Tiamat,
> He scattered her forces, he dispersed her host.
> As for the gods her allies, who had come to her aid,
> They trembled, terrified, they ran in all directions,
> They tried to make a way out(?) to save their lives,
> There was no escaping the grasp that held (them)!
> He drew them in and smashed their weapons.
> They were cast in the net and sat in a heap,
> They were heaped up in the corners, full of woe,
> They were bearing his punishment, to prison confined.[3]

The "Lord" in this passage is Marduk, the principal Mesopotamian deity whom the text exalts and who here battles the sea monster Tiamat. The

1. See, for example, F. I. Andersen, *Job*, TOTC (Downers Grove, IL: InterVarsity Press, 1976), 234; Nancy Declaissé-Walford, Rolf A. Jacobson, and Beth Laneel Tanner, *The Book of Psalms*, NICOT (Grand Rapids: Eerdmans, 2014), 907–8; John H. Walton, *Job*, NIVAC (Grand Rapids: Zondervan Academic, 2012), 171; Elmer B. Smick, "Job," in *1 Chronicles–Job*, REBC 4, ed. Tremper Longman III and David E. Garland (Grand Rapids: Zondervan, 1988), 700; Ludwig Koehler, Walter Baumgartner, and Johann J. Stamm, eds., *The Hebrew and Aramaic Lexicon of the Old Testament*, trans. M. E. J. Richardson, 4 vols. (Leiden: Brill, 2000), 1193.

2. "Enūma Elish," trans. Benjamin R. Foster (*COS* 1.111:398).

3. "Enūma Elish" (*COS* 1.111:398, lines 93–114).

connection to Job's words goes beyond the reference to a primeval sea monster and extends to the context where Job has used ancient cosmological language in Job 9:6–9, concepts also found immediately following the above passage from "Enūma Elish" where part of Tiamat's corpse is used to create the heavens.

The reference in Job's speech to "the cohorts of Rahab" is also paralleled in "Enūma Elish" by reference to Tiamat's cohorts in lines 107–114 above (together with more in what follows the portion quoted above). The parallels make it clear that Job moves in the thought world of the ancient Near East, and that the earliest readers of the book of Job would also have understood the fundamentals of this worldview.

This view extends to other aspects of the cosmos. The ending of Job's cosmic speech (Job 10:20–22) makes reference to the underworld as a place of "gloom and utter darkness." This reflects Mesopotamian thinking about the underworld, which held it to be a place of misery, as revealed in the epic of "Gilgamesh" where the dying Enkidu describes his journey there when relating the contents of a dream to his friend Gilgamesh:

> [He bound] my arms like (the wings of) a bird,
> to lead me captive to the house of darkness, seat of Irkalla:
> to the house which those who enter cannot leave,
> on the journey whose way cannot be retraced;
> to the house whose residents are deprived of light,
> where dust is their sustenance, their food clay.
> where they are clad like birds in coats of feathers,
> and they cannot see light but dwell in darkness.[4]

As Andrew George explains:

> The famous beginning of Enkidu's description of the Netherworld describes the dismal conditions in which the shades of the dead eke out their pitiful existence. . . . Slightly different versions of these lines are found in "Ištar's Descent to the Netherworld" and "Nergal and Ereshkigal," showing them to be standard material in the Babylonian poetic repertoire.[5]

4. SB tablet VII, 183–190; from George, *The Babylonian Gilgamesh Epic*, 1:645. "Irkalla" (mentioned on the second line quoted) is a reference to the Mesopotamian underworld.

5. George, *Babylonian Gilgamesh Epic*, 1:481.

EXPLAIN the Story

Can You Win an Argument with God? (9:1–35)

Job does not interact at length with Bildad's words but does acknowledge one thing: he knows that "this" is true. It is not immediately clear what "this" refers to in verse 2. Is it all of what Bildad said, part of it, or what Job is about to say? Verse 1 implies that Job's words are in reply to Bildad, so it is likely that Job begins by affirming at least something that Bildad said to him, and that is most likely Bildad's assertion that God does not pervert justice (8:3).

Job's agreement with Bildad is, however, also dismissive. He immediately reframes the issue, revealing his primary concern. Job is concerned less with the justice of God than with showing himself to be righteous. Although these two may seem to be inextricably linked, in Job's mind he believes he has a case to present, and God has a case to answer. We will see this juxtaposed again when Elihu argues for God's justice (chs. 32–37) immediately after Job has presented the case for his own righteousness (chs. 29–31).

Job faces the problem of not knowing how to demonstrate his righteousness before God (9:2b). The NIV differs slightly from most other English translations at this point. The Hebrew simply reads "But how is a person justified with God?" The meaning of the phrase itself is clarified by the following verses, indicating that Job's difficulty is primarily that God is far wiser and more powerful than any human, and so a mere human has no hope of successfully presenting a case to him.

Job proposes one potential means by which one might seek to establish that they are right before God: a dispute (Hebrew *rib*). The term here carries the connotation of a legal case presented in the context of a court (although in the ancient world such may have taken place at the town gate). In such a dispute, witnesses could be called and evidence cited, so this would appear to be an eminently reasonable approach to the problem facing Job.

And yet Job knows that things would not be so straightforward if God was on the stand. Even if the scenario played out a thousand times, not even once could someone answer God (v. 3)! An expression like "one in a thousand" is a common expression in the Old Testament for a task with overwhelming odds (e.g., Deut 32:30; Josh 23:10; Eccl 7:28; Isa 30:17). Job's younger friend, Elihu, will later refer to the same odds, but will do so positively to express the hope that God does readily deliver (Job 33:23–28).

Job's next words (9:4–13) preempt in some ways the series of questions he will be asked by Yahweh toward the end of the book. There Yahweh will ask

Job whether he can answer a series of questions that Job clearly cannot, all in order to demonstrate the limits of Job's knowledge (and by extension, the limited knowledge of all human beings). Implicit in Yahweh's questions is the idea that Yahweh does know the answer, and Yahweh alone. In this passage Job lists a series of things that only God can do that no human can do, so also highlighting the uniqueness of God. The difference here arises from Job's focus on power—he identifies things God can do that mark him as omnipotent and so infinitely more powerful than humans—rather than as omniscient (the focus of Yahweh's questions in chs. 38–41). The point here is that Job believes that God is an insuperable opponent in a legal dispute.

Job begins to illustrate God's power by noting that he moves (the Hebrew verb *'tq* could also mean "removes") mountains and shakes the earth's foundations (v. 5). In Job's cosmology the earth is supported on pillars and should be immobile, and the mountains themselves support the heavens. Job is claiming that God is capable of shaking the heavens and the earth. Shaking the mountains "without their knowing it" probably refers to an action so sudden and overwhelming that they are taken completely by surprise (Job is obviously anthropomorphizing the mountains here).

The cosmological scope of Job's words continues in verses 7–8, now referring to God's work in governing day and night. Broadly speaking, the verse indicates that it falls within God's power to prevent the sun from rising and to "seal up" the stars (so preventing them from shining). This may be a reference to eclipses or other phenomena that hide the sun, but it is likely a reference to the daily activity of the sun and stars. The sun, of course, does not appear to shine at night, and the stars do not appear to shine during the day. Job attributes this to God's work of maintaining the universe. While our understanding of the universe differs considerably to Job's, this should only increase our appreciation of the power involved in keeping things running. This power extends to God's solo creation of the heavens. Verse 8 recalls not only Genesis 1 but also the language of Isaiah (40:22; 42:5; 44:24; etc.), where the heavens are also said to be stretched out by God.

The final clause in verse 8 refers to God treading on the back of the sea, often understood to mean the waves of the sea. The word *bamah* is most often translated "high place" and can mean "hill" but is not used elsewhere for "waves" (there is another Hebrew word for that [*gal*]). And given the cosmological background here and the use of aspects of ancient mythology, the reference may be to God's standing victoriously on the back of the sea monster Yam (Hebrew *yam* means "sea"; see Isa 63:3 where such defeat is also referenced in terms of trampling the enemy). Understood this way, the verse refers to the waters above (the heavens) and the waters below (see Gen 1:6–8), and so cosmologically to the entire universe.

The first half of verse 9 makes reference to a number of prominent astronomical constellations and ascribes their creation to God. (For details on the constellations, see the discussion at 38:31–32 below.) The point, however, is to reflect further on the absolute power of God and hence on the inadequacy of Job in facing God in court.

If the second half of the verse is parallel with the first, then it likely refers to some constellations of the southern sky (as seen from Israel or thereabouts). The suggestion that it refers to cosmic storehouses where wind, snow, and hail are stored seems improbable given the different language used to refer to them in 38:22.

In 9:10 Job summarizes the point of these observations about the power of God: it is beyond Job's ability to comprehend. While his words are strongly reminiscent of Eliphaz's words in 5:9, his focus is different and far more personal. For Job this is not overwhelmingly something to celebrate but instead the grounds for lament at his inability to call God to justify Job's suffering.

This inability of Job to contend with God in court is not just limited to the problem of God's power and wisdom, as Job notes in verses 11–12. The other problem is finding God to challenge him to answer at all. As Job says, even if God were to pass right by him, he would not even know it had happened. Even when God does something that strikes at Job's very core—such as when he snatches away, as he has done to Job's possessions and children—Job has no idea where to find God as these terrible things happen!

Job returns to reflecting on God's power and the manner in which it makes it impossible for Job to call God to account in verse 13. Job has felt that he is subject to God's anger and notes that nothing can turn that back once it is unleashed. Rather than merely point to his own experience, he looks to the ancient Near Eastern thought world, wherein God defeated all opposing forces, in this case Rahab.

Rahab is not to be confused with the woman of Jericho (in Hebrew her name is spelled differently). Rahab here is a reference to a mythological monster associated with the sea and sometimes connected to differently named deities from elsewhere throughout the ancient Near East, including the Mesopotamian Tiamat (see Listen to the Story above). The meaning of the Hebrew word *rahab* here is something like "raging, surging" and so may be more a description of this creature than its name.[6] Nonetheless, there are

6. See Clines, *Job 1–20*, 233; "רהב," *HALOT* 1192–93; "רהב I" and "רַ֫הַב," *DCH* 7:424–25.

other references in the Bible that provide some more information on what is going on here. Isaiah 51:9 identifies Yahweh as the one who "cut Rahab into pieces," and Psalm 89:10 also indicates that Yahweh defeated Rahab. Those passages make it clear that Yahweh's power is unmatched even against the most powerful conceivable supernatural foe.

In Job 9:13b the helpers of Rahab (presumably also monstrous evil creatures) are those left behind after the defeat of Rahab and by implication are less powerful than Rahab. It is not clear whether they are cowering at God's feet (so NIV and many other English translations) or crushed and defeated along with their master (NET, NLT). The point of the verse, however, is that even mighty primordial forces in nature cannot resist God's anger, so Job or any mere mortal stands no chance whatsoever.

In light of all he has noted, Job highlights the problem that began his speech: How could he answer God, and where would he find the right words to challenge God (vv. 14–15)?

Job's point in verse 15 is not so much that he is innocent, but rather that even in the situation where he were innocent, such is the nature of God and his relationship with Job that he could not question God's actions. All he could do is appeal for mercy.

The reference to Job's "Judge" here is sometimes understood to refer not to the judge in the court but to his opponent in the court (so, "accuser" in ESV, NRSVue), largely to preserve the metaphorical associations Job has set up thus far in his speech—after all, one would not question the judge in court but rather one's opponent. Yet, the designation as judge here is not misplaced, for Job must recognize that in any legal dispute with God, God serves not only as his opponent but also as the judge, thus backing Job further into a corner from which his only option is to appeal for mercy.

Job continues to expand on his hypothetical court case against God in verse 16. Now he envisions God answering the summons and attending the court, only to expect that he would not listen to Job's specific questions or answer them.

Job's expectations of any confrontation with Yahweh are set forth in verses 17–18 and are somewhat prescient for what will take place in 38:1, where Yahweh will indeed come in a storm (the same word for storm is used both here and there with a minor change in spelling).[7] In addition, Job's ideas here recall the devastation of the prologue when a violent wind struck the

7. Clines argues that the Hebrew should be read slightly differently to mean "for a hair." This does not really seem to make any better sense and fails to note the likely link to Job 38:1. See Clines, *Job 1–20*, 235.

house in which his children were gathered, and there lies the logic that allows Job to fear being crushed by a storm, for his children suffered just such a fate!

Job 9:17 carries a second allusion to the prologue, for there Yahweh complained that the Satan had provoked him to afflict Job "without any reason" (2:3). Here Job reflects on his own experience, believing there can be no justification for the suffering he is enduring, and so he accuses God of afflicting him without cause.

In some sense Job's anticipation of the outcome of any confrontation with God is built upon his experience to date. He thus expects that in such a scenario he would find himself with no opportunity to catch his breath (indeed, the barrage of questions from God in chs. 38–41 somewhat justifies this), for there would be no chance to escape the misery that he is in. What we will see in chapters 38–41 is that God's response is not quite what Job anticipates here. It will not involve an exercise of power but rather a revelation of Job's ignorance, and that difference will prove crucial for Job to come to some acceptance and understanding of his predicament.

Job proceeds in 9:19–20 to highlight again the imbalance that exists between himself and God that, he expects, would mean any case is lost before it begins. There is no question about who is stronger between God or Job, and if it comes to the question of justice, no one would choose Job over God! As the footnote in the NIV indicates, the translation has opted for a variant reading of the text (reading "him" [i.e., God] instead of "me"), but this is not necessary. The Hebrew makes good sense, reading "if concerning justice, who would summon me?" Job essentially asks a rhetorical question making the point that in any question about justice, no one is going to put Job's word above God's!

Furthermore, verse 20 makes clear that Job does not expect that he could stand in the face of God and offer a valid defense. Rather, he believes that he is incapable of arguing with God and that his attempts would always end up confused and weak. His words echo what he had said a few verses earlier (v. 15), but this time his innocence would be obscured by his own inability to defend himself in the face of the Almighty.

Up until this point, Job has expressed his own innocence in somewhat tentative terms (beginning verses 19–20 with "if," as though to express his innocence in hypothetical terms). In verses 21–24, however, he moves to outright assertion, restating the claim of verse 20 as an unequivocal "I am blameless," with the same word used to describe Job in the prologue (see 1:1, 8; 2:3). Hence we know that Job is correct in his own assessment here.

The meaning of the next line, "I have no concern for myself," is unclear.

Rendered woodenly, Job simply says, "I do not know myself," so it could mean that he now expresses some doubt over the confident assertion he had just made—perhaps he is not as blameless as he thinks. More likely, however, is that he is simply stating that he cares little to prove the point any further, for in his mind he can make no progress in proving the point before the might and wisdom of God. As a result of his conundrum, he despairs and despises his life. There is for him no way out of his present situation, and because he can make no difference, he concludes that God does not care, sweeping up the blameless and the wicked in travail (see Eccl 9:1–3 for similar conclusions from the Teacher).

The "scourge" of Job 9:23 is a word that usually refers to a whip (although the word is obscure and could possibly refer to a flood[8]) but is used by Job to represent any sudden calamity that sweeps away the righteous and the wicked. Job argues that God's apparent disdain for the victims reflects his contempt for the innocent, an observation reinforced by another example: corruption among those who should dispense justice. Job lays this at God's feet, again (correctly) recognizing that God's sovereignty extends to all matters of justice and so injustice reflects on God himself. Job experiences this situation in his own life and can see no way to make sense of it aside from concluding that God does not care.

It should be easy to see both why Job feels as he does and why his friends are incensed by his claims. Yet the solution will not be found in the attempts made by his friends to correct Job, for their answers do not grapple with the complexities underlying God's sovereign rule of the world. The true answer will only be hinted at by Elihu later in the book and ultimately drawn out when God himself appears.

Job returns to his present experience in verses 25–26, noting just how swiftly time is passing (a point he had already mentioned in 7:6) using three images: a runner, papyrus or reed boats on a river, and a bird of prey swooping from the sky.

Messengers were sometimes referred to as "runners" (e.g., 1 Sam 22:17), as were foot soldiers employed as guards (e.g., 1 Kgs 1:5). In general, the focus here in Job 9:25–26 falls on the runners' speed, as they either convey information quickly or else respond adeptly to threats. The second clause of verse 25 reveals that Job's complaint here is not merely related to the speed with which the days pass, but the fact that their rapid succession sees only misery and no good. Day after day after day there is nothing Job finds enjoyable, only unrelenting pain and trouble.

8. See Clines, *Job 1–20*, 218n23.a; "שׁוֹט II," *HALOT* 1441; "שׁוֹט II," *DCH* 8:304.

Bracketing this lack of joy are more depictions of speed. The papyrus boats referenced in 9:26 are most likely lightweight Egyptian boats (see Isa 18:2). Being made from papyrus reeds meant they were light and fast. The final image is that of an eagle (the Hebrew word can refer to either eagle or vulture, but the focus on swooping speed here rules out the vulture). There are several different types of eagles indigenous to the region, and they are at their fastest when they dive to capture prey.

Job reveals in verses 27–28 that he has thought about trying to break out of the misery he is in by forgetting his complaint and putting on a happy face. The words "change my expression" employ a word that elsewhere is used of restoring or repairing (e.g., Neh 3:8), but it is clear that Job can only envision changing his appearance without changing his inner experience of misery. This realization reveals the futility of any attempt by Job to change his experience, and ultimately he knows that while God is against him nothing will change.

The second-person singular reference ("you") in Job 9:28 makes it clear that in this portion of his speech Job has moved from talking about God to speaking directly to God.

Job next reiterates the futility of taking any action against God—he has shared similar sentiments earlier in the speech (see vv. 14–20). He is convinced that he has already been tried and found guilty, and the punishment has been dealt. The word "vain" (*hebel*) in verse 29 is the word found frequently on the lips of the teacher in Ecclesiastes (five times in Eccl 1:1 alone!) and conveys both futility and senselessness. Job recognizes that to fight against God is to fight not merely a losing battle but a battle that has already been lost.

To reinforce his point, Job elaborates in 9:30, suggesting that even were he to use the best cleaning agents known, it would make no difference to God. The Hebrew word for "soap" (*sheleg*) is the common word for "snow" (cf. the footnote in the NIV84), but it probably refers not merely to frozen water but to soapwort, a plant used to produce a form of soap and hence a cleansing agent.[9] This makes better sense of the parallel in the next line where lye is used. The use of soapwort and lye to clean skin is extreme but serves to drive home Job's point: there is no conceivable action he could take to remedy his situation, for even if he were to make himself this clean, God would make him filthier than ever!

In verse 32 Job returns to third-person speech about God and reiterates the consequences of the imbalance between himself and God. There is no way

9. See Clines, *Job 1–20*, 220n30.b.

that facing God in a court of law would allow him to adequately present his case; the imbalance between them is too great.

In light of this imbalance, Job realizes that the only hope he has would be if there could be someone to mediate between him and God who would somehow overcome the disparity that exists between them. The Hebrew of verse 33 begins with the words, "there is not . . . a mediator," but the Hebrew expression for "there is not" is unusual, and it is probably better to understand the phrase with the NIV, expressing a hope that Job believes to be impossible: "If only there were someone to mediate between us [although I know there is none]."

Such a mediator would, Job anticipates, level the playing field. He would be empowered to remove God's rod from Job. The "rod" (v. 34) is representative of God's disciplinary wrath on Job (the same term is used in Prov 13:24, "whoever spares the rod hates their children," where it is a symbol of discipline; see also Isa 10:5; 30:31). From the Christian's perspective, the temptation is immediately to identify Jesus as the mediator Job is looking for, but we need to take care. Job is not suffering under the wrath of God over his sins—that much has been unequivocally established by the narrator and by God himself in the opening of the book! On the other hand, Jesus is literally the human face of God, the one who makes him known to us, and so the mediator Job seeks is ultimately Jesus after all!

Job Rehearses His Opening Statement (10:1–22)

Aware that he would be incapable of confronting God in a formal legal setting, yet also placing no value on his life, Job proceeds to give voice to the words he would want to say to God. It is important to note at this point that despite the move to second-person speech to God, Job 10 is all framed as a speech directed to his friends explaining what he would say to God if he could rather than as Job actually speaking directly to God—hence the opening words of verse 2, "I say to God" (the Hebrew verb translated "say" here should be read in a modal [i.e., possibility] sense: "I would say"). This allows Job to address God indirectly and so escape the conundrum he described in the previous chapter. The remainder of the chapter records speech directed to God, but the impact of these opening words on how we read the remainder of the chapter should not be overlooked.

The other thing that becomes clear in verse 2, however, is that Job already feels he is part of a formal legal proceeding with God. He wants to tell God not to treat him as guilty—for clearly Job feels that he has already been judged thus—and to explain the grounds for this case that has been brought against him.

The first question Job would ask God is whether he benefits from oppressing Job (v. 3). The Hebrew is simply "is it good for/to you?," which is a broad question seeking to know how God benefits from his treatment of Job. Implicit in this question—as is clear from the remainder of verse 3—is Job's belief that he does not deserve his suffering and that justice has been inverted, for while he, an innocent man, suffers, he sees the wicked go free. The Teacher of Ecclesiastes (known as Qoheleth in Hebrew) witnessed the same thing (see Eccl 7:15), and like Job, it made no sense to Qoheleth either. Consequently, Job's circumstances lead him to question God's justice.

How does Job account for this apparent failing on God's part? He proceeds in Job 10:4–7 to question God's sovereignty by asking if he is constrained as mortals are, seeing only as much as a person might and living only as long as a human. Job, of course, knows that these limitations do not apply to God (as is apparent by Job's admission in verse 7 that God knows he is not guilty), but feels that his treatment by God does not reflect his nature. Job feels as though he is being interrogated so that God might discover what he ought to already know—that Job is innocent. Regardless of all this, Job also knows that no one can deliver him from God's power.

Here, in essence, is Job's quandary. He knows that God knows he does not deserve his present suffering, and yet he is suffering. He struggles to make sense of the incomprehensible by questioning God's omniscience and omnipotence, despite knowing that his questions are baseless.

Job proceeds to contrast his awareness that he was carefully created by God with how he feels that he is being destroyed by God in verses 8–12. Job's language is reminiscent of the creation accounts (the Hebrew verb translated "shaped" by the NIV in v. 8 [*ʿtsb*] is similar to the noun for "painful labor" [*ʿetseb*] in Gen 3:16; the references to being made from clay and returning to dust in Job 10:9 also recall Gen 2–3) as well as the poetic account of the formation of a new human life in Psalm 139. But Job moves beyond the familiar language about creation to include more poetic reflections on creation in Job 10:10.

The connection between "milk" and "cheese" in verse 10 and Job's creation is usually held to see a parallel between the milk and semen, from which life springs and which, poetically, solidifies into a new human child, much as milk forms cheese. Job continues to reflect on this process in verse 11 by describing the completion of the formation of his body and finally, in verse 12, that body being imbued with new life. "Kindness" (*khesed*) here conveys an element of loyalty from God to Job as reflected in God's providential care. Job has not forgotten how blessed his life had been, and he does not forget that God was responsible for that as much as he is responsible for this change in circumstances. And it is that change that leaves Job so perplexed, for the care and kindness that had been lavished upon him is impossible for him to reconcile with a God who would so quickly allow his creation to endure such terrible loss and suffering.

This apparent goodness of God's creation of Job is contrasted with something more sinister in verses 13–17. Job feels that God had a hidden agenda, something hidden in his heart. It is important to remember that "heart" in Hebrew encompasses more than the seat of the emotions but is often more adequately translated as "mind" (which the NIV has achieved by supplying the word "mind" in the second half of verse 13).

What was God's hidden agenda? Job believes he was waiting to catch him as a wrongdoer. Although it is to be expected that God punishes sin, as Job notes in verse 14, punishment is not Job's primary concern here. Rather, it is the attitude of God who, in Job's eyes, seems only to be waiting for him to fail and to sin. That much becomes clearer over the remaining verses of this section, for even if Job is innocent, he would feel incapable of facing God (as he noted in 9:2–3, 14–20, explaining that he would not be able to confront God, and hence why in 10:15 he is presenting the hypothetical argument, which he would present if he were able).

To reinforce this point, in verses 16–17 Job explains how he feels stalked by God as a lion would stalk him. Reference to a lion makes clear that Job feels that God is a predator and he the prey. Building on the idea of verse 14, Job feels God is out to get him.

Job also thinks that God's response to his suffering and any attempt by Job to appeal the court case would only result in his situation deteriorating further. In verse 17 the identity of the new witnesses God would bring to reinforce Job's supposed guilt (remembering that we are hearing Job's voice and so his perception of the world and not God's at this point) is not made clear. Many scholars believe that it refers to additional suffering that God would inflict if Job were to stand before him and insist upon his innocence. In short, Job feels that there is no course of action open to him. Even an attempt to question his suffering is likely only to result in his situation deteriorating.

Where does all this leave Job? He can see no hope. To his mind, appealing to God is futile and only destined to make his life even worse. And so, in verses 18–22 he returns to his earlier lament, wishing that he had never been born (see 3:11–19).

Job repeats his understanding that his life is almost over (10:20; see 7:21) and again asks that God would leave him alone and thus give him some respite before his end (see 7:16). A similar sentiment is found in Psalm 39:13, where David also appeals to God that he be left alone before he dies so he may enjoy some respite from his woes. The major difference between Job and David in Psalm 39 is David's recognition that he deserves God's judgment. Job, we know, does not.

The final two verses of Job's speech, Job 10:21–22, reveal something of his expectations of what is to come for him after his death. The Old Testament's view of what is to come after death is limited, and Job's own expectations here reveal there is nothing he hopes for in his future. Death for Job is a place of no return and of utter darkness so deeply felt that he emphatically reiterates this idea of darkness six times in the final six lines of the poem: "place of no return," "land of gloom," "utter darkness" (twice), "land of deepest night," and "darkness."

Job's wish to be left alone to die and then to dwell in Sheol, a place of utter darkness, serves to highlight just how miserable his present situation is. Even that beleaguered existence in Sheol is preferable to continuing in the life he now has. Even death is to be preferred despite the prospect of endless darkness that it—as far as Job is concerned—holds for him. While Paul could say, "to live is Christ and to die is gain" (Phil 1:21), Job lived before God had revealed enough of what comes after death for him to hold any real positive belief about the afterlife. Thus, Job might be paraphrased as saying, "to live is to suffer, and to die is to suffer less!"

LIVE the Story

Speaking Truth to Power

In the movie *A Few Good Men*, the actor Tom Cruise plays a junior rank legal prosecutor in the US Army. At one point he is cross-examining a colonel (played by Jack Nicholson) who resents having to answer Cruise because he holds him in contempt (not legal contempt) because of his age, lack of military experience, and junior rank. For a moment in the film, Cruise appears to question his own standing and is on the verge of caving to the pressure he is under.

Job in this chapter constructs a hypothetical scenario somewhat reminiscent of this scene—he wishes to cross-examine God but believes he is so far beneath God that he has no way to get the answers he wants or feels he needs. This should not surprise us, unless we have completely domesticated God in our own lives. The foundational concept of biblical wisdom—the fear of

God—should help us to understand where Job is coming from here. And it is important to note that this concept is not one restricted to the Old Testament and abrogated by the arrival of the Messiah; it is foundational for knowing God in the New Testament as well, and in a few places is made explicit (e.g., Luke 12:5; 2 Cor 5:11; 1 Pet 2:18).

Job spends much of chapter 9 recounting the power of God. It is a good reminder for us, too, for all too often we limit and domesticate God, forgetting just how powerful he really is. Job's reflections here will not allow us to do that. And there are positives to remembering how powerful God is. It means that, no matter how uncertain life is, we know that God is powerful enough to ensure that his promises for the future will be fulfilled. There is no opponent who can derail God's plans, and we are assured of this as we look back through history, for that one point where it may be tempting to think God had lost control, as his Son was beaten and executed, is revealed not as a loss of control, for we know that it was the very goal of God's plans that began with him sending his Son to live among us!

Job, however, does not find comfort in God's overwhelming power. Rather, he sees that power as an obstacle to being heard, preventing him from calling on God for an answer. While there is a logic to Job's point, it also fails to appreciate the implications of God's power and preeminence over the creation. For what Job fails to appreciate here is that God is not threatened or afraid of being challenged. God can be confronted, can be questioned, can be challenged because he is *not* threatened in any way by such actions. Violent responses to such challenges are far more likely to arise when the one being challenged *is* threatened and feels the need to reassert their dominance. Later in the book, as the feeling that he has nothing to lose grows, Job will become bolder in challenging God. And even there God is not threatened. This ought to be a lesson for us: do not hide from God, do not even try to hide when we question what God is doing. He is not threatened by our honesty.

Yet that is not the end of the problems Job faces if he is to confront God. The whole experience is so overwhelming that when we read of such encounters between people and God elsewhere in the Bible, the people are almost struck dumb and at a loss for how to respond. This is inherent in the warning to Moses up the mountain against looking directly at God, and it is ultimately reflected in Peter's response at the transfiguration, where he seems to have no idea what to say and ultimately sounds as though he is clutching at straws for the appropriate way to respond to the scene unfolding before him. Job, already cognizant of God's power and exalted state, recognizes that were he to find himself in a situation where he finally was confronting God, then he, too, would be unable to present his own case. We see this born out when Job does finally find himself standing in the presence of God in chapters 38–41 of the book. There the theophanic vision of God has Job reevaluate all that he sought to do in his plans to confront God.

This realization by Job of his powerlessness in the face of God's power prompts him to wish that there would be a mediator who was truly capable of taking on the task that he himself feels unable to take up (9:32–34). At this point he has no real expectation that such a mediator would appear. It is, for the New Testament believer, tempting to see here a valid call for the mediator who would come to stand before God, Jesus, but Job's expectations here do not quite fit with the mediation Jesus offers. Job is not looking for someone to take away his sin; he is looking for someone to defend his virtue before God and convince God that he is not deserving of the suffering he is now enduring. Now, theologically speaking, Job's salvation depends as much on Jesus as does our own, but we need to take care not to read into the story of Job answers to questions it is not raising. Job's faith and faithfulness, recounted in some detail in the opening of the book, provides the assurance that his sin will be forgiven, and that same faith was, just as with Abraham, credited to him as righteousness.

Having said that, mediation goes in two directions. As such, Job does need a mediator as much as we do, only not to present his case to God but to make God known to him. Jesus has fulfilled this role. Although God had revealed himself to his people in the Old Testament, it remained for God to send his one and only Son to finish that revelation, to make him fully known (John 1:18). When we find ourselves in circumstances even vaguely reminiscent of Job's—actually, whatever circumstances we find ourselves in—it is to Jesus we should look to best understand where God is working in our lives. We may not find the answer we are looking for, but we do see God become flesh, walking and suffering and teaching among us, and resetting our understanding so that we can grasp the essentials of God's purposes for us.

The Problem of Providence

Job 9:23–24 makes reference to the apparently undiscriminating administration of providence—the good and the wicked are caught up in the same disasters. For Job, this is evidence of God's contempt for the innocent who are not spared. It is an issue that is real for us too. In early 2023 an earthquake struck Syria and Türkiye (Turkey) in which tens of thousands died. Were they all equally evil and deserving to die in that way? On the day after Christmas in

2004, a tsunami in the Indian Ocean killed over 225,000 people. Were they all equally evil and deserving to die in that way? Were they somehow worse than the greedy, corrupt people who prosper in various places in the rest of the world? Clearly the answer to all these questions can only be "No!"

But can we not also feel Job's outrage here? Do not such indiscriminate events trouble us and prompt us to ask how it is God can allow these things to happen and what possible justification there can be for such things? The author of the book of Job wants us to feel the power of Job's concern here, and it should not be difficult for us to feel it. In essence, this is the heart of the problem the book seeks to address—Job feels he is the victim of the same sort of apparently indiscriminate treatment that many victims of such apparently indiscriminate events must also have been.

How do we address such issues? It might be tempting to take a theological perspective that all have sinned, and so even the most upright person swept away by the tsunami was not ultimately innocent. Yet, such an answer is far from adequate. It fails to address the apparent indiscriminate nature of such events, for surely some among the many victims were among those who called Jesus "Lord"—their sins were dealt with on the cross. And yet they were not spared, just as Job was not spared. Why?

Job painfully understood the power of this line of questioning. After all, he was one of God's faithful people; indeed, as the prologue to the story makes clear, he was preeminent among them. He was scrupulous in ensuring the sins his family committed were dealt with in accord with the sacrificial requirements of the time. His virtue was extolled by God in the prologue, and so we know his confidence was not a delusion.

The weight of circumstances here, and his consideration of the apparently indiscriminate nature of God's activity in the world, prompts Job to conclude that confronting God—even were he to overcome the other challenges such a task had already raised for him—would be futile. God would not be swayed, no matter how deserving or compelling Job's case. But was Job right in feeling this? Ultimately, the answer can only be "No," simply because Job's understanding of what is happening to him is based on a faulty premise. God is not punishing him; God is not oblivious to his circumstances.

But what is the answer to Job's charge about God's apparently indiscriminate behavior in governing the world? At this point in the story we have no answer. We, like Job, ought to be contemplating the question. The answer will come, but it will have to wait until Yahweh speaks later in the book, and even then it will take some unpacking for us to fully appreciate the point of all the questions Yahweh poses to Job.

In Anticipation of Death

Chapter 10 returns to some of the themes of chapter 3 and Job's complaint there. Did you notice how many ways he speaks of darkness at the end (vv. 20–22)? Job's poetry is often like that, reinforcing something through repetition. Job, it seems, does not hold out hope for anything good beyond death:

> Are not my days few?
> So stop it and leave me alone
> So I can have a little happiness
> Before I go, and never return,
> To the land of darkness, of deepest shadow
> the land of gloom, like utter dark without order,
> and even light shines like darkness. (my translation)

What is clear is that Job is certain that God is responsible for his predicament. And in some ways, this is true because at the end God approves of Job's words!

The end of Job's speech in chapter 10 reflects Job's place in the story of God. What he knows—or thinks he knows—of the afterlife is a reflection of common beliefs in the ancient world. In their conception, the underworld (Sheol) is not a place of joy or hope but a place of utter darkness. This reflects Babylonian beliefs in the miserable state of those in the underworld.

Through time God revealed more to his people about our fate and what awaits us after this life is done, but as we read Job's words it helps to remember where he is coming from and just what it is he knows and believes about what lies before him once he reaches the end of his time on earth.

CHAPTER 7

Job 11

Zophar's First Words

LISTEN to the Story

1Then Zophar the Naamathite replied:

2"Are all these words to go unanswered?
Is this talker to be vindicated?
3Will your idle talk reduce others to silence?
Will no one rebuke you when you mock?
4You say to God, 'My beliefs are flawless
and I am pure in your sight.'
5Oh, how I wish that God would speak,
that he would open his lips against you
6and disclose to you the secrets of wisdom,
for true wisdom has two sides.
Know this: God has even forgotten some of your sin.

7"Can you fathom the mysteries of God?
Can you probe the limits of the Almighty?
8They are higher than the heavens above—what can you do?
They are deeper than the depths below—what can you know?
9Their measure is longer than the earth
and wider than the sea.

10"If he comes along and confines you in prison
and convenes a court, who can oppose him?
11Surely he recognizes deceivers;
and when he sees evil, does he not take note?

[12]But the witless can no more become wise
than a wild donkey's colt can be born human.

[13]"Yet if you devote your heart to him
and stretch out your hands to him,
[14]if you put away the sin that is in your hand
and allow no evil to dwell in your tent,
[15]then, free of fault, you will lift up your face;
you will stand firm and without fear.
[16]You will surely forget your trouble,
recalling it only as waters gone by.
[17]Life will be brighter than noonday,
and darkness will become like morning.
[18]You will be secure, because there is hope;
you will look about you and take your rest in safety.
[19]You will lie down, with no one to make you afraid,
and many will court your favor.
[20]But the eyes of the wicked will fail,
and escape will elude them;
their hope will become a dying gasp."

Listening to the Text in the Story: "The Great Cairo Hymn of Praise to Amun-Re"; "Purifying a House: A Ritual for the Infernal Deities" (Hittite)

Zophar's first speech, like those presented by the other speakers in the debate, draws on imagery from the ancient worldview in which the speakers lived. We see this in 11:8–9 with Zophar's reference to the full extent of the world described from the "heavens above" and the "depths below" being "longer than the earth" (or "the land"; the Hebrew term is the same, and for the ancient reader, there would likely have been little conceptual difference between these ideas) and "wider than the sea." Similar expressions are found elsewhere in the Old Testament (e.g., Amos 9:2–4; Ps 139:8–9) and further afield in ancient literature, all expressing the entirety of creation. For example, in "The Great Cairo Hymn of Praise to Amun-Re" we read:

> Hail to you—by all flocks,
> Jubilation to you—by all foreign lands,

To the heights of heaven, to the breadth of the earth,
To the depths of the ocean.[1]

The terminology used in this passage simply serves as a means to express totality, and Zophar's point is that the mysteries of God are greater than all of creation and so ultimately beyond Job's reach (although, as I shall note below, Zophar does not quite apply his own logic to himself).

In verse 14 Zophar makes reference to the need for Job to "allow no evil to dwell in your tent." This assumes that Job is, as head of his household, in some way responsible for all that takes place within that household. It is, Zophar implies, his responsibility to ensure the purity of his family. We have already seen Job assume this responsibility in the prologue, where we are told that he would regularly offer sacrifices on behalf of his children (1:5). The idea that the sin of one person could contaminate others was not unusual in the ancient world (cf. Jer 31:29–30; John 9:2). The need to offer a remedy for such sin is recorded outside of the Bible as well. For example, there are Hittite incantations designed to purify a physical house:

§4 He says as follows: "O Sun Goddess of the Earth, we are taking this m[atter . . .]. Why is this house gasping? Why does it look upward to heaven?

§5 Either a human has perjured (himself), or he has [shed] blood and has turned [up] his *šeknu*-garment to these houses, or someone has made a threat, or someone has spoken a curse, or someone having shed blood or having committed perjury has entered,

§6 or someone has practiced (witchcraft(?)) and [has] en[tered], or bloodshed has occurred in the house.[2]

In ancient Near Eastern culture, the most senior male in the household generally held the responsibility for such matters, particularly prior to the establishment of more formal social structures such as the priesthood (and so in the patriarchal times in which Job is set).[3] Zophar here ascribes this responsibility

1. "The Great Cairo Hymn of Praise to Amun-Re," (*COS* 1.25:39).

2. "Purifying a House: A Ritual for the Infernal Deities," trans. Billie Jean Collins (*COS* 1.68:168).

3. See, for example, Andrea Zammit, "What Were the Powers of the Paterfamilias over His Children?," unpublished paper, January 1, 2011, https://www.researchgate.net/publication/336085568_What_were_the_powers_of_the_Paterfamilias_over_his_children. The antecedent manifestation of this in the ancient Near East is referred to by I. Mendelsohn, "The Family in the Ancient Near East," *BA* 11.2 (1948): 24, where he says, "the absolute authority of the father who, within his own

to Job and sees his acceptance of this responsibility as prerequisite to his restoration. We, thanks to the details found in the prologue that explicitly refer to Job undertaking this task, already know that Job's predicament cannot be ascribed to any failure on his behalf in this area.

EXPLAIN the Story

Making More Extreme Claims to Prove a Point (11:1–11)

Zophar is the third of Job's friends to speak, but he has little of merit to add to the arguments of his two friends. He is certain that Job's suffering is warranted by his sin and, despite the depths of that suffering, claims that God has been gracious, for he has actually overlooked some of Job's sin (see 11:6)! If Job would only repent and fall on God's mercy his life would be restored. Along the way he implies that Job is bordering on "witless" (v. 12) and in danger of falling in with the wicked (v. 20). Compared to his two friends who have already spoken, Zophar is perhaps the most blunt and least willing to allow that Job's culpability may be mitigated by other factors. In other words, Zophar is the most black and white of the three of Job's friends who speak in the first half of the book.

Zophar starts out by belittling Job's words, initially mocking them through reference to Job's verbosity ("all these words" [v. 2]; compare Prov 10:19; Eccl 5:3, which both use the same phrase in a context where many words are bad), and then both dismissing them as "idle talk" (Job 11:3) and, rather ironically, characterizing them as mockery without stating precisely who or what Job is mocking. In the midst of these opening words, Zophar makes it clear that he sees a failure to respond as tantamount to conceding that Job is right (NIV "vindicated," or "righteous," which carries more legal overtones). So, Zophar opens his words with the clear implication that Job is wrong, that Job has said little of any value, and that Job must be corrected.

From this point Zophar proceeds to paraphrase in two points what he appears to believe Job's claim to be: that his beliefs are flawless and that he is pure in God's sight (v. 4). The latter point does reflect what Job had said in 9:20–21 and 10:7, but the former claim does not explicitly reflect anything

---

domain, had the physical power and the legal right to treat his wives and children as he pleased and even to dispose of them as he saw fit." See also Tikva Frymer-Kensky, "Patriarchal Family Relationships and Near Eastern Law," *BA* 44.4 (1981): 210, who similarly notes, "In the case of the daughter, [the father] has unlimited authority to dispose of her in any way he sees fit, whether by contracting a marriage for her or even by giving her as a slave."

Job has already said. Here, in referring to Job's "beliefs" (v. 4a), Zophar is suggesting that Job has claimed to have faultless knowledge about God, what we might call doctrine. The term for "beliefs" (*leqakh*) appears in Proverbs 4:2; 16:21, 23, and elsewhere with this sense, but it depicts Job's claims in a far too clinical manner that ultimately misrepresents him. While, at one level, this may represent the fact that Job's claims do arise out of his beliefs, at another level they do not reflect the fact that Job's claims arise out of his desperate situation—he is like a drowning man grasping at anything to keep afloat. And ironically it is Zophar and the other friends who answer Job out of the certainty of their own beliefs!

Job, thus far, has avoided calling on God to answer him directly, fearing that the power imbalance inherent in such a conversation would overwhelm him, and he would concede despite the merits of his case. Zophar, however, has no such qualms and believes that were God to speak to Job, then he would have to admit that his friends had been right all along (Job 11:5–6).

Part of the need for God to speak, according to Zophar, is the fact that "true wisdom" (v. 6b; the Hebrew word here, *tushiyyah*, is rare but usually refers not merely to wisdom but emphasizes the sound wisdom of God, see Isa 28:29; Prov 8:14) has two sides: (1) that which is available to people, and (2) the secret wisdom of God that Zophar wishes would be revealed to Job. At this point, at least, Zophar is not far from the ultimate point of the book to be revealed in Job 28 and when God does finally speak in chapters 38–41. Where Zophar falls short, however, is in his conviction that the revelation of God's secret wisdom will vindicate his own argument when, in fact, it shall overturn the friends' claim that Job suffers because of his sin.

Zophar's claim that God has already forgotten some of Job's sin (11:6c) functions to reinforce the friends' claims about Job's sinfulness and so the justification for his suffering: Job has sinned, so much so that God has overlooked some of his sin, and so his present suffering is actually less than he deserved, not more, as Job claims.

Zophar elucidates this view that God's wisdom is incomprehensible in verses 7–9. This stanza opens with a rhetorical question addressed to Job, asking whether he can "fathom the mysteries of God." The Hebrew phrase here is reminiscent of the Greek in 1 Corinthians 2:10 ("the depths of God") and is asking whether Job is able to discover those things for which God searches. The meaning is not that there are things God cannot discover but, as captured by the NIV's translation, that there are things about God that are incomprehensible to mere humans.

The second line of Job 11:8 parallels the first, imagining God in physical terms as a being without limit. In this, Zophar makes the point that finding a limit to the Almighty is beyond our capacities. From here he expounds upon those limits: they are beyond the heavens and deeper than Sheol. The two lines of verse 8 each close with a question addressed to Job, which could be paraphrased, respectively, as "How could you discover such a limit?" and "How could you comprehend such a limit?" Verse 9 fills out the stanza, adding the remaining dimensions of width and breadth to the image of God's size.

In verses 10–11 Zophar presents an application of his claims about God in the preceding verses that picks up on some of the legal themes encountered earlier in the book. For starters, were it God's intention to arrest someone and bring them before a legal gathering, who would be able to turn him from this course of action? The target of the comment is usually provided in translation by the insertion of "you" in verse 10a, but this is left unstated in the Hebrew. This is relevant largely because, from Zophar's perspective, Job has already been found guilty, and the metaphorical account of arrest and trial has already passed in Job's situation.

The target of God's legal proceedings is clarified in verse 11: deceivers and those who do evil. Zophar's obvious implication is that this applies to Job in some way—he has sinned, God has noticed, judged him, found him guilty, and meted out the appropriate punishment. Job's present circumstances are, for Zophar (and his friends), unequivocal evidence of the truth of this assertion.

Zophar Advises Job to Repent and Outlines the Rewards He Will Then Reap (11:12–20)

Many commentators read verse 12 as the conclusion to the preceding portion of Zophar's speech, which then has Zophar asserting that all that he has said about Job in the opening verses leads to the conclusion that witless Job cannot become wise. This presents a contradiction to verses 13–20 where Zophar expects Job to grow in wisdom (see particularly on v. 13). As such it is better to follow Seow and read verse 12 as an introductory warning to Job for the words of verses 13–20. Job should heed Zophar's words, lest he show himself to be witless and incapable of wisdom.[4] He begins with an aphorism that parallels two impossibilities such that its initial assertion—that the witless become wise—is made out to be as likely as a wild donkey giving birth to a human. "Witless" here translates a term essentially meaning "empty"—we might say an "empty-headed person." Zophar states that for such a person to become

4. Seow, *Job 1–21*, 603.

wise and knowledgeable (the verb here [*lbb*] makes out that they would grow a heart, where *heart* in the ancient world encompassed both thought and emotion) is impossible.

Zophar closes his speech offering Job advice on how to remedy his situation. That he does so indicates that he does not believe Job to be so lost as the empty-headed fool of the aphorism he quoted in verse 12. Rather, he believes there is still hope for Job. On the other hand, the line of argument is somewhat manipulative: he is telling Job that an empty-headed fool would not change his mind but then explains that if Job were to follow Zophar's advice, he would prove not to be empty-headed. The reverse implication remains, however: if Job does not listen to Zophar, he is indeed—in Zophar's view—an empty-headed fool!

The Hebrew phrase (the verb *kwn* [translated variously] plus the noun *lebab* ["heart"]), translated as "devote your heart" in verse 13, appears elsewhere a number of times (2 Chr 6:12–13, 29; Pss 10:17; 57:7[8]; 78:8; 108:1[2]; 112:7; Job 11:13; 2 Chr 12:14). The term "devote" here points to a "heart" that is set on God. The heart in biblical terms encompasses more than our emotional selves but particularly includes what we may more commonly think of as our minds. Thus, Zophar is calling on Job to make a conscious decision here: to plan his thoughts and actions to turn to God. In essence, Zophar is calling on Job to repent.

"Stretch out your hands" is also a common expression depicting prayer in the Old Testament (see Exod 9:29, 33; 1 Kgs 8:22, 38, 54; 2 Chr 6:12–13, 29; Ezra 9:5; Ps 44:21; Isa 1:15; Jer 4:31). It is, then, Zophar's advice that he call out to God in prayer and repent.

Zophar is quite convinced that Job has sinned (that much he has already made clear in Job 11:6), and so now he presents Job with a clear choice to either persist in his sin or to turn from his sin (v. 14). From Zophar's perspective, were Job to persist in his protestations of innocence, then he is essentially persisting in his sin and would reveal him to be witless rather than wise (cf. v. 12).

Zophar's appeal to Job here is that he both identify his sin and get rid of it—and not just personal sin but any sin in his household ("in your tent"). Job's actions in the prologue indicate that he, too, held to these ideals, for there we were told that he preemptively sacrificed to deal with possible sins committed by his children (1:5). The belief that familial sin had consequences for the individual was common in the Old Testament and continued into the New Testament (e.g., Josh 7:13, 24–25; Jer 31:29–30; John 9:2), but later revelation made it clear that we are answerable for our own sins and not those of others. Nonetheless, to most of us this would be valid and good advice, but for Job we know he did already take sin in his household seriously and deal with it. Zophar's advice here was simply not relevant to Job and clearly no basis for him to be held to account and punished by God.

Zophar then recounts the consequences of Job eradicating sin (Job 11:15–19). As is common in the wisdom writings of the Bible (and, indeed, elsewhere in the ancient world), an upright life will be rewarded in the present with prosperity and health. Although there are proverbs that seem to support this view (e.g., Prov 9:11–12; 10:3–4, 6, etc.), it is a simplistic misreading of Proverbs to claim from these that there is some sort of absolute rule or one-to-one correspondence of reward to uprightness and of punishment to sin as Zophar and his friends seek to apply to Job.

The description of the prosperity that Zophar holds out to Job is indeed attractive. Job will lift his face (where his face had been downcast, Job 10:15). The NIV's "free of fault" is rendered woodenly as "without blemish," which can refer to moral defect (e.g., Prov 9:7) or physical defect (e.g., Lev 21:17), both of which apply to Job in Zophar's thinking. Job will "stand firm," the Hebrew here uses language associated with casting iron as if Job is being made into a statue and so emphatically describes the strength Zophar claims Job will have once he eradicates sin from his life and home. With such strength he will no longer fear as he now does (see Job 5:21–22).

Zophar then goes on to tell Job that he will forget his trouble, which he cleverly parallels with a description of how Job will remember his trouble. But the remembering is really equivalent to forgetting, as it will be like water that has flowed away (11:16).

Whereas Job had referred to darkness in 10:22, in 11:17 Zophar points to life in the light as a further consequence of Job's repentance, should he follow Zophar's advice. Indeed, although there are dark times (perhaps Zophar is thinking of night), they will not truly be dark but rather be like the morning when the sun's breaking light illuminates the world afresh.

In verse 18 the aspect of Zophar's idyllic future for a repentant Job is security, for without security there can be no peace for Job. Zophar's implication is that Job was experiencing the manifestation of just such a lack of security: he had lost everything without warning. So, the promise of a future without confidence that it would remain secure is a hollow promise. But what is the basis for the security Zophar holds out? It would be hope. Hope features in the speeches of all three friends—Eliphaz suggested Job's hope was in his blameless life (Job 4:6), and Bildad warned that the hope of the godless perishes (Job 8:13). Zophar, in tying hope to Job's repentance, also makes hope contingent upon Job's renouncing his (supposedly) sinful path. For Job this can serve as little more than a cruel taunt, for he is aware of no sin to renounce, and yet his hope has vanished (Job 7:6). Zophar will remind Job of his hopelessness in 11:20.

Zophar concludes his account of the blessings a repentant Job could expect by highlighting the untroubled rest he will have, a further manifestation of the security of this future. This same expression is used to describe an idyllic future in Zephaniah 3:13, and it was clearly a dream for the sages (see Eccl 2:22–23). Furthermore, Job's standing in the community will be restored as many will seek his favor (see Prov 19:6). The point here is that Job will be admired and envied by those around him, as indeed he once had been.

Rather than leave Job with this account of a prosperous future, Zophar concludes in Job 11:20 by reminding Job of the alternative. For all the good that awaits the repentant and righteous Job, in Zophar's simplistic retributive world a Job who fails to repent has no hope—aside from the hope Job himself has noted, and that is for his life to be over soon.

LIVE the Story

When Hubris Trumps Humility

The Dunning-Kruger effect is a cognitive bias most notably described by the psychologists David Dunning and Justin Kruger in 1999. It refers to the phenomenon where people with limited knowledge or experience in a certain area overestimate—sometimes grossly overestimate—their level of expertise in that area. While the description is relatively new, the effect itself is not. In fact, we can see it in all of Job's friends and, to some extent, even in Job himself. They each make claims to a level of understanding about God that is ultimately shown to be wrong. Not only is this apparent in Zophar's first speech, but it is also somewhat surprising given what he says in verses 7–9. In those words, he anticipates the conclusion of the book by making the same point that the narrator makes in the poem in chapter 28, that God makes in his speeches, and that Job finally comprehends in chapter 42:

> Can you fathom the mysteries of God?
> Can you probe the limits of the Almighty?
> They are higher than the heavens above—what can you do?
> They are deeper than the depths below—what can you know?
> Their measure is longer than the earth
> and wider than the sea. (Job 11:7–9)

Despite this, however, Zophar and his friends do not seem to have taken these words to heart. They appear to claim a level of understanding that has transcended the need to apply this realization about God to their own beliefs about God. They remain convinced (as does Job at this point) that they have it right, that they understand the truth about Job's situation, and that they can offer him a way out.

It is here that Zophar gets things terribly wrong. He is a hypocrite in that he applies his awareness of human limitations to Job but fails to apply the same awareness to his own thinking. Where he questions Job's beliefs, he unquestioningly affirms his own beliefs—perhaps bolstered by the certainty already expressed by his friends. He appears certain that Job's predicament has come about because of his own sin. Moreover, he argues that Job was so completely oblivious to his sinfulness that he was not aware that God had forgotten some of his sins (Job 11:6). Yet even excluding the sins that God had forgotten, his present suffering was testimony to the fact that there were even more sins for which Job needed to repent. According to Zophar, God was showing mercy to Job in that the suffering he was currently experiencing was less than he deserved!

We see this all too often in the world around us and, even worse, in the church. Whether it be from academics, ministers, Bible study leaders in small groups, or anyone who walks into a church building. People are so often overly confident in the truths they espouse, particularly about God.

The consequence of this type of hubristic thinking for Zophar (much like the other two friends we have met thus far) is that his words lack any real empathy for Job. He even lacks understanding of Job's loss. The idea that restoration following repentance would have Job "forget your trouble" (v. 16) is difficult to accept—would Job really have forgotten the loss of his children even following restoration? The danger for us is the same: when we fail to approach God's word in humility, recognizing the limitations of our own understanding, our application to and assessment of the lives of those around us suffers, and those around us suffer as a result.

Zophar's rhetoric is already, in his first words to Job, reflecting a degree of frustration with Job's stubbornness. He comes across as annoyed that Job has not conceded to the arguments of Eliphaz and Bildad, arguments that align with Zophar's understanding of God and Job. With frustration comes escalation, as we indeed see in the claims about the degree of Job's sinfulness in verse 6, the claim that Job is a "deceiver" (v. 11) and that he is "witless" (v. 12). Zophar's message to Job is then essentially reduced to: "Job, you're actually worse than even we have made out; you need to repent and fix things with

God now before making an even bigger fool of yourself!" With this it is clear that the friends and Job are not moving toward any agreement but further away from one as Job stubbornly (but correctly) refuses to listen to the words of his three friends. Their rhetoric ramps up, with the friends increasingly arguing that he is more deserving of the suffering he has encountered. As Job has repeatedly failed to accept the assertions of his friends that he must repent of his sinfulness, in their eyes he has moved from merely ignorant to stubbornly refusing to be taught their own wisdom. He is, for them, in very real danger of becoming so irredeemably foolish that there is no hope of him ever learning wisdom.

Every January the New South Wales branch of the Australian Church Missionary Society holds a summer school in the Blue Mountains west of Sydney. Those who attend have the opportunity to meet and hear from missionaries at home on furlough about their experiences. Missionaries sometimes speak of the blind spots of those in the countries where they have served—things that locals are oblivious to yet that run counter to the way that God wants us to live. And one of the most common questions the missionaries are asked by those attending is what they think *our* blindspots are. It is a great question, for it recognizes that we are often so immersed in our culture that we cannot easily see where we are out of step with God, where we are at odds with the way God would have us live.

It is all too easy to see Zophar's errors and to think that we would never repeat them. And perhaps that is right—we may be unlikely to repeat this particular error. We are, after all, quite unlikely to encounter someone as upright and blameless as Job! Yet, we are often all too ready to see the speck in our sister's or brother's eye while being completely blind to the log in our own (Matt 7:1–4)!

Finally, it is important to note that Zophar's conclusion—his promise of health and prosperity for Job if he returns to an upright life—is echoed by false teachers down through history and, indeed, into the present. It is, however, a lie today, and it always has been a lie. To be sure, God promises these things, but not here and not now. The consistent message of the Bible—both Old and New Testaments—is that the righteous can and do suffer in this life. Indeed, this is an essential component of the message of Job. Suffering does not invariably arise from a sinful life; there are other causes and, without divine revelation, it is often impossible to determine why we suffer.

CHAPTER 8

Job 12–14

Job's First Reply to Zophar

LISTEN to the Story

12:1 Then Job replied:

2 "Doubtless you are the only people who matter,
and wisdom will die with you!
3 But I have a mind as well as you;
I am not inferior to you.
Who does not know all these things?

4 "I have become a laughingstock to my friends,
though I called on God and he answered—
a mere laughingstock, though righteous and blameless!
5 Those who are at ease have contempt for misfortune
as the fate of those whose feet are slipping.
6 The tents of marauders are undisturbed,
and those who provoke God are secure—
those God has in his hand.

7 "But ask the animals, and they will teach you,
or the birds in the sky, and they will tell you;
8 or speak to the earth, and it will teach you,
or let the fish in the sea inform you.
9 Which of all these does not know
that the hand of the LORD has done this?
10 In his hand is the life of every creature
and the breath of all mankind.
11 Does not the ear test words

as the tongue tastes food?
12Is not wisdom found among the aged?
Does not long life bring understanding?

13"To God belong wisdom and power;
counsel and understanding are his.
14What he tears down cannot be rebuilt;
those he imprisons cannot be released.
15If he holds back the waters, there is drought;
if he lets them loose, they devastate the land.
16To him belong strength and insight;
both deceived and deceiver are his.
17He leads rulers away stripped
and makes fools of judges.
18He takes off the shackles put on by kings
and ties a loincloth around their waist.
19He leads priests away stripped
and overthrows officials long established.
20He silences the lips of trusted advisers
and takes away the discernment of elders.
21He pours contempt on nobles
and disarms the mighty.
22He reveals the deep things of darkness
and brings utter darkness into the light.
23He makes nations great, and destroys them;
he enlarges nations, and disperses them.
24He deprives the leaders of the earth of their reason;
he makes them wander in a trackless waste.
25They grope in darkness with no light;
he makes them stagger like drunkards.

13:1"My eyes have seen all this,
my ears have heard and understood it.
2What you know, I also know;
I am not inferior to you.
3But I desire to speak to the Almighty
and to argue my case with God.

4You, however, smear me with lies;
you are worthless physicians, all of you!
5If only you would be altogether silent!
For you, that would be wisdom.
6Hear now my argument;
listen to the pleas of my lips.
7Will you speak wickedly on God's behalf?
Will you speak deceitfully for him?
8Will you show him partiality?
Will you argue the case for God?
9Would it turn out well if he examined you?
Could you deceive him as you might deceive a mortal?
10He would surely call you to account
if you secretly showed partiality.
11Would not his splendor terrify you?
Would not the dread of him fall on you?
12Your maxims are proverbs of ashes;
your defenses are defenses of clay.

13"Keep silent and let me speak;
then let come to me what may.
14Why do I put myself in jeopardy
and take my life in my hands?
15Though he slay me, yet will I hope in him;
I will surely defend my ways to his face.
16Indeed, this will turn out for my deliverance,
for no godless person would dare come before him!
17Listen carefully to what I say;
let my words ring in your ears.
18Now that I have prepared my case,
I know I will be vindicated.
19Can anyone bring charges against me?
If so, I will be silent and die.

20"Only grant me these two things, God,
and then I will not hide from you:
21Withdraw your hand far from me,

and stop frightening me with your terrors.
22Then summon me and I will answer,
or let me speak, and you reply to me.
23How many wrongs and sins have I committed?
Show me my offense and my sin.
24Why do you hide your face
and consider me your enemy?
25Will you torment a windblown leaf?
Will you chase after dry chaff?
26For you write down bitter things against me
and make me reap the sins of my youth.
27You fasten my feet in shackles;
you keep close watch on all my paths
by putting marks on the soles of my feet.

28"So man wastes away like something rotten,
like a garment eaten by moths.

14:1"Mortals, born of woman,
are of few days and full of trouble.
2They spring up like flowers and wither away;
like fleeting shadows, they do not endure.
3Do you fix your eye on them?
Will you bring them before you for judgment?
4Who can bring what is pure from the impure?
No one!
5A person's days are determined;
you have decreed the number of his months
and have set limits he cannot exceed.
6So look away from him and let him alone,
till he has put in his time like a hired laborer.

7"At least there is hope for a tree:
If it is cut down, it will sprout again,
and its new shoots will not fail.
8Its roots may grow old in the ground

and its stump die in the soil,
[9]yet at the scent of water it will bud
and put forth shoots like a plant.
[10]But a man dies and is laid low;
he breathes his last and is no more.
[11]As the water of a lake dries up
or a riverbed becomes parched and dry,
[12]so he lies down and does not rise;
till the heavens are no more, people will not awake
or be roused from their sleep.

[13]"If only you would hide me in the grave
and conceal me till your anger has passed!
If only you would set me a time
and then remember me!
[14]If someone dies, will they live again?
All the days of my hard service
I will wait for my renewal to come.
[15]You will call and I will answer you;
you will long for the creature your hands have made.
[16]Surely then you will count my steps
but not keep track of my sin.
[17]My offenses will be sealed up in a bag;
you will cover over my sin.

[18]"But as a mountain erodes and crumbles
and as a rock is moved from its place,
[19]as water wears away stones
and torrents wash away the soil,
so you destroy a person's hope.
[20]You overpower them once for all, and they are gone;
you change their countenance and send them away.
[21]If their children are honored, they do not know it;
if their offspring are brought low, they do not see it.
[22]They feel but the pain of their own bodies
and mourn only for themselves."

Listening to the Text in the Story: "Ba'alu Myth" (Ugaritic); "Inanna and Enki" (Sumerian); "Coronation Hymn and Prayer" (Neo-Assyrian); "The 'Aqhatu Legend"

Job in this long speech touches on a number of themes that are unique neither to the book of Job nor even to the Bible but are reflections of subjects discussed in ancient Near Eastern literature. However, as is almost always the case, the Bible offers a theological corrective to the beliefs of the nations in whose midst the Israelites found themselves.

Job, for example, picks up on the idea that wisdom is particularly the possession of the aged, the elders in society (Job 12:12). The same idea will be reflected in the words of the young friend Elihu when he begins to speak in chapter 32, but the idea is present throughout the ancient world. For example, we find in the Ugaritic account of Baʿal a reference to the wisdom of the father deity ʾIlu, whose description makes his age clear:

> The Great Lady, ʾAṯiratu of the Sea, replies:
> Great indeed, ʾIlu, is (your) wisdom,
>   your gray beard surely instructs you,
>   the respite that is yours alone (surely instructs you).[1]

The link between the two is as ancient as written language itself. It is also expressed in Sumerian literature in the tale of "Inanna and Enki" where it is included in a list of the basic tenets of civilization, there described as "the (wise) state of old age."[2] This adage, however, is questioned in Job both here by Job himself and later by Elihu. Wisdom, based on the testimony of the Bible, is a gift of God neither restricted to nor guaranteed for the older members of society. Age is not the source of wisdom so much as the fear of God (see Prov 1:7).

The "fear of God" brings us to another aspect of Job's thinking in this speech—that the "splendor" of God is terrifying (Job 13:11). In the ancient Near East, the splendor of divine beings could also be described as being terrifying. In one particular Neo-Assyrian coronation hymn, the "terrifying

1. Both the reference to the "gray beard" and "respite" are taken by the translator (Dennis Pardee) as references to the great age of ʾIlu, one of the deities in the myth. See "The Baʿlu Myth" (*COS* 1.86:259–60).

2. "Inanna and Enki," trans. Gertrud Farber (*COS* 1.161:523).

splendor" of the deity Ninurta is bestowed upon the king.[3] This idea is also present in a much older Sumerian inscription commemorating the construction of a temple of the god Nergal in Ur. In this inscription he is described as one with "a perfect fearsome splendor."[4] In short, the people of the ancient world shared a view that their gods and goddesses were terrifying in their splendor (and in some instances the king was also viewed as terrifying in his splendor). This reflected a general view of the transcendence of the divine, a view that would only have been heightened for Job and his friends who recognized that Yahweh was the one sovereign God of the universe and so was clearly far more powerful than the gods and goddesses of the ancient world, none of whom were attributed with sole credit for all of creation!

One other facet of Job's speech is that which raises the question of whether Job or his contemporaries held to any clear view of an afterlife. Job will dream of the idea in 14:14, yet it is clearly only a dream for Job (see the discussion below). Views on an afterlife vary throughout the ancient world, but of particular interest here is the response of the young man Aqhat (or ʾAqhatu) to the offer of immortality from the Ugaritic goddess Anath in "The Aqhat Legend." In attempting to convince the young man to give her his bow, she says:

> Ask for life, O valiant ʾAqhatu,
> ask for life and I'll give (it to) you,
> for immortality and I'll make it yours;
> I'll make you count years with Baʿlu,
> with the son of ʾIlu will you count months;
> (You will be) like Baʿlu (who), when he comes
> (back) to life, feasts:
> they give a feast to the living one, give him drink,
> the goodly one chants and sings in his honor.
> So I, for my part, will answer (the request),
> I will give life to valiant ʾAqhatu.

to which the young man responds:

> Don't lie to me, girl,
> your lies are despicable to a real man;
> What after(life) can one obtain?

3. "A Late Piece of Constructed Mythology Relevant to the Neo-Assyrian and Middle Assyrian Coronation Hymn and Prayer," trans. Alasdair Livingstone (*COS* 1.146:477).
4. "Rim-Sin," trans. Douglas Frayne (*COS* 1.102B:253).

> what can a man obtain hereafter?
> (For) they will pour glaze [on] (my) head,
> white stuff over my cranium.
> [And] I'll die the death of every man,
> I also must surely die.[5]

Aqhat's offer here seems not to be for an unending afterlife but for a means to return to this life following death (the Ugaritic phrase translated "immortality" above is literally "not dying," and her suggestion that he would be like Baʿal, who was held to return to life, suggests this understanding of the offer). In the thought world of this tale, eternal life beyond death held no appeal. Rather, an eternal continuation of *this* life was the ideal the goddess used in an attempt to convince the young man to surrender his bow.

EXPLAIN the Story

Job Reacts to His Friends (12:1–6)

Job's opening words in this, his fourth speech and third response to his friends, make it clear that he is not addressing Zophar alone. His use of the plural "you" frames what follows as directed to them all. The meaning of the opening phrase, "Doubtless you are the only people who matter," is expressed woodenly as "Truly you are people," and its meaning is not entirely clear. However, the second line reveals Job's meaning: out of Job and his friends, the friends alone are the true sages, for they alone hold claim to true wisdom (and so when they die, wisdom will be gone). Job is quite clearly being sarcastic and so somewhat contemptuous of his friends, having been finally provoked by Zophar's speech.

Job's sarcasm makes it clear that he does not actually believe that all wisdom resides with his friends. Rather, he reminds his friends that he, too, has a brain (the Hebrew word refers concretely to the heart but is correctly translated by the NIV as "mind," for the heart in ancient thought was held to be where rational thought took place). More disparagingly, Job makes it clear that nothing his friends have said is particularly insightful by reminding them that everyone knows the things they are telling him.

"Laughingstock" (v. 4) is not a word used all that often in the modern world, but it refers here to an object of public mockery and derision (not a comedian!). The laughter need not be literal in this case, but Job's depiction

5. "The 'Aqhatu Legend," trans. Dennis Pardee (*COS* 1.103:347).

of his friends' response to his suffering in this way tells us as much about his perception of their response as their actual response. They doubtless felt they were upholding the truth and looking to help Job (after all, they believed that getting him to repent would ultimately lead to his restoration). Yet Job felt them to be sorely lacking in empathy and only listening to him so as to rebuke and correct him. Such treatment of others—even when they are wrong—is a failure to love.

Job's claim to be one who called on God and whom God answered (12:4) seems at odds with the events that have thus far transpired in the book of Job. The best understanding of these words is that they are a reflection by Job of his life before the events of the prologue. He contrasts his previous standing with the way he is perceived by others now—he has gone from one so lofty as would readily call on God and receive a reply to someone who is mocked and ridiculed. Verse 5 has Job elaborate on this: to add to his calamity he is derided by his friends (rather than comforted), and they trip him up when his foot slips. The Hebrew of the second half of verse 5 is difficult. The word rendered "feet" is singular in Hebrew, and the word translated "fate" (*nakon*) by the NIV is not well understood—parallelism suggests the sense here is that when Job's foot slips, his friends compound matters and trip him.

To make matters worse for Job, he feels that he suffers while those who truly deserve suffering—"marauders" and "those who provoke God" (v. 6)—sleep soundly and safely in their beds. The last line of verse 6 is either understood as saying that "those God has in his hand" (so NIV) or "those who carry their god in their hands" (ESV, NRSVue). The NIV is more likely because the shift from the plural references of the previous clauses to the singular one who carries in v. 6 (Heb. *hebi'*) marks a transition which more naturally would be understood to be a reference to God. Thus, Job is here expressing his feeling that God actively helps the unrighteous while opposing him, a reflection of Job's belief that he is suffering a failure of divine justice.

Job's Thoroughly Conventional Wisdom (12:7–11)

The main point of Job's words in verses 7–11 seems to be to remind his friends that the claims about wisdom that he is making are uncontroversial—animals, birds, the earth itself, even fish would be able to teach this. Job's situation can ultimately be attributed to God himself. Curiously, this is the only place in the dialogues of Job that the name of God, Yahweh, is used. Furthermore, it repeats a phrase found elsewhere only in Isaiah 41:20—"The hand of Yahweh has done this" (NIV modified). Job reminds his friends that the claim that God is sovereign over his creation is not a novel teaching and is not something he has made up; it is fundamental to all wisdom and knowledge shared throughout creation.

Job closes these words with an observation that is also trivially obvious: the ear does "test words" (that is, as one listens to words, one judges their veracity) and "the tongue tastes food" (Job 12:11). Nothing Job has claimed about wisdom here is in any way controversial and, as such, claiming that God is ultimately responsible—as Job has consistently done—should not be a surprise to his friends, and so they should not object to the way he speaks.

Job Contests Conventional Wisdom (12:12–25)

Job moves from one piece of self-evident wisdom to a piece of wisdom that is widely accepted in the ancient world but which he clearly is unhappy about. Verse 12 is quite terse and as such has the flavor of a traditional aphorism that Job is quoting. The notion that old age is accompanied by wisdom is widely assumed (e.g., 32:7 where Elihu refers to the age of Job and his three friends), but it has not proven to be true in Job's present experience. As such, Job quotes this in order to qualify it by asserting that the ultimate source of wisdom, power, counsel, and understanding is God, not old men. Job points out that the best human wisdom (that of counselors and judges, 12:17) and the most powerful people (the kings of 12:18) are nothing when compared to God.

The following verses serve to illustrate what Job says of God in verse 13 by providing examples of God's unmatched power (vv. 14–15). What is striking about these examples, however, is that they are destructive—they involve tearing down, imprisoning, drought, and devastation rather than God's work of creation (vv. 14–16). While Job is correct to affirm God's power, it would appear that his present circumstances have pushed him to overwhelmingly see the negative side of God's power. Beyond the physical, God's power extends to the human realm as well (vv. 17–21). Again, Job's view is negative: all humanity is divided into those who deceive and those who are deceived. Job's view leaves no place for truth since human beings do not have access to it, or at least as far as Job is presently concerned. Furthermore, Job reiterates God's power, for all people are his (whether deceived or deceiver).

God's surpassing power and wisdom is also expressed in the fate of counselors (the NIV's "rulers" in v. 17 is better understood to refer to those who advised the king) and "judges" (the term, used of the rulers God raised up in the book of Judges, encompasses more than those making decisions in courts of law). The counselors are led away naked, demonstrating their complete humiliation, while the judges—who were supposed to be among the wisest people—are made out to be fools (vv. 19–20). The contrast is between the best humans have to offer and God, who stands incomparably superior.

Job's point is expanded to every possible category: kings, priests, officials, advisers, elders, nobles, and the mighty in verses 18–21. Each and every one of these individual in positions of authority is in the hands of God and is belittled by God. In Job's presentation, all the best of humanity is depicted negatively next to God.

Concluding this part of his argument, in verses 22–25 Job expands his view from individuals to nations and the world in general. Yet, with the broadened field of view, Job maintains his negative perspective. For one, nothing is hidden from God, and what is more, that which is hidden is exposed by God for all to see. The language of dark and light is somewhat reminiscent of the opening of John's Gospel (e.g., John 1:5), for nothing can be hidden from God. His power extends over the nations, both making them and breaking them. The leaders of the nations have no real power, for God is in control and they merely stumble around in the dark.

In all these examples, God subverts the human world—making the powerful powerless, the wise foolish, the strong weak. The negative depiction of God by Job corresponds with his recent experience: his world had been turned upside down and God was responsible. Job thus concludes that God is a force for disruption in the world, undermining human achievement rather than rewarding it.

Job Appeals to His Friends to Stop Lying (13:1–12)

Job turns his attention more directly to his three friends, beginning with an affirmation of his equality with them. Job's statement comparing their knowledge with his own in verse 2 is emphatic: what they know, he certainly knows. They are not superior to him, they are not more knowledgeable than he is, and they do not have greater wisdom. After asserting their equality, however, Job moves on to highlight their differences.

Like many of the Hebrew verbs translated with the future tense in English, Job's words in verse 3 should be understood modally: he wants to speak to God, even to argue with God. Instead, he finds himself arguing with his friends who, Job makes clear, have no interest in his needs or desires and certainly do not countenance him taking up his cause with God. As a result, in verses 6 and 8 Job continues to speak about arguing (in a legal sense), repeating his desire to so argue and the friends' failure to act as adequate respondents on God's behalf. For them, this is an open and shut case—Job simply needs to swallow his pride, accept the situation is as they describe it, and repent.

As such, Job's friends are no help. In verse 4 he states that they cover the truth with lies (the NIV's "smear me with lies" is too specific; the Hebrew does not specify Job as the one smeared, even if their words have that effect). They, who aim to heal, do no such thing. Compared to what they have done, silence would have demonstrated greater wisdom (v. 5).

Having called on them for silence, Job also calls on them to listen to him (v. 6). More than this, however, he accuses his friends of telling lies for God (vv. 7–8). The sense of these questions from Job is not that he is asking the friends about what they might do in the future—he is questioning them about things they have already said! The words are better understood as bordering on accusation: "How can you speak wickedly on God's behalf?"[6] From Job's perspective, their diagnosis of his condition and their representations of God's view have been wrong. And, as it will turn out, God will agree with this (see Job 42:7).

Woodenly translated, in verse 8 Job asks, "How can you lift his face?" The expression refers to showing partiality and is condemned in legal contexts (see Lev 19:15). It might sound odd to complain about showing God favor or being partial to him, but Job's point here, as is made clear in the second clause, is that the friends have not only contravened due process and chosen not to be impartial but have done so by presenting their own arguments, not God's. These arguments, Job claimed in the previous verse, are simply wrong. Indeed, Job notes, if God were to turn on them and question them, they would find that he would rebuke them too!

Job's analysis of his friends' arguments here will turn out to be spot on, for at the end of the book God's verdict on the friends' claims is given, and they are found to have (inadvertently) lied about God. It will turn out that both Job and his friends have the same failing that has manifested itself differently: neither Job nor his friends have an adequate understanding of God to be able to comprehend what is happening to Job.

Job concludes his evaluation of the friends' words and actions here by consigning them to the dustbin. Though claiming to be wise, they show themselves to be fools (Rom 1:22).

Job Will Take His Chances with Confronting God (13:13–19)

Job now moves from directly addressing the friends (after one final plea that they remain silent so that he may speak), explaining that he is willing to

---

6. The form of the Hebrew verb here frequently expresses a modal sense. Waltke and O'Connor describe this particular sense as the "non-perfective of capability." See Bruce K. Waltke and M. O'Connor, *An Introduction to Biblical Hebrew Syntax* (Winona Lake, IN: Eisenbrauns, 1990) §31.4.c.

face the consequences of confronting God. While earlier he expressed some reticence to do this, even claiming it would be futile (see 9:14–20), now he is ready to move forward, fully aware that he is putting himself in danger. The question "Why do I put myself in jeopardy?" (13:14) renders a somewhat obscure Hebrew phrase, which woodenly reads, "Why do I take my flesh in my teeth?" The meaning of the idiom is made clear, however, by the parallel line where Job admits he is taking his life in his hands (see Judg 12:3; 1 Sam 19:5; 28:21). Aware of the risk, he presses on as he realizes he has nothing left to lose.

The well-known words of verse 15 are made difficult by the presence of some uncertainty with the original Hebrew text that either reads "not" or "to him" and so presents the two possibilities: "though he slay me, yet will I hope *in him*" or "he will surely slay me, I have *no* hope" (as in the NIV footnote; italics added). In the end, the choice can only be made by judging which fits better in the context. Even then, scholars are divided, so perhaps the context is not as clear as we would like it to be. Nonetheless, there are some salient points to be made from the immediate context that do favor one understanding above the other.

First, it is quite clear from the preceding verses that Job believes that the course of action upon which he is about to embark is perilous. He is taking his life in his own hands, which means there is, in his mind, a risk that he may lose it. Second, the first phrase in verse 15 is not an expression of certainty, as though Job believes it is certain that God will kill him. Once again, the Hebrew verb here should be understood modally, reading as "even if he kills me." Job is about to enter into a course of action in which his life may be lost. Third, Job's words here in verse 15 are presented as an answer to the question of verse 14 where he asked why he would imperil his life in this way. Whatever these words mean, they should answer that question.

These considerations suggest that Job is justifying his choice to confront God in legal dispute on the basis that, even though his life is in danger, he has nothing left to lose. As such, the first line of verse 15 is best read as, "It does not matter if he kills me, I have no hope anyway." And so, Job is determined, as the second half of verse 15 makes explicit, to stand up to God and defend his ways.

Job proceeds to explain what he hopes to achieve in all of this in verse 16: his deliverance. The word translated "deliverance" is elsewhere translated "salvation," but it is not entirely clear what Job imagines that he would be delivered or saved from. It is certainly anachronistic to imagine he is thinking of any sort of eternal salvation. He is either referring to his chance at surviving an encounter with God or the rescue of his reputation, for he recognizes that even his determination to confront God speaks of his piety, as a "godless" person would not undertake such action.

Furthermore, Job is certain that he has a legitimate case. He tells his friends here that he is prepared for court, and he is certain that he is right. So certain, in fact, that in verse 19 he asserts that if someone should successfully be able to win a case against him, then he will be silent and die. Job here uses the image of someone taking up a legal case against him in the way he plans to press charges against God. Job knows that he would not lose such a challenge. He is right, and so in pressing his case against God, he would not be found wrong.

Job Turns to Speak Directly to God (13:20–27)

Job turns from addressing his friends to speaking directly to God. What we learn here is a little surprising after all the bravado of Job's preceding words to his friends. It turns out he is not quite as prepared to present his case as we might have been led to believe. Instead, he begins by asking that God would do two things for him before he proceeds: withdraw his hand far from him and stop terrifying him (vv. 20–21).

The mention of God's "hand" reminds us of the fact that the Satan had in the prologue challenged God to send his hand to strike Job (1:11; 2:5; cf. 19:21). While a different Hebrew word (*yad*) is found in 1:11 etc., the word in 13:21 (*kaph*) is also used in contexts of power (e.g., 1 Sam 4:3; 2 Sam 14:16), and so it is likely that Job is asking to be freed, at the least, from his physical suffering. The second request reflects Job's belief that no one can face God and give a satisfactory defense (see Job 9:34). The requests appear reasonable; it would be hard to give a fair defense while feeling unwell and terrified.

Job makes it clear that if these conditions are met, he is prepared for God to initiate proceedings ("summon me"), or else he will initiate them himself ("let me speak, and you reply to me," v. 22). Indeed, as Job is already speaking, he continues on into a series of questions for God, effectively starting the proceedings without waiting for his initial requests to be answered.

Job's questions tell us something about what he thinks God has been doing to him. The first questions (13:23) indicate that Job shares the same presuppositions about suffering as his friends do, and so the fact that he is suffering must mean that God believes he is accountable for some sin. Furthermore, the precise meaning of Job's first question here is ambiguous. While Job may be asking how many sins God believes he has committed, given the present legal context, he may be asking for clarification of the charges against him, essentially saying, "What sins am I charged with?" What is abundantly clear is that Job is not aware of any sin that would warrant the punishment he feels he is receiving.

Hiding one's face, as Job believes God has done to him (13:24), is elsewhere God's response to sin and an indication of withdrawal of his protection and favor (see Deut 31:17–18; 32:20; Isa 8:17; 54:8; 59:2). All this leaves Job believing that God sees him as his enemy. Job likens himself to a windblown leaf or dry straw—things which are untethered and insignificant and probably, in Job's view, things that God should not be interested in tormenting. Job elaborates on the nature of this torment in verse 26, where he notes that God writes down bitter things against him. Precisely what Job means by "things written down" is not immediately clear. In 31:35 Job will wish to see a document written by his accuser, so perhaps that is what he imagines here, namely, that God has such a document filled with the bitter accusations that have prompted him to visit calamities upon Job.

Job's reference here to "the sins of my youth" (13:26b) should not be understood to provide some explanation for his present suffering, for that would simply make nonsense of the rest of the book, particularly the repeated assertion both in the prologue by the narrator and God, and throughout Job's own speeches, of Job's blamelessness. The prologue had made clear that Job was scrupulous in attending to the sacrifices appropriate for any sins he or his children had committed. Rather, Job's point here is that it appears as though God has failed to forgive those sins and holds him accountable for actions that he ought not to be held accountable.

Job concludes this section in verse 27 by describing God's treatment of him as though he is bound in stocks and his every movement scrutinized. The purpose of engraved marks on the soles of Job's feet is debated, but whatever it does refer to, it likely connotes the further restriction of the movement of his feet. Job is not free; he is imprisoned by God and has no idea why.

Job Reflects on Mortality (13:28–14:6)

The chapter breaks in the Bible were not part of the original text but were added later. By and large the breaks make good sense, but in a few places they are not quite where they should be, and this is one example. The change in Job's speech to refer to someone in the third person connects 13:28 with the opening words of chapter 14. A large portion of this chapter reflects on mortality—how human beings live and then die, and (as far as Job is aware) that is the end. Furthermore, that brief life is filled with trouble. While it reads as Job's thoughts on human life in general, it is ultimately a reflection on his own life, a reflection dominated by the trouble that has come upon him.

The fleeting, pain-filled life described in 13:28–14:2 serves primarily as a foil for Job's observation of God in 14:3. While not formally a question, Job's words express incredulity, surprise that God would bother to expend energy on something so insignificant as the fleeting existence of one person. Job is building on an idea he had already canvassed back in 7:17–19, and again he cannot grasp why God would bother with a mere human. The NIV's "fix your eyes on them" renders Hebrew that may be woodenly rendered as "open your eyes," a common expression that carries no negative connotations but refers to becoming aware of something. In this case, Job cannot believe that God bothers to make himself aware of the ins and outs of individual human lives and thus bring people—and particularly Job—to judgment.

Job builds on this argument, making his case for why God should look away and stop judging frail, fleeting human beings. First, Job feels in 14:4 that God's expectations of human beings are unrealistic: "Who can bring what is pure from the impure?" Furthermore, Job recognizes that human life is itself determined by God who has numbered our days and imposed limits on us. Job is essentially arguing that human beings have no chance to stand God's scrutiny, and that it is largely God's fault that this is the case! He sets the limits; he has placed us in an impure world from which we cannot escape.

So, Job asks (if not almost insists) that God should leave human beings (and by extension Job himself) alone (v. 6). He has asked for the same thing before (see 7:16; 10:20). The meaning of the final line of verse 6 is not immediately clear. A hired laborer's relief comes not during the time of toil but at the end of the day. Yet, from Job's perspective it would at least be better for him if God were simply to leave him alone with his troubles, and so he asks that God would now leave him alone until his troubled days are at an end.

Job's Imaginary Hope (14:7–17)

Job next makes it clear that he has no hope for any postmortem existence, no afterlife from which he may return vindicated. Unlike a tree, which when cut down may sprout and grow again, Job is certain that such new life is not available to human beings (v. 7; cf. Isa 6:13 in which the regrowth of a tree is an image of hope that destruction is not final). Although we know that trees do eventually die and not sprout again, that misses the point of this illustration in Job. Here his point is merely that for human beings—and specifically for Job—there is nothing after death (Job 14:10–12).

The other point to remember is that this is a clear reminder of Job's place in the overall story of redemptive history. Looking back from this side of the cross, we know that there is indeed hope beyond the grave, that though we lie down, we do rise again. Job, however, did not know that, and as far as he knew, death was the end. Whatever existence in Sheol looked like, it was not something Job considered to be on par with this life.

In verses 13–17 Job imagines a way out of his predicament by dreaming up a future in which he could escape what he (mistakenly) understands to be God's anger against him. We know that Job's suffering has not come about as a result of God's anger, but Job, without any real understanding of what is going on and only his (and his friends') belief in retributive justice, has arrived at this conclusion. And Job cannot see any way out before he dies, leaving him to long for an escape *through* death, an escape beyond Sheol (the word "grave" in the NIV of Job 14:13 is the Hebrew *Sheol*).

It is clear that, as far as Job is concerned, his thinking here is entirely hypothetical. He has only just finished proclaiming his confidence that death is the end for him, and that death will arrive soon. In verse 14, reflecting on the finality of death in his present predicament has Job wishing things were different, wishing that there could be some hope beyond death, at which point God would have moved past whatever it is that has caused him to oppose Job, as Job feels he does. Moshe Greenberg writes:

> But must containment in Sheol be final? Might it not be a temporary shelter from God's wrath? "If a man dies, can he revive?" (14:14)—hope wells up in the question, and the fantasy of reversal continues: When wrath subsides, God would call and Job would answer, God would long for his creature. But this anticipation of a doctrine whose time was not yet ripe, this flight of mind liberated by the collapse of its concept of order, is a momentary flash. Job falls back into despondency.[7]

The nature of this conjecture is, from Job's perspective, entirely hypothetical. He has repeatedly expressed his conviction that death is the end for him (see 7:7–10, 21; 10:21–22; 14:7–12), and he will repeat that belief in the speeches to come (e.g., 16:22). He does not here say, "When a person dies, they *will* live again!" No, for Job death is final, and here he is simply imagining a different future where he could return to a life without the suffering he now endures.

As such, the remainder of 14:14 should be read modally. Job describes his remaining days before death as "hard service"—the language is usually associated with military service—but if there were life after death, he would

7. Moshe Greenberg, "Job," in *The Literary Guide to the Bible*, ed. Robert Alter and Frank Kermode (Cambridge: Harvard University Press, 1987), 290.

endure (the word "wait" in the NIV conveys a sense of hope), knowing that relief would come. The apostle Paul, living on the other side of the cross, confidently knows that there is indeed life after death, and thus he can express a hope Job can only dream of:

> I consider that our present sufferings are not worth comparing with the glory that will be revealed in us. (Rom 8:18)

Job's dream continues in verse 15, where Job imagines that God would call and he would answer, freeing Job from the alienation he currently feels and from the suffering he now endures. In that imagined future, God would once again enjoy Job's company to the point where God himself would long for it.

The NIV (and some other translations) present the opening clause of verse 16 as if it were a future comment: "Surely *then* you *will* count my steps." The reference to counting one's steps conveys the notion of close scrutiny (cf. the varying descriptions of close scrutiny in 7:17–19; 13:27; 31:4). This is precisely what Job has been wishing that God would stop doing, and so it seems odd that Job would imagine with such scrutiny this idealistic future scenario continuing. Furthermore, the second clause of verse 16 expresses the desire that God would not keep track of his sins. Rather than read the opening clause as a reference to the future, however, the Hebrew of verse 16 is better understood as portraying a contrast between the present, as Job was then experiencing it, and the hypothetical future, which he hoped for: "While now you number my steps, [then] you would not keep track of my sin."

Aside from not keeping track of sin, Job finishes describing his imagined future in verse 17 by wishing that at that time even any past sins that he may have committed would be concealed and forgotten. Though the Hebrew words are different, the idea of "covering" (the verb *tpl* in v. 17) over sins is shared with the notion of atonement found elsewhere in the Old Testament (see, e.g., the use of the root *kpr* regarding the Day of Atonement in Lev 23:28). While Job here uses different terminology, the idea of covering sin signifies dealing with it, such that it no longer has any bearing on the person's relationship with God.

Job's Dreams of the Future Give Way to the Reality of the Present (14:18–22)

Verse 18 begins with a sharp disjunction marking the end of Job's short-lived flirtation with hope in an idyllic afterlife. Reality comes crashing back, and in the real world Job knows he has no hope. Job depicts the destruction of his own hope in terms of the slow and relentless wearing down of a mountain of rock by the elements. What is more, Job boldly claims that human hope is worn down and eroded by God himself.

That which finally defeats human hope here, according to Job, is death. God overpowers "once for all" (v. 20)—that is, forever. Death is final and, as Qoheleth (the teacher who speaks in Ecclesiastes) noted, it undoes all hope and meaning from life (e.g., Eccl 2:14–16; 3:19; 9:1–6). As Job notes here, the dying will not know what will become of their children, and they are consumed by their own suffering. The change in "countenance" mentioned in verse 20 is most likely a reference to a change in appearance associated with death. While it may refer to changes as one ages and approaches death, Job does not believe he will see old age, and so it is likely referring primarily to death.

Job thus concludes that death, which is brought about by God, undermines any hope human beings may have.

LIVE the Story

How Should We Respond to God and to Others?

How should we respond to others when we disagree with them? It is a question raised in Job's responses to his friends, particularly in chapter 12 where Job's response includes stinging sarcasm, rebuke (see 13:4–5), and the claim that his friends are essentially lying for God (vv. 7–8). Now, we have no reason to believe that Job's friends are disingenuous in anything that they are saying to Job; there is no indication that they do not truly believe all that they are saying—unlike so many people in the modern world who seem to be willing to say just about anything with distinctly dubious motives. These are not three TV evangelists whose teachings to Job are designed to dupe him into supporting them financially. These friends really do seem to have Job's best interests at heart! Most of us would, in (hopefully) different circumstances, endorse their theology and not just their motives.

And yet they are wrong in what they say to Job. And because they were wrong, Job was right to say that they were effectively lying for God or, at the very least, about God. Their problem was that they were unable to see outside of the restrictive theological understanding that they held to be fundamental. This is not to say that we should let go of all of our theological moorings or that we should render all of our understanding of God—built (hopefully) on careful reading of God's word—as contingent and subject to revision under difficult circumstances. A wise church minister once said to his congregation that as he got older, he was less and less certain about more and more, but more and more certain about that which remained. His point was that there are central truths from which lines that should not be crossed can be constructed. We need to be careful that we draw the right lines, for many create boundaries out of theological hobbyhorses and set up boundaries that they enforce mercilessly. And such an approach often goes further than can be justified by what God has made known in the Bible. We may even be right about our hobbyhorses, but we may be wrong to let them override God's grace and mercy by making them our "hills to die on." We all need to choose those hills very, very carefully.

How should we respond to God when we disagree with him? Is that even an option? It is difficult to reconcile such an approach to God with any traditional theological understanding of God at all. We acknowledge that God is omniscient and omnipotent. If he truly knows all and is all powerful, then, how could he be wrong? Should we ever consider God to be our enemy as Job does? What is the danger inherent in making such judgments too hastily and without all the information? We know that God was not Job's enemy, and Job himself will come to understand that by the end of chapter 41. Despite this, sometimes the way things feel—even the way things appear—does not match up to what is true.

Job's response is to search for some way to hold God to account, to force God to explain to him what is going on. His means to this end is to call God to account in what is essentially a legal court. Previously he had expressed a hope to do this but acknowledged the impossibility of winning the case or even bringing it before God (see 9:14–20). As time passes, and perhaps as Job grows more desperate, his reticence wanes and his determination grows. He becomes increasingly determined in his desire to confront God, and the belief that this would be pointless diminishes.

Fortunately, we will never be in the same position as Job finds himself in. That is not to say that we will not face difficult times of loss and suffering in our lives, but instead it is to say that when we do face such times, we will always do so knowing far more than Job ever could have. We have the great benefit of living after the arrival of Jesus. We begin with far more information and (hopefully) with far more understanding than Job could have had at his point in history. And some of that understanding comes from Job's own story, as we progress through the chapters and learn what Job learned about God.

One place this strikes a chord with Job's thinking in this section is in his desire that God would deal with human sin in such a way that we do not bear the brunt of God's wrath ourselves (14:16–17). We now know that God ultimately does do this. God cannot ignore sin or else justice is abrogated and

God—as Elihu will later rightly argue at length—is certainly just. Rather, God will take sin away from frail human beings and place it on his beloved Son, making him "who knew no sin" to be sin "so that in him we might become the righteousness of God" (2 Cor 5:21). God will not ignore sin and will not ignore justice, but through his love for us and mercy he found a way that sin could be forgiven and dealt with, that we might live and yet justice served. That is where the story of God is leading.

Job and the Resurrection of the Dead

For a modern Christian reader of the book of Job, it may come as a surprise that Job does not believe in the resurrected life of the new heavens and earth. But it should not be a surprise. God's revelation to us has been progressive. We know now more than people, even the most faithful of believers, did in Job's day (see Matt 13:17). Job's expression of his hopes and beliefs needed to correspond at least with those of the original audience of the book so that they could relate to what was written. They had to come to understand how their faith was to work within their worldview while they awaited more complete answers and a fuller revelation of the nature of God's universe.

In light of these considerations, we need to try and make sense of Job's words within that context before leaping to apply them today. We should not conclude that Job's words about life after death are the whole story simply because they are in the Bible, for we know that they are not. The whole story is found in the whole Bible!

That is not to say that Job or the author's contemporaries had never contemplated the possibility or hope of life after death. Most ancient Near Eastern cultures held to some form of postmortem existence, even if merely as a shade in the underworld. Yet, particularly in Mesopotamia, that existence did not ultimately equate to this life, and any postmortem existence had the great potential to be thoroughly miserable and a poor shadow of life here and now—an idea depicted clearly in Enkidu's report of the netherworld to Gilgamesh in the poem of "Bilgames and the Netherworld" (referenced in the discussion of Job 3, above) and in the offer made by the goddess Anath to the youthful Aqhat, which amounted to a promise that he would not die or return to this life after death, and so live forever in this life rather than the in the next (see above under Listening to the Text in the Story).

The result is Job's expressed loss of hope in the face of death (14:1–14). This echoes some of Qoheleth's thought (probably at a later time). For Qoheleth (the title of the character who speaks throughout the book of Ecclesiastes), any advantage in this life is undone by death, for whether one was rich or poor, wise or foolish, everyone winds up dead. Those who toil and those who are lazy end up dead and without any ability to enjoy the fruits of their labors beyond the present (see, e.g., Eccl 4:13–16; 5:10–20). Job, as Qoheleth did, lays the blame for this situation squarely at the feet of God (Job 12:13–25).

What is more, the eventual conclusion to the story of Job does not quite offer a complete or satisfying answer to this problem. While Job does live a long life restored to the status he enjoyed before his travails began, he will still die, and he knows of no hope beyond the grave. This unsolved problem will persist throughout the Old Testament. Yet hope for some resolution grows, and the anticipation that God will do something about the problem mounts until finally a baby is born in an insignificant town called Bethlehem. That child shall ultimately provide the complete answer to Job's problems. For now, however, Job struggles in life to understand what is happening to him.

This unsolved problem is brought to the fore in this speech of Job's as he imagines a future beyond death (14:13–17). In that imagined future Job finds the possibility of a hope that would transcend his present troubles, a hope in new life beyond death. Here, in Job's longing for a better future than the one he believes lies before him, we encounter one manifestation of the longing that Jesus spoke to his first disciples of when he said to them:

> For truly I tell you, many prophets and righteous people longed to see what you see but did not see it, and to hear what you hear but did not hear it. (Matt 13:17)

Job longed for exactly that which Jesus would bring—a true hope and a true understanding of what really did lie beyond the grave. Job's words, "if only you would hide me in the grave, and conceal me till you anger has passed, if only you would set me a time and then remember me" (14:13) did express a hope that was ultimately fulfilled in Jesus. And while Job was not suffering for some specific sin he had committed, he was suffering nonetheless. From that suffering he sought release, an escape, and regardless of the reasons for his suffering, it would turn out that the ultimate escape would lie beyond death thanks to the work of the Messiah.

Job's Understanding of God

The connections to Isaiah in Job are numerous, and in this speech (and elsewhere throughout the book) Job reflects a notion, espoused a number of times in Isaiah 40–55, that God is ultimately in control of the universe. As Isaiah writes in Isaiah 45:5–7:

5I am the LORD, and there is no other;
 apart from me there is no God.
I will strengthen you,
 though you have not acknowledged me,
6so that from the rising of the sun
 to the place of its setting
people may know there is none besides me.
 I am the LORD, and there is no other.
7I form the light and create darkness,
 I bring prosperity and create disaster;
 I, the LORD, do all these things.

Job is right to turn to God for answers, for ultimately it is God who is in control. Yet, where Isaiah records God's own words asserting his greatness in order that his people might love and serve him, Job's purpose in Job 14 is different. Job understands the implication of this truth about God to be that, in his own situation, God is the one who must provide the answers he is looking for. The friends have failed to listen to him or to take him seriously, and their wisdom has come up short. They chastise him for ignoring their advice and speaking brusquely to God, and so Job presents an argument to demonstrate that his approach is valid.

While Job is right to acknowledge that God ultimately stands behind all that has happened to him, there is no promise in the Bible that God must explain his actions to Job (or, for that matter, to us). Job—and we as readers of his tale—will learn this by the end of the book, for no explanation is given to Job. And even though we readers have been allowed into God's heavenly court in the opening chapters to witness some of the hidden proceedings that in part instigated Job's suffering, we are left with both more questions and awareness that we do not have a complete account of God's purposes in allowing Job to suffer.[8]

This applies to us as well. There is no guarantee in Scripture that we shall know why it is that we may suffer at any point in our lives. What we do have is assurances as to the faithfulness of God, his love for us, and his purposes for the future. Our faith in God ought not to be founded in how comprehensive our understanding of the reasons we may suffer is but rather in the clear demonstration of God's commitment to us and love for us. Job's faith was

8. For more on the incomplete nature of the prologue's rationale for Job's suffering, see the discussion in the subsection What Is God up to in Job 1–2 in Live the Story on Job 1–2 (Ch. 1); also Shields, "Malevolent or Mysterious?"

founded in what he knew of God's actions in the past. Given his place in history, Job's knowledge base for understanding was more limited than is ours, and part of his growth in faith takes place through the events recorded in this book, culminating in his encounter with God in chapters 38–41. In those chapters Job will learn something that he already knew in principle, but he will learn it in such a way that he better understands the complex nature of God's control of the whole universe plays out for his own life.

For us, living at the other end of history compared to Job, we look to the clearer demonstration of God's love and faithfulness shown to us in the life, death, resurrection, and ascension of Jesus. Here we see the level of God's commitment to us as the one who is willing to endure death, even death on a cross, in order to rescue us from the desperate mess we have made of our own lives.

CHAPTER 9

Job 15

Eliphaz's Second Speech

LISTEN to the Story

1Then Eliphaz the Temanite replied:

2"Would a wise person answer with empty notions
or fill their belly with the hot east wind?
3Would they argue with useless words,
with speeches that have no value?
4But you even undermine piety
and hinder devotion to God.
5Your sin prompts your mouth;
you adopt the tongue of the crafty.
6Your own mouth condemns you, not mine;
your own lips testify against you.

7"Are you the first man ever born?
Were you brought forth before the hills?
8Do you listen in on God's council?
Do you have a monopoly on wisdom?
9What do you know that we do not know?
What insights do you have that we do not have?
10The gray-haired and the aged are on our side,
men even older than your father.
11Are God's consolations not enough for you,
words spoken gently to you?
12Why has your heart carried you away,
and why do your eyes flash,
13so that you vent your rage against God
and pour out such words from your mouth?

[14]"What are mortals, that they could be pure,
    or those born of woman, that they could be righteous?
[15]If God places no trust in his holy ones,
    if even the heavens are not pure in his eyes,
[16]how much less mortals, who are vile and corrupt,
    who drink up evil like water!

[17]"Listen to me and I will explain to you;
    let me tell you what I have seen,
[18]what the wise have declared,
    hiding nothing received from their ancestors
[19](to whom alone the land was given
    when no foreigners moved among them):
[20] All his days the wicked man suffers torment,
    the ruthless man through all the years stored up for him.
[21]Terrifying sounds fill his ears;
    when all seems well, marauders attack him.
[22]He despairs of escaping the realm of darkness;
    he is marked for the sword.
[23]He wanders about for food like a vulture;
    he knows the day of darkness is at hand.
[24]Distress and anguish fill him with terror;
    troubles overwhelm him, like a king poised to attack,
[25]because he shakes his fist at God
    and vaunts himself against the Almighty,
[26]defiantly charging against him
    with a thick, strong shield.

[27]"Though his face is covered with fat
    and his waist bulges with flesh,
[28]he will inhabit ruined towns
    and houses where no one lives,
    houses crumbling to rubble.
[29]He will no longer be rich and his wealth will not endure,
    nor will his possessions spread over the land.
[30]He will not escape the darkness;
    a flame will wither his shoots,

and the breath of God's mouth will carry him away.
[31]Let him not deceive himself by trusting what is worthless,
for he will get nothing in return.
[32]Before his time he will wither,
and his branches will not flourish.
[33]He will be like a vine stripped of its unripe grapes,
like an olive tree shedding its blossoms.
[34]For the company of the godless will be barren,
and fire will consume the tents of those who love bribes.
[35]They conceive trouble and give birth to evil;
their womb fashions deceit."

Listening to the Text in the Story: "The Adapa Story"

Eliphaz returns to some ideas from the ancient world that we have already encountered in earlier speeches of the book, but he also alludes to ideas we have not encountered thus far. In verse 7 he asks if Job is the first man ever born, which may initially seem to be a reference to Adam except, of course, that Adam was not "born" so much as "formed." This is more likely a reference to the idea that wisdom could be anthropomorphized as a perfectly wise man born before the creation of the world (hence the question of the second part of verse 7). Clines suggests that this idea may lie behind the association of wisdom with the figure of the King of Tyre in Ezekiel 28:11–19 and perhaps even the description of wisdom in Proverbs 8.[1] Some scholars point to the Mesopotamian story of the semi-divine sage Adapa (who nonetheless himself finds some parallels with the biblical Adam).[2]

The wisdom imparted to Adapa by the god Ea is clearly recounted in the fragmentary opening to a fourteenth-century BC text from Amarna:

> [Wis]dom . . . [. . .].
> His command was indeed . . . [. . .] like the command of [Ea].
> Wide understanding he had perfected for him to disclose the designs of the land.

---

1. Clines, *Job 1–20*, 349.

2. Walton, *Job*, 211; Seow, *Job 1–21*, 700–701.; cf. "The Adapa Story," trans. Benjamin R. Foster (*COS* 1.129:449).

To him he had given wisdom; eternal life he had not given him.
In those days, in those years, the sage from Eridu,
Ea, created him as the *model* of men.
The sage—his command no one can vitiate—
The capable, the most wise among the Anunnaki is he;
The blameless, the clean of hands, the ointment priest, the observer of rites.[3]

Some version of this primordial figure likely stands behind the notion that Eliphaz is appealing to here. Regardless of the precise details behind his reference to the first man, the context in Job 15 makes it clear that Eliphaz is pointing to a sage of unrivaled wisdom who existed in primordial times and, as such, stood well above Job in terms of wisdom. Eliphaz essentially states that Job's claims to knowledge are equivalent to making a claim to have the wisdom of this mythical figure of antiquity, a claim that is patently absurd. Job, in Eliphaz's estimation, is making claims that stand at odds with the wisdom known from and known since the kin of Adapa. And for Eliphaz such claims simply do not stand scrutiny for Job's claims contradict the wisdom that has been established from antiquity.

EXPLAIN the Story

Eliphaz Questions Job's Piety (15:1–13)

Whereas Eliphaz began his first reply to Job with some amount of care and gentleness, this second speech evinces no such care and rather directly challenges Job's wisdom, which he had defended in the preceding speech (e.g., 13:2). The east wind metaphor Eliphaz uses in verse 2 characterizes Job's wisdom as empty or insubstantial, a point made particularly clear in the second line, for if wind fills one's belly, then their hunger is not sated. The second question from Eliphaz forsakes metaphor to be more direct, noting that the wise do not engage in useless or valueless speech. Although he has not stated it directly, he is clearly pointing at Job here—this is his assessment of his words, revealing that he has not heard Job in any meaningful way and has dismissed all he has had to say.

But Eliphaz does not stop there. Job, he says, goes even further than this: "you even undermine piety" (v. 4). "Piety" here (*yir'ah*) is the word commonly

3. "Adapa," trans. E. A. Speiser (*ANET*, 101).

translated "fear, reverence," and so Eliphaz's claim is that Job not only speaks empty words but impairs his own (and possibly others') relationship with God. He claims in verse 5 that Job's words are prompted by his sin; Job speaks as one who is "crafty" (*'arum*), a word that, although used positively throughout Proverbs (e.g., Prov 12:16; 13:16), can describe the worst aspects of wisdom (so it describes the serpent in Gen 3:1; cf. Job 5:12). In the end, Eliphaz feels that Job has condemned himself by his own words (15:6).

What is it that Job has said that prompts Eliphaz to speak thus? He asserts that Job has repudiated the wisdom of his friends and has directly called out God for his behavior. To Eliphaz, Job appears more interested in defending himself and seems blind to the obvious implication of his suffering, namely, that he has sinned.

Eliphaz continues to call Job's wisdom into question in verses 7–10. While the reference to the "first man" (v. 7) would immediately make us think of Adam, as noted above Adam is probably not exactly who is being referred to here. The parallel in the second part of the verse has this first man existing before the hills, which clearly Adam did not, and so the reference is something less concrete. Some have suggested an association with the king of Tyre as depicted in Ezekiel 28:12–13, but perhaps the reference to "before the hills" (Job 15:7) and the subsequent question about being part of God's council refers to a private group of advisors to God (v. 8; cf. Jer 23:18, 22) suggest that the overall image is of one who was party to God's plans concerning creation and so whose wisdom surpasses all others.

This idea is reflected in Proverbs 8:22–25 when it describes wisdom as the firstborn of creation that God brought forth in order to subsequently create a world founded on wisdom (cf. Col 1:15). Understanding the natural world is an important part of biblical wisdom (cf. 1 Kgs 4:33; Job 38–41), and so Eliphaz sarcastically asks Job if he had been part of the planning committee for the creation and so can justify his bold claims to superior wisdom. Driving this point home, he asks Job what wisdom he has that his friends are lacking (Job 15:9)—with the clear insinuation that there is no such knowledge! Completing the point, Eliphaz claims that all conventional wisdom supports their case.

For the reader who comes to Eliphaz's words here after reading the prologue, it is hard not to be reminded that we have indeed listened in on God's council (1:6–12; 2:1–6). Further, this should remind us that what we overheard there actually proves Eliphaz to be wrong in what he here says to Job.

Who are the grey-haired men who are older than Job's father (v. 10)? First, the reference to age is an appeal to authority in wisdom circles (see 12:12;

32:4). Second, the terms here are singular and have prompted some to suspect that Eliphaz is referring either to himself or to his friends.[4] The difficulty with this view is that he says that these people are "with us" (v. 10), implying that they are distinct from the three friends. Most likely these are collective references to the aged sages of the world. Thus, the friends claim that they are not alone, but all the wisest sages would back them up, and so Job stands alone and against the best minds of the world.

In verses 11–13 Eliphaz turns to Job's attitude toward an understanding of God. The word "consolations" refers to comfort derived from trusting in God and specifically in his word (as the parallel line makes clear). Eliphaz quite probably feels that he is speaking about the words spoken by himself and his friends, which he seems to think are gentle and comforting, and that God is speaking through them. Comfort is something of a theme throughout the book of Job. Job is looking for comfort, and Eliphaz seems to think that Job's behavior reflects a refusal to find comfort in God. Eliphaz is not wholly wrong here. Job will ultimately find comfort after hearing from God himself toward the end of the book (see 42:6 in the commentary below). Yet Eliphaz is wrong if he thinks either his words or the words of his friends will help Job in any way.

Job's refusal to find comfort in God through his friends is evidence, at least to Eliphaz's way of thinking, that Job's mind has led him astray (15:12). Once again, the Hebrew word "heart" used here is more closely aligned with what today would be referred to as our "mind," and so it is Job's thoughts to which Eliphaz refers. The second line in verse 12 is difficult to understand, as it contains the Hebrew verb *rzm*, which is found nowhere else. Many English translations render it "flash," but that is by no means certain, and it is not immediately clear what it would mean that Job's eyes flash. In the end it is probably best, following the common pattern of Hebrew poetry, to understand this line as paralleling the preceding one as another way of accusing Job of having led himself away from the truth.

Eliphaz turns to explain the evidence that he sees in support of his contention in verse 13. Although the NIV (and many other English versions) renders the Hebrew "so that you vent your rage against God" or something similar, the Hebrew simply says, "for you have turned your spirit/breath [*ruakh*] toward God." As with many parts of Job, scholars have some difficulty understanding this passage, but here it is probably better to read verse 13 with

4. E.g. Clines, *Job 1–20*, 351.

Eliphaz depicting Job turning toward God to vent. The same words appear in Proverbs 29:11:

> Fools give full vent to their rage [*ruakh*],
> but the wise bring calm in the end.

In short, Eliphaz feels that Job's words amount to nothing more than venting his uncontrolled anger against God in much the same way as the fool is depicted doing in Proverbs 29:11.

Eliphaz Explains Retributive Justice to Job (15:14–35)

Having chastised Job, Eliphaz moves to explain in verses 14–16 that no one is innocent or blameless before God. The "holy ones" of v. 15 are clearly spiritual or angelic beings rather than people, and yet neither they nor the heavens themselves attain God's standard of purity. To our ears his logic may appear unassailable, and yet we also know that God himself has identified Job as "blameless and upright, a man who fears God and shuns evil" (1:8). Even in Job's day, God had made a way for sinful human beings to be right with him so that they might enjoy fellowship with him. Today we know that such a relationship is only possible through Jesus and that, although they did not know it, in Job's day it was ultimately Jesus's sacrifice on the cross that enabled them to be blameless and upright in God's eyes (cf. Rom 3:25). Through faith, however, expressed through obedient observance of sacrifice, Job's sins (and those of his household) had been dealt with (see Job 1:5).

The remainder of Eliphaz's speech, 15:17–35, is devoted to a description of the life of the wicked person. After an introductory remark (v. 17), he begins in verse 18 with another appeal to authority, claiming that the view he is about to share is one that is endorsed by all wise people and which has been passed down from their forefathers. The meaning of the end of verse 19 is not entirely clear. It is likely an affirmation of the purity of the wisdom passed down, asserting its unadulterated nature by asserting that this wisdom was not compromised by foreign input.[5] This wisdom is, in Eliphaz's view, uncontroversial, universally accepted among the sages, and compelling. Furthermore, at many points the words are chosen to point to Job's present travails, making it clear where Eliphaz believes that Job stands.

---

5. Presumably "the land" is Eliphaz's homeland, not Israel, although the author may have held that the same truism applied to both.

Eliphaz's depiction of the wicked here is a textbook rendition of the simplistic understanding of retributive justice that he and his friends espouse. The wicked are both consumed by troubles in the present (vv. 17–26). Even if they presently prosper, they are destined to fall (vv. 27–35).

The present troubles of the wicked do not, by and large, exclude the prospect of material prosperity. Rather, they are predominantly related to anxiety and uncertainty together with an impending sense of doom (v. 20). Furthermore, whatever his material circumstances, the wicked live in darkness (v. 22)—a common metaphor in the Bible that ultimately represents alienation from God and all that is good—and have no hope of escape from that darkness.

The meaning of verse 23 is also difficult. The word translated "vulture" here (*'ayyeh*) could also simply mean "where is it?" (so ESV). The early Greek translators understood the verse to be saying: "he has been appointed to be food for vultures." This is probably the best understanding of the verse, paralleling the ideas in the surrounding material, which declare the wicked person to be destined for disaster: marauders attack, he is marked for the sword, and he is destined to be food for vultures. Vultures are birds of prey that feed on carrion (i.e., decaying flesh). And if you are destined to be vulture food, it does not bode well for you!

In verses 25–26 Eliphaz makes the point that the ultimate doom of the wicked is that they set themselves up in opposition to God. It is clear here that Eliphaz sees this behavior in Job, who has questioned God's justice and made accusations against God.

The last stanza in Eliphaz's poetic speech (vv. 27–35) highlights the possible disparity between the outward appearance of the wicked versus their inward appearance. Having a face "covered with fat" (v. 27) may not sound appealing to us, but here it is a sign of prosperity, as is the bulging of his waistline. The wicked man is no pauper, starving and desperate for food. Rather, he has all he needs in the present, and his physical appearance reflects his wealth. Yet, Eliphaz notes, this outward appearance is a facade that masks a deeply troubled and troubling inner life (v. 28). All this material wealth in the present is fleeting and will soon pass (vv. 29–30). The final verses (vv. 31–35) reflect Job's personal experience—all his wealth and good fortune were taken from him, and Eliphaz makes it clear that this is precisely what the wicked have always been destined for.

Eliphaz's words are targeted directly at Job. He was wealthy, living the good life. Yet, according to Eliphaz, this was a facade destined to crumble as Job's sin caught up with him, and God inevitably struck him and took all he had, consigning him to the miserable life he now endured.

But Eliphaz was wrong.

LIVE the Story

The Danger of Lies That Sound like the Truth

Again, we see the rhetoric amp up as Eliphaz also grows in his frustration over Job's stubbornness and the friends' inability to bring Job around to their way of thinking. Eliphaz begins by blatantly questioning Job's wisdom, but more than that, his continued failure to accede to their arguments has become for them such a point of irritation that Eliphaz claims that it "undermines piety" (v. 4). In some ways, this is akin to the modern put-down of saying that listening to someone has the effect of lowering everyone's IQ. Eliphaz's assertion that Job undermines piety and hinders devotion to God is not merely claiming that Job is undermining his own devotion to God but rather all devotion to God!

Sometimes, of course, it is true that someone's words may be empty or just hot air. But in making this claim of Job, Eliphaz is really playing the man. Instead of rebutting Job's claims or arguments he is now simply calling him a fool. Eliphaz does, however, respond to some of Job's actual thoughts, as expressed in his preceding speech. Job had made reference to the supposed sources of wisdom (e.g., 12:12) but noted that ultimately it was God's wisdom that trumped all (vv. 13–25). Eliphaz responds by essentially asking how it is that Job knows so much about God's wisdom—is he privy to the secret counsel of God's council (15:8)? He argues that Job claims too much for himself, and yet, like all of the friends, he fails to recognize that he makes claims that are no less bold or sure about the behavior of God when he calls Job to acknowledge his sin and repent!

Eliphaz also returns to his primary argument in chapter 15: human beings are sinful and to claim otherwise simply reveals one's ignorance. It is hard for us not to be sympathetic once again to this line of argument. It is the rationale by which suffering in the world is explained to us, and sometimes it is the rationale provided for individual suffering in the world, just as it is used here by Eliphaz for Job. How can anyone claim to be sinless? We might hear similar logic from any pulpit in any church on any given Sunday today:

> What are mortals, that they could be pure,
>   or those born of woman, that they could be righteous?
> If God places no trust in his holy ones,
>   if even the heavens are not pure in his eyes,
> how much less mortals, who are vile and corrupt,
>   who drink up evil like water! (Job 15:14–16)

This seems to be exactly what Paul says in the New Testament: "All have sinned and fall short of the glory of God" (Rom 3:23). Or we might think of the words of John: "If we claim to be without sin, we deceive ourselves and the truth is not in us" (1 John 1:8). So, is this surely true of Job, as Eliphaz and his friends claim?

As noted before, however, Job has not claimed to be sinless, but he is said to be blameless (Job 1:1). This points to the fact that Job, through the means set down by God, had made sure that any sin in his household was dealt with. He had offered the appropriate sacrifices (1:5). He had repented in faith and so had been forgiven and so was blameless. As such, there was no punishment for sin owing to him. Indeed, were Job to be further penalized for the sin from which he had repented and for which he had made amends through the offering of sacrifices, then that would be a sign that God would not accept these as the means through which sin could be dealt with. It would be akin to claiming that a repentant person today who, in faith, calls Jesus Lord would still bear the penalty for their sin—it would be a claim that Jesus's atoning death was ineffectual. In this Eliphaz misunderstands Job's predicament.

There is more that he and the friends get wrong. The book of Job repeats the point, and so it bears repeating here. It is a syllogistic fallacy to argue that if the punishment for sin is suffering, then all suffering indicates sin in the life of the sufferer. In effect, Eliphaz and the friends argue this:

> The consequence of sin is suffering.
> Job is suffering.
> Therefore, Job has sinned.

It does not take too much thought to recognize that this claim is fallacious. It is akin to the following claim:

> Smoking causes cancer.
> John has cancer.
> Therefore, John is a smoker.

Clearly there are more causes of cancer than just smoking! Similarly, we know there are other causes of suffering than personal sin from which a sufferer has failed to repent and make atonement. Yet Job's friends cannot find any way out of this argument and continue to insist that they have it right.

Speaking for God

It is a dangerous thing to claim to be speaking for God. Eliphaz and his friends clearly think that they are defending God and speaking for him throughout the book of Job, and here in particular Eliphaz makes the claim that the words he and his friends speak are gentle, comforting, and ultimately derived from God himself (Job 15:11). Many today continue to make this claim, some more boldly than others. And yet it is the more subtle among these claimants today who are the more dangerous. *Half-truths are more dangerous than blatant lies. The line between understanding the Bible to be God's word and our interpretation or application of the Bible being God's word is all too often overstepped by preachers.*

How is this error to be avoided? At the heart of the answer lies humility, for it is pride that results in us putting ourselves above the word of God and placing greater authority in our own interpretation than is warranted. It is pride that pushes us to hold to a position for longer than we would otherwise do so in the face of information to the contrary. It is pride that has us ignore differing viewpoints and voices, surrounding ourselves only with those who sing from the same song sheet, who hold to the same position. Instead, if we see ourselves as always the student, learning from God's word, rather than as the master, authoritatively explaining God's word, and if we make this position clear to those who listen to our words, then we are in a position to avoid the pride that promotes false teaching.

Of course, there is much more that can be said on this matter. We need to recognize that we do not stand alone but listen to the voices of the past. We need to understand that the words we seek to teach to others must first strike home in our own lives and must first challenge us and our way of thinking. We must be quick to listen and slow to speak. But in all of these, if we do not begin with humility and being open to the possibility that we are wrong, then we shall inevitably fail.

This also means that we should remain open to being challenged and questioned by others. Rather than simply rejecting the thoughts of others because they do not fall into our own personal list of the approved, we ought to listen to those with whom we disagree, to understand their arguments, and to be ready to change our understanding if their arguments stand up to scrutiny and the measure of Scripture. It is not a matter of accepting everything everyone says, but it is a matter of testing everything—and in particular our own cherished beliefs—against Scripture, recognizing that *our interpretation is not the same as "what the Bible says."* What we might label as "the plain meaning" of a text may only be plain to us and not to others, or to those to whom the passage was originally written.

CHAPTER 10

Job 16–17

Job's Second Reply to Eliphaz

LISTEN to the Story

16:1 Then Job replied:

2 "I have heard many things like these;
you are miserable comforters, all of you!
3 Will your long-winded speeches never end?
What ails you that you keep on arguing?
4 I also could speak like you,
if you were in my place;
I could make fine speeches against you
and shake my head at you.
5 But my mouth would encourage you;
comfort from my lips would bring you relief.

6 "Yet if I speak, my pain is not relieved;
and if I refrain, it does not go away.
7 Surely, God, you have worn me out;
you have devastated my entire household.
8 You have shriveled me up—and it has become a witness;
my gauntness rises up and testifies against me.
9 God assails me and tears me in his anger
and gnashes his teeth at me;
my opponent fastens on me his piercing eyes.
10 People open their mouths to jeer at me;
they strike my cheek in scorn
and unite together against me.
11 God has turned me over to the ungodly
and thrown me into the clutches of the wicked.

12All was well with me, but he shattered me;
he seized me by the neck and crushed me.
He has made me his target;
13 his archers surround me.
Without pity, he pierces my kidneys
and spills my gall on the ground.
14Again and again he bursts upon me;
he rushes at me like a warrior.

15"I have sewed sackcloth over my skin
and buried my brow in the dust.
16My face is red with weeping,
dark shadows ring my eyes;
17yet my hands have been free of violence
and my prayer is pure.

18"Earth, do not cover my blood;
may my cry never be laid to rest!
19Even now my witness is in heaven;
my advocate is on high.
20My intercessor is my friend
as my eyes pour out tears to God;
21on behalf of a man he pleads with God
as one pleads for a friend.

22"Only a few years will pass
before I take the path of no return.

17:1My spirit is broken,
my days are cut short,
the grave awaits me.
2Surely mockers surround me;
my eyes must dwell on their hostility.

3"Give me, O God, the pledge you demand.
Who else will put up security for me?
4You have closed their minds to understanding;

therefore you will not let them triumph.
5 If anyone denounces their friends for reward,
the eyes of their children will fail.

6 "God has made me a byword to everyone,
a man in whose face people spit.
7 My eyes have grown dim with grief;
my whole frame is but a shadow.
8 The upright are appalled at this;
the innocent are aroused against the ungodly.
9 Nevertheless, the righteous will hold to their ways,
and those with clean hands will grow stronger.

10 "But come on, all of you, try again!
I will not find a wise man among you.
11 My days have passed, my plans are shattered.
Yet the desires of my heart
12 turn night into day;
in the face of the darkness light is near.
13 If the only home I hope for is the grave,
if I spread out my bed in the realm of darkness,
14 if I say to corruption, 'You are my father,'
and to the worm, 'My mother' or 'My sister,'
15 where then is my hope—
who can see any hope for me?
16 Will it go down to the gates of death?
Will we descend together into the dust?"

Listening to the Text in the Story: "Enūma Elish"; "The Destruction of Mankind" (Egyptian)

Chapter 17 includes particularly striking military imagery used to describe God's attack upon Job. The Old Testament frequently depicts God in military terms—the common "LORD Almighty" (e.g., Ps 24:10 in NIV, or "LORD of hosts" in ESV) depicts Yahweh as the head of the combined forces of heaven and earth—a supreme commander of sorts (indeed, the title itself may well be a military title something like "general" or, perhaps better, "commander in chief").

It was common in the ancient world to associate one's deity with military struggle, and in the polytheistic religious context of the ancient Near East the battles were frequently between the gods themselves rather than directed toward humans.[1] In one of the most famous of these tales, the Babylonian "Enūma Elish," the battle between the primordial gods and the other gods is recorded and results in Marduk's victory and the creation of the cosmos. There are, however, examples of deities targeting humans. From Egypt there is a text known as "The Destruction of Mankind" in which the god Re arranges for the destruction of those people who were plotting against him.[2]

In the Old Testament, military language is commonly used of God. One prominent example is the song declaring God's victory over the Egyptian army in Exodus 15:1–3. Note especially the reference to the Yahweh as a "warrior" (the Hebrew may be rendered woodenly "man of war"). In using such language and concepts of God, Job has a long tradition behind him, even if the specific enemy in this instance is an individual human.

The surprising thing about Job, however, is that he turns the military metaphor on its head. Instead of using this language to depict God as one who defends his supposed ally, Job uses it to depict God as the one who attacks him. This, however, is not entirely unparalleled in the Old Testament. The prophets depict Yahweh attacking his people, proclaiming to the people that Yahweh is coming in judgment against his people with the might of an invading army. The stark difference for Job, however, is that Job is blameless whereas Judah was guilty.

EXPLAIN the Story

Job Rebukes His Friends (16:1–7a)

Job responds to Eliphaz for the second time but directs his words to all three of the friends. Here he trades sarcasm for blunt and direct speech: they are miserable comforters whose longwinded speeches go on and on with no relief. The act of shaking one's head that Job refers to in verse 4 is here an act of mockery (see 2 Kgs 19:21; Ps 22:7; Matt 27:39). Yet Job makes the point that if they traded places, if he were the one who had come to comfort them in their troubles, then he would speak words of encouragement and relief.

1. The distinction is complicated, particularly in Egypt where Pharaoh was considered divine, so that human battles were thus implicitly fought by a divine warrior.

2. "The Destruction of Mankind" (Egyptian), trans. Miriam Lichtheim (*COS* 1.24:36–37).

Job, in making this point, shows that his desire would be that his friends would do this for him, yet they do not.

In contrast to the way Job would speak if he and his friends could change places, he notes how neither speaking nor remaining silent from where he is, in the midst of pain and suffering, offer him comfort. Job feels that his words are powerless to change his life and that silence will make no difference. Job's powerlessness here leads into his view of the way God has dealt with him in the next stanza.

The first part of verse 7 serves as a transition to the next section. Though the NIV has Job addressing God directly in verse 7a (supplying "you" and the word "God" to specify the subject), in Hebrew Job speaks of God in the third person, "*he* has worn me out"; the shift to singular marks a segue into direct speech to God, in which Job lists the attacks he feels that God has made on him. The words "surely now" that open verse 7 serve both to mark a contrast with that which has been said before and to highlight for the reader that Job has reached the end of his tether. God has now worn him out; he is exhausted and cannot continue (although he will continue nonetheless).

Job Addresses God as His Enemy (16:7b–17)

In the second half of verse 7, Job turns to speak directly to God. While the Hebrew text does not explicitly mention God, the shift from plurals in the previous verses to the singular in this section marks a change from addressing the friends to God, although by verse 9 Job reverts to speaking about God in the third person, perhaps feeling that his words are falling on deaf ears.

Job lists the things he believes God has done to him through verses 7b–14. He has devastated his entire household (the word encompasses more than just his children and recalls the events of the prologue wherein Job's servants were also wiped out). There are a number of difficulties in understanding the precise meaning of the Hebrew for much of verse 8, but the gist of the text is captured by the NIV. Job's emaciated state, a result no doubt of his illness and suffering, stands as witness against him.

What does he mean by this? How is his physical condition a witness against him? Both Job and his friends hold to the idea that God operates in this world according to a strict application of retributive justice. Those who suffer deserve to be suffering because of some offence they have committed. Hence, to Job's friends at least, his physical condition reflects his guilt. Job does not dispute this idea; what he questions is God's apparently unreliable application of this rule. So, for Job, his physical condition stands as witness against his innocence.

Verse 9 switches back to referring to God in the third person, describing him as a wild animal who attacks Job (similar imagery is used of God in Hos 5:14; 6:1). God is also described here as an "adversary" (the word here is *tsar*, not the word *satan* used in the prologue, which was used as a title to describe the supernatural adversary who prompted God to attack Job). As Job's adversary, God—like a predator—has locked his eyes on Job, his prey. Tying these images together, Job makes it clear that God is his opponent who attacks him as a wild carnivore attacks its prey. The imagery highlights just how powerless and victimized Job feels at this point.

In the midst of Job's words about God he reflects momentarily on the way he has been treated by other people (Job 16:10). The switch is subtle. In Hebrew it is only indicated by the switch from singular to plural verb, essentially "they [men] open their mouths." His treatment at the hands of other people is, for Job, ultimately an outworking of God's treatment of him anyway, a point he clarifies by noting that he has fallen into the hands of evil people only because God has put him there (v. 11).

The next few verses use wartime imagery of God's attack on Job. The "neck" (v. 12) is a place where one can be yoked and so held captive (e.g., Deut 28:48). From Job's perspective, he is the target of God's attacks; the odds against him are overwhelming and his inevitable fate is death (Job 16:13). That Job's kidneys are a particular target reflects the severity of the attack—the kidneys are both essential to life and the seat of a person's emotions in Hebrew thought (see Job 19:27 where "kidneys" [NIV "heart"] is used to represent Job's deepest desire). Today such a play on words might be made by writing something like "his axe broke my heart." The military imagery concludes with God breaking through the city walls that metaphorically represent Job's defenses.

"Sackcloth" (v. 15) is a traditional sign of mourning and reminds us of Job's losses in the opening chapters, which understandably prompt his mourning. "Dust" may remind us of the friends' initial response upon sighting Job (Job 2:12), although here Job's "horn" (*qeren*, NIV "brow") is buried in the dust. The horn is often symbolic of strength and power (e.g., Jer 48:25), and so the metaphor here expresses more than Job's head being covered in dust (as would be appropriate in mourning) but goes further and speaks of his strength and power being lost as well.

Mourning is accompanied by grief in Job 16:16, and so Job describes his grief through its physical effects, where his tears have reddened his face and darkened his eyes. Job closes these verses noting just why his grief and despair are so great—they are undeserved. Job's claim to have committed no violence and to have prayed what is pure are reminiscent of the acts of the suffering servant of Isaiah, of whom we are told:

> He was assigned a grave with the wicked,
> and with the rich in his death,
> though he had done no violence,
> nor was there any deceit in his mouth. (Isa 53:9)

Job's innocence makes the suffering all the more unbearable. It is not as though he knows he deserves all that has happened—quite the reverse.

Job's Heartfelt Desire for an Intercessor (16:18–17:1)

The final verses of chapter 16 have Job contemplating his impending death. That he believes he shall soon die has already been revealed (e.g., Job 7:21; 10:20–22). The image of his blood spilt on the earth and crying out in 16:18 is reminiscent of Abel's blood crying out from the ground (Gen 4:10). In essence Job is pleading that he not be allowed to die and be forgotten. Formally, Job here seems to express a desire that his vindication take place even if he dies first (when his blood is on the ground), but at the heart of the plea is first that he would be vindicated, and second that it would take place soon.

At this point (Job 16:19) we are met by a somewhat surprising expression of hope from Job, hope that there is someone to stand up to God and argue his case. He appears confident that there is a witness, an advocate, an intercessor who will stand before God and plead his case. This intercessor is his friend and pleads with God with all the vigor that a friend would plead (vv. 20–21).

Part of the surprise is that Job had previously expressed hope for a mediator with the realization that there was no one to fulfill that position (9:33–34). Has Job now changed his mind? It is certainly possible. Job has persisted in calling upon God to answer him despite making it clear that he knows that he would not be able to stand before God and answer him, suggesting that Job can be prone to waver in his certitude over various matters. Of this we ought not to be surprised, for under the extraordinary circumstances in which Job finds himself, who would not struggle to sustain completely consistent thought?

There is another reading, however, that makes better sense of the passage. Job has opened verse 18 by expressing a desire that his blood would not be covered before he is vindicated, and so he has set the tone that this section expresses his desires as opposed to stating something that will be certainly accomplished. He does not know that he will be vindicated; rather, he only wishes that it would happen. In light of this, it is best to read the "also" (*gam*; NIV "even") in verse 19 as a continuation of this desire, this wish.[3] Thus Job hopes that he will be vindicated before he dies (if not soon after), and he hopes that this can be achieved now by someone to represent him before God in heaven.

This understanding also has in its favor the fact that no mediator ever appears for Job and that it fits well with Job's earlier expression of hope that there might be a mediator to stand before God on his behalf in 9:33–34.

But who is this intercessor? A common claim is that the intercessor is God himself. While theologically tempting, the conclusion is difficult to sustain from the text itself. Job has just identified God as his enemy (16:7–17), and this intercessor pleads with God, a point from which the original reader of Job (living before Christ) would have inferred that it must be someone other than God.

As readers living after the cross, we might also be tempted simply to conclude that the intercessor is obviously Jesus. And we would not be wrong, except in so much as to say that there is no way that this answer would have occurred to either Job himself, the author of the book, or to the original readers of the book of Job.

However, if we are to understand these words as an expression of hope on Job's part rather than a statement of certainty, then the precise identity of the witness in heaven is of less import. Job simply hopes that there would be someone on his side in heaven who would argue his case as a friend and obtain justice for him before God, for he has recognized that he cannot do it himself.

The chapter closes with Job reiterating his belief that he does not have long to live. His reference to a small number of years remaining should not be pushed too literally—it is not as if Job knows that he has years and not months to live. Instead, it presents a stark contrast to God who, according to 36:26, has years without number.

Job continues in his bleak assessment of his future in 16:22–17:1. That his spirit is broken is likely not a statement that he has lost the will to fight but rather another way to say that he sees death approaching (see 12:10 where "spirit" [*ruakh*; NIV "breath"] is parallel to "life" [*nephesh*]). His next destination is the grave.

Job Complains of God's Treatment of Him (17:2–9)

In 17:2–9, Job turns from speaking about his impending demise to the way he is being treated by those around him. The "mockers" around him must refer

3. There are no verbs in the Hebrew of Job 16:19. This, together with the particle "also" suggest that the verbal sense of verse 18 ought to continue to apply in verse 19.

to, at the very least, his friends, for they do not listen or take Job seriously. Job repeatedly characterizes those around him as mocking him (see 11:3; 21:3; 30:1, 9).[4]

In 17:3–4 Job addresses a single person. His subsequent words make it clear that he is now addressing God directly. A "pledge" here is a surety to be reclaimed once a task is fulfilled or a debt repaid (see Gen 38:17–20). It would appear that Job believes that he must pay a bond to secure the opportunity to prove his innocence, for there is no one else to do it. In part this comes down to God's actions, for in Job's mind it is God who has prompted his friends to mock him by preventing them from comprehending the truth.

The purpose of verse 5 is not immediately clear. David Clines suggests that it is likely to be a traditional proverb quoted by Job.[5] Regardless of its origin, the reason it appears here is difficult to determine. Who is the man who denounces his friends? It is most likely that Job is quoting a proverb to make the point that the behavior of unfaithful friends will ultimately come back to bite them. Job seems to alternate his attention between God and his friends over these verses, but that likely reflects his feeling that God and his friends are together his opponents.

So, in verse 6 Job switches to speaking about God in the third person, once again laying the blame for his predicament squarely on God, who has made him a "byword." The Hebrew word here is the verb form of the noun often translated as "proverb" (indeed, the Hebrew name for the book of Proverbs is the plural form of this noun). Already within Job's lifetime, his suffering had become proverbial, although the second half of the verse suggests that what was known to those around him was in accord with the claims of his friends that he stubbornly refused to repent of sin. As such, people spit in his face, and for Job this is a direct result of God's treatment of him.

The expression "my eyes have grown dim with grief" (17:7) could easily be interpreted as meaning that Job's eyesight was failing (and quite a few commentators take it this way).[6] The idea would then be prompted by the reference to eyes failing in verse 5. However, the two verses use different language, and so the meaning of this expression should not be controlled by that. This is perhaps better understood to mean that Job's eyes had become

---

4. The Hebrew word here, *hatulim*, which is found only here in the Hebrew Bible, is different from those found in the other verses listed (the verbs *l'g* [11:3; 21:3] and *skhq* [30:1] and the noun *neginah* [30:9]), but the meaning overlaps.

5. Clines, *Job 1–20*, 395; Hartley, *Book of Job*, 269.

6. E.g. Hartley, *Book of Job*, 269; Lindsay Wilson, *Job*, Two Horizons Old Testament Commentary (Grand Rapids: Eerdmans, 2015), 99.

inexpressive.[7] In modern parlance we might say that he had cried so much that he had run out of tears.

Verses 8–9 make reference to the upright and the righteous but do so using verbs that should probably be read modally as, "the upright *would be* appalled at this" rather than understood to imply that there is some group of upright people to whom Job may appeal. The point is made clear when Job turns to address his friends directly in the next verse: the upright would be appalled, but now let us hear from you again! Job backs this up in verse 9 by noting that the righteous remain steadfast in their view (they "hold to their ways"), maintaining their view in the face of ridicule. They do not participate in the ridicule and closed-mindedness of the friends. Indeed, were there any such upright, righteous people impartially looking on at Job and his friends, Job feels confident that they would only be strengthened in their conviction (they will, in the words of verse 9, "grow stronger").

Job Surrenders His Hope (17:10–16)

Job concludes his speech by goading his friends to continue in their ways but makes it clear that he does not believe they are wise. He is past caring, considering his life to be all but over (v. 11). The NIV treats the following words as an expression of some hope, as it has Job stating that the desires of his heart can turn night into day and suggesting that the time of his suffering may soon come to an end. Yet, this does not fit the context well, particularly with the words that follow. Rather, "the desires of my heart" should be understood as parallel to "my plans" in the preceding clause, such that Job is stating that his plans, the desires of his heart, have been shattered. Verse 12 should then be read as explaining what his plans and desires could have done: "they would have turned night into day." Job had hopes and plans that things would turn around and night be turned into day, but they have been shattered. He no longer has any hope.

To make this even clearer, Job poses a question. The hypothetical part of the question for Job is not about whether he will make Sheol his home—he certainly believes that to be true. Rather, knowing that Sheol will soon be his home, the hypothetical part of the question comes as Job asks whether he then has any hope (v. 15). It needs to be noted here that verse 14 parallels verse 13. The word translated by the NIV as "corruption" in verse 14 renders a Hebrew noun (*shakhat*) most commonly translated "the pit." This mirrors the reference to the "grave" (Sheol) in verse 13. Although verse 16 is phrased

7. See "כהה," *HALOT* 461; note also the use of the *piel* form to mean "colorless" in Lev 13:6, 56.

as two questions in the NIV, it is better to read them as a statement about what has happened to Job's hope. His hope will descend to the gates of Sheol if he does: "If I go to Sheol, so too goes any hope I have."

LIVE the Story

Compassion for the Powerless and Weak

To this point, a lot has been said by both Job and his friends. Through all this, it has become apparent to Job that his words are powerless. From his perspective, nothing he can say makes any difference to his situation—"If I speak, my pain is not relieved; and if I refrain [from speaking], it does not go away" (16:6). Before this all began, Job was used to his words having an impact, making a difference. He sat at the town gate where he was respected and heard, where his words did make a difference (see 29:7–11). Job has experienced life at both the top and the bottom of society, and he has come to understand how power, respect, and status are linked. It is a true reflection of the way in which human society has treated people throughout time. Even today, in the most affluent countries in the world, there are many at the bottom of society who have no voice, for whom Job's experience is true. If they speak, their pain is not relieved, and if they refrain from speaking, it does not go away.

And it is not hard to find people living in precisely that situation all around us from those who through all manner of circumstances are forced to live on the street to those we simply see as too different to be accepted into mainstream society. There are voices in society that argue that such people have only themselves to blame for their situation. Some believe that such people are serial victims who through laziness have chosen to rely on government handouts and that they could, if they simply put their minds to it, escape the situation they have chosen to live in. Some believe that the opportunities are there for the taking for all of us, and so those who are at the bottom of society deserve no special treatment. In the case of some people, certainly a very few, there may be some truth to this. But for the majority, these claims rightly ring hollow and reflect more the thinking of Job's friends than that of either Job himself—now that he has learned the hard way—or even of God.

Job's life is a loud rebuke to such thinking. How could we claim that he is where he is and could readily escape his suffering if only he put his mind to it? That runs counter to everything we know about him, and to what God has said about him in the prologue. Conversely, it parrots the claims of his friends, who argue that it is in Job's power to acknowledge his sins and repent and be restored. Yet we will hear at the end of the book that they are wrong in this thinking. No, Job is not where he is because of his own actions or choices, and he does not remain in the state he is through lack of motivation or action on his part. He is trapped there with no way of escape, just as many today are trapped in poverty or desperate circumstances. We are not masters of the universe, or even our own small parts of the universe. Job is not able to escape simply through putting an end to his complaining and seizing the opportunities that are presented to him. His words are powerless, and unless we feel the weight of this powerlessness, we have missed the pathos of the speeches of Job and need to return to the beginning and start again.

What could possibly help the powerless? Job comes to realize by the end of chapter 16 that there is at least one answer: the intervention of a powerful mediator, one who can be heard, one who can plead for him as a friend would, one who is of sufficient status to have a voice that will be heard, one of sufficient power such that God will take notice (16:19–21). It is a valid conclusion, and true for the powerless today. They have no hope in their own capacity to escape their circumstances, but if only there were someone who could intervene on their behalf, then they would have some hope of escape. In the material world that hope might be manifest through charities, family, friends, churches, or government social supports. It might be found in the provision of social housing, or the microloans made to the impoverished to give them a chance to escape their poverty.

Spiritually, the situation is even more broadly applicable. We are, Paul tells us, dead in our trespasses and sins (Eph 2:1). The dead are clearly powerless and so have no hope of being able to rescue themselves from that state. So, we are all utterly dependent upon outside help if we are to have any hope of finding life, and we all need someone who is powerful enough to be able to rescue us. It is not possible to tell the dead to fix their own problems. Fortunately, the one who is powerful enough to rescue us does intervene and offer us life. For those who believe that we have sufficient power within ourselves to effect our own salvation, this whole line of thinking is difficult to accept, just as Job's friends found it difficult to accept that Job could not, through repentance and confession, persuade God to restore him to his previous state.

While Job realizes that his best hope for vindication before God would be to have a friend who could stand up before God in heaven and plead his case, he also believes that there is no such person who could do this. Yet, in this he is anticipating the coming of one who would be able to do exactly what Job realized was needed. While Job's problem was not his own sin—that much was made abundantly clear in the prologue of the book—he nonetheless lacked representation in the heavenly court and so struggled to bring his case before God. In this way Job's hope ultimately anticipated the intercessory work of Jesus, who would bring about reconciliation between human beings and their Creator.

For each of us, however, our biggest problem is sin. It alienates us from God, and it leaves us powerless before him. God clearly concurs with Job's logic here. We who were powerless to come before God needed someone who has a voice in the heavens, who has the power to restore us from being dead in our transgressions and sins, and who could restore us to our place in God's family. Thanks be to God for the Lord Jesus, the mediator he appointed, "for there is one God and one mediator between God and mankind, the man Christ Jesus" (1 Tim 2:5).

CHAPTER 11

Job 18

Bildad's Second Speech

LISTEN to the Story

1Then Bildad the Shuhite replied:

2"When will you end these speeches?
Be sensible, and then we can talk.
3Why are we regarded as cattle
and considered stupid in your sight?
4You who tear yourself to pieces in your anger,
is the earth to be abandoned for your sake?
Or must the rocks be moved from their place?

5"The lamp of a wicked man is snuffed out;
the flame of his fire stops burning.
6The light in his tent becomes dark;
the lamp beside him goes out.
7The vigor of his step is weakened;
his own schemes throw him down.
8His feet thrust him into a net;
he wanders into its mesh.
9A trap seizes him by the heel;
a snare holds him fast.
10A noose is hidden for him on the ground;
a trap lies in his path.
11Terrors startle him on every side
and dog his every step.
12Calamity is hungry for him;
disaster is ready for him when he falls.
13It eats away parts of his skin;

death's firstborn devours his limbs.
14He is torn from the security of his tent
and marched off to the king of terrors.
15Fire resides in his tent;
burning sulfur is scattered over his dwelling.
16His roots dry up below
and his branches wither above.
17The memory of him perishes from the earth;
he has no name in the land.
18He is driven from light into the realm of darkness
and is banished from the world.
19He has no offspring or descendants among his people,
no survivor where once he lived.
20People of the west are appalled at his fate;
those of the east are seized with horror.
21Surely such is the dwelling of an evil man;
such is the place of one who does not know God."

Listening to the Text in the Story: "Descent of Ishtar to the Nether World" (Babylonian); "The Ba'lu Myth" (Ugaritic)

Bildad's speech makes a rather obscure reference in verse 14 to the "king of terrors." It turns out that the meaning of this phrase might be elucidated by the ancient Near Eastern context in which Job's story is situated. Nahum Sarna, building on earlier work by William Irwin, argues that the term "terrors" in the phrase "king of terrors" that appears in Job 18:14 should be understood as a reference to the ruler of the underworld or Sheol, based on similar terms found in the Babylonian tale of "The Descent of Ishtar to the Underworld" where Ereshkigal reigns as queen of the "land of no return."[1] The relevant portion of that text reads:

> To Kurnugi, land of [no return],
> Ishtar daughter of Sin was [determined] to go;
> . . .

1. A strong association between "terrors" and the underworld is made in the text "A Vision of the Nether World," which includes the line, "the nether world was filled with terror" (see "A Vision of the Nether World," trans. E. A. Speiser [*ANET*, 110]).

Ishtar, when she arrived at the gate of Kurnugi,
Addressed her words to the keeper of the gate,
"Here gatekeeper, open your gate for me,
Open your gate for me to come in!
If you do not open the gate for me to come in,
I shall smash the door and shatter the bolt,
I shall smash the doorpost and overturn the doors,
I shall raise up the dead and they shall eat the living:
The dead shall outnumber the living!"
The gatekeeper made his voice heard and spoke,
He said to great Ishtar,
"Stop, lady, do not break it down!
Let me go and report your words to queen Ereshkigal."[2]

While Irwin recognized that Bildad's reference to a king where the Babylonian text described a queen seems to undermine Sarna's claim, Sarna noted that the book of Job tends to reflect some degree of conflation of a number of ancient Near Eastern cosmological and theological ideas, and so the disparity in gender between Bildad's ruler and the Babylonian does not, in fact, pose any particular problem for allowing the one to inform our understanding of the other. For this, Sarna notes that Cassuto had also suggested that the phrase "death's firstborn" (*bekor mawet*, woodenly, "firstborn of death") in verse 13 may be a reference to "the firstborn of Môt," Môt being the Canaanite deity who ruled the underworld (i.e., the Canaanite equivalent to Sheol).[3] If these references are accepted, then the "firstborn of Môt" of verse 13 would be a reference to Môt's first child, who corresponds to the deity Namtar in Babylonian mythology, a demon of evil fate whose task was the conveying of souls into the underworld.[4]

Furthering these connections is a Ugaritic reference to Môt devouring his victims, as noted:

2. "The Descent of Ishtar to the Underworld," trans. Stephanie Dalley (*COS* 1.108:381).

3. Nahum M. Sarna, "The Mythological Background of Job 18," *JBL* 82.3 (1963): 316; William A. Irwin, "Job's Redeemer," *JBL* 81.3 (1962): 217–29; U. Cassuto, *The Goddess Anath*, trans. Israel Abrahams (Jerusalem: Magnes, 1971), 63. See also Clines, *Job 1–20*, 417; John Barclay Burns, "The Mythological Background to Job 18,5–61," *BeO* 33.3 (1991): 129–40; Nicholas Wyatt, "The Expression Bĕkôr Māwet in Job XVIII 13 and Its Mythological Background," *VT* 40.2 (1990): 207–16. The Hebrew word *mot* is translated by English versions as "death."

4. See John Barclay Burns, "The Identity of Death's First-Born (Job XVIII 13)," *VT* 37.3 (1987): 363.

> But take care, divine servants:
> Do not get too close to Divine Mot,
> Lest he take you like a lamb in his mouth,
> Like a kid, you be crushed in the chasm of his throat.[5]

The imagery found in this text and in Job 18:13 is reflected elsewhere in the Old Testament (e.g., Isa 5:14; Hab 2:5). Bildad is using these ideas to instill the dread over the fate of the wicked (see Job 18:5) in Job: the wicked one's perilous fate includes being devoured by the demonic forces of Sheol. Sarna summarizes Bildad's words as:

> In short, what Bildad is saying is that Môt, king of the nether world, sends his first-born as his emissary to slay the unrighteous one and to march him off to the infernal regions. The world of the wicked collapses about him and dissolves into oblivion.[6]

In New Testament terms adjusted to modern parlance, he might have said to Job, "You're on a highway to hell, and when you get there, your present suffering will be as nothing compared to what you shall then experience."

As we have noted previously, the inclusion of such ideas in the account of Job ought not to surprise us since the story is set outside of Israel in the time of the patriarchs. Job's original audience would have understood the ideas conveyed within the text even if they did not endorse the theology that underpinned those ideas in their original contexts. What these do highlight, however, is the strength of this imagery that the author of the story of Job has included in this text.

EXPLAIN the Story

The Fate of the Wicked (18:1–21)

Bildad's second speech is largely occupied with a poetic account of the fate of the wicked man. He makes his thinking clear, and it is quite simplistic in its application of the doctrine of strict retribution: the good are blessed and the wicked are punished, and it all happens in the here and now.

---

5. *KTU* 1.4:8, lines 14–20. See Mark S. Smith and Wayne T. Pitard, *The Ugaritic Baal Cycle*, 2 vols., VTSup 114 (Leiden: Brill, 2009), 2:703–4.

6. Sarna, "Mythological Background of Job 18," 318.

There are at least two ways that this could be read in the context of his debate with Job. He could be implying that Job is a wicked man and so his current predicament and future life reflect that of the wicked that he describes in his speech.[7] Alternatively, he could be issuing a warning to Job that he is in danger of becoming like the wicked he describes, and so the fate he describes may ultimately become his.[8]

There is little standing between these two options. The fact that he tells Job that he must think about what they have said before they can have further discussion (18:3), together with the fact that many of Job's present circumstances are reflected in the descriptions made by Bildad throughout this chapter, suggest at the very least that Bildad thinks Job is among the wicked, yet his leaving open the option for further discussion also makes it clear that he has not given up all hope for Job.

Although it appears that Bildad's first words in verse 2 are addressed to Job, the verbs are plural and so a more natural inference is to understand them as addressed to both Job and the other friends. The NIV's "be sensible" here might be read as more pejorative than necessary, and it is better to read the Hebrew's meaning along the lines of "you should all understand this, and then we can talk." Bildad is making an appeal to Job and his friends to listen to what he has to say now and understand it. He seems to think that what he is about to say should put an end to the debate—if he is listened to and understood there will be nothing more the friends need to add and nothing to which Job can object.

In verse 3, however, Bildad reverts to addressing Job alone. Cattle were proverbially stupid (see Ps 73:22), and Bildad feels that Job's failure to take heed of their arguments is an indication that he does not treat them with the respect that they deserve—he is treating them as though they were as stupid as cattle. Rather, Job's anger is self-destructive, and his expectations are, according to Bildad, an inversion of the moral order of the universe tantamount to the land (NIV "earth"; Hebrew uses the same word, *'erets*, to mean "earth" or "land") being abandoned just for him, or like expecting a boulder or perhaps even a rocky hill to be moved from one place to another. The essence of his objection here is that Job's expectations lie against the natural order of things.

Bildad turns from directly addressing either Job or his friends to a description of the lot of the wicked in an extended poetic discourse in verses 5–21,

---

7. So, for example, Roland E. Murphy, *Wisdom Literature: Job, Proverbs, Ruth, Canticles, Ecclesiastes, and Esther*, FOTL 13 (Grand Rapids: Eerdmans, 1981), 32.

8. So, for example, Clines, *Job 1–20*, 409.

a discourse laced with metaphors. The substance of these words is simply that the wicked invariably suffer the consequences of their actions.

The first two verses (vv. 5–6) appeal to the metaphor of the lamp (remembering that fire was the only man made source of light in the ancient world). The metaphor itself appears elsewhere (see Job 21:17; Prov 13:9) and its meaning is quite broad, with light ultimately a reference to life as opposed to the darkness of death. In Job 18:5–6 the lamp being snuffed out thus ultimately presents the notion that the wicked, if not already dead, are as good as dead. The verbs throughout the remainder of this chapter should probably be read as future—"The lamp of the wicked man will be snuffed out" (NLT)—rather than the present (NIV). For Bildad, premature death is the inevitable fate of the wicked.

Verses 7–10 revolve around the idea of tripping one's feet. The opening verse associates the traps for the wicked person's feet with their own advice (NIV "schemes," v. 7), reminding us of the strong link between action and punishment in Bildad's thought.

Along with these consequences of wickedness, Bildad adds that the wicked will be terrified, presumably by the increasing awareness of the consequences of their actions. Calamity devours the wicked person, and the idea of hunger continues to eat away at the skin of the wicked. "Death's firstborn" (v. 13; see Listening to the Text of the Story above) gives a terrifying image of the inevitable fate of the wicked slowly gnawing away at their body until they succumb. These terrors culminate in verse 14 with an encounter with the "king of terrors"—death itself.[9]

Having been taken from his earthly dwelling (his "tent"), all trace of his existence is eradicated as fire burns in his tent and it is covered in "sulfur" (v. 15, what older translations rendered as "brimstone"). There is nothing left for others to take up or occupy, nothing to be inherited from the wicked. Neither "roots" nor "branches" (v. 16) or, more concretely put, children or "descendants" (v. 19) remain, nor even a "memory" (v. 17), so complete is his eradication from the earth.

Bildad's speech concludes with the impact of the destruction of the wicked on the onlooker. The reference in verse 20 to people of both the east and west is a poetic way to say that everyone is appalled at the fate of the wicked, so overwhelming is it in Bildad's depiction. And for Bildad, this is the path on which Job is traveling.

---

9. For more of the complex background to this section, see Listening to the Text of the Story above.

LIVE the Story

Strong Emotions and Sin

Bildad's second speech is noticeably shorter than his first, a trend that will continue as the back and forth of the speeches continues through the first half of the book. Unlike his previous speech, this time Bildad makes virtually no mention of God at all, referring to him only near the end in verse 21, and there only as part of a descriptive label for the wicked person (i.e., "one who does not know God"). The bulk of Bildad's speech describes the fate of the wicked, real fire-and-brimstone preaching (in Job 18:15 he even uses the same word used in Gen 19:24 to describe the burning sulfur that rained down on Sodom and Gomorrah). The picture he paints is indeed bleak: the wicked person is destined to deteriorate physically, fall into traps, be terrified by all manner of things, and ultimately be taken away to Sheol, leaving behind no family, no progeny to carry on a legacy, nothing. Such is the fate of the wicked that all who see it are appalled. It is difficult not to see in Bildad's words a representation so extreme that it clearly does not accord with reality—clearly some of the wicked do have descendants, some prosper, and some live long lives. That much is apparent from other wisdom literature such as Ecclesiastes where Qoheleth (the title given the speaker in the book) struggles to comprehend the absurdity of his observations that the wicked do sometimes prosper while the righteous sometimes fall. This ought to have been enough for Bildad and his friends to have identified a substantial flaw in their argument, but perhaps it indicates that they have lived sheltered lives!

On the other hand, Bildad's description of the fate of the wicked does accord with the larger view of the fate of the wicked that is revealed through the remainder of the Bible. The book of Isaiah ends with a view that for the wicked who rebelled against God "the worms that eat them will not die, the fire that burns them will not be quenched, and they will be loathsome to all mankind" (Isa 66:24). Later still we hear from Jesus that those who do not know him "will go away to eternal punishment" (Matt 25:46) while John writes in Revelation that "anyone whose name was not found written in the book of life was thrown into the lake of fire" (Rev 20:15). Bildad unknowingly, it would seem, given his place in history, speaks with some truth on the eschatological fate of the wicked who persist in rebelling against God. We would have to acknowledge that his theology is consistent with the biblical witness; what he says of the wicked is—at least in one sense—true. The fate he describes may not befall those who rebel against God in this life, but they shall not escape it when they ultimately face judgment on the day that is coming.

Because of this, we might think that Bildad has a good point and that he is speaking biblical truth. However, where Bildad fails—again—is in his application of his theology. First, his description of the fate of the wicked does not correspond to the actual experience *in this life* of many wicked or, for that matter, innocent people. Good things do sometimes happen to bad people, and bad things happen to good people, to people who do profess deep trust in God and live with Jesus as their Lord. Second, and more immediately relevant, the application of his theology completely misses the mark when applied to Job. Bildad continues to get things backward by assuming that circumstances in this life attest to one's spiritual standing before God. If there is anything we should be learning from Job, it is that this is not true. We cannot look around and see someone suffering and conclude that they must be wicked.

And that, ultimately, is the lesson to be drawn from Bildad here. We might be tempted to judge others based on their circumstances. For Bildad and the friends of Job here, the response of Job to his suffering: his questioning of God, his anger, his failure to follow their advice to confess sin and repent, all serve as evidence to bolster their belief in his guilt. If he continues down this path, then he will go down to Sheol and share the fate of all the wicked. But they never stop to consider that there might be some truth to Job's claims, and so they end up labeling as sin that which never was sin. Is it a sin to cry out to God, to open up to him about one's innermost feelings?

The answer to that is not straightforward, and if we are angry or upset or disappointed, there is doubtless a line that can be crossed beyond which these do become sinful. I like to quote a saying I have dubbed "Shields's Axiom," which is simply that "the truth lies halfway down the slippery slope." There is a place for expressing such things, for hiding them from God is pointless, so there is no way to bottle them up and pretend God is not aware of them. This idea is found in some advice found in the pages of the Bible. For example, we are told, "In your anger do not sin" (Eph 4:26), a piece of advice that implies that it is possible to be angry and *not* sin.

In many cultures people are uncomfortable with strong expressions of emotion, and there can be a tendency to label that with which we are uncomfortable as sin. And there is no doubt that Job does express a whole range of emotions and express them strongly. It does not, however, make Job's words or actions sinful just because we, or his friends, are uncomfortable with them. If we look beyond Job, we find confronting expressions of emotion throughout the Bible. One clear and confronting example is Psalm 137:8–9:

> Daughter Babylon, doomed to destruction,
> happy is the one who repays you
> according to what you have done to us.
> Happy is the one who seizes your infants
> and dashes them against the rocks.

Peering beyond a superficial reading of these words, we are invited to feel the author's pain, for the horrific image of infants being dashed against rocks is not merely one imagined for the author; it has happened to them at the hands of the Babylonians. The words are confronting because they seek to convey the intensity of the experience of the Israelites whose infants had suffered the fate here wished upon those who had inflicted this on them.

Beyond this we find Jesus himself expressing intense emotions that we may well be uncomfortable with (e.g., Matt 21:12–13; 26:37–38; Mark 3:5; Luke 14:21). Jesus's actions could even be said to be violent as he overturned the tables in the temple precinct, tables presumably sanctioned by those who administered the temple. To many onlookers this act would have appeared to be opposed to the religious order of the day, his actions seeming excessive and out of control. But do we label as sin that which God does not so label? That is the danger we face when we too quickly judge strong emotional expression as sinful—whether it be anger, sorrow, or any other emotion.

Job's friends judge Job guilty of some sin which initially invoked his suffering and then of further sin in his response to his suffering. On both counts they were wrong. Their failure can all too easily be our failure, and hence the wise person is slow to speak and slow to judge the other. May God forgive us all for the times we have failed at this.

CHAPTER 12

Job 19

Job's Second Reply to Bildad

LISTEN to the Story

1Then Job replied:

2"How long will you torment me
and crush me with words?
3Ten times now you have reproached me;
shamelessly you attack me.
4If it is true that I have gone astray,
my error remains my concern alone.
5If indeed you would exalt yourselves above me
and use my humiliation against me,
6then know that God has wronged me
and drawn his net around me.

7"Though I cry, 'Violence!' I get no response;
though I call for help, there is no justice.
8He has blocked my way so I cannot pass;
he has shrouded my paths in darkness.
9He has stripped me of my honor
and removed the crown from my head.
10He tears me down on every side till I am gone;
he uproots my hope like a tree.
11His anger burns against me;
he counts me among his enemies.
12His troops advance in force;
they build a siege ramp against me
and encamp around my tent.

13"He has alienated my family from me;
my acquaintances are completely estranged from me.
14My relatives have gone away;
my closest friends have forgotten me.
15My guests and my female servants count me a foreigner;
they look on me as on a stranger.
16I summon my servant, but he does not answer,
though I beg him with my own mouth.
17My breath is offensive to my wife;
I am loathsome to my own family.
18Even the little boys scorn me;
when I appear, they ridicule me.
19All my intimate friends detest me;
those I love have turned against me.
20I am nothing but skin and bones;
I have escaped only by the skin of my teeth.

21"Have pity on me, my friends, have pity,
for the hand of God has struck me.
22Why do you pursue me as God does?
Will you never get enough of my flesh?

23"Oh, that my words were recorded,
that they were written on a scroll,
24that they were inscribed with an iron tool on lead,
or engraved in rock forever!
25I know that my redeemer lives,
and that in the end he will stand on the earth.
26And after my skin has been destroyed,
yet in my flesh I will see God;
27I myself will see him
with my own eyes—I, and not another.
How my heart yearns within me!

28"If you say, 'How we will hound him,
since the root of the trouble lies in him,'

[29]you should fear the sword yourselves;
for wrath will bring punishment by the sword,
and then you will know that there is judgment."

Listening to the Text in the Story: "A Sumerian stele from Lagash"; a funerary inscription from "Khirbet el-Qom"; "The Behistun Inscription"

This response by Job contains some of the book's most famous words—"I know that my redeemer lives" (Job 19:25). They are included in Handel's major work, *The Messiah*, and can similarly be found in other more recent musical works.[1] They are accorded profound significance by many, seeing here an expression of Job's own immutable faith in God such that he expresses—somewhat surprisingly—his unwavering confidence that, in the end, God will come through for him.

However, there are a number of problems raised by this understanding of Job's words here, and their context within the book of Job and in the ancient world will help us interpret Job more accurately and should make us hesitant to leap to any conclusions about the meaning of Job's words based on modern traditions.

First, Job's reference in verse 6 to God having "drawn his net around me" presents a metaphor depicted visually on a Sumerian stele from King Eannatum of Lagash. This stone pillar presents an image of the deity Ningirsu, below whom is a net filled with the bodies of naked men.[2]

Second, Matthew Suriano has pointed out some relevant material from ancient Israel related to funerary rites or burial practices that has a bearing on how we ought to read these rather famous words from Job.[3] As he says,

> In vv. 23–24, the terms "inscription" and "rock" in the parallel verses are both objects of the verbs "engrave" and "hew," respectively, and together they describe a single location of writing that is consistent with a tomb inscription. This idea is described again in v. 24b, where the permanency of writing Job's words is ensured by its locus, the "rock," and the use

1. See Seow, *Job 1–21*, 793, for some examples.

2. Izak Cornelius, "Job," in *The Minor Prophets, Job, Psalms, Proverbs, Ecclesiastes, Song of Songs*, ZIBBCOT (Grand Rapids: Zondervan Academic, 2009), 5:274.

3. Matthew J. Suriano, "Death, Disinheritance, and Job's Kinsman-Redeemer," *JBL* 129.1 (2010): 49–66.

of metal implements ("iron stylus and lead"). The creation of a tomb inscription, or epitaph, was an important component of funerary rites in ancient Judah.[4]

Third, Suriano points to a funerary inscription from Khirbet el-Qom (biblical Makkedah, cf. Josh 10:10) for someone named Uriyahu that includes an apparent attribution to the person responsible for making the tomb inscription (one Oniyahu) who may have been Uriyahu's kinsman-redeemer.

Fourth, on the reference to the metal "lead" in Job 19:24, a long-standing understanding of this is in reference to engraved text being filled with lead to ensure its permanence. This notion is not entirely speculative, for Seow points out that the Behistun Inscription (also known as the Bisitun, Bisotun, or Bisutun Inscription), commissioned by Darius I around 515 BC, employed just this technique.[5]

EXPLAIN the Story

Job Complains of His Friends' Persistence (19:1–6)

Job's response begins, as is often the case, with an address directed to his friends, turning Bildad's opening "how long" (Job 18:2) back on him—the incessant and persistent speech comes from both sides of this debate, and from Job's perspective he suffers the more for it. Clines notes that Job's words here reveal to us that he is growing in his anger toward his friends and, as such, the accusations leveled against his friends in verse 2 ought to be read as modal, "How long will you *try* to torment me."[6]

Job's reference to being reproached "ten times" (v. 3) is not a literal count of the interactions he has had with his friends but instead a figurative use of the number to represent a full amount. In essence, Job complains about their incessant verbal attacks upon him that aim not to care for him but to crush him. So, Job pushes back, essentially saying that if he had sinned—and he is certainly not agreeing with the friends that he had—then the matter would be between him and God and none of their business. As it is, in verse 5 he sees them as lording it over him, exalting themselves and using his circumstances for their own ends. Rather than conceding, Job plainly states his view: God has

4. Suriano, "Death, Disinheritance, and Job's Kinsman-Redeemer," 51–52.

5. Seow, *Job 1–21*, 802–3. Seow also notes that the suggestion itself is at least as old as the comments of the medieval rabbi known as Rashi.

6. Clines, *Job 1–20*, 439.

treated him unjustly—a point that is certainly true from Job's perspective if it is true that he is being punished for some sin as the friends maintain. The verb translated here as "has wronged" (*'wt*) in verse 6 is the same as that used by Bildad in 8:3 and so serves as Job's answer to the question of whether God perverts justice. In Job's opinion, if the friends are right and he is being punished for some sin (19:4), then the suffering he now experiences is unjust. While we may balk at this claim, remembering that all have sinned, Job's meticulous offering of sacrifices for sin outlined in the prologue (1:5) means that Job had followed God's instructions for dealing with any sin, and so further penalties should not apply.

Job Returns to the Claim That God Is His Enemy (19:7–12)

This prompts Job to turn his focus to God in verses 7–12, depicting him as a violent enemy who, in his anger, has destroyed him. God has failed to help when Job needed help (v. 7). The references to Job's "way" and "paths" in verse 8 are images representing the path his life would take. Job perceives that God has blocked the normal unfolding of his life—the Hebrew depicts this as a wall being built across the path of Job's life. Exacerbating Job's predicament, God has not only blocked his path but shrouded him in darkness so that any possible escape is obscured, trapping Job in the dire situation in which he currently finds himself.

Job next elaborates on the situation he is in in verses 9–10. God has stripped him of his status and reputation such that he falls from the rank of ruler to one who has been brought down to near death! God has demolished him like a building, or uprooted any hope he had like one uproots a tree—both images present different views of destruction. Job's life and hope are lost, destroyed by God.

Verses 7–12 close by depicting God as a military foe of vastly superior power who has, for an unknown reason, become angry at Job and marshaled his troops to bring about Job's destruction. The one-sided nature of this battle is revealed, for God's mighty armies surround Job's feeble tent—the disproportionate nature of this battle is made eminently clear.

The important thing to remember through this is that God is not really Job's enemy and is not working to destroy him—this much we know (but Job does not) from the opening chapters of the book. Yet just as clearly Job, in his ignorance of God's purposes, feels very much that God is treating him as his enemy. He does not understand what God is doing and can do nothing more than process his experience through the only theological framework he has, and that is one in which God operates exclusively according to the idea of retributive justice. It is a struggle Job will continue with until the truth finally dawns on him after hearing Yahweh's long array of questions from the whirlwind. But we have many chapters more before we get there!

Job's Isolation from His Family (19:13–20)

The next part of Job's response (verses 13–20) is characterized by repeated references to Job's extended family and his utter isolation from them. Most significantly, however, is that Job lays the blame for all of this squarely at God's feet in his opening words of verse 13. The drastic inversion in circumstances is reflected in the manner in which his former servants now treat him—those who once depended upon him for their livelihoods are now not even responding to Job begging them for help. Job's "family" in verse 17 is not a reference to his children (who all perished) but to his siblings (see 42:11). The Hebrew for NIV "to my own family" is woodenly "to the sons of my womb," where "my womb" is most likely a reference to the womb that Job once occupied, i.e., his mother's womb (see Job 3:10 where the same expression appears).

Job is alone, abandoned by his family. He feels as though he is God's enemy, and the friends who have come to him have turned out to be miserable comforters. It is no wonder he has no hope and expects his life to come to an end soon.

Job's Plea for Compassion (19:21–22)

Job calls on his friends to treat him with compassion (verses 21–22), telling them that the "hand of God" has struck him and that thus far they have pursued him in the same way that he feels God has. The term translated "pursue" (v. 22, *rdp*) here is negative, frequently used elsewhere in military contexts, to the point where some translations use "persecute" elsewhere to translate this word.[7] The Egyptian army pursued the Israelites as they fled from Egypt (Deut 11:4; Josh 7:5; 8:24). God is said to pursue people in judgment (Deut 28:22, 45). Job here feels subject to such treatment by God.

Christopher Ash has suggested that Job is mistaken, for the prologue recorded Yahweh saying to the Satan that Job was now "in your hands" (Job 2:6), and so Job should not be attributing responsibility for his present plight directly to God.[8] Appealing as it might be to find such a simple way to let God off the hook (so to speak), it faces a number of difficulties which make it untenable. For one, in 42:7 God tells Job's friends that Job did speak the

7. See., e.g., Deut 30:7; Pss 69:26; 119:157, 161. One notable exception is Ps 23:6 where goodness and mercy "will follow" (*rdp*) the psalmist.

8. Ash, *Job*, 213.

truth about him. While it might be feasible to argue that that comment may not validate everything Job ever said, it would need to be shown why it excludes some of Job's words—such a point should not simply be assumed because some of Job's words do not fit our preconceptions. Furthermore, this reading moves too far toward a dualistic reading of Job where Satan is free to act without permission from God—a point that the prologue quite clearly counters by definitively noting that the Satan may only act with God's express permission.

The expression "in your hand" is an idiom meaning "in your power." It appears numerous times in the Bible and several times in Job. And in the end, Job is right. While the immediate cause of his affliction may have been the Satan, the ultimate cause was God. The Satan could have done nothing without Yahweh's approval and permission, and had Yahweh wished to stop the Satan at any point, he clearly could have. Attributing Job's plight to the Satan does not resolve the questions about why God has allowed these things to befall his faithful servant.

Finally, Job is also clearly right because the challenge issued by the Satan was completed by the close of chapter 2. The Satan did not present himself before God on a third day and extend his challenge. The fact that Job continues to suffer now, some considerable time after he had uttered the words "shall we accept good from God, and not trouble?," and the narrator had declared him not to have sinned in his response to his suffering (2:10) is only because God has not brought the suffering to an end. It is the question of why *that* has not taken place that prompts both Job—and us as readers—to ask for an explanation from God, and for that we shall have to wait until Yahweh finally appears and speaks at the end of the book (although we shall get a hint in chapter 28).

I Know That My Redeemer Lives (19:23–27)

Facing the apparent hopelessness of his situation, Job believes that any hope of vindication is lost (verses 23–27). He finds this outcome distressing and so wishes that there would be some way for his words, his protestations of innocence and injustice, to be recorded. If this were possible, then perhaps his case would not be forgotten and one day, somehow, he would be vindicated.

Job announces that he knows that his redeemer lives in what are perhaps the most famous words of the book. But who is his redeemer? The Old Testament uses the term "redeemer" (*go'el*) in a couple of ways. First, it describes a relative whose responsibility it is to restore the family's fortunes: whether that be to effect justice when a member of the family had been murdered (e.g., Num 35:12, 19–27), reclaim property sold through financial hardship (Lev 25:25–34), or care for a widow (such as Boaz does in the story of Ruth). Second, the Psalms and prophets frequently identify God as the redeemer of his people (e.g., Ps 19:14; Isa 41:14).

Many commentators argue that this second meaning applies here, and that Job refers to God as his redeemer. These words are then an expression of his faith in the face of all that he has suffered.[9] It is certainly an appealing idea, the basis for a rousing sermon, and even more for an astonishing oratorio—as found in Handel's magnum opus, *Messiah*. These are not, however, particularly strong exegetical reasons in favor of understanding these words of Job to be referring to God or even Jesus. Rather, it is the type of interpretation that arises out of a need to find some relevance for the modern reader in the ancient text, even at the expense of misreading the text itself. For up to this point Job has repeatedly viewed God as his opponent, the source of his troubles. He has given no indication of any expectation of salvation or redemption. Furthermore, as we continue to hear from Job in the coming chapters, there is nothing he says that reflects this thinking about God.

Instead, everything in this passage points to Job referring to a relative ready to step in when he dies. Job has already made it clear that he does not expect to live for much longer (see Job 7:21; 10:20). He will leave behind a widow, his lands, and any other remaining possessions will need to be distributed to those in his extended family. The reference in 19:24 to inscribed stone could even be suggesting that Job desires that his arguments be included on his tomb.[10] In this context, the reference to his redeemer is yet another way for Job to let us know that he expects his life will soon be over. And although Job has just explained that he is alienated from his extended family (19:13–20), this does not mean that the need to appropriately distribute his estate and care for his widow will be ignored.

Furthermore, as readers of Job's story, we have seen its origin—the encounter between Yahweh and the Satan in the opening chapters of the book—so we know that Job does not need anyone to plead his case with God, for God knows Job is the most upright and blameless person there is. What is more, no redeemer will appear for Job as we read on. In the end, God will appear to challenge and instruct Job, but not to intercede on Job's behalf. If these verses truly reflected the presence of a heavenly redeemer for Job, then the absence

9. E.g. Ash, *Job*, 216; Hartley, *Book of Job*, 295; Andersen, *Job*, 209; Smick, "Job," 787. Robert L. Alden, *Job*, NAC 11 (Nashville: B&H, 1993), 207, suggests that both options may be intended, but given the problems with proposing God as Job's redeemer here that would seem unlikely.

10. See Suriano, "Death, Disinheritance, and Job's Kinsman-Redeemer."

of that redeemer anywhere later in his story would seem to undermine his certainty. The only other reference to a possible heavenly "redeemer" (although not described in those terms) will be mentioned by Elihu in 33:23–26.

Once Job has died, "in the end" (19:25), this redeemer will stand on the earth. The Hebrew word translated "earth" (*'apar*) in the NIV is often translated "dust," as in "for dust you are and to dust you will return" (Gen 3:19) and "I will lie down in the dust" (in reference to Job's own death, Job 7:21). In essence, Job's redeemer will stand on his grave. To make it even clearer, Job reinforces this with the first line in verse 26. The clause is notoriously difficult in the Hebrew, but the sense seems to be to parallel the previous lines by reinforcing the idea that the Job's postmortem arrangements are all taken care of. The redeemer will arise once his skin has rotted away from his body—when he is dead.

Thus, when he has died the kinsman-redeemer will arise and fulfill his obligations to Job and his family. So, Job is now ready to die—there remains only one thing he hopes and longs for now: to see God before he dies. This hope is clearly expressed in verses 26b–27, and Job has previously made clear this desire (e.g., 13:3). While most English translations express Job's words as simple future tense verbs, the better understanding of the Hebrew is that here Job is expressing a future hope, and this understanding is confirmed by the final clause of verse 27. A clearer translation of verses 25–27 would thus be:

> I know that my kinsman-redeemer lives,
>   and after me he will stand on the dust,
>   after they have stripped my skin from this (body/corpse).
> Yet from my flesh I want to see God,
>   I want to see him for myself,
>   see *him* with my eyes, not a stranger's!
> [For this] my innards yearn within me.

The reference to Job's innards' yearning here uses the common Hebrew idea that one's deepest feelings are felt in the pit of your stomach and in your innards (NIV "my heart"; Hebrew *kilyotay*, woodenly "my kidneys"). This same idea of yearning is found in other passages using the same verb (*klh*) (see 2 Sam 13:39; Pss 84:2; 119:81). Job longs to meet with God before he dies, so that God can give an account of his actions to him (cf. Job 13:3). Although Job does not know it, this longing will ultimately be fulfilled before the end of this story.

Job Warns His Friends (19:28–29)

Job addresses his final words in this speech (vv. 28–29) directly to his friends (the "you" at the beginning of verse 28 is plural). While the Hebrew text is unclear here (Andersen goes so far as to say, "these verses are largely unintelligible"),[11] Job's words are clearly a warning to his friends. He notes the friends' intent to pursue him after identifying him as the problem (the NIV's opening "if" should be construed as "if you continue to"). Should they continue, Job notes that they themselves will be the guilty ones. The clause "for wrath will bring punishment by the sword" in v. 29 is more woodenly rendered, "for anger is a sin of the sword," where "of the sword" is likely a qualitative description highlighting the severity of the sin they would be committing, similar to "sin worthy of death" (Deut 22:26; cf. Job 31:11, 28).

Job thus finishes this speech by warning his friends that in their growing anger and continued pursuit of him, in the false accusations they make, that they are themselves sinning. And their sin is serious (see Exod 20:16; Ps 5:6). If they are not going to stop out of compassion for Job, here he appeals to them to stop out of fear of judgment. We shall see that they do not heed his warning!

LIVE the Story

Learning from Job's Faith

While Job's talk of a redeemer and hope to present his case directly to God may not hold the meaning that many modern readers have been led to expect (see under Explain the Story above)—he is not speaking of God as his redeemer in this passage—, nonetheless the very fact that he holds onto these hopes reflects his underlying faith in God. Although the redemption he speaks of in this passage is not the same as the redemption we speak of in New Testament terms—Job simply expects a relative to fulfill the social task of redeemer and manage his estate after his demise—the hope he has to present his case to God and be found right does reflect his underlying faith in God's justice. He believes that, when presented with Job's case, God will acknowledge that Job is right, and he will be vindicated.

Without saying too much, it is worth noting that when God does appear at the end of the book, Job's conviction that there is nothing in his life that warrants the suffering he is experiencing as retribution is vindicated. It will become clear from God's words in chapter 42 that Job is not here suffering for

11. Andersen, *Job*, 210.

something he has done wrong, and so his claim is right and the friends were wrong. Where Job failed was in his simplistic understanding of the way God works that believed that all suffering was a consequence of personal sin—the same understanding the friends have, but one Job struggles with, because he is the one suffering and cannot reconcile that understanding of his suffering with what he knows to be true about the way he has lived his life.

One lesson, perhaps *the* lesson, to be learned from Job here is about faith. Despite all that has happened to him, he holds out hope. And Job lived in relative darkness, for, as the New Testament says, the least under the new covenant is greater than even the greatest under the old because we have seen the coming of the Messiah (Matt 11:11; Luke 7:28). The great mystery of the gospel has been revealed to us. Job knew nothing of this, yet he holds out hope that he will be vindicated.

In the final analysis, Job's faith is not heralded through an upbeat hope in God as his redeemer; his faith is shown in the depths of his struggles. Like Jacob who struggled all night with God (Gen 32:22–32), Job struggles with God throughout the book of Job, never giving up, never abandoning his faith. He questions God, he complains, he laments, but he does not give up through all the uncertainty of his circumstances. He does not walk away from God; he walks toward him with all his pain, questions, and heartache. That is the path of faith.

There are many other lessons to be learned from Job's experiences here, not the least that those claiming to be God's representatives do not always do a good job of representing him. We have seen this, and will continue to see this, as we hear from Job's three friends. While some in our society would claim to reject God on the basis of his representatives, Job does not.

Job, Job's Redeemer, and Life Beyond Death

Job's words, "I know that my redeemer lives," are taken up in music in celebration of Jesus's resurrection.[12] Yet that interpretation of these words does not fit well with Job's words here. For Job, speaking of a redeemer at this point is essentially a confident assertion of his own impending death, after which he is certain that his estate will be taken care of by a relative who had been appointed as the redeemer of his estate—a "kinsman-redeemer." It is not a cry of faith in personal redemption, and his redeemer is not God.

It is understandable that reading this passage to be saying that Job's

12. Aside from their recitation in Handel's *Messiah*, they are found in numerous more recent musical works. For a list of some of these, see Seow, *Job 1–21*, 793.

redeemer is God or the Messiah is attractive to Christian readers of Job. We know that all Scripture is given by God for our benefit, and we know that Job is part of Scripture, so we rightly ask how these words benefit us? What assurance do they give us? What do they teach us? How do they point us to Jesus? Surely an interpretation which provides easy answers to these questions has to be the right one?

Believers have long struggled with such questions, and not just over this passage or the book of Job, but with the entire Old Testament. We need to be wary, however, of assessing the worth of an interpretation only on how directly it fulfils our need to have these sorts of questions answered, or to make it easy for us to relate to the text and apply it to ourselves. Otherwise, we would return to the allegorical readings of the early church, which provided rather imaginative interpretations of Old Testament passages to find a direct link to Jesus and then to the reader. Rather, we need to ask whether the original recipients of these words of Scripture would have understood them the way we're proposing. In this case, it is exceedingly unlikely that the original readers would have understood these verses to be pointing to a (for them) future messiah who would rescue sinners and reconcile them to God! James Wharton offers a salient warning on approaching this passage:

> The words have simply achieved a life of their own in the heart-language of Christian faith, and that language is not finally subject to correction by technical exegesis of Job 19:25. It is important for Christians, however, to recognize that when we identify the "Redeemer" of Job 19:25 with the risen Christ of the Gospels, it is *our* faith we are expressing, not the faith of Job.[13]

The most straightforward reading of these verses is that Job is expressing his belief that he is soon to die—he is essentially saying that his last will and testament is in the hands of the executor of his estate. Preparations have been made. He knows he has a kinsman-redeemer ready to take control of his estate, one who will stand on the dust (perhaps Job's way to refer to what's left of all he once had) after Job's flesh has been destroyed. Yet, in light of his belief that he will not live much longer, Job now forcefully expresses his desire to see God before he dies, before his flesh is gone.

It would seem commendable for Job to wish to fix his relationship with God before he dies—from our perspective that is certainly something we

13. James A. Wharton, *Job*, Westminster Bible Companion (Louisville: Westminster John Knox, 1999), 89.

are all called to do. Yet, we also know that Job does not actually need this. His problem is not that he is alienated from God but rather a simple lack of understanding about what is happening in his life, a lack of understanding that is exacerbated by his and his friends' commitment to their theology, in particular to their commitment to the notion of retributive justice. They view God's actions and Job's suffering through that lens and conclude that either God has made a mistake (so Job) or that Job has sinned (so the friends). Yet, neither of these positions is correct, and none of them has yet come to the place where they question the theological position they have taken. Until that happens, they shall continue to disagree, argue, and misunderstand God.

These are the consequences of bad theology. Indeed, in Job's situation we see just how damaging bad theology can be. He feels that God is his enemy; he feels his friends are attacking him; he feels despair and hopelessness. Still today these are just some of the consequences of bad theology. The danger for us is that we all too easily see the bad theology of those around us—as Job's friends saw what they considered to be Job's bad theology—without first measuring our own position. And because it is from our theology that we judge others, we ought to be humble rather than unteachable. We should be open to correction and kind in our correction of others. Bad theology afflicts the innocent and ultimately alienates people from God. We need to hear God's voice and seek to understand what he is saying, and then listen carefully to those we disagree with and understand what they are saying before we jump to make judgments about our brothers and sisters who may disagree on this point or that.

CHAPTER 13

Job 20

Zophar's Second Speech

LISTEN to the Story

1Then Zophar the Naamathite replied:

2"My troubled thoughts prompt me to answer
because I am greatly disturbed.
3I hear a rebuke that dishonors me,
and my understanding inspires me to reply.

4"Surely you know how it has been from of old,
ever since mankind was placed on the earth,
5that the mirth of the wicked is brief,
the joy of the godless lasts but a moment.
6Though the pride of the godless person reaches to the heavens
and his head touches the clouds,
7he will perish forever, like his own dung;
those who have seen him will say, 'Where is he?'
8Like a dream he flies away, no more to be found,
banished like a vision of the night.
9The eye that saw him will not see him again;
his place will look on him no more.
10His children must make amends to the poor;
his own hands must give back his wealth.
11The youthful vigor that fills his bones
will lie with him in the dust.

12"Though evil is sweet in his mouth
and he hides it under his tongue,

13though he cannot bear to let it go
and lets it linger in his mouth,
14yet his food will turn sour in his stomach;
it will become the venom of serpents within him.
15He will spit out the riches he swallowed;
God will make his stomach vomit them up.
16He will suck the poison of serpents;
the fangs of an adder will kill him.
17He will not enjoy the streams,
the rivers flowing with honey and cream.
18What he toiled for he must give back uneaten;
he will not enjoy the profit from his trading.
19For he has oppressed the poor and left them destitute;
he has seized houses he did not build.

20"Surely he will have no respite from his craving;
he cannot save himself by his treasure.
21Nothing is left for him to devour;
his prosperity will not endure.
22In the midst of his plenty, distress will overtake him;
the full force of misery will come upon him.
23When he has filled his belly,
God will vent his burning anger against him
and rain down his blows on him.
24Though he flees from an iron weapon,
a bronze-tipped arrow pierces him.
25He pulls it out of his back,
the gleaming point out of his liver.
Terrors will come over him;
26total darkness lies in wait for his treasures.
A fire unfanned will consume him
and devour what is left in his tent.
27The heavens will expose his guilt;
the earth will rise up against him.
28A flood will carry off his house,
rushing waters on the day of God's wrath.

[29]Such is the fate God allots the wicked,
the heritage appointed for them by God."

Listening to the Text in the Story: "Instruction of Amenemope" (Egyptian)

We come to the last of the friends' speeches in the second round, the words of Zophar. His speech, which he admits arises out of feeling dishonored by Job's words (cf. 20:2–3), largely serves to establish that the idea of retributive justice has been universally accepted since the dawn of time. A look into the ancient Near Eastern background bears out Zophar's claim, at least as far as we are able to delve with any certainty. One good example is to be found in the Egyptian "Instruction of Amenemope" from the latter part of the second millennium. This text repeatedly connects moral act and consequence according to the principle of retributive justice. It even has rather specific thematic connections to some of the words of Zophar here. For example, it includes the idea that the wicked, who have "consumed" the poor, will ultimately vomit up the material goods they have stolen, an idea we see in Job 20:15. Zophar describes the apparent prosperity of the wicked (the "mirth of the wicked" in v. 5), as temporary, for "his food will turn sour in his stomach . . . he will spit out the riches he swallowed, God will make his stomach vomit them up" (vv. 14–15). In the "Instruction of Amenemope" we read a similar account of the consequences of evil actions, in this case the exploitation of the poor:

> Do not covet a poor man's goods,
> Nor hunger for his bread;
> A poor man's goods are a block in the throat,
> It makes the gullet vomit.[1]

As Hernández points out, this parallel with Zophar's description of the consequences of exploiting the poor and innocent by the wicked here serve as "emphasizing Zophar's unique goal of portraying God's intimate involvement

1. "Instruction of Amenemope," trans. Miriam Lichtheim (*COS* 1.47:118); cf. Cornelius, "Job," 5:275; Dominick S. Hernández, "The Expression of Moral Judgments through Imagery in Job and Ancient Near Eastern Literature," in *Teaching Morality in Antiquity: Wisdom Texts, Oral Traditions, and Images*, ed. T. M. Oshima and Susanne Kohlhaas, Orientalische Religionen in der Antike 29 (Tübingen: Mohr Siebeck, 2018), 154.

in divine retribution."[2] Indeed, the "Instruction of Amenemope" reflects a clear understanding of retributive justice as foundational in the world, a belief that underpins all of the debates in the book of Job.

EXPLAIN the Story

Zophar Takes Offense (20:1–3)

Zophar begins his speech with the familiar justification for offering yet another response to Job (see Job 4:2; 8:2; 11:2–3; etc.). This time around he claims that Job's words are deeply disturbing him ("troubled thoughts" recalls Eliphaz's description of his nightmare in 4:13). The troubling thing to Zophar about Job's words, it would seem, is that Job has insulted him by not conceding that he is right nor accepting his reproof! He feels dishonored and so takes Job's words as a personal attack.

Zophar Appeals to Tradition (20:4–29)

Zophar begins a defense of his position by returning to the claim that the information he imparts is well established and universally accepted. The same claim has already been made by Bildad (8:8–10). That which has been known since time immemorial is simply this: that the wicked do not prosper (unless it is ever so briefly), and they shall inevitably and imminently become undone and suffer the consequences of their wickedness. In this speech, Zophar focuses only on the fate of the wicked rather than including any description of the blessings of the godly.

Verse 7 has Zophar liken the fate of the wicked to that of their dung. The comparison seems odd. Why use this as an image of disappearing forever? Part of the answer may be that Zophar is reaching for an offensive image to express his own disdain for the wicked. Excrement, whether human or not, will dry and then burn or be scattered to the wind, thus disappearing. Beyond this it is difficult to elaborate on whether Zophar believes in some form of blessed afterlife for the righteous. More likely, in the context of the ancient world, Zophar would be claiming that the memory of the wicked will be lost forever, they would have no progeny to remember them, and that their existence in Sheol would also be lost.

That verse 10 has troubled translators is reflected in the differences that English Bible versions present. There are two alternatives: the wicked man's

2. Hernández, "Expression of Moral Judgments," 154.

children will either repay the poor or else seek the favor of the poor. The first view (followed by the NIV, CEB, NET, and others) is ultimately difficult to fit with the second line of the verse, which indicates that the wicked man himself has had to return his wealth and so is presumably impoverished at death and leaves nothing of any value to his children. The second view (followed by the CSB, ESV, KJV, and others) likely means that the wicked man will leave his children so destitute that they are forced to beg for food from the poor. The latter is preferable, for it also fits with what Zophar says later in verse 18, but either way the wicked man loses everything. Furthermore, the wicked man dies prematurely (v. 11)—while the vigor of youth is still in his bones. According to Zophar, all is lost for the wicked, and it is lost quickly.

The next section (verses 12–19) is tied together through the imagery of the consuming and digesting of food. Zophar considers the wicked man who is addicted to evil. For such, that evil has an insidious effect: food meant to sustain is like poison, and (segueing to the metaphorical) the wicked man regurgitates the wealth he has consumed. In the end, the evil and wealth consumed are likened to sucking poison from snakes—they result in the death of the wicked man.

Zophar continues to use the symbology of food in verse 17. The reference to "streams" is often understood to refer to "streams of olive oil" based on language used elsewhere (such as 29:6), but at the very least the language speaks of an abundance of "honey" (which often, in biblical Hebrew, referred to a sweet syrup distilled from dates rather than the produce of bees) and "cream" (*khem'ah*, sometimes translated as "butter," could also refer to cream or curds). The point is simply that the wicked are deprived of these foods, which reflect the delights expected from the promised land (see Exod 3:8). Further, in Job 20:18 that which he has worked hard to acquire (likely through commercial transactions, as made clear at the end of the verse, and those possibly done dishonestly depending on the nuance of the Hebrew word translated "toiled for"), he cannot consume but must return. While we may feel the need to ask who he returns it to, it is a question unanswered by Zophar, whose emphasis is on the fact that the wicked man cannot benefit from it and loses it quickly, even before he has consumed it.

Only in verse 19 do we discover some of the details of the wicked man's actions: he has oppressed the poor, taking from them that which was not his to take, and then left them to their fate. The most curious thing about the specifics here is that it is difficult to imagine that either Zophar or his friends would attribute this behavior to Job (it certainly runs counter to the character of Job as revealed in the opening chapters). Yet the disturbing truth is that we are seeing an escalation in their accusations of what they believe Job was capable of doing that would result in his situation.

The following few verses (vv. 20–22) reflect the notion that the desire for more is never satisfied. When that desire is for wealth and prosperity, it becomes all-consuming to the point that, when the appetite can no longer be satisfied; it becomes self-destructive. While devouring more and more, Zophar says that God will inflict his judgment upon this wicked man. The NIV's past tense in v. 23, "when *he has filled* his belly" (italics added), from which the reader might infer a completed action, should probably be understood as a present tense, "when *he fills* his belly," reflecting the ongoing insatiable desire to devour more, as reflected in v. 20. This wicked man can know no satisfaction, and in the midst of his insatiable craving judgment will fall on him.

Zophar speaks of this judgment in terms of God's anger falling on the wicked. Job has previously described himself as the target of God's anger (14:13; 16:9; 19:11). He speaks of the wicked as engaged in combat with God, with the blows of combat leading to the flight of the wicked, only to be struck as he flees with a divine arrow into his liver (or more precisely, his gallbladder, see 16:13). Such an injury would invariably be fatal, and realizing this, the wicked man is overcome with terrors.

Death is, then, the end of the wicked, and is a death under God's judgment. The total darkness will conceal the wicked man's treasures so that they are lost to him, and then fire will consume the one who had previously devoured and consumed others (20:26). That the fire is unfanned implies that it is supernatural in origin and not made by man. It also reminds us that fire fell from heaven and devoured Job's sheep and servants (1:16).

The final verses (vv. 27–29) continue to confirm all that has been said to this point. To vindicate the judgment that has consumed the wicked, the heavens and the earth (v. 27) themselves will testify to his sin, such that there will be no doubt remaining as to the dispensation of justice. The wicked will thus lose his possessions and ultimately his life as a consequence of his wickedness.

LIVE the Story

When Responding to Provocation Is Wrong

When I was nearing the end of high school, my physics class worked out that if anyone were to ask our teacher about UFOs, then the remainder of the lesson would depart from the syllabus and be spent discussing UFOs. This was clearly a topic of some interest for our teacher, so much so that he would neglect to teach the very thing we were there to learn in order to discuss it. For many of us there are similar topics—I dare say that the book of Job, through the course of writing this commentary, has become just such a topic for me! Mention an appropriate subject to us, and we leave behind any former discussion, no matter how important, and head off down a path that is ultimately neither relevant nor necessarily helpful.

Zophar reveals that his response here is something like this. He recognizes in Job's words "a rebuke that dishonors me" (Job 20:3), and so he reacts. It is a natural response to feeling attacked, but such a response is often unhelpful—as Zophar's words are here. From the outside it is easy to judge. On the one hand, we have Job, who has suffered unimaginable loss and continues to suffer from both those losses and the ongoing health problems and the pain associated with them. On the other hand, we have Zophar and the other friends, who come in their wealth and privilege to "comfort" Job. Even if we disagree with the tone of some of Job's words, it is hard not to be sympathetic in his circumstances. Yet instead of showing sympathy and support, his friends are consumed by their own anger arising from their perception that Job has attacked them and so respond in a cruel and vindictive manner.

From the inside it is not so easy to see this, and it is from the inside that we, just like Job's friends, can find ourselves succumbing to this form of response. When someone needs us but strikes out in pain, our first response can easily be to strike back, to justify ourselves, to be blind to their needs and their pain. We all too easily fall into the trap that Job's friends have fallen into, and that Zophar even admits to in this speech. Sometimes it is not even a personal attack that prompts such a response, but an attack on a cherished belief, something we hold dear and feel the need to defend. For the friends, this is also apparent in their confident adherence to the doctrine of retributive justice. For us it can easily be any of a number of doctrines that, when raised, trigger a response that displaces the more appropriate compassionate response.

One curious detail about this speech of Zophar's is the apparent lack of direct reference to Job. The point comes to a fore when in verse 19 Zophar describes the crimes of the wicked man for whom he has provided an extensive discussion of the consequences of his wickedness as being one who oppressed the poor, stole their homes, and left them with nothing. This is one of Job's friends speaking, and it seems unlikely that he believes that Job has actually treated the poor in this way. As readers we know it to be wholly outside of Job's character as described in the opening chapters, where God boasts about him as being upright and blameless. Job himself will later claim his treatment of the poor (as well as widows and others) is a reflection of his righteousness (29:12).

Yet, unimaginable as it seems, his friends' ideas of what it is that Job could have done to warrant his fall from grace seem also to be growing in magnitude. Here, his treatment of the poor is called into question, even if only indirectly. Later, Eliphaz will make even more extreme accusations about Job's behavior (22:4–11). Job's stubborn refusal to concede to his friends' arguments would seem to be provoking them to more and more extreme claims. The tragedy of this is that instead of moving toward some form of resolution, the friends and Job are moving apart, and they are becoming less and less helpful and more and more damaging to Job. Their stubborn refusal to exhibit any humility in regard to their understanding of the nature of God and his justice and the way in which he works it out in the world is profoundly troubling.

The pattern repeats itself—both in the Bible and beyond. In the first century, the Jewish leaders grew in their distrust of and hatred for Jesus. And in our own lives there is always the danger of problems in relationships growing rapidly when, if cooler heads could prevail, reconciliation and trust should have (or could have) been found.

Why Are the Speeches in Job So Repetitive?

If you have not already asked—along with Job and his friends—how long can this endless, repetitive cycle of back and forth between Job and his friends continue, how long can they persist in repeating what are substantially the same arguments over and over, then by now you are likely starting to raise this question. It is a good question, and doubtless one that the author of Job wanted the audience to ask.

There are at least two responses that ought to be made on this point. First, the repetition and persistence of Job's friends reflects just how deeply ingrained the idea of retributive justice was in the author's context. The friends persist in the face of Job's insistence that he does not deserve what is happening to him because their understanding of God and, indeed, their entire worldview is built around this notion that God will reward good and punish evil and that these outcomes are invariably worked out in the present, in this life, for they have no firm notion of what could possibly come after this life.

The second response, however, is just as important for us. Profound suffering deserves more than a simple answer. A brief response ultimately fails to comprehend the depth of pain that anyone experiencing such suffering endures. That is certainly not to say that the responses of Job's friends—apart from their initial seven days in silence just sitting with Job—are the appropriate responses. But there is something to say about grappling deeply with the problem of suffering, and the repetition of the book of Job forces the patient reader to do that for themselves. And we ought also to recognize that the enduring and sustained account of Job's suffering and struggles with that suffering force us, as readers, to dive more deeply into Job's experience. We come to more fully appreciate his pain and struggle. We get to know Job in a way that a superficial, brief description fails to convey.

Zophar's View of the Afterlife

While Zophar says nothing of the fate of the righteous, it is generally accepted that the Old Testament as a whole has no clear concept of an afterlife. However, his insistence in verses 7–9 that the wicked will "perish forever" seems meaningless if that is also the ultimate fate of the righteous once they die. The truth is that we cannot say much in detail about the state of the dead in the Old Testament. It may simply be that the reference to "perish forever" refers to the family line by implying that God would prevent the wicked from having any descendants, so their name would disappear forever.

We do know, however, that death was not the end in an absolute sense in the thought of the ancient Near East. In Mesopotamia the dead were believed to dwell in the underworld, and various aspects of their life in this world influenced their state there. In Egypt there was a sophisticated understanding of an afterlife. So, it is unlikely that Job and his friends would have believed that death was an absolute end, but we cannot say much more than that. Furthermore, we should be wary of placing too much stock in Zophar's words here—after all, he is declared by God to have not spoken correctly (see 42:7). Nonetheless, Zophar's words do here seem to reflect a notion that the righteous will go on to some form of afterlife, even if there is very little definite we can say about it.

From the perspective of the New Testament, however, we can draw some points from Zophar's speech. As noted above, in a general theological sense he is both right and wrong at points. Yet his notion that a wicked person would "perish forever" (20:7) reflects an expectation that justice will be done in the long term and that any present prosperity enjoyed by the wicked will ultimately be undone. Presumably Zophar and his friends (including Job himself) would have understood in greater detail the implications of his words here, implications we probably do not fully appreciate being so removed from their historical and cultural context.

The expectation that justice will be done and that any prosperous wicked people would meet their comeuppance does reflect an expectation of God that is ultimately substantiated as time unfolds. What is perhaps surprising is that Zophar can hold the view that the wicked may enjoy temporary prosperity without also holding that the righteous could enjoy temporary suffering that may not arise from disobedience or sin. After all, he is not suggesting that the prosperity of the wicked arises because of a brief flirtation with righteous behavior!

The details of Zophar's confidence in just outcomes in life (vague as they are here) is a reflection of the nature of God as the just, sovereign ruler of all creation. The paucity of detail reflects the limited understanding available at his place in history, but that will change—and Job's story is part of that change. As this expectation—namely, that just earthly outcomes result from God's justice—unfolded in history, we come to see how this progression took place. The idea referenced by Zophar that the wicked will ultimately "perish forever" (v. 7) leads to the eschatological view that all will be judged and the righteous go to eternal life and the wicked to eternal punishment that is revealed later in history (e.g., Matt 25:31–46). What Zophar does not understand, it would seem, is that what God requires is beyond the capacity of any human being to achieve, and so all are inherently destined for destruction. Salvation does not, in the end, depend on our good works but on the Messiah's work on our behalf.

CHAPTER 14

Job 21

Job's Second Reply to Zophar

LISTEN to the Story

1Then Job replied:

2"Listen carefully to my words;
let this be the consolation you give me.
3Bear with me while I speak,
and after I have spoken, mock on.

4"Is my complaint directed to a human being?
Why should I not be impatient?
5Look at me and be appalled;
clap your hand over your mouth.
6When I think about this, I am terrified;
trembling seizes my body.
7Why do the wicked live on,
growing old and increasing in power?
8They see their children established around them,
their offspring before their eyes.
9Their homes are safe and free from fear;
the rod of God is not on them.
10Their bulls never fail to breed;
their cows calve and do not miscarry.
11They send forth their children as a flock;
their little ones dance about.
12They sing to the music of timbrel and lyre;
they make merry to the sound of the pipe.
13They spend their years in prosperity
and go down to the grave in peace.

14Yet they say to God, 'Leave us alone!
We have no desire to know your ways.
15Who is the Almighty, that we should serve him?
What would we gain by praying to him?'
16But their prosperity is not in their own hands,
so I stand aloof from the plans of the wicked.

17"Yet how often is the lamp of the wicked snuffed out?
How often does calamity come upon them,
the fate God allots in his anger?
18How often are they like straw before the wind,
like chaff swept away by a gale?
19It is said, 'God stores up the punishment of the wicked for
their children.'
Let him repay the wicked, so that they themselves will
experience it!
20Let their own eyes see their destruction;
let them drink the cup of the wrath of the Almighty.
21For what do they care about the families they leave behind
when their allotted months come to an end?

22"Can anyone teach knowledge to God,
since he judges even the highest?
23One person dies in full vigor,
completely secure and at ease,
24well nourished in body,
bones rich with marrow.
25Another dies in bitterness of soul,
never having enjoyed anything good.
26Side by side they lie in the dust,
and worms cover them both.

27"I know full well what you are thinking,
the schemes by which you would wrong me.
28You say, 'Where now is the house of the great,
the tents where the wicked lived?'
29Have you never questioned those who travel?

Have you paid no regard to their accounts—
30 that the wicked are spared from the day of calamity,
that they are delivered from the day of wrath?
31 Who denounces their conduct to their face?
Who repays them for what they have done?
32 They are carried to the grave,
and watch is kept over their tombs.
33 The soil in the valley is sweet to them;
everyone follows after them,
and a countless throng goes before them.

34 "So how can you console me with your nonsense?
Nothing is left of your answers but falsehood!"

Listening to the Text in the Story: "The Babylonian Theodicy"; "The Song from the Tomb of King Intef" (Egypt)

In his reply to Zophar, Job questions the implementation of retributive justice on the wicked, noting that there are too many examples where those deserving of punishment do not experience it, enjoying instead a long and prosperous life. Their lack of devotion to God does not result in them suffering or experiencing discipline. Instead, they get what they should not. These are the roots of the skepticism that appears more fully in the words of Qoheleth, the teacher whom we hear speaking in the book of Ecclesiastes. Such skepticism was not confined to Israel or biblical thought in the ancient world; there are indications in other ancient Near Eastern literature that the long-held beliefs about the justice of the gods was, at various times throughout history, called into question.

One example is found in "The Babylonian Theodicy," which expresses similar ideas to Job 21:7–9:

> Those who seek not after a god can go the road of favor,
> Those who pray to a goddess have grown poor and destitute.[1]

The idea reflects the inversion of what is expected when the devout suffer and the irreligious prosper. Such skepticism toward beliefs and traditions was

1. "The Babylonian Theodicy" (*COS* 1.154:493).

also found in some literature from ancient Egypt—particularly "Contrasting Harper Songs from the Tomb of Neferhotep" (also known as "The Good Fortune of the Dead"), although there it tended to be more around the afterlife. These texts suggest that those who had gone before were slowly being forgotten and enjoyed no ongoing existence. The author of these works reached this conclusion in part as he saw the tombs crumbling around him, showing no signs of perpetuity.[2]

EXPLAIN the Story

The Prosperity of the Wicked (21:1–22)

Job responds to Zophar, in part, by contradicting what he has claimed. Instead of conceding that the world operates according to the principle of retributive justice, where good is rewarded and evil punished, Job points to situations where evil and wickedness are not only not punished, but the wicked actually prosper! Although it may initially seem that Job's points reveal that he does not adhere to the doctrine of retributive justice, the actual nature of his accusation here is that God fails to adequately implement retributive justice—he allows the wicked to escape the consequences of his actions, and so God is behaving in an unjust manner (so 21:17, 19).

Following the usual pattern, Job's words begin with some introduction appealing to his friends to at least listen to him (vv. 2–3). The plural forms of the verbs "listen" and "bear with" (English commands have an implied "you," which can be either singular or plural; Hebrew distinguishes singular and plural) clearly indicate that these words are addressed to the friends—although Job could also be including God with his friends in the opening, since the final word of verse 3, "mock," is a singular verb. Typically, when Job switches to the singular he addresses God directly. While it is possible that this should be corrected to a plural, it is also possible that Job ultimately feels mocked by God (recalling 9:23 where he does claim that God mocks).

Before digging into Zophar's argument, Job again offers some justification for the nature of his responses in 21:4–5. Job notes that he is contending with God, not people, and as such he is disheartened by the lack of progress in his case. The Hebrew phrase here translated "impatient" may be woodenly rendered "my spirit is short." In this context, it likely conveys

2. See "Contrasting Harper Songs from the Tomb of Neferhotep," trans. Robert K. Ritner (*COS* 2.13:64–66).

the idea that Job is not so much impatient but at a loss as to how to proceed and dispirited by the apparent failure of his pleas to be heard by God (see Exod 6:9 and the similar expression in Judg 16:16).[3] Job asks his friends to understand how he is feeling and, in doing so, to keep quiet and listen to him. Job, at this point, is looking for someone to understand him and show a little empathy.

The bulk of Job's response to Zophar is just that: a response to Zophar's argument claiming the wicked do get their recompense. This is surprising; most of Job's responses turn quickly from the friends to God himself. Yet, this time around he barely makes any reference to God (possibly making reference to him at the end of v. 3, see above), let alone make any attempt to address him directly. Perhaps he finds Zophar's claims to be so divorced from reality that he cannot but offer an extended answer, and so he does.

Job observes, much as Qoheleth (the teacher in Ecclesiastes) also noted, that there are times when wicked people prosper, and so Zophar's claim is disproven by simple observation.

> In this meaningless life of mine I have seen both of these:
> the righteous perishing in their righteousness,
> and the wicked living long in their wickedness. (Eccl 7:15)

For Job, this is terrifying, for it means that there is no justice in the world, and so he has no hope.

Job elaborates on the fortunes of the wicked who escape judgment, live in prosperity and peace, and are blessed with many descendants. They have no regard for God and yet suffer no ill consequences for doing so (Job 21:15). Perhaps most galling for Job is that he recognizes that the prosperity of the wicked is not founded on their own efforts but comes by God's hand (v. 16). As such, the "counsel of the wicked" has nothing to offer Job, for that is not the source of their good fortune. Rather, it is simply God's unpredictable and apparently amoral choice (or so Job here surmises). Job, like Qoheleth in the book of Ecclesiastes, cannot make moral sense of the world into which he has been plunged.

In verse 19 Job presents a possible objection to his argument (the Hebrew lacks the words "it is said" supplied by the NIV to make this clear). In the

3. David J. A. Clines, *Job 21–37*, WBC 18A (Nashville: Nelson, 2006), 523. In Exod 6:9, NIV "discouragement," rendered woodenly is "from shortness of spirit," and in Judg 16:16, NIV "he was sick of it," uses a similar expression rendered woodenly, "his soul was short."

situation where the wicked prosper, the punishment is meted out on their children. Job, however, finds this answer unsatisfying—how is justice really served in this scenario? Job notes that such people are not overly concerned over the fate of their children, and so such action hardly penalizes them for their behavior. If justice is truly to be served, the one who sins should be punished for their sins. Indeed, the prophets also recognized the problems with the innocent being punished for the sins of others, and in particular the children bearing the penalty for the sins of their parents. They proclaimed that such a situation would no longer be acceptable in God's world:

> In those days people will no longer say,
>
> "The parents have eaten sour grapes,
> and the children's teeth are set on edge."
>
> Instead, everyone will die for their own sin; whoever eats sour grapes—their own teeth will be set on edge. (Jer 31:29–30; cf. Ezek 18:2)

Despite recognizing this problem, Job feels powerless, since he is in no position to contend with God—can any mortal offer instruction to God (Job 21:22)? And yet, from Job's perspective that is what needs to happen. God, Job believes, is in need of a good lesson in basic morals. He should not be blessing the wicked and punishing the good, and from what Job can see, that is exactly what is going on!

Death, the Great Leveler (21:23–26)

In verses 23–26 Job arrives at the conclusion that death is the great leveler. Whether wicked or upright, no matter how blessed one's life has been or how filled with pain and loss, in the end everyone lies in the grave as equals. This conclusion is shared with Qoheleth:

> All share a common destiny—the righteous and the wicked, the good and the bad, the clean and the unclean, those who offer sacrifices and those who do not.
>
> As it is with the good,
> so with the sinful;
> as it is with those who take oaths,
> so with those who are afraid to take them.

> This is the evil in everything that happens under the sun: The same destiny overtakes all. The hearts of people, moreover, are full of evil and there is madness in their hearts while they live, and afterward they join the dead. (Eccl 9:2–3)

Some claim that Job holds out a hope for an afterlife. While there may be some truth to this (for there was a widespread belief that death was not the end of one's existence throughout the ancient Near East), it is clear that if Job did have such an expectation, then he held no hope for redemption after death—any afterlife was not, in Job's expectation, a preferable existence to this life, if this life was largely trouble free. To go further into detail about Job's eschatology descends into almost pure speculation. What we do know is that Job held out no hope for judicial vindication after death and so can see no ultimate expression of justice.

The Friends' Claims Undermined by the Prosperity of the Wicked (21:27–34)

Job closes his speech by turning to his friends (the second-person references throughout this section are all plurals), emphasizing his point that in reality there are many examples of the wicked prospering (vv. 27–34). Job claims to know what his friends are thinking—not a difficult claim given that it is completely in line with all of their arguments to this point. Job's quote in verse 28 is not directly from anything the friends have already said. It is a summary of their argument that any success of the wicked is now gone, and they have received their just rewards.

Job counters the argument of the friends by appealing to the knowledge gained by those who have wider experience of the world—"Those who travel" (v. 29). Were the friends to speak to such people, they would quickly find that the idealistic world they had constructed was unrealistic. There are, Job says, many examples of the wicked prospering, living long lives, being spared from calamity. This observation stands in contrast to the numerous verses which seem to indicate that divine judgment would be enacted in the present life rather than at some eschatological judgment (see Deut 32:5; Jer 18:17; 46:21) and delivered from the day of wrath (see Ezek 7:19; Zeph 1:15, 18). As such, Job implicitly questions divine justice but is nonetheless certain that the wicked do not all experience divine judgment for their wickedness in this life (as had been claimed by the friends).

Even in death, Job argues, the wicked are honored—so much so that he describes the soil in which they are buried as "sweet" (v. 33). The tomb of the wicked will be protected ("watch is kept over their tombs," v. 32), making it clear that these people are not quickly forgotten. The identity of all who follow and the countless number who precede the wicked into the grave is not entirely clear. Are they simply those taking part in the funeral procession? Are they those who have died before and who will die after the wicked? Or are they those who came before and those who will come after who also share this rather fortunate end despite being wicked? What is clear is that Job is certain that the fate of the wicked is, in many cases, far more blessed than his friends have claimed.

Having argued that his friends' claims are based on a demonstrably false premise—that the wicked are punished for their wickedness and the upright are rewarded—in verse 34 Job declares that their efforts are futile; they can offer him no consolation or comfort. There is nothing for him in all the words they have spoken.

LIVE the Story

How Should We Think About the Apparent Triumph of Evil in the World?

We, like Job, can readily observe examples in the world around us where the wicked appear to prosper and the innocent suffer. Even while we acknowledge that all fall short of the glory of God, it is not hard to see that sometimes those who best manifest the fruit of the Spirit nonetheless suffer more than those governed by the ruler of the kingdom of the air, the spirit who is now at work in those who are disobedient (Eph 2:2). If we expect to see justice at work in this world, in this present age, then we shall often be disappointed. And it is precisely to this problem that the book of Job is addressed, and while to this point we have not yet arrived at the book's answer to this issue, we nonetheless must grasp the problem and acknowledge the truth it presents.

This observation of the nature of the world in which we live was acknowledged elsewhere in the Bible, perhaps most notably by Qoheleth, the teacher whose words are preserved in the book of Ecclesiastes. For him, the toil of this life was rendered meaningless by the inevitability of death, a fate that was shared by all no matter whether one had lived a good or wicked life. For him, this called into question any endeavor aside from simply trying to enjoy the present moment (see Eccl 8:15).

Like Job in this speech, Qoheleth noted times when justice does not appear to be implemented:

> In this meaningless life of mine I have seen both of these:
>
> the righteous perishing in their righteousness,
> and the wicked living long in their wickedness. (Eccl 7:15)
>
> There is something else meaningless that occurs on earth: the righteous who get what the wicked deserve, and the wicked who get what the righteous deserve. This too, I say, is meaningless. (Eccl 8:14)
>
> I have seen something else under the sun:
>
> The race is not to the swift
> or the battle to the strong,
> nor does food come to the wise
> or wealth to the brilliant
> or favor to the learned;
> but time and chance happen to them all. (Eccl 9:11)

Job goes beyond this observation to note that there are consequences for the wicked who prosper. There is no motive for them to fear God or serve him. They see no benefit for themselves in serving God (Job 21:15). They present a clear contrast to the Job we met in the prologue, where the Satan had argued that Job's devotion to Yahweh was a result of the good he experienced in his life. Instead, Job here points to those experiencing good in their lives despite their lack of devotion to Yahweh. Rather than gratefully accepting the good gifts of God, these people accept them with no gratitude or recognition of the source of the good in their lives. And without the prospect of judgment, it is difficult to reconcile this situation with the idea that God is good rather than merely arbitrary or even absent altogether. Job cannot yet, given his place in history, share Paul's perspective on the way the world is, for Paul (as with any believer after Jesus's time on earth) could see God's map for the future and so could claim with assurance that "our present sufferings are not worth comparing with the glory that will be revealed in us" (Rom 8:18).

Paul knew this because he lived after Jesus had come as the one who, being in very nature God (Phil 2:6), had shown more clearly than ever before the nature of God and how that played out both in this life and the next. Jesus made it clear that in the present age, God causes "his sun to rise on the evil and the good, and sends rain on the righteous and the unrighteous" (Matt 5:45). Jesus himself addressed the very situation of the righteous suffering while the unrighteous prospered when he taught his disciples the parable of the rich man and Lazarus (Luke 16:19–31). There he depicts a diseased beggar whose entire existence is somewhat akin to Job's present situation—a man beset by a miserable skin condition, condemned to an existence of begging for every meal and whatever he needed to live. When he and the rich man die, they then find their fortunes reversed, with the rich man in agony and Lazarus in paradise. What is more, unlike the temporary situation faced by the two in this life, their reversal is presented as permanent.

Once again Job's situation and his and his friends' analysis of his situation highlight their place in God's story as it unfolds through history. They highlight to us our own need to understand this point. For Job and his friends, this future that is revealed later in Scripture remains unknown. Once we acknowledge this point, we realize the greater challenge to their faith in the goodness of God that Job's tragic circumstances, and the events that transpire in the lives of many Old Testament believers, presented. Yet even in the darkest of circumstances, we find powerful expressions of such faith. After the Babylonians had murdered Jewish infants and the Edomites destroyed their homes (Ps 137:7–9), and after Job had lost his children, health, and home, they continue their struggle with God and in doing so express a profound faith.

From Job's limited perspective comes the point of his observations about the prosperous wicked around him: it clearly undermines the arguments of his friends. Not only do they share Job's belief in retributive justice, they also maintain that God infallibly implements it in the lives of people everywhere. Yet Job speaks from personal experience to insist that it is not just his own circumstances that count against his friends' arguments but simple observation of the actual lives of wicked and godless people around them that should quickly cause them to rethink their position.

Job's whole point is summed up in the last verse of this chapter:

> So how can you console me with your nonsense?
> Nothing is left of your answers but falsehood! (Job 21:34)

He is simply aiming to refute the argument of his friends. This is not a case of "if the facts do not fit the theory, the facts must be changed" (sometimes erroneously attributed to Albert Einstein)!

What we do know, with the benefit of both hindsight and further revelation, is that neither the theory nor the facts were sufficiently complete for Job or his friends to understand accurately what was happening to Job. This should prompt us to ask whether we can still make a similar mistake.

Are we able, living with the benefit of the revelation that came through the establishment of the new covenant and the full revelation of God's Son, to still reach wrong conclusions because we lack the facts we need to correctly reach an understanding of suffering in either our own lives or in the lives of those around us?

The answer necessarily remains a clear "Yes!" Although much more has been revealed to us than was to Job and his friends, we do not know everything. Even the apostle Paul could still note that

> For now we see only a reflection as in a mirror; then we shall see face to face. Now I know in part; then I shall know fully, even as I am fully known. (1 Cor 13:12)

Part of the additional revelation that we have received has made it clear that there is much we do not know and cannot know. We do not have a detailed account of how every event in our lives plays out in eternity. As such, we need to see in Job and his friends a warning against drawing conclusions about what God thinks of us and our friends—or even those outside our immediate circle of friends—based merely on what we see or our own pet theories about what God might think about them. We need to be careful not to judge others as Job's friends judged him when we do not have all the facts.

CHAPTER 15

Job 22

Eliphaz's Third Speech

LISTEN to the Story

1 Then Eliphaz the Temanite replied:

2 "Can a man be of benefit to God?
Can even a wise person benefit him?
3 What pleasure would it give the Almighty if you were righteous?
What would he gain if your ways were blameless?

4 "Is it for your piety that he rebukes you
and brings charges against you?
5 Is not your wickedness great?
Are not your sins endless?
6 You demanded security from your relatives for no reason;
you stripped people of their clothing, leaving them naked.
7 You gave no water to the weary
and you withheld food from the hungry,
8 though you were a powerful man, owning land—
an honored man, living on it.
9 And you sent widows away empty-handed
and broke the strength of the fatherless.
10 That is why snares are all around you,
why sudden peril terrifies you,
11 why it is so dark you cannot see,
and why a flood of water covers you.

12 "Is not God in the heights of heaven?
And see how lofty are the highest stars!
13 Yet you say, 'What does God know?

Does he judge through such darkness?
14Thick clouds veil him, so he does not see us
as he goes about in the vaulted heavens.'
15Will you keep to the old path
that the wicked have trod?
16They were carried off before their time,
their foundations washed away by a flood.
17They said to God, 'Leave us alone!
What can the Almighty do to us?'
18Yet it was he who filled their houses with good things,
so I stand aloof from the plans of the wicked.
19The righteous see their ruin and rejoice;
the innocent mock them, saying,
20'Surely our foes are destroyed,
and fire devours their wealth.'

21"Submit to God and be at peace with him;
in this way prosperity will come to you.
22Accept instruction from his mouth
and lay up his words in your heart.
23If you return to the Almighty, you will be restored:
If you remove wickedness far from your tent
24and assign your nuggets to the dust,
your gold of Ophir to the rocks in the ravines,
25then the Almighty will be your gold,
the choicest silver for you.
26Surely then you will find delight in the Almighty
and will lift up your face to God.
27You will pray to him, and he will hear you,
and you will fulfill your vows.
28What you decide on will be done,
and light will shine on your ways.
29When people are brought low and you say, 'Lift them up!'
then he will save the downcast.
30He will deliver even one who is not innocent,
who will be delivered through the cleanness of your
hands."

Listening to the Text in the Story: KAR 307 (Mesopotamian); pottery sherd from Tell Qasile; "The Vassal-Treaties of Esarhaddon" (= "Esarhaddon's Succession Treaty"); "The Annals of Shalmaneser III"

Eliphaz's mention of the "vaulted heavens" (22:14) is another of the book's references to ancient Near Eastern cosmology, references that appear a number of times throughout the book (see, in particular, Job 38:4–38).[1] In Mesopotamian cosmology the heavens were generally understood to consist of multiple (usually three) layers.[2] The lowest of these, which would form the sky above us, was said to be made of a form of the mineral jasper that was sky-blue in color. One primary source detailing the way the heavens were thought to be constructed is *KAR* 307.30–33, which reads thus:

> 30 The Upper Heavens are *luludānītu*-stone. They belong to Anu. He settled the 300 Igigi inside.
> 31 The Middle Heavens are *saggilmud*-stone. They belong to the Igigi. Bel sat on the high dais inside,
> 32 in the lapis lazuli sanctuary. He made a lamp? of electrum shine inside.
> 33 The Lower Heavens are jasper. They belong to the stars. He drew the constellations of the gods on them.[3]

It might seem a stretch to associate this text with Eliphaz's reference to a "vaulted heavens" here were it the only time such a reference is made, but as noted above these ideas are reflected elsewhere throughout the book. Job and his friends clearly exist in a time and a culture where these ideas were

1. David J. A. Clines, "One or Two Things You May Not Know About the Universe: The Cosmology of the Divine Speeches in Job," in *Joban Papers*, Hebrew Bible Monographs 102 (Sheffield: Sheffield Phoenix, 2023), 328–42. https://www.academia.edu/6854753/One_or_Two_Things_You_May_Not_Know_about_the_Universe_The_Cosmology_of_the_Divine_Speeches_in_Job.

2. See Wayne Horowitz, *Mesopotamian Cosmic Geography*, Mesopotamian Civilizations 8 (Winona Lake: Eisenbrauns, 1998).

3. Horowitz, *Mesopotamian Cosmic Geography*, 4. The proper nouns here (such as Anu, Igigi, Bel) are names of deities associated with those levels of the heavens. The Igigi were a class of gods who served Anu. The italicized words are transliterations of the Akkadian names of the stones referenced (the precise identification of which is not always clear). For more information see Douglas R. Frayne and Johanna H. Stuckey, *A Handbook of Gods and Goddesses of the Ancient Near East: Three Thousand Deities of Anatolia, Syria, Israel, Sumer, Babylonia, Assyria, and Elam* (University Park, PA: Eisenbrauns, 2021).

common. What is more, for the author of Job to have included them in this account indicates that, for people living at the time Job was written, these ideas were generally accepted. One temptation today might be to suppose that these descriptions were originally understood metaphorically and so were never thought to reflect the actual material construction of the heavens. For such a claim to be true, however, would require that these descriptions in Job be clearly marked as metaphorical to counter the natural inference of the audience that the result of the universal belief throughout the ancient Near East that these details were accurate reflections of reality.

What do we make of them today? They clearly do not correspond with a modern understanding of the universe. The same could be said, however, for the language used when Job was written—even modern Hebrew speakers do not speak the same language that Job was written in (that is, there are significant differences between modern and biblical or classical Hebrew). It would have been quite unhelpful for Job to have been written in modern Hebrew, much less modern English, and still distributed to an audience millennia in the past when neither of these languages were understood, unless the point of the text was to teach modern English. To communicate effectively with the ancient audience, the message of Job had to be written in a language they understood, and this applies to both the use of Hebrew and the ideas employed within the story to communicate its message. In the same way it would have been quite unhelpful to have written a text about innocent suffering infused with alien ideas (such as a modern cosmology) unless the purpose of the text was to teach modern cosmology, and that is clearly not the purpose of the text.

The point is that these ancient ideas found in the text are there to ensure that the original audience got the message. The ideas are not there to teach that those widely accepted cosmological ideas were true any more than to teach that the biblical or classical Hebrew language was somehow "true" and all others false. The ideas and the language were necessary components of effectively transmitting the actual message of the text to an audience that lived and thought in a world where these ideas were common. In short, the book of Job never sets out to teach a specific cosmology; it sets out to engage with ideas of innocent suffering and God's sovereign rule of the world. To get its message across in the most effective manner, the author has employed language and ideas that the (ancient) audience could relate to and understand. We could even argue that part of the process of translating the ancient language in the modern world could include translating the ancient cosmology into a modern one to allow the modern reader to be more fully immersed in the message of the text, but that would then be a decision for the translators of any particular version of the book into the modern world. The point here can be summarized by the idea that *the biblical text is written for us but not to us. Both its language and ideas need to be translated into our worldview for us to correctly understand what God is saying to us.*

Eliphaz accuses Job of following the path (or way) of the wicked (22:15–16), which ultimately is undone when a flood undermines their foundations. While probably metaphorically representing the general destruction of the wicked, the image of destruction by flood (and not necessarily the great flood) appears in literature throughout the ancient Near East. It is somewhat reminiscent of the curse of Esarhaddon for those vassals who would break their treaty with him:

> Whoever changes, neglects, violates (or) voids the oath of this tablet . . .
>
> May Adad, the canal inspector of heaven and earth, bar rain showers from your land! May your fields be deprived of grain! May he submerge your land in a severe flood for no good end![4]

Flood imagery is also used often as a metaphorical description of an overwhelming military attack on an enemy.[5] From the Neo-Assyrian annals of "Shalmaneser III," for example, we read:

> I departed from the city of Gurgum. I approached the city of Lutibu, the fortified city of Ḫayāni, the Sam'alite. Ḫayāni, the Sam'alite, Sapalulme, the Patinaean, Aḫuni, (the man) of Bît-Adini, (and) Sangara, the Carchemishite, put their trust in each other. They prepared for war. They marched against me to do battle. With the exalted power of the divine standard which goes before me (and) with the fierce weapons which Aššur, my lord, gave, I fought with them. I decisively defeated them. I felled with the sword their fighting men. Like Adad, I rained down upon them a devastating flood.[6]

4. "Esarhaddon's Succession Treaty," trans. Jacob Lauinger (*COS* 4.36:162–63); cf. Clines, *Job 21–37*, 560.

5. Some further examples may be found in the account of Sennacherib's first campaign against Merodach-Baladan; see "Sennacherib's First Campaign Against Merodach-Baladan," trans. Mordechai Cogan (*COS* 2.119A:301); more from Esarhaddon (see "Esarhaddon's Thompson Prism," trans. Victor Hurowitz [*COS* 4.39:176]); and in the letter to the God Ashur recounting Sargon's eighth campaign (see "The Letter to the God Aššur Recounting Sargon's Eighth Campaign," trans. F. M. Fales [*COS* 4.42:199, 202, 206]).

6. "The Kurkh Monolith," trans. K. Lawson Younger Jr. (*COS* 2.113A:262, see 1.i. 41b–50). Adad was the Sumerian god of storm and thunder (hence the connection to rain here).

For dwellers in the ancient world (at least for those outside of Egypt where the annual flooding of the Nile was anticipated and, to some extent, welcomed), floods always caused trouble. It is clear that Eliphaz's appeal to floodwaters as a judgment upon the wicked is entirely appropriate against this backdrop.

Another reference in Eliphaz's speech that is not immediately clear to the modern reader is that to the gold of Ophir (cf. Job 28:16). We do not have a lot of information to elucidate the significance of this phrase, but reference has been found on a sherd of pottery at archaeological excavations that took place at Tell Qasile between 1948 and 1950. This makes mention of gold from Ophir, which was apparently provided for a location named Beth-Haran (perhaps connected to the Haran of Gen 11:26–31, but see also Num 32:36).[7] This indicates that Ophir was known for its (presumably) high quality gold in the ancient world.

EXPLAIN the Story

God's Impartiality Proves Job's Sinfulness (22:1–20)

Upon first reading, these opening rhetorical questions in verses 2–5 from Eliphaz may sound as though he is arguing that God does not care whether someone is righteous or wicked, but that misses the point of his argument. Rather, he asserts that God is impartial and not swayed in his judgments by anything he might gain from them. God does not benefit from the wisdom of the wise, as if he were lacking in wisdom himself. God does not benefit from the righteousness of the upright, as if he were lacking in righteousness himself. There is no way that any human can interfere in God's judgments. He cannot be bribed or coerced or influenced. He is impartial in his judgments.

Eliphaz's point here is simple. God's judgments are sound, and so the outworking of his judgments can be trusted. If Job is suffering in this world, there is (from Eliphaz's point of view) no doubt that he has acted in a way that warrants that suffering. So now Eliphaz reveals what he believes to be the full extent of Job's wickedness to a degree that none of the friends has even contemplated to this point. So extreme are the accusations that Job will feel it necessary to rebut these claims in his final speech (31:16–21).

The irony in Eliphaz's question in verse 4 should not be lost on the reader, for it is precisely because of Job's piety (or "fear of God") that Job finds himself in the situation he is in (see 1:9)! This is a reminder to the reader of just how

7. B. Maisler, "Two Hebrew Ostraca from Tell Qasîle," *JNES* 10.4 (1951): 265–67.

far from right the friends' arguments are, none more so than the words of this portion of Eliphaz's response to Job. The various sins listed by Eliphaz are clearly not sins he has actually observed Job commit. They are more likely deduced from both the severity of Job's suffering and the apparently hidden nature of Job's wickedness. As Clines notes, "they are not . . . the observed sins of the real man Job but the kinds of sins a person in his position can be imagined as committing."[8]

The first specific accusation against Job comes in verse 6. Eliphaz claims that Job has "demanded security from [his] relatives for no reason." The "security" here is a guarantee against a debt and, in the case of the poor, potentially consisted of the very clothes off their backs. The nature of this charge brings to mind the law of Exodus 22:26–27, wherein a garment may be taken as a pledge, but if the person from which it is taken has no other clothing, it must be returned by sunset. The two parts of verse 6 ought to be read in parallel, and so Job's behavior is all the worse because he demands the security from his relatives rather than show them mercy in their need and give without the need for a guarantee at all. Perhaps the most damning indictment here, however, is that Eliphaz claims that Job has demanded security "for no reason." The accusation is that Job has exploited his relatives when there was absolutely no need for him to do so.

The remainder of Job 22:7–9 reflects similarly on Job's supposed behavior to the vulnerable who were not part of his extended family but who nonetheless sought his help. Eliphaz imagines that Job has deprived those in need of food and water, even when they were widows or orphans (v. 9). For these reasons, deduces Eliphaz, Job has been struck down as he has. The language he uses in verses 10–11 recalls that previously used ("snare" in 18:9; "darkness" in 12:25; 15:22; 18:18; a "flood" [*yebul*] in 20:28, cf. 38:34 [*shiph'ah*]) or that found elsewhere in the Bible ("sudden disaster" in Prov 3:25; although the "disaster" part of this phrase appears frequently throughout Job, see Job 3:25 [NIV "what I feared"]; 15:21 [NIV "terrifying"]).

Eliphaz moves on to challenge Job regarding his attitude toward God in 22:12–20. Surprisingly, Eliphaz begins this section by (almost) accurately identifying the one problem Job has—that Job overestimates his own wisdom and underestimates God's by asking, "What does God know?" (v. 13). Job has accused God of misjudging him and seeks opportunity to set God right. However, Job has never actually uttered the words Eliphaz accuses him of speaking in verses 13–14, although they do reflect something of Job's argument in chapter 21. While Job has not suggested that God was unaware of what was

8. Clines, *Job 21–37*, 555.

taking place on earth as Eliphaz here implies, he did suggest that God simply allowed the wicked to prosper and the upright to suffer. Ironically, Eliphaz also overestimates his own wisdom by presuming to understand how God operates.

Eliphaz counters his understanding that Job thinks God is blind to the deeds of humans by noting that God has a vantage point from which he can view all that happens in the world, and so he knows all. In arguing thus, Eliphaz has erected a straw man against which to argue rather than addressing Job's actual arguments—a technique commonly used in debates but that primarily serves to tarnish the opponent by associating them with views they do not actually hold. Ultimately it reflects a failure to listen carefully and understand before responding—an important lesson for us all.

Eliphaz, ignoring Job's actual argument from the preceding chapter, returns to accusing Job of following the way of the wicked (22:15–17) and making the claim that the wicked do suffer the consequences of their actions. The reference to a "flood" in verse 16 is not a reference to Noah's flood (which did wipe away one generation, but Eliphaz is referring to all generations who have preceded them).[9] Rather, it is a metaphor for the destruction that comes upon the wicked, the destruction that Eliphaz believes has now made its way into Job's life. He has already claimed that Job has lived following the path of the wicked (22:6–9), and so here he asks whether Job will continue in this way that will lead to his destruction.

The wicked, according to Eliphaz, fail to appreciate that any good things they possess were given to them by God (22:18), instead thinking that they need nothing from God. The second half of verse 18 (woodenly, the Hebrew reads "the counsel of the wicked is far from me") mirrors Job's words in 21:16. Whether Eliphaz is deliberately quoting Job's words to make a point is not entirely clear, but while Job claimed to have no interest in the advice of the wicked, since he felt that their fortune was ultimately rooted in divine ambivalence rather than any inherent success derived from their wickedness, Eliphaz has different motivation. His avoidance of the advice of the wicked is founded in his conviction that any success they have is short-lived.

In 22:19–20, ultimately Eliphaz maintains his unshaken faith that the fate of the wicked is ultimately destruction, a fate that is witnessed by the righteous. Moreover, those righteous are said to rejoice at the ruin of the wicked. In context this is disturbing, given that Eliphaz is clearly identifying Job as

9. Some translations imply that the reference is to Noah's flood (e.g., NET), but there is no article in the Hebrew (it is not "the flood" but "a flood"), and the Hebrew here has the word *nahar*, usually translated "river," rather than the term used of Noah's flood, *mabbul*. Flood imagery was commonly used in the ancient world to depict all manner of destruction—see above under Listen to the Story.

among the wicked at this point. If Job was seeking comfort, these words from Eliphaz announcing the delight he would feel at Job's comeuppance must dash any hope Job had that the friends would help at all.

Eliphaz Calls on Job to Repent (22:21–30)

Eliphaz closes in verses 21–30 by once again offering advice to Job on how to remedy his situation. Job must be reconciled to God and make peace with him. Job can achieve this, says Eliphaz, through obedience (22:22) and repentance (22:23; the verb "return" [*shwb*] is used in reference to repentance, e.g., 1 Kgs 8:33, 48; Jer 3:7; 4:1; etc.), which go hand in hand with removing wickedness and ill-gotten gains (Job 22:24). The result of such action would be prosperity (v. 21), which means far more than mere material wealth, as Eliphaz explains in verses 25–30. Job will delight in God, his prayers will be heard and answered in a way that will turn others in trouble to him, and his intercession with God will result in their rescue—even those who are themselves not innocent will be saved by Job's intercession.

The identity of the person whom Job's prayer could deliver (v. 30) is complicated by the unusual language the author has used at this point. Somewhat reminiscent of the name Ichabod (1 Sam 4:21; this name is simply a transliteration of the Hebrew *'i kabod*, meaning "where is the glory?"), the phrase rendered "one who is not innocent" (*'i naqi*) in Job 22:30 could mean "where is the innocent?" probably in reference to those who do not know innocence. As such, the NIV's "not innocent" likely captures the meaning of the phrase well. The final expression of verse 30, "the cleanness of your hands," refers to one's righteousness (see the parallel in Pss 18:20, 24; 24:4) and so here points to the righteousness of the restored Job, who had followed Eliphaz's advice. Eliphaz envisions that Job would then be able to intercede effectively and plead on behalf of those who were guilty before God.

The last words of Eliphaz in Job 22:30, namely, that God will deliver one who is not innocent at Job's request, will prove to be ironically accurate when, at the end of the book, God will say to Eliphaz, "My servant Job will pray for you, and I will accept his prayer and not deal with you according to your folly" (42:8)—and that without Job's needing to repent!

LIVE the Story

Eliphaz begins the third cycle of speeches in fine form, and Job will respond in the next two chapters. But beyond that point the third cycle descends into disarray. Whether that is the result of damage to the original text or is a deliberate ploy by the author is disputed. There is, for example, no third speech from Zophar, and we shall see more difficulties appear as we move into chapter 24 and beyond.

In the meantime, Eliphaz doubles down and, rather than attempting to argue against Job's strenuous assertion that the wicked do indeed often prosper, largely just reasserts his original position, denying Job's claim (22:12–24). Before getting to that, however, he makes direct accusations about Job's behavior that has resulted in him losing everything (vv. 4–11). His estimation of Job has fallen considerably, and the claims he makes are the most extreme thus far. The escalation we see here, however, has its roots earlier in the book. Already in chapter 20 Zophar had implied that Job oppressed the poor, stole from them, and left them destitute (20:19). As readers who have shared the heavenly insights into Job's character revealed in chapters 1–2, it should be clearer than ever that the friends are completely wrong about Job and that their case against Job is more and more detached from reality and so less and less compelling. This has Eliphaz closing with yet another exhortation that Job repent and so be restored.

Reaching Wrong Conclusions with Insufficient Information

We know that Eliphaz's argument must be faulty given that we know Job is upright, and it is precisely for this reason that he suffers. Despite this, it is not quite so obvious to the reader exactly why it is faulty. Consider his first point: God is impartial and not open to influence or bribery. It is difficult to dispute that. Then we know that Job is suffering terribly, and Job and his friends all agree that this suffering is a result of God's actions. We know that as well, although we have been made aware of an intermediary—the Satan—in the prologue. Yet, it was also made clear that the Satan only operates within the confines of God's sovereignty, as he was required to gain God's permission before he acted, and so ultimately what happens to Job only takes place with God's approval.

The problem with the logic is not so much with the points being made as with what is left out. Eliphaz's world is too simple—he lives unaware of the big picture. He does not grasp the full complexity of the universe (neither, for that matter, does Job . . . yet). As such he makes simplistic connections that do not stand close scrutiny and so ultimately do not reliably represent the way God works.

It is easy enough to point the finger at Job's friends. It is also too easy to be blind to our own shortcomings and assumptions about the way God works in the world today. It is always easier to see the speck in our sister's or brother's eye than the plank in our own (Matt 7:3–5). For example, the argument is sometimes made that if we have enough faith, we can ask for anything—if we are sick we can be healed, if only we have enough faith. After all, everyone who came to Jesus when he walked the earth and asked for healing was healed, and Jesus is the same yesterday, today, and forever, so should not people be healed today?

And the claim is not limited to health. Some preachers today promote the idea that sufficient faith (often expressed through financial contributions) will ultimately result in God blessing us and making us wealthy. The claim even seems to make some sort of sense: Paul tells us that our God, the Creator of the universe, works in all things for our good (Rom 8:28), so it makes sense that he wants to bless us. Jesus even tells us not to worry about our needs since God will provide for them (Matt 6:26, 30; verses carefully extracted from their context by those who espouse these views). So, trust in God now, show your faith, and you will be blessed, God will provide for all your needs. It makes sense.

But it is wrong.

The problem with this argument is the same as the problem with the argument of Job's friends. It works with incomplete information and so draws premature and faulty conclusions. It fails to account for the consequences of living in a world alienated from its creator and the fact that reconciliation and restoration are tasks that involve dealing with the complexities that such alienation introduces. The quick solution to human sinfulness and rebellion against the divine King would simply be eradication, but God loves us and so has found another solution to the problem, a solution that stretches across the millennia from Adam through Job to Jesus and then forward to us, so that no one that God chooses to rescue will be lost. As this plan unfolds, we live while sin and its consequences have yet to be fully eradicated and so must deal with the complexities that entails.

Eliphaz's words in Job 22:19–20, read in a context where he has identified Job as wicked and deserving of the suffering he is enduring, should also be a troubling reminder to us of the dangers of self-righteousness. To see suffering in the lives of those around us as a sign of God's displeasure in them and to even rejoice in their fate not only lacks empathy but also presents God in a way that is incompatible with his character as revealed in the Bible. Using it as an excuse to avoid showing compassion is a failure to understand that there, but for the grace of God, go we.

Prayer and Intercession

Eliphaz ends his words with an interesting claim: the prayer of a restored Job would have the capacity to mediate with God on behalf of those in trouble, even to the point where, because of the cleanness of Job's hands, those who are guilty can be delivered (22:27–30). We have to remember that these words come from Eliphaz who is, in the end, declared to be wrong in what he has said. As such, we would be mistaken were we to conclude that the righteous can themselves atone for the sins of the wicked, at least in general.

Eliphaz's suggestion is nonetheless intriguing—that someone who is guilty would be delivered by Job's righteousness. Job himself had imagined an intercessor in 16:20, looking for someone to represent him in God's presence. There, however, Job was not looking for someone to excuse his guilt, for his suffering, as we have known from the beginning of the book, was not a consequence of any sin he had committed. Eliphaz, by contrast, specifically suggests that Job's righteous standing before God would carry such weight that God would forgive the guilty were he to ask him to do so.

The Old Testament contains few indications that such an appeal could succeed, but there is one famous phrase:

> Therefore I will give him a portion among the great,
> and he will divide the spoils with the strong,
> because he poured out his life unto death,
> and was numbered with the transgressors.
> For he bore the sin of many,
> and made intercession for the transgressors. (Isa 53:12)

The New Testament picks up this and points clearly to Jesus as the one whose intercession, on account of his righteousness, is able to "deliver even one who is not innocent" (Job 22:30; cf. Heb 7:25). As such, Eliphaz's words do reflect something far more important and fundamental to the prospect of reconciliation with God, an idea that will be further developed as God's story unfolds through history. There will be one whose "cleanness of hands" will allow him to atone for the sins of the wicked. The one who not only suffered as Job had suffered but who suffered vicariously, who took the penalty for sin that we all deserved, and who made it possible for our rescue to be effected.

At this point the parallels between Job and Jesus are more readily apparent. Job suffered undeservedly, as did Jesus. Job will intercede on behalf of others (Job 42:8), and they will be forgiven, and Jesus has interceded with the Father on our behalf, and we have been forgiven. At the macroscopic level Job does clearly prefigure Jesus. The differences, however, reflect the differences between the Old and New Testaments. So, while reconciliation between sinner and Creator is achievable in the Old Testament through obedience to the law and to the requirements of the sacrificial system, that reconciliation is, ultimately, achieved through the work of the Messiah in the New Testament (as explicitly detailed in Rom 3:25–26). Similarly, while Job's intercession may result in forgiveness and reconciliation, as the New Testament makes clear, that forgiveness is ultimately only possible through the demonstration of God's righteousness at the cross.

Thus, we ought to note that the efficacy of Job's prayers on behalf of others, whether as proposed by Eliphaz here or as actuated on God's instructions in chapter 42, is founded on the atonement wrought by the Messiah centuries later. Here Job both anticipates his work and models it, reflecting it and depending upon it. Job could not have understood the details here, but we are privileged to know this, such that when we intercede for others with God, pleading for their reconciliation with him, then we do so, not depending upon our own righteousness but on that of the King who suffered, who bore the sins of many and made intercession for transgressors.

And thank God that we can rely on the righteousness of another rather than our own, for otherwise all would be lost.

CHAPTER 16

Job 23–24

Job's Third Reply to Eliphaz

LISTEN to the Story

23:1 Then Job replied:

2 "Even today my complaint is bitter;
his hand is heavy in spite of my groaning.
3 If only I knew where to find him;
if only I could go to his dwelling!
4 I would state my case before him
and fill my mouth with arguments.
5 I would find out what he would answer me,
and consider what he would say to me.
6 Would he vigorously oppose me?
No, he would not press charges against me.
7 There the upright can establish their innocence before him,
and there I would be delivered forever from my judge.

8 "But if I go to the east, he is not there;
if I go to the west, I do not find him.
9 When he is at work in the north, I do not see him;
when he turns to the south, I catch no glimpse of him.
10 But he knows the way that I take;
when he has tested me, I will come forth as gold.
11 My feet have closely followed his steps;
I have kept to his way without turning aside.
12 I have not departed from the commands of his lips;
I have treasured the words of his mouth more than my
daily bread.

13"But he stands alone, and who can oppose him?
He does whatever he pleases.
14He carries out his decree against me,
and many such plans he still has in store.
15That is why I am terrified before him;
when I think of all this, I fear him.
16God has made my heart faint;
the Almighty has terrified me.
17Yet I am not silenced by the darkness,
by the thick darkness that covers my face.

24:1"Why does the Almighty not set times for judgment?
Why must those who know him look in vain for such days?
2There are those who move boundary stones;
they pasture flocks they have stolen.
3They drive away the orphan's donkey
and take the widow's ox in pledge.
4They thrust the needy from the path
and force all the poor of the land into hiding.
5Like wild donkeys in the desert,
the poor go about their labor of foraging food;
the wasteland provides food for their children.
6They gather fodder in the fields
and glean in the vineyards of the wicked.
7Lacking clothes, they spend the night naked;
they have nothing to cover themselves in the cold.
8They are drenched by mountain rains
and hug the rocks for lack of shelter.
9The fatherless child is snatched from the breast;
the infant of the poor is seized for a debt.
10Lacking clothes, they go about naked;
they carry the sheaves, but still go hungry.
11They crush olives among the terraces;
they tread the winepresses, yet suffer thirst.
12The groans of the dying rise from the city,
and the souls of the wounded cry out for help.
But God charges no one with wrongdoing.

[13]"There are those who rebel against the light,
who do not know its ways
or stay in its paths.
[14]When daylight is gone, the murderer rises up,
kills the poor and needy,
and in the night steals forth like a thief.
[15]The eye of the adulterer watches for dusk;
he thinks, 'No eye will see me,'
and he keeps his face concealed.
[16]In the dark, thieves break into houses,
but by day they shut themselves in;
they want nothing to do with the light.
[17]For all of them, midnight is their morning;
they make friends with the terrors of darkness.

[18]"Yet they are foam on the surface of the water;
their portion of the land is cursed,
so that no one goes to the vineyards.
[19]As heat and drought snatch away the melted snow,
so the grave snatches away those who have sinned.
[20]The womb forgets them,
the worm feasts on them;
the wicked are no longer remembered
but are broken like a tree.
[21]They prey on the barren and childless woman,
and to the widow they show no kindness.
[22]But God drags away the mighty by his power;
though they become established, they have no assurance of life.
[23]He may let them rest in a feeling of security,
but his eyes are on their ways.
[24]For a little while they are exalted, and then they are gone;
they are brought low and gathered up like all others;
they are cut off like heads of grain.

[25]"If this is not so, who can prove me false
and reduce my words to nothing?"

Listening to the Text in the Story: "The Hittite Laws" 2.19; "Instruction of Amenemope"; "The Poem of the Righteous Sufferer"

We have seen in the previous chapter that in Mesopotamian thought the gods were understood to dwell in the various layers of the heavens above the precious stone of the vaulted heaven. The relevance of that understanding to Job's words here is that it was understood in the ancient world that the abode of the gods was inaccessible to human beings. We see this reflected in Job 23:3, as Job recognizes that he cannot initiate an audience with God because, as a mere mortal, he has no way of making his way into God's presence. As Michael Hundley notes, "In order to influence the gods, people required contact with them. However, consonant with normal human experience, (living) humans generally had little to no access to the divine realm."[1] Job was faced with precisely this problem. In the ancient world, the solution to this problem was usually to build a temple for the gods as a place that would bridge this gap, a place where the gods could come to dwell and so where the devotee could come to present their petitions. Job, however, lived before there was a temple for Yahweh (or, for that matter, even a tabernacle). Job knew of no way to confront God in such a way that would prompt God to explain himself, and so felt at a loss for how he might resolve his differences with God.

Job's admission of being terrified before God (23:15; using a term [the root *pkhd*] distinct from that typically used to describe the "fear [*yr'*] of God" elsewhere in the Bible) is reflected in the words of "The Poem of the Righteous Sufferer," a tale that parallels Job's story in a number of ways. There we read of the suffering inflicted upon an individual by the Babylonian deity Marduk:

> He cut off the benevolent angel who (walked) be-side [me],
> My protecting spirit was frightened off, to seek out someone else.
> My vigor was taken away, my manly appearance became gloomy,
> My dignity escaped and lit on the roof.
> Terrifying signs beset me:
> I was forced out of my house, I wandered outside.
> My omens were confused, they were contradictory every day,
> The prognostication of diviner and dream interpreter could not
> explain what I was undergoing.

1. Michael B. Hundley, "Divine Presence in Ancient Near Eastern Temples," *RC* 9.7 (2015): 203.

> What was said in the street portended ill for me,
> When I lay down at night, my dream was terrifying.[2]

Job's terror is more directly focused on God than is this more circumstantial account of the righteous sufferer, but this terror produces the same result, namely, an inability to confront either God or (for the righteous sufferer) Marduk. For both Job and the righteous sufferer, there are no means available to redress the situations in which they find themselves.

Beyond this, there are other aspects of Job's speech here that reflect its ancient context. His catalog of offenses (Job 24:2–17) committed by evildoers contains numerous ancient parallels, a few of which illustrate the point. His concern over the location and integrity of boundary stones (v. 2) was not merely a concern in Israel (e.g., Deut 19:14; 27:17) but throughout the ancient world. Hittite law included the following detailed description of the penalty for violating a boundary:

> If anyone violates the boundary of a field and takes one furrow off (the neighbor's field), the owner of the field shall cut 0.25 square meters of field (from the other's field)the owner of the violated field shall cut off a strip of his neighbor's land 0.25 meters deep along their common boundary (= ca. 0.1 shekel) and take it for himself. He who violated the boundary shall give one sheep (= 1 shekel), 10 loaves, and one jug of . . . beer and re-consecrate the field.[3]

Similarly, the Egyptian "Instruction of Amenemope" warns against moving "the markers on the borders of fields," that is, boundary stones:

> Do not move the markers on the borders of fields,
> Nor shift the position of the measuring-cord.
> Do not be greedy for a cubit of land,
> Nor encroach on the boundaries of a widow.[4]

Moving such markers was not only theft of land but also that which was on the land, and so potentially could be linked to the livestock referenced in the second half of Job 24:2.

---

2. "The Poem of the Righteous Sufferer," *COS* 1.153:487, tablet I, lines 46–55.
3. "The Hittite Laws," trans. Harry A. Hoffner Jr. (*COS* 2.19:116, no. 168).
4. "Instruction of Amenemope," *COS* 1.47:117.

EXPLAIN the Story

The Impossibility of Challenging God (23:1–17)

Following Eliphaz's speech, Job speaks but does not respond directly to Eliphaz. He speaks as though Eliphaz had said nothing. This perhaps reflects the fact that he had really said nothing new, and Job felt no need to dignify his words with a response.

The Hebrew of verse 2 presents a couple of problems. While most translations have Job describing his complaint as "bitter" (from the root *mrr*), the Hebrew has a similar word that means "rebellious" (from the root *mrh*). As such, it seems better to understand Job as recognizing that his complaint is defiant. He recognizes that he is not dispassionately attempting to call God to account but is acting in a more confrontational manner, a subject that occupies him through the opening section of this speech.[5]

Job has only referred to his groaning once before (3:24). It refers not to the specifics of his complaint against God but more to his visceral response to his suffering. The heavy hand (NIV "his hand") that rests on his groaning is, however, Job's hand (the Hebrew has simply "my hand"). When the phrase "a heavy hand appears" elsewhere, it opposes that which it rests on (e.g., Judg 1:35 [NIV "the power . . . increased"]; 1 Sam 5:6–11 [NIV "the . . . hand was heavy"]; etc.). Thus, we find here Job attempting to suppress his groaning in order to express his defiant complaint. He is attempting to maintain self-control in order to present a more compelling argument.

Job outlines his preferred course of action in Job 23:3–17 based on a single condition: that he could know where to find God (v. 3). Armed with that knowledge, Job would confidently present his case to God. Furthermore, Job feels that the case is now winnable. If he could find the place where God is, God would listen to him, see the truth of Job's claims, and save him (v. 7).

The attentive reader will see that Job's thinking has changed over time. Initially he felt that there was no point in bringing a case against God (e.g., 9:3–4), for who could argue with God? Job, however, has become more desperate, more certain of the rightness of his position, more rehearsed in his arguments, and so he has become more confident that there is some chance that his case could succeed. What this also means, of course, is that Job remains ultimately convinced that God is just, and this is the ultimate sign of the strength of Job's faith. Despite all that has happened, even despite the

5. See Clines, *Job 21–37*, 593.

prolonged silence from God, he retains a deep belief that God is just and will do what is right, if only he has the opportunity to argue his case.

Yet Job does not know where to find God and so cannot present his case to him. In 23:8–9 he expresses this clearly. Conversely, God does know where to find Job (v. 10) and, more than just a geographic location, God knows the paths of his life and that Job has always lived an upright life following God's way, obeying his commands and treasuring his word.

Despite his initial bravado, however, Job revisits the nature of his opponent in verses 13–17. The Hebrew of verse 13 begins with the simple statement "he stands alone" (woodenly, the Hebrew reads, "he is as one"). Translations grapple with this in different ways, but the remainder of the verse makes it clear that Job is referring to God being both aloof and unchangeable. Faced with the might of God, Job is rightly terrified. Nonetheless, now Job is determined to overcome his fear.

The final verse of chapter 23 again presents difficulties in the Hebrew. Probably the best understanding is that Job declares that, in the face of encompassing darkness, he will not disappear and be silenced. Elsewhere, darkness was that which would remove something from sight and so make it as though it did not exist (e.g., 3:4–6). Job is thus determined to speak despite the overwhelming odds against him.

Job's Reflections on the Lack of Justice in the World (24:1–25)

In chapter 24 Job turns to reflect on the lack of justice in the world. To some extent this is a progression from reflecting on the lack of justice he has experienced in his own life and so serves to enhance his claim. He had previously presented the argument that the wicked are not called to account for their evil deeds (ch. 21). Here he advances this by reflecting on the consequences for their victims and of the failure to hold the wicked to account.

Judgment is frequently held to be a bad thing in the modern world. "Do not judge me," it is said, often with reference to Scripture to support the assertion (Matt 7:1; Luke 6:41–42). But in the Bible, judgment is what holds the wicked to account, reins in evil, and brings justice to the downtrodden (Ps 1:5; Isa 11:4). As such, Job laments the apparent lack of judgment in the world, for that allows the wicked to prosper (the Hebrew here more woodenly reads, "why are appointed times not set by the Almighty?"—lacking any word for "judgment," which the NIV correctly infers from the context). At this point, of course, it is important not to judge Job for his own ignorance, for we stand at a privileged point in history—the point after Jesus has come, died, risen, and ascended—that affords us rather more information than Job had access to and allows us to answer some of these questions. Nonetheless, there is a warning here for us as well: we must not assume that we know more than we do!

Job lists a series of examples of evil behavior that he feels are not judged in verses 1–8. Moving boundary stones amounts to theft of land from one's neighbor and is explicitly proscribed in Deuteronomy 19:14; 27:17; Proverbs 22:28; 23:10. One feature of the wicked described in Job 24 is their theft from the poor and needy. Both the orphan's donkey and the widow's ox in verse 3 would have been instrumental in their well-being, but they are taken by the wicked as a "pledge," which means that they were taken in payment for a debt.[6]

The path from which the needy are thrust (v. 4) is likely, in light of the second half of the verse, a public thoroughfare. The meaning is that the wicked force the needy out of the public eye, away from the place where they can be seen. "Out of sight, out of mind," could be their motto. This leads into the description of the poor in verses 5–6 as foraging for food at a subsistence level, their time and energy wholly occupied by the task of gathering just enough food to keep their families alive. These poor are naked, exposed, and vulnerable (vv. 7–8).

So terrible is the plight of these poor that they are required to make devastatingly difficult decisions in order to survive (verses 9–12). The worst of this for widows is the necessity to allow their children to be taken in order to service a debt to their corrupt overlords. Beyond this, the irony of their plight, according to verses 10–11, is that they work to gather food for the wicked but do not receive any of the bounty for themselves. Their nakedness (v. 10) highlights the injustice they face, for clearly they are so poorly remunerated for their labors that they cannot adequately provide even basic clothing for themselves. They cannot feed, clothe, or shelter themselves or their families—despite being engaged in employment.

One of the other ways in which the poor were employed was in the production of olive oil (v. 11a). This important commodity was produced through a physically demanding process that involved the gathering of the olives from the trees, transporting them to the oil presses, and then the storage of the oil.[7] Similarly, wine production involved gathering the grapes and taking them to the presses. Yet, despite their labor to produce olive oil and wine, the poor were deprived of access to the benefits of their labors (v. 11b). As David Clines notes, "Deut 25:4 prohibits a landowner from muzzling an ox when it treads out the grain, but here the farmworkers are depicted as being treated worse

6. Hartley, *Book of Job*, 346.
7. Clines, *Job 21–37*, 609.

than oxen."[8] The poor are treated contrary to God's own law (see Lev 19:9–10; 23:22), and yet God does not intervene on their behalf.

In Job 24:12, Job returns to his disdain regarding God's inaction on behalf of the wicked. The poor and downtrodden of the opening verses of chapter 24 are, in Job's eyes, wounded and dying. They call out for help, but their calls are not answered. And in all this, Job notes that God does not intervene. There is no justice; only death awaits.

In verses 13–17 Job turns from the lot of the oppressed poor to recount further the behavior of their wicked oppressors using the overarching image of darkness as the realm in which the wicked practice their evil. The themes of light and dark recur not only through the book of Job but throughout the Bible. In Job, darkness either represents death (e.g., 10:21; 17:13) or, as here, the place where the wicked carry out their evil deeds (e.g., 34:22; cf. Isa 5:20; John 3:19).

Job catalogs the deeds of the wicked, which they hide from the light. First listed is "the murderer" (*rotseakh*) who waits until dark (Job 24:14), whose victim is specifically identified as the poor and the needy. No reason is given as to why these victims are chosen by the murderer, but in the context of this chapter it is possible that Job is using the verb "kill" (*qtl*) as a metaphor to cover all the evil deeds of the wicked, which ultimately deprive the poor victims of their lives (v. 12).

Second is an "adulterer" who also waits for dark, explicitly to hide his evil deed (v. 15). Likewise, "thieves" wait until dark to break into houses (v. 16). For all of these wicked, the normal order of things is reversed—their "morning" comes as daylight ends, and daybreak brings for them the terrors that deep darkness brings for those who are not wicked (v. 17).

The final portion of Job's speech, recorded in verses 18–25, is fraught with difficulties. Superficially it seems to present an argument that runs counter to Job's claims in the opening verses of the chapter, mainly that the gains of the wicked are short lived and that they soon wind up in Sheol. The verses jump around between singular and plural referents, and in some places it is almost impossible to make any sense of the text. Some translations omit verses where the Hebrew is considered nonsensical (e.g., NAB 2002). Some scholars move these verses to chapter 27 to form part of an otherwise missing third speech from Zophar. Most translations (including the NIV) insert God into the text (see Job 24:22–23) despite the absence of any word for "God" in the Hebrew of this text.

8. Clines, *Job 21–37*, 609.

David Clines explains the problem well:

> In its present position in the book, it is so hard to see what these verses have to do with Job's argument in this speech, indeed with Job's argument at any point in the book. If they are really saying that the wicked get their just deserts, that is not only the position of the friends and not of Job, but it is also the very opposite of what Job has been arguing in this very speech in chaps. 23–24.[9]

The textual problems surrounding the third speech cycle do not end here, and these have prompted a number of suggested changes to the text throughout chapters 24–27, but no consensus has been reached. It seems likely that there are questions about these verses of Job 24 concerning which we will not ever have certain answers.

That is not to say that we cannot take a stab at understanding the gist of the passage. If we aim to make sense of the verses with minimal disruption, leaving them in the mouth of Job and expecting them to make some sense, there are at least a few comments that can be made.

The beginning of verse 18 in the NIV is rendered as "Yet they are foam on the surface of the water." This reflects a more wooden rendering of the Hebrew, "he is quick on the surface of the water." The "he" here would seem to be any one of the wicked described in the preceding section. That they are "quick . . . on the water" could mean, as the NIV has it, that they exist only briefly, like bubbles (i.e., "foam") floating on the water surface. Alternatively, waters may carry the connotation found elsewhere of that place of foreboding evil. Over such, the wicked skim with ease as it is their natural abode.

In the same verse the wording switches to a plural subject, "*their* portion" (italics added), which would imply that the subject is not the same as that for the opening verse. If that is the case, then the cursed land does not belong to the wicked. Further confusing things, the subject becomes singular again when referring to the way to the vineyards. The phrase translated "no one goes to the vineyards" (NIV) is better understood as "he does not clear a way to the vineyards."[10] The reference here to vineyards reminds us of Job's earlier words about the poor working to tread out the grapes to produce wine (v. 11).

What Job may be saying here is that the portion of the land that had belonged to the poor is cursed, possibly by the wicked, and the wicked further

---

9. Clines, *Job 21–37*, 667.

10. The same expression is translated this way in most of its other occurrences. For example, see Isa 40:3; 57:14 (NIV "prepare the way/road").

prevent the poor from gleaning in their vineyards (as a result of which they thirst, as stated in v. 11).

The dominant idea through the remainder of these verses appears to be the death of the wicked. Superficially this might seem to be recounting them getting their just desserts, but Job notes that this is the shared fate of everyone (v. 24). From Job's perspective, death comes to all, and if it arrives without any punishment or reward, then there has been no justice. It is all too easy to forget that Job knew nothing of a final judgment—that was only revealed later in history. The fact that the wicked die is not, for Job, a sign of judgment upon them, and so does not contradict his opening words in the chapter. If there are any negative outcomes for the wicked in these words, it is likely only that they are not remembered (v. 20). Yet Job has already observed that the wicked are unperturbed by this and enjoy their lives regardless (21:21).

LIVE the Story

Speaking to God

In this speech, Job expresses confidence that if he were indeed able to present his case to God then he would be vindicated and so shows confidence in the righteousness of God. It implies that, in Job's mind, his present circumstances must be the result of some sort of cosmic mistake, something that God has missed and that, when brought to his attention, will be remedied. It is a tempting thought that, given the scale of the universe and the manner in which it appears to simply keep running without the need for obvious divine intervention, God may be detached from the day-to-day minutiae of running every aspect of the universe, such that sometimes, at least on occasion, something might escape his attention.

The words of 23:3–7 suggest that, in Job's mind, finding God's dwelling would give him an opportunity to force God to hear his case and concede that Job's complaint has merit, for he suggests that in that place, and perhaps there alone, the upright can establish their innocence before him. Job's thinking here does prompt us to ask what Job thinks about prayer. We know he is aware of it; after all, prayer is mentioned in Job (16:17; 22:27; 33:26) and is commanded by God in 42:8, 10. Thus it is clear that Job and his friends understand the concept of prayer as a means to address God. The rationale behind Job's thinking here is that he believes that God is ignoring him or not hearing him (13:24), and so he has concluded that he must physically confront God—face to face, as it were—in order to ensure that his case is heard. God is ignoring Job's calls, so Job wishes to go pound on his front door until he gets an answer. The problem is there is no way for Job to get to God's front door!

Job's conclusion would be valid if his presuppositions were valid. If God only allowed suffering when it was deserved as a result of unrepented and unatoned sin, if divine discipline was always and only connected to behavior that warranted correction, then Job's logic would be valid—it could only be that God was ignoring him. And so, if Job was right—as we know he was, thanks to the backstory we are given in the prologue to the book—then turning up at God's door and demanding an audience would seem to be the best and perhaps only course of action available to remedy his situation. But Job was not right in this. Furthermore, we know that God does not overlook the minutiae of day-to-day life for any of his creatures (e.g., Lam 3:37–39; Matt 10:29–31), so whatever was happening to Job was not an accident of divine oversight.

Stepping back, however, we see that the problem Job had was not that God was ignoring his prayers or not hearing them. God begins his words to Job in Job 38 making reference to Job's words. He has heard them. The problem was not that Job's prayers—together with all his other words—had not been heard. The problem, revealed in those very first words of Yahweh to Job, was one of a lack of understanding, of Job's insufficient knowledge of the way the universe works and the purposes of God.

Job had an excuse, of course. He did not know everything that we do. That is a fundamental premise underlying the story of God, that there is progressive revelation from the garden in Genesis 2–3 all the way through to the cross and resurrection. This means that we should not make the same mistakes that Job made, and yet it is all too easy—at least at an emotional level—to fall into the thinking that God is ignoring us. "If you believe, you will receive whatever you ask for in prayer," says Jesus (Matt 21:22), and yet we ask and do not receive. If the universe is inexpressibly complex—and the more we understand of the universe from modern scientific investigations the clearer this truth becomes—then we fall prey all too easily to simple answers offered by deceptive but equally simple teachers around us. Such answers can give us the illusion of control over our own lives in exactly the same way the simple answers offered by Job's friends held out the hope of control to Job: repent, turn back to God, and you will be restored. Today we are told that if we ask and do not receive, we simply need more faith. People are reluctant to dive deeper into the teaching of Scripture and to see the context in which the words of Jesus were originally spoken. The simplistic teaching about asking and receiving fails to relate to God on a personal level as a loving heavenly Father; it instead treats him—as Job's friends depicted him—as an automaton whose responses could be assured by providing the correct set of inputs. If, on the other hand, we recognize that God loves us as a perfect parent loves their children, then our expectations and our understanding of the events of our lives is immediately changed. Whereas we think we know what is good for us, we cannot truly know this. If we believe that material wealth would be good for us, we cannot know the future impact such wealth would have on us or on those around us. But God does know this. A child can ask for things that the parent knows are not ultimately for their benefit, and so a good parent does not grant every request.

Job does not fall prey to the simplistic teaching of his friends—his circumstances would not allow it. We should heed this warning and be wary of easy answers to complex and difficult problems. We should trust God as a child trusts his or her father to have our best interests at heart.

Justice in the World

All this leads Job, who feels a lack of justice in his own life, to lament the lack of divine judgment in 24:1–17. He does so because he lives in a world at a time when the details of the future remained obscure at best. He certainly makes assumptions about the future, for he reaches conclusions based on the idea that there can be no future existence in which all are called to account and judged. He operates from the belief that this life is pretty much all that there is, and from that perspective he is right to lament a lack of judgment, for it allows the wicked to prosper without being held to account, and it allows the righteous to suffer without any reward. And while his conclusion is understandable, for he reaches this conclusion based on observation and cannot observe what will happen beyond death, he is attributing greater certainty to his conclusions than the evidence he has at hand warrants. He does not know what is in store for all people beyond death, but we now know, for God did choose an appropriate time to make that known to us.

As I noted in the comments on 24:1–8, judgment is often held out to be a bad thing in the modern world. "Don't judge me!" we are told (often appealing to Jesus's words in Matt 7:1 as an attempt to lend authority to the imperative). Yet a lack of judgment, a failure to hold the guilty accountable for their wickedness, is universally decried. We all know just how wrong that is. We keenly feel the weight of injustice when we are its victims, and in this experience we should understand at least some of the magnitude of Job's own feelings of being a victim of injustice. Job's belief in his own victimhood here will ultimately be assuaged by knowledge he learns through divine revelation. In Job's case it will come when God himself speaks from the whirlwind directly to him. Similarly, any sense of injustice we may feel can also be alleviated by divine revelation from God through Jesus and recorded for us as the Bible. From that revelation we learn that God is just (e.g., 2 Thess 1:6), powerful (e.g., 2 Cor 4:7), and loving (e.g., John 3:16). We learn that nothing escapes his attention, and nothing takes place outside of his sovereign rule. We will discover from the book of Job that the world we live in, the world God created and actively sustains, is vastly complex beyond our comprehension. We are told that things are not the way they should be—the creation is at odds with the Creator, since we creatures have rebelled against him. And we are told that God will not allow the situation we now find ourselves in to persist indefinitely—indeed, he has already taken decisive steps to resolve the situation. Those steps have made a way for the rebellious creatures to be reconciled and forgiven and restored, but this will also involve a final day when all are judged and held accountable. Justice will be done, and the day of judgment is coming. Prepare now!

Injustice in the World

Job's observations about the behavior of the wicked toward the poor and those in need in chapter 24 should also speak both to us as individuals and to us as a society. It is all too easy to turn a blind eye to those around us in need, including the homeless, the hungry, and anyone who falls outside of the comfortable and safe circles of society. There are places in most major cities where such people are hidden, sometimes they are even hidden from us in plain view, living on the streets and in desperate circumstances. Job's critique here should trouble us all, for we all participate—often tacitly—in such injustice. People in these circumstances are easily made someone else's problem or written off as perpetuating their own poverty and suffering, and so we blame the poor for their poverty. Job here points to these people as an example of the failure of God's justice, an oversight on his part that needs to be addressed. Even then, however, for those who live in affluent societies, the resources to help are not far off, but the will to help is hard to find.

In light of the injustices that persist in our world, we must ask with Job, "Where is God in all of this?" Is God's lack of action a sign of his lack of care or a lack of power on his part to intervene? Is it a concession by God, who demonstrates love centered on the other person by permitting free agency to the creatures he had created? Or is it, as Job intimates, a simple oversight in God's sovereign rule over creation that, if brought to his attention, would be rectified because of his just nature? Is God just too transcendent and distant from us to note such injustices that are occurring on a relatively small planet in a distant corner of a vast, vast universe?

These are questions explicitly raised by Job's circumstances and highlighted through Job's words here, particularly in chapter 24. There is a problem with justice in this world. And, as Job notes, that problem ultimately lies at God's feet. While the catalog of injustices presented by Job—moving boundary stones, taking an orphan's donkey or a widow's ox—may lie outside of our own day-to-day experience, the modern world has no shortage of equally unjust actions perpetrated by those who appear to escape justice. And so, we ask, where is God in all of this?

We do get answers to these questions if we are willing to hear them, answers that Job could not have heard in his day but that have since been revealed. We know that justice is coming and that judgment is both taking place today (according to Rom 1:24–32 one aspect of God's judgment on the world is *not* intervening and allowing sin to take its course, allowing us to bear the consequences of the sinful decisions we make) and ultimately to be dealt out at the end when the final day of the Lord arrives (Acts 17:31). And as much as we might long for that day when justice is finally and fully manifest, we should also be careful what we wish for, since we, too, will be held to account. We will be held to account for the times we turned a blind eye to those in need, or when we stole from others by cheating on our taxes or misrepresenting our own situation to others. In the end, the only way we can be prepared to face this judge who knows all and requires justice is to accept his offer of clemency, wherein the judge himself pays the penalty we deserve in order to fulfill the demands of justice.

The full expression of God's justice, we now know, is to be found both in the future and the past. In the future there will be a judgment for that which we have all done in this life. Justice will be done and will be seen to be done. It will be clear that God has not turned a blind eye, and that evil will reap its reward and, as such, evil will be fully and finally dealt with. The injustice of inaction of which Job laments in his speech will ultimately be met with clear and decisive action on God's part.

But as I noted, this justice is found both in the past and future. Job has highlighted the injustice of some, but in reality when we look closely at our own lives, we know that we are ourselves guilty. We may not consider our transgressions to be as heinous as those of people we consider to be truly evil, and such a self-assessment may well have elements of truth. But relative guilt is not the same as complete innocence. As such, we could only anticipate that we, too, will inevitably be subject to a judgment that will find us guilty. Yet, God has always been known as a loving God, as he had already said to Moses, "Yahweh, Yahweh, the compassionate and gracious God, slow to anger, abounding in love and faithfulness, maintaining love to thousands, and forgiving wickedness, rebellion and sin" (Exod 34:6–7a).

This is where many would like the description of God to stop, but it does not. To stop here would be to leave us with a world without justice. And so, we need to hear the remainder of Exodus 34:7: "Yet he does not leave the guilty unpunished; he punishes the children and their children for the sin of the parents to the third and fourth generation." Punishment cannot simply be hidden, forgotten, or ignored. Justice will be done and sin, rebellion, wickedness will all be punished. How, then, is this apparently insurmountable problem of expressing both mercy and justice to be resolved?

Job's situation points us down this path by recognizing the problem of injustice, the apparent lack of anyone being truly held to account. At this point we see that the story of Job is part of a bigger story. It is one episode of a longer series, each of which leads us to the cross of God's Messiah, where justice, mercy, and love find their ultimate and unique meeting place. For only here can our own culpability for the things we have done or left undone both be addressed with the penalty to ensure justice is done and seen to be done. It is only here that the mercy and love necessary for us to escape ultimate condemnation are found.

The idea is well represented in the final verse of the hymn "The End of Things Created," a verse penned by William Collyer:

> Great God, what do I see and hear!
>   The end of things created!
> The Judge of mankind doth appear,
>   On clouds of glory seated:
> Low at his cross I view the day
>   when heaven and earth shall pass away,
>   and thus prepare to meet him.[11]

This is not, however, an excuse for our own inaction in the present world. We as individuals, as the church, and as a society cannot hide from the truth that God does expect more from us. Just because the immensity of God's grace has been shown in the way he forgives our sin, we should not then sin more as if our continued sin could be perceived as demonstrating even more of God's grace (see Rom 5:20–6:14). No, for now that sin has been dealt with in our lives, we ought to live by his rules as citizens of God's kingdom. We are ambassadors of that kingdom in this world and ought to live as such, seeing need and seeking to meet those needs.

---

11. Lyrics from *The Baptist Hymnal* (Philadelphia: American Baptist Publication Society, 1883), 336.

CHAPTER 17

Job 25

Bildad's Third Speech

LISTEN to the Story

1Then Bildad the Shuhite replied:

2"Dominion and awe belong to God;
he establishes order in the heights of heaven.
3Can his forces be numbered?
On whom does his light not rise?
4How then can a mortal be righteous before God?
How can one born of woman be pure?
5If even the moon is not bright
and the stars are not pure in his eyes,
6how much less a mortal, who is but a maggot—
a human being, who is only a worm!"

Bildad's remarkably short speech has prompted some to suggest that an originally longer speech has been corrupted—possibly by assigning the second part to Job in the next chapter. A reasonable alternative understanding, however, is that Job interrupts Bildad, taking over the argument skewed somewhat to highlight his point.[1] What Bildad does say recalls words said before (cf. Job 4:17–21; 15:14–16), so he makes no new points. What he does do, following the pattern we have already seen in Eliphaz, is remove any nuance he had in earlier speeches and become more extreme in his arguments.

Bildad opens with reference to the terrifying might of God using military language. His reference to "awe" (*pakhad*) in verse 3 is elsewhere used in the context of a holy war (e.g., 2 Chr 20:29), and "forces" translates a term (*gedud*)

1. See Greenberg, "Job," 293; Patrick W. Skehan, "Strophic Patterns in the Book of Job," *CBQ* 23.2 (1961): 141.

used elsewhere of military units (e.g., 2 Chr 25:9, 10). Such language was often used to accentuate the power of a deity in the ancient world as it was something to which the audience could relate. For more detailed discussion, see Listen to the Story on Job 16–17, above.

From noting God's power, Bildad also returns to the themes of light and dark to point further to the vast difference between God and human beings by highlighting that difference by noting that God is far more pure than even the heavenly bodies such as the moon. If God is so far beyond heavenly bodies (see also Job 15:15), how much further is he beyond mere human beings.

Elsewhere in the ancient world, the brilliance of the moon was praiseworthy. One example can be found in the Sumerian "The Exaltation of Inanna," where the moon goddess is described:

> Like the light of the rising moon,
> how she was sumptuously attired!
> When Nanna (Moon) appeared in proper view,
> They (all) blessed her (Inanna's) mother Ningal.[2]

That Bildad here contrasts God's brilliance with that of the moon provides an emphatic affirmation of God's glory and of the vast chasm between God and human beings.

EXPLAIN the Story

The Magnificence of God (25:1–6)

Bildad begins by noting the magnificence of God. The Hebrew text does not mention God explicitly until verse 4, but it is patently clear that God is the subject of Bildad's words here. First, he points to God's sovereign rule and the fear that God inspires in his creatures. That this response is more than simple awe is made clear in other places where this terminology appears (see the reaction to this awesome God in passages such as Isa 2:10, 19, 21). Such is his power and majesty that he establishes order (Hebrew *shalom*) in his high places. The point is not to say that this is the only place where God effectively rules, but rather that if God rules effectively in these heavenly places, then his rule beyond is trivial by comparison. The point is emphasized at the end of verse 3.

2. "The Exaltation of Inanna," trans. William Hallo (*COS* 1.160:522).

Bolstering God's sovereignty are his extensive forces, an army beyond number (v. 3). There is no way anyone could imagine standing in opposition to such might. That everyone is included is made clear in this rhetorical question, for God's light indeed shines on everyone. It may be here that Bildad is reflecting Job's comments in the previous chapter about the wicked who lived in the dark. Bildad makes it clear that even they cannot escape the light of God and so are subject to his rule whether they like it or not.

The remainder of Bildad's short speech revolves around the inevitable impurity of human beings as an apparent consequence of God's sovereign power. The implication of this is that, according to Bildad's way of thinking, purity requires power, and so ultimate purity comes with God's ultimate power. For any lesser being, purity is thus unattainable. Although that appears to be Bildad's argument here, this does not mean that he is correct. His conclusions about purity appear to be a non sequitur, but we should hardly be surprised that he is attempting an argument that cannot stand scrutiny, for God will himself declare the friends to be mistaken in chapter 42.

Nor is there anything new in Bildad's words here—the same assertions have been made earlier by Eliphaz (see Job 4:17; 15:14). Bildad states that neither the moon nor the stars, heavenly bodies that in ancient thought were far above mere human beings, are pure in God's eyes. The parallels from verse 4 to verse 5 build on the notion that righteousness and purity are metaphorically paralleled in the concept of the brightness and clarity of the moon and the stars. Hartley notes that the full moon was sufficiently bright to allow a traveler to navigate at night.[3] His point here is not that the moon and stars are somehow morally suspect in God's sight, but rather that even the light they shine, which appears pure and bright to our eyes, is dull in God's sight.

If that is true of the heavenly creations, then how much more is it true of mere human beings? Bildad drives the point home by equating a human being with a maggot or worm. Dire as that sounds to our ears, the association is worse in the ancient world, where maggots and worms were unclean through their associated with death (see Lev 11:41; cf. Job 17:14; 21:26; 24:20; Isa 14:11). Thus, Bildad leaves us with the clear understanding that, from his perspective, to be human is to be inherently unclean. Consequently, there is simply no way that Job's claims could be true.

---

3. Hartley, *Book of Job*, 357.

LIVE the Story

Trying to Win an Argument by Shouting Louder

The arguments in Job have gone around and around in circles without making any headway. For the reader it would be easy to have lost sight of who is saying what. There is a well-known comedy routine that has two people arguing. Eventually the argument descends into simple contradiction—one says "Yes," the other says "No." This cycle repeats at increasing pace until one finally switches the answer prompting the opponent to switch inadvertently to the other answer. By this stage of the book of Job, we are almost in this position.

Bildad's short and blunt speech fails at a couple of significant points. First, there is no logical connection between his observation about our lack of sovereign power and being unclean. If this were true, then the first humans of the Genesis account would invariably have been unclean. Second, and more significantly, Bildad fails to acknowledge here that God had made a way for Job (and everyone else in the ancient world) to be pure through obedience and sacrifice.

There is a lesson to be learned at this point: blind repetition does not make for a good argument. Bildad simply ups the ante in the argument, pushing the rhetoric further but making no new substantive points. He is doing little more than yelling louder, as if the loudest voice wins the debate. In this process he loses any nuance his arguments may have had as well as any vestiges of compassion his words may have had for Job. Sadly, that mode of argument is all too common in the modern world, particularly when such arguments are carried out impersonally over social media. We ought to take the advice that Desmond Tutu's father gave him: "Don't raise your voice. Improve your argument."[4] Instead of listening and engaging, learning and compromising, and sometimes even admitting to error, we often dig our heels in and let our pride prevent us from admitting that we have failed to represent the truth. We cannot change our minds even when it is desperately apparent that we need to. It is ultimately the problem many have with repentance. Admitting we are wrong—even slightly wrong—is all too difficult. And yet it is at the heart of what it is to be Christian.

It might be noted that Job also digs his heels in and refuses to back down. The difference, of course, is that Job is actually in the right! So perhaps the

4. See Desmond Tutu, "Address by Archbishop Emeritus Desmond Tutu" (presented at the Second Nelson Mandela Annual Lecture Address, Johannesburg, South Africa, 23 November 2004), https://www.nelsonmandela.org/news/entry/the-second-nelson-mandela-annual-lecture-address.

problem at the heart is not merely pride, which makes it almost impossible to resolve an argument. Instead, the problem is twofold. First, it is that Bildad and his friends have not really heard Job and are intent on making their case almost without any concern for what Job says at all. Second, it is that they treat their theology as infallible, much as some treat their interpretation of the Bible as infallible and ultimately assign the authority to that interpretation which truly belongs to God's word alone.

How do we avoid these problems in our own interactions with others? The first problem—the issue of not hearing the other person—requires us to take the time to listen carefully to what the other person is saying by seeking to understand where they are coming from and by considering what circumstances are prompting them to say what they are saying. If we do not listen to and understand their argument, then we will do only damage and not help. The philosopher Daniel Dennett summarized the psychologist Anatol Rapoport's advice on arguing well here: "You should attempt to re-express your target's position so clearly, vividly, and fairly that your target says, 'Thanks, I wish I'd thought of putting it that way.'"[5] If you are unable to do that, then perhaps it is best to hold off responding until you arrive at the point where you can.

The second problem derives from our own pride and sometimes from our tendency to listen only to interpretations and points of view that affirm our own. To combat this, we need to learn humility, to expose ourselves to people with different ideas, to read different interpretations of the Bible. We do not need to agree with others, but we do need to understand them. If we do not end up agreeing with them, then at least we will either have improved our confidence in our own interpretation or recognized that our interpretation is not as certain as we had thought and thus be more circumspect and humbler in our approach to others.

Ultimately, however, we need to start by loving the person we are debating.

5. Daniel Dennett, *Intuition Pumps and Other Tools for Thinking* (New York: Norton, 2013), 33.

CHAPTER 18

Job 26–27

Job's Third Reply to Bildad

LISTEN to the Story

26:1 Then Job replied:

2 "How you have helped the powerless!
How you have saved the arm that is feeble!
3 What advice you have offered to one without wisdom!
And what great insight you have displayed!
4 Who has helped you utter these words?
And whose spirit spoke from your mouth?

5 "The dead are in deep anguish,
those beneath the waters and all that live in them.
6 The realm of the dead is naked before God;
Destruction lies uncovered.
7 He spreads out the northern skies over empty space;
he suspends the earth over nothing.
8 He wraps up the waters in his clouds,
yet the clouds do not burst under their weight.
9 He covers the face of the full moon,
spreading his clouds over it.
10 He marks out the horizon on the face of the waters
for a boundary between light and darkness.
11 The pillars of the heavens quake,
aghast at his rebuke.
12 By his power he churned up the sea;
by his wisdom he cut Rahab to pieces.
13 By his breath the skies became fair;
his hand pierced the gliding serpent.

14And these are but the outer fringe of his works;
how faint the whisper we hear of him!
Who then can understand the thunder of his power?"

27:1And Job continued his discourse:

2"As surely as God lives, who has denied me justice,
the Almighty, who has made my life bitter,
3as long as I have life within me,
the breath of God in my nostrils,
4my lips will not say anything wicked,
and my tongue will not utter lies.
5I will never admit you are in the right;
till I die, I will not deny my integrity.
6I will maintain my innocence and never let go of it;
my conscience will not reproach me as long as I live.

7"May my enemy be like the wicked,
my adversary like the unjust!
8For what hope have the godless when they are cut off,
when God takes away their life?
9Does God listen to their cry
when distress comes upon them?
10Will they find delight in the Almighty?
Will they call on God at all times?
11"I will teach you about the power of God;
the ways of the Almighty I will not conceal.
12You have all seen this yourselves.
Why then this meaningless talk?

13"Here is the fate God allots to the wicked,
the heritage a ruthless man receives from the Almighty:
14However many his children, their fate is the sword;
his offspring will never have enough to eat.
15The plague will bury those who survive him,
and their widows will not weep for them.
16Though he heaps up silver like dust

and clothes like piles of clay,
17what he lays up the righteous will wear,
and the innocent will divide his silver.
18The house he builds is like a moth's cocoon,
like a hut made by a watchman.
19He lies down wealthy, but will do so no more;
when he opens his eyes, all is gone.
20Terrors overtake him like a flood;
a tempest snatches him away in the night.
21The east wind carries him off, and he is gone;
it sweeps him out of his place.
22It hurls itself against him without mercy
as he flees headlong from its power.
23It claps its hands in derision
and hisses him out of his place."

Listening to the Text in the Story: "The Sarcophagus Inscription of Tabnit, King of Sidon"; "The Patrons of the Ugaritic Dynasty"; "The Code of Hammurabi"; "The Ba'lu Myth" (Ugaritic)

This, Job's final speech in direct response to his friends, again includes some mythological references that point back to the ancient world that Job inhabited. The opening reference to "the dead" in Job 26:5 uses the Hebrew word *repha'im*, which refers to the departed spirits of people existing in the underworld or Sheol (the term is also found in Ps 88:10; Prov 2:18; 9:18; 21:16; Isa 14:9; 26:14, 19). A cognate term appears in both Ugaritic and Phoenician literature with similar meaning.[1] The Phoenician example appears as part of a warning against violating the coffin of King Tabnit of Sidon, who reigned in the fifth century BC. That text reads:

> I, Tabnit, priest of ʿAshtart, king of the Sidonians, son of ʾEshmunʿazor, priest of ʿAshtart, king of the Sidonians, am lying in this coffin.

1. For Ugaritic, see "The Patrons of the Ugaritic Dynasty (KTU 1.161)," trans. Baruch A. Levine, Jean-Michel de Tarragon, and Anne Robertson (*COS* 1.105:357–58); Philip S. Johnston, *The Shades of Sheol: Death and Afterlife in the Old Testament* (Downers Grove: IVP Academic, 2002), 127–30, 134–41.

> Whoever you are, any man who comes upon this coffin, do not, do not open my cover and disturb me, for no silver is gathered with me (and) no gold is gathered with me or any kind of riches. I alone am lying in this coffin. Do not, do not open my cover and disturb me, for such a thing would be an abomination to ʿAshtart! And if you do open my cover and disturb me, may you have no offspring among the living under the sun or a resting place with the Repa'im.[2]

These parallels, together with the instance in Isaiah 14:9, suggest that the reference is not merely to any dead, but specifically to dead rulers, that is, rather notable figures among the dead.[3] If that is the case, then the reference here enhances the significance of these dead who tremble before God—even the greatest of human rulers tremble with terror in the presence of the Almighty!

One example of the Ugaritic use of the term in reference to rulers who had passed to the netherworld is from *KTU* 1.161, "The Patrons of the Ugaritic Dynasty," where the Ugaritic sun god Shapash gives instruction on descent to the netherworld where various ancient rulers are listed, including the Rephaim:

> Shine bright, O Shapash!
> Shine bright, O great luminary!
> On high Shapash cries out:
> After your lord, from the throne;
> After your lord, to the netherworld descend!
> To the netherworld descend;
> And go down low into the earth.
> Below is SDN-w-RDN;
> Below is Ṯ R-KLLMN;
> Below are the most ancient Rephaim.
> Below is Ammishtamru, the King;
> Below is Niqmaddu, the King, as well.[4]

The underworld or netherworld is referred to in Job 26:6 using two names, Sheol and Abaddon (see Rev 9:11), both of which refer to the place of the dead

2. "The Sarcophagus Inscription of Tabnit, King of Sidon," trans. P. Kyle McCarter (*COS* 2.56:182).

3. See Clines, *Job 21–37*, 634. It seems that those who produced the ancient Greek translation of the Old Testament (often called the Septuagint) understood this and so rendered the Hebrew term has using the plural of the term *gigas* (i.e., *gigantes*, "giants").

4. "The Patrons of the Ugaritic Dynasty," *COS* 1.105:358.

in ancient thought. The Hebrew conception of the underworld shared much with that of the nations in Israel's immediate vicinity. The location, identified as being "beneath the waters," reflects the ancient Near Eastern cosmological view that the realm of the dead (Sheol in the Bible) lay below the primordial ocean upon which the land floated.[5] As noted earlier in this commentary, such use of cosmological language should not be read as endorsing such a view as the correct understanding of the universe. Rather, it should be understood as part of the language used to communicate the message of the book to an audience who thought in these terms. To use modern cosmological language would have resulted in the true message of the speech being obscured from the original audience. For us to understand the original story involves translation both of the words in the Hebrew and the ideas, metaphors, and other figures of speech used to convey the message.

The "northern skies" of Job 26:7 translates the Hebrew word *tsaphon*, often simply transliterated "Zaphon" in Bible versions (e.g., Josh 13:27 [ESV]; Judg 12:1 [NIV, ESV]; and in NIV also Ps 48:2[3 Hebrew]; Isa 14:13). There is no word for "skies" in the Hebrew text, and it has been inferred by the translators.[6] This becomes significant when we realize that the term was also the name of the mountain noted in Ugaritic texts that was the abode of the gods. This idea may be in the background here (see also Isa 14:13). There, in the heights of that mountain, dwells Baal and the other gods. As a result, many Ugaritic texts make reference to Zaphon. As an example, here is a portion of "The Baʿlu Myth":

> He arises, chants, and sings,
> cymbals (being) in the hands of the goodly one;
> The good-voiced youth sings
> for Baʿlu in the heights of Ṣapānu.[7]

With its ancient context in mind, the point in Job 26:7 would then be that Yahweh's power is such that not only does the netherworld lie bare before him, but he is also the one who established the place that many thought to be the abode of the gods. In the minds of the original audience, this would

5. Clines, *Job 21–37*, 635. For further discussion of Sheol and the netherworld/underworld, see Listen to the Story for Job 3.

6. Tremper Longman, *Job*, BCOTWP (Grand Rapids: Baker Academic, 2012), 316. The Hebrew *tsaphon* is most commonly translated "north" or with similar expressions.

7. "The Baʿlu Myth," *COS* 1.86:250 (i 18–22). In this translation, Zaphon (Ugaritic *ṣpn*) is rendered Ṣapānu.

have established Yahweh's preeminence above all other deities. While we may question whether any in ancient Israel (i.e., the original audience for the book of Job) would have believed that other gods existed, it is indeed likely to some extent, as evidenced by some parts of the Old Testament (e.g., Exod 12:12; Num 33:4; Judg 11:24; Ps 86:8). From a New Testament perspective we also recognize that there are spiritual forces at odds with God, and so the idea that these were, in earlier times, identified as the gods of the nations should not make us too uncomfortable.

In the same verse, however, we hear Job affirm that God "suspends the earth over nothing." In ancient cosmology the earth (or land—the same Hebrew term is used for both ideas with "earth" really just meaning "all of the lands") was supported on pillars, and so some take Job's words here as an indication that he had a more modern cosmological understanding of the world than many commentators credit him with (although as we read on we still find clear references to supporting pillars in v. 11). This understanding, however, reads too much into Job's language here for, as David Clines points out, the terminology used here is elsewhere used in connection to the erection of tents. He explains,

> There are "pillars of the heavens" at the four corners of the earth . . . , but what supports the "tent" across the vast expanse of the sky, from one horizon to the other? Nothing! There is no center pole to the tent that is the sky. Here then is an example of the power of God, that he can spread out the skies with nothing to hold them up.[8]

Similarly, Job's description of the earth (or "land") being suspended over nothing may point to the belief that there was a vast cavity below the earth (i.e., Sheol), over which the land of the living was suspended. Despite attempts to extract Job from his historical and cultural context, it turns out he remains embedded there, and appropriately his words remain comprehensible to the ancient audience.

Job 26:12–13 refers once again to the mythical sea monster Rahab. (For more information on this creature, see the earlier discussion on Job 9:13.) The final section of this passage includes an imprecatory poem against Job's enemy. While the Old Testament contains a number of examples of this type of speech (see, for example, Pss 5; 10; 17; 35), such imprecations are also found elsewhere in the ancient Near East, where they appear commonly on

8. Clines, *Job 21–37*, 635–36.

monuments and in treaties. One notable example is the imprecatory section at the end of "The Laws of Hammurabi," where we read,

> (But) should that man not heed my pronouncements, which I have inscribed upon my stela, and should he slight my curses and not fear the curses of the gods, and thus overturn the judgments that I judged, change my pronouncements, alter my engraved image, erase my inscribed name and inscribe his own name (in its place)—or should he, because of fear of these curses, have someone else do so—that man, whether he is a king, a lord, or a governor, or any person at all, may the great god Anu, father of the gods, who has proclaimed my reign, deprive him of the sheen of royalty, smash his scepter, and curse his destiny.[9]

Thereafter follow many more curses called down on whoever would ignore the laws contained therein.

Throughout the ancient world, then, imprecations were used when the person making them had no power to carry them out but felt strongly about the justice of their position against various opponents. Job fits well into this scenario, convinced in the rightness of his position while feeling opposed by everyone—both the people around him and even God.

EXPLAIN the Story

Job Mocks His Friends (26:1–4)

The third cycle of speeches ends with words from Job and is missing any contribution from Zophar. Following Bildad's short speech in chapter 26, it may be that Job has interrupted Bildad before he could finish, and some of these words attributed to Job do sound more like the friends than Job himself. As such, some attribute some parts of this speech to Zophar rather than Job, concluding (with some justification) that the text we have in our possession has been damaged during its history. David Clines, for example, assigns verses 2–14 to be a continuation of Bildad's speech and claims that verse 1 is a later interpolation.[10] Job 27:13–23 could very easily be an argument made against Job by one of his friends. Indeed, it would make the task of understanding the book simpler to make such an adjustment.

---

9. "The Laws of Hammurabi," trans. Martha Roth, starting at line xlix.18 (*COS* 2.131:352).
10. Clines, *Job 21–37*, 626.

Another view is to note that the debate between Job and his friends has been going in circles for a while, and finally things are falling apart. The lack of progress, the failure to concede even a small point, and the pig-headed obstinacy of the participants inevitably lead to the point where the words being spoken are essentially meaningless. They are just noise, the debate collapses into the noise, and the author of Job has reflected this in the disintegration of form.[11]

In addition to all this, Job likely mimics or parodies his friends. He has not been afraid to use sarcasm—indeed he opens this speech with some. In his frustration it is not surprising to see him resort to somewhat childish debating techniques. One might imagine him speaking their words back to them using the voice of a child taunting a friend. Certainly, the argument has descended to this level. As such there is no compelling reason to change the text as it is preserved in the Hebrew.

Job once again begins with sarcasm. The objects of his lines—"The powerless," "the arm that is feeble," and so on—are all singular, so pointing quite clearly to Job himself. The subject is also singular, so perhaps should be read as singling out Bildad in his last speech. Job has elsewhere highlighted his own weakness (e.g., 6:11–12) and his need for help (e.g., 6:13) but will soon speak of the way he did help those in need (29:12).

By way of contrast, however, with his sarcasm in chapter 26 Job does not think of himself as lacking in wisdom but clearly questions the wisdom of his friend, who has given him no help and offered no wisdom of any value. Furthermore, Job questions the source of the words offered to him by Bildad, probably reflecting the fact that they simply echo the earlier words of Eliphaz (compare 25:4–6 with 4:17; 15:14). There is nothing new or original in Bildad's words; they are simply the words of the other friends repeated. There is no new argument, no wisdom, no help.

Job Describes the Might of God (26:5–14)

In verses 5–14 Job turns to recount the might of God. He has previously made reference to God's might and power as reasons why he feels incapable of calling God to account (see 9:2–20), so his words here are in keeping with this earlier thought. For Job at this time, the might and power of God do not

11. Long presents a good argument for this view (V. Philips Long, "On the Coherence of the Third Dialogic Cycle in the Book of Job," in *Studies on the Text and Versions of the Hebrew Bible in Honour of Robert Gordon*, ed. Geoffrey Khan and Diana Lipton, VTSup 149 [Leiden: Brill, 2012], 113–25).

offer comfort. They do not assure him of a resolution to his problems; they only appear as an obstacle.

Verse 6 makes reference to Sheol, "the realm of the dead." In the ancient world, the dead were thought to reside "beneath the waters" (v. 5), which does not mean somewhere in the sea itself but rather deep below the ocean in a realm below, the underworld or netherworld. These verses make it clear that, in Joban thought, death was not the absolute end—that is, nonexistence—, for the residents of Sheol could be said to be in "deep anguish" (v. 5). Yet, from a broader perspective existence in Sheol was not comparable to living under the sun; as Hartley notes, "its inhabitants eked out a wretched, meagre existence . . . for while they have existence and identity, they are weak and helpless."[12]

Job's point here is that even the most inaccessible places, the hidden realm of the dead, is naked and bare before God. The "anguish" of the dead here (and likely dead kings or rulers who would be the most immune to terror; see above under Listen to the Story) refers to their being made to tremble as a result of laying exposed before God. The verb used here (*hyl*) is often associated with physical or emotional pain (e.g., Isa 26:18, "writhed in labor"; Esth 4:4, "she was in great distress").

The "northern skies" in verse 7, as mentioned above, is considered by some to be a reference to Zaphon, the Ugaritic mountain of the gods, which is cognate to the Hebrew term used here. A difficulty with this view is that Job states that the north is spread out over empty space, which seems an unlikely description of the mountain, even if a similar description applies in the same verse to the earth. Whichever way the name "Zaphon" is taken, the point is that God has the power to do the unimaginable and impossible. This verse, together with the remainder of this chapter, all speak poetically from the perspective of the ancient cosmology, which reflected the way Job and his friends would have thought about the universe. The point of these words of Job is not to correct their cosmology in accordance with modern conceptions but rather to speak to them in language they understood of God's power in creation.

Job's description of God's power over his creation in verses 7–10 has him supporting the world, holding vast amounts of water in clouds by his power—so much so that the full moon can be concealed by them. The horizon is a boundary established by God that separates light and darkness, the latter possibly a reference to the darkness of the deep waters below the horizon,

12. Hartley, *Book of Job*, 365.

which is contrasted to the illumination of the sky.[13] The "pillars of the heavens" (v. 11) were the cosmological structures thought to support the sky. That they shake at God's rebuke again reflects the awesome power of God (see 2 Sam 22:16, Ps 18:15).

Verse 12 further depicts God's vast power over the sea, a place that was imbued with significant meaning in the ancient world. The sea was a place of dark chaotic powers often held to be at odds with the purposes of God. Yet, even these are subdued by God.[14] In this sea is the powerful Rahab (see comments above on Job 9:13; also see Ps 89:10; Isa 51:9). And again, this powerful creature is defeated by God, along with its counterpart, the "gliding serpent" (v. 13), which is also used to refer to Leviathan (see Isa 27:1). The clearing of the skies as a counterpoint to God's power over Leviathan parallels the stilling of the waters and his victory over Rahab. God's power is absolute.

Job, however, is not satisfied with this depiction of God's power, so in verse 14 he makes it clear that these are demonstrations of the barest edges of God's power. In actuality, these depictions of God's power barely scratch the surface, and yet they already stretch human imagination to its limit. Job points out that God's power extends way beyond that which he has depicted. It is limitless.

And for Job we already know that this is a problem. How could he stand and argue before one such as this (see 9:2–20)?

Job Protests His Innocence (27:1–6)

Chapter 27 begins with an unexpected interruption from the narrator in the middle of Job's speech. This is the only clear example of this happening anywhere in the book.[15] The purpose of this break may be to reiterate that what follows continues Job's speech where we may have otherwise expected Zophar to take over, a further sign that the debate has decayed into disarray.

Job makes a final statement of his innocence and his determination to persist with his case in verses 2–6. He begins by swearing an oath to affirm the truth of his statements (vv. 2–4). Such an oath as the one Job here swears

13. The meaning of the Hebrew here is not entirely clear.

14. The NIV's "churned up" here renders a term that could either mean this or else "become/make still" (see "רגע," *HALOT* 1188). The latter is to be preferred in a context where God's power over the sea is being depicted (see CEB, ESV, GNV, LEB, NASB; Longman, *Job*, 316; Clines, *Job 21–37*, 638.). Such so-called contranyms—words whose meanings include their own opposites—exist in English too, such as *cleave*, which can mean "cling to" or "divide."

15. I say "clear" because the same words appear at Job 29:1 which, if Job 28 is assigned to Job, would do the same. However, it is unlikely that chapter 28 is spoken by Job. See the discussion on chapter 28 for more detail.

highlights the depth of Job's determination, for he ties it to God in such a way that the consequences for breaking the oath would be dire (cf. Lev 19:12). Ironically, this appeal to God to demonstrate the profound veracity of the claim Job makes about his truthfulness comes amid his claims that God has not treated him with justice.

Job makes it very clear that he considers any agreement with his three friends over their diagnosis of the cause of his woes to be tantamount to lying. His sworn oath that he has and will speak only the truth is presented in contrast to admitting that they were right. Job's final declaration is that he will not waver in his testimony; he will not concede even one point to his friends.

Job Calls for Justice to Be Done (27:7–23)

For many readers, having Job speak the words found in verses 7–23 seems at odds with what he has said earlier in the book and seem more to reflect the views of his friends. Furthermore, the preceding words from Job read as a climactic declaration of his determination never to concede. Consequently, some assign these words to Zophar, who is otherwise missing from the third cycle of speeches.[16] Others think the text of these chapters has been scrambled so thoroughly during the history of its transmission that its original form cannot be recovered.[17] Greenberg, however, suggests that Job engages in mimicry here, demonstrating that he has so thoroughly mastered the arguments of his friends that he speaks their words for them.[18]

The diverse array of readings of these verses highlights the difficulties, and so however we decide to interpret these words, some amount of humility is called for, and thus we ought to tread carefully. Nonetheless, all we ultimately have to go on is the text before us, which clearly ascribes these words to Job.

The passage itself opens with an imprecation on Job's enemy. Words such as these are uncomfortable for modern readers but are an expression of the depth of emotion of the speaker in the face of entrenched opposition (a number of psalms include such language, e.g., Pss 69; 109). They often express a strong desire for justice on the part of the speaker where it has otherwise failed, such as in Psalm 137:8–9, and so their words should not be read as a promise that the outcome will be achieved but more as a rhetorical expression

16. Clines, *Job 21–37*, 651–77.

17. See Wharton, *Job*, 111. who writes, "the entire block of material from 24:18 . . . through 27:23 has been rather hopelessly scrambled . . . somewhere in the process of copying, preserving, editing, and transmitting the text."

18. Greenberg, "Job," 294. In similar vein, Janzen suggests that Job herein parodies Zophar in anticipation of his final speech and so denies him the opportunity to make that speech, see J. Gerald Janzen, *Job*, IBC (Louisville: Westminster John Knox, 1985), 185–86.

of the depth of feeling that stands behind the words. Furthermore, the focus is not so much on whether God reliably implements retributive justice (for Job has clearly stated that he does not) but on the desire to have his enemy brought to justice.

Understood this way, perhaps the best approach to this section of Job's speech is to understand it as an expression of Job's desire for justice. This desire is not limited to a hope that his enemy would be brought to justice but that God himself would implement the justice he (and his friends) had always understood to be inherent to God's nature. As such, the opening "may," expressing strong desire, sets the tone for the remainder of the chapter.[19]

So, who is Job's enemy? The term is singular rather than plural, but it is unlikely to be God, given the repeated references to God as the one Job wants to implement justice (e.g., v. 8, "when God takes away his life"), despite that Job refers to God as an enemy (13:24; 33:10). It cannot be the Satan of the prologue (the word translated "adversary" in v. 7 is a different Hebrew word [*mithqomem*] from the one used for the Satan in the prologue), for Job knows nothing of him or his role in his circumstances. Most likely, following on from the preceding section, Job's enemy is anyone who persists in accusing him of sin. As such, each of the three friends falls perilously close to fitting this description. That they do not yet fit this description is made clear when Job explicitly refers to them from verse 11 onward.

Verses 8–10 and 13–23 describe Job's hope for how the wicked, unjust, or "godless"—the Hebrew word means "profane, impious"[20]—ought to be treated by God and so describes the fate Job wishes upon his enemy. In an ideal world imagined by Job, God does not listen to them when they need help. Their children bear the consequences of their sin (vv. 14–15), while the righteous reap the benefits of their labors (vv. 16–17). Their house is fragile as is their entire life (vv. 18–19), such that it can end prematurely in a moment (vv. 20–23).

In the midst of this, Job breaks his train of thought to address directly his friends in verses 11–12. He refers to them all (the pronouns are plural) using verb forms that should be understood modally so that they do not express certainty—Job is not claiming that his instruction will be successful but is rather expressing his desire. He would like to teach his friends about the power of God, even admitting that he should not have to teach them, as they have all seen God's power. This realization prompts Job to question why so

19. See Andersen, *Job*, 221.
20. See "חנף I," *DCH* 3:277, §3.

much time has been wasted (v. 12). The phrase "meaningless talk" translates an intensive expression, which is also repeated throughout Ecclesiastes and here labels everything that has been said by the friends to this point as futile.

Job simply wants his enemy to face justice, the justice his friends say God delivers, the justice that Job had believed and still wishes God would deliver. And he wants his friends to hear him, learn, and understand the implications of God's power in the world.

LIVE the Story

Standing Firm in the Face of Opposition

Job begins this speech by speaking about God's power over creation (26:5–14). In doing so Job is reiterating his earlier points about God's greatness and power, factors that have kept him from expecting any answer from God, since we know from what Job has already said that this all makes God unapproachable and undermines any hope Job has had in his ability to plead his case. For Job, God's power is not a consolation but a problem. Job's focus here presents a subtle but significant contrast to God's own speeches later in the book where the emphasis is not on his power but on his wisdom and knowledge. This difference reflects the true problem that Job faces: it is not his lack of power in the face of powerful deity but his ignorance before a supremely wise God who sovereignly manages the affairs of the entire universe.

Job closes his words to his three friends here by making his final stand, declaring his determination to maintain his insistence on his innocence and persist in his upright and blameless ways (27:4–6). He will maintain his integrity. He will not concede to the friends' insistence that he must repent of his sin, for there is no sin in Job's life of which he must repent. Job declares that he will not budge from his position; he will not concede to their claims.

Such stubbornness can be either good or bad. A stubborn refusal to compromise the truth, to call righteous that which is unrighteous, to label a wrong as right, or to commit a sin as a good thing it is to be applauded and supported. When Job insists that this is where he will stand and that he will not budge from his position; he is in the right. For Job to have repented of something at this point would have been to lie simply to accede to the pressure of his friends. Such an action on Job's part may have silenced his friends, but it would not have solved Job's problem.

On the other hand, a stubborn refusal to acknowledge wrongdoing, repent, or make amends is clearly bad. And, to be quite honest, that is a far more real danger for any of us. We are far more likely to want to justify our poor choices, our bad behavior, and our sin in such a way that it is whitewashed. Our pride pushes us to turn a blind eye to the true nature of much of our behavior. As Yahweh made clear in the prologue of Job, there is none like Job who is blameless and upright. When we find ourselves in difficult circumstances holding on to our integrity, we may just need to step back a little and acknowledge that our integrity is not quite as intact as we would like to believe or would like others to believe. We need to be prepared to admit to our failings, repent, and call upon the mercy of God.

Understanding Ancient Cosmological Language

The extensive use of language reflecting an ancient cosmology, both in this speech by Job and elsewhere in the book, presents a helpful lesson in reading the Bible. Should we read this language as somehow authorizing this view of the universe? Should we dismiss it as poetic metaphorical language? Or should we understand it in some other way? The answer is to be found in understanding the purpose of the passage, and that purpose is to communicate the power of God using language the ancient audience would understand. Were the author to use modern cosmological language and concepts to make the same point, it would make no more sense to the ancient audience than it would have had the author written in Spanish. The cosmology we read of here is ultimately part of the language used to communicate the message. Were it written today it would use different terminology and concepts about the universe, and it would have been written in a modern language using concepts from modern culture. But it was not written today, and we ought to recognize and accept the fact.

Some might then ask why it is not possible for God to have moved the author to write in a way that transcends such cultural constraints, to make his word more universal and readily understood throughout time. The limit, however, is not on God but endemic to humanity, for since Babel all human communication is bound up with our language and culture. The original words of Job were written down in the ancient Hebrew language, a language that represented an expression of a culture and worldview that existed millennia before us. God chose to make this revelation to those people in that time. These words were written to them but are also for all of us. Yet the process of making them available to us requires translation from that ancient cultural and linguistic context into our own, so that we might understand the intended meaning invested by God in his words to us.

Similar considerations surround the use of mythical ideas, like the references here and elsewhere in Job to the sea monster Rahab. God chose to express his message through the use of concepts and ideas that, in the poetry of Job, best expressed the message he sought to convey to the original audience of the book. Had he chosen to use ideas and concepts that were more immediately relevant to readers in the twenty-first century, the meaning would have been lost on the ancient audience. We can, at least, see into the past and thus recover the meaning from the ancient Hebrew text and culture and translate that into our own world. We can, with a little work, understand how these words apply to us.

Beyond this we can see that we do the same thing today. If we listen to some of the songs sung in churches, we find language about God that would have made no sense two or more thousand years ago but they convey to a modern audience the same ideas we find in the Bible, though using more relatable language. If we were to talk about God laying down the laws of physics, the fusion of atoms, or the igniting stars, then we would be employing our own cosmology to convey the same truths that the author of Job did using his cosmology.

When Is Imprecation Okay?

Job's conclusion to this speech, found in Job 27:7–23, contains an imprecation upon Job's enemy. This raises at least two questions: (1) Who is Job's enemy (the references are all singular)? and (2) Is it appropriate to speak of our opponents in such terms where we call down God's judgment on others? Above I have argued that Job's enemy is a rather generic reference by Job to anyone wrongfully accusing him of sin, and so each of his friends is clearly in danger of becoming Job's enemy. Upon such as these, Job is here calling for God's judgment; that God would treat them like the wicked and the unrighteous (27:7), that God would not hear them in their distress, and that their children would be hungry and cut off and ultimately brought to their death.

Is this how we are to think about our enemies? The New Testament makes it clear that we will have enemies, but it also makes clear how we are to treat our enemies:

> You have heard that it was said, "Love your neighbor and hate your enemy." But I tell you, love your enemies and pray for those who persecute you. (Matt 5:43–44; cf. Luke 6:27, 35)

Ultimately, Paul makes it clear that each and every one of us had a time when we were God's enemies:

> For if, while we were God's enemies, we were reconciled to him through the death of his Son, how much more, having been reconciled, shall we be saved through his life! (Rom 5:10)

So yes, we do have enemies or will have enemies at some point in life. But we are to love them and pray for them, to treat them with kindness and show them love. This, however, is not the whole story, for the New Testament also contains imprecatory speech. In Acts 1:20 we find Peter quoting Psalm 69:25 and applying the imprecation to Judas (although here Peter speaks these words after Judas's death, unlike Job who looks to a future judgment of his enemy). While it may be a little circumlocutive, it is nonetheless an example of the apostle speaking judgment on someone. Another example is found in Acts 8:20–23 where Peter responds to Simon the sorcerer by saying,

> May your money perish with you, because you thought you could buy the gift of God with money! You have no part or share in this ministry, because your heart is not right before God. Repent of this wickedness and pray to the Lord in the hope that he may forgive you for having such a thought in your heart. For I see that you are full of bitterness and captive to sin.

What is revealing here is that, despite the imprecation of the opening verse, Peter ultimately makes a call on Simon to repent and be forgiven—the two are not mutually exclusive. This implies that the imprecation is, at least to some extent, a warning of the consequences of continued failure to submit to the lordship of the Messiah. What we do observe here, however, is that the New Testament reserves such strong language for those who undermine the gospel rather than those who are for any other reason considered the speaker's enemy. The case with Job's words is not so clear.

Is Job, then, together with the other imprecations found in the Old Testament (commonly through the Psalms, for example), wrong to speak this way about his enemy? To answer this question, it is important to be clear about precisely what Job is seeking here. He is not seeking an opportunity to persecute or destroy his enemy. Rather, he is calling for God to pass judgment on his enemy (Job 27:13–23).

The question then becomes: Who is our enemy that we would want God to judge them? The danger for us is that we are likely to think some to be our enemy who are not or do so on grounds that are simply wrong, entirely selfish, or even hypocritical. One rather egregious example of this can be found in the 1727 prayer of the British Member of Parliament John Ward who, among other things, prayed, "And because Thou hast said: 'The days of the wicked are but short,' I trust Thee that Thou will not forget Thy promise, as I have an estate in reversion on the death of the profligate young man, Sir J . . . L . . ."[21] We should not treat God as a personal avenger of wrongs, for all too often we are susceptible to equivalent wrongs to those that others commit, and so are in danger of the same judgment. As Jesus taught: "In the same way you judge others, you will be judged, and with the measure you use, it will be measured to you" (Matt 7:2; cf. Mark 4:24; Luke 6:38).

Yet there are clearly those who are enemies of God's people, even if the enmity is passive. That much is clear from Jesus's parable about the sheep and the goats. If that is our guide in this discussion, then perhaps we can make some headway. When Jesus explains the negative judgment on the goats, he does so in terms of their treatment of his brothers and sisters, and those who are goats are surprised (Matt 25:31–46). The implication of that surprise is that some of them (perhaps all of them) expected to be among the sheep. When we think of Job's friends and ask where they would stand, they come perilously close to being among the goats who, when Job needed clothes and was hungry, did not clothe or feed him. This implies that there are grounds for calling God to judge the enemies of his people, for that will ultimately take place, and it is an implicit call made whenever we cry, "Come, Lord!" (1 Cor 16:22). Yet while we may call for God's judgment on his enemies, let us also call on them to repent.

21. Peter Bowler, *The True Believers: Oddities and Curiosities of Religious Faith* (Malton, UK: Methuen, 1986), 146.

CHAPTER 19

Job 28

Where Is Wisdom to Be Found?

LISTEN to the Story

28:1 There is a mine for silver
and a place where gold is refined.
2 Iron is taken from the earth,
and copper is smelted from ore.
3 Mortals put an end to the darkness;
they search out the farthest recesses
for ore in the blackest darkness.
4 Far from human dwellings they cut a shaft,
in places untouched by human feet;
far from other people they dangle and sway.
5 The earth, from which food comes,
is transformed below as by fire;
6 lapis lazuli comes from its rocks,
and its dust contains nuggets of gold.
7 No bird of prey knows that hidden path,
no falcon's eye has seen it.
8 Proud beasts do not set foot on it,
and no lion prowls there.
9 People assault the flinty rock with their hands
and lay bare the roots of the mountains.
10 They tunnel through the rock;
their eyes see all its treasures.
11 They search the sources of the rivers
and bring hidden things to light.

12 But where can wisdom be found?
Where does understanding dwell?

13 No mortal comprehends its worth;
it cannot be found in the land of the living.
14 The deep says, "It is not in me";
the sea says, "It is not with me."
15 It cannot be bought with the finest gold,
nor can its price be weighed out in silver.
16 It cannot be bought with the gold of Ophir,
with precious onyx or lapis lazuli.
17 Neither gold nor crystal can compare with it,
nor can it be had for jewels of gold.
18 Coral and jasper are not worthy of mention;
the price of wisdom is beyond rubies.
19 The topaz of Cush cannot compare with it;
it cannot be bought with pure gold.

20 Where then does wisdom come from?
Where does understanding dwell?
21 It is hidden from the eyes of every living thing,
concealed even from the birds in the sky.
22 Destruction and Death say,
"Only a rumor of it has reached our ears."
23 God understands the way to it
and he alone knows where it dwells,
24 for he views the ends of the earth
and sees everything under the heavens.
25 When he established the force of the wind
and measured out the waters,
26 when he made a decree for the rain
and a path for the thunderstorm,
27 then he looked at wisdom and appraised it;
he confirmed it and tested it.
28 And he said to the human race,
"The fear of the Lord—that is wisdom,
and to shun evil is understanding."

Listening to the Text in the Story: "Enki and Ninmaḫ" (Sumerian); "The Ba'lu Myth" (Ugaritic)

This poem introduces a marked change in tone from all that has gone before. As such it should not be read as a speech by one of the characters (see further discussion below). It begins by making reference to mining. Precious metals and gemstones were mined in the ancient world, an activity used in this poem to highlight the ingenuity of human beings. One particularly well-documented site for such mining was the Timnah Valley, where there remains evidence of thousands of mineshafts used to search through the earth for copper ore, or to follow veins of copper ore that breached the surface in various locations.[1] As the basis for the greatest technological milestones in the ancient world—the extraction of ore from the earth to produce metals key to the advance of civilization—the activity forms a fitting illustration of the wisdom of human beings.

In some ancient Near Eastern cultures there was also a connection between wisdom and deep places (indeed, the association lives on in modern English, where describing something as "deep" means it is profound and comprehensively thought out). Greenstein points to the opening words of the "Code of Hammurabi," where he identifies himself as "the wise (literally, 'deep'), the effective, who reached the source of wisdom."[2] Earlier we find the Sumerian text, "Enki and Ninmaḫ," which praises the god Enki, who is described in the text in the words:

> At that time, the one of immense wisdom,
> the creator of all the senior gods,
> Enki, in the deep E-engura,[3]
> in the flowing water, a place
> whose inside no god has ever seen . . . [4]

Here in Job 28, the connection between mining and wisdom appears also to reflect something of this. The ingenuity required to find precious metals and gems deep in the earth is itself a reflection of a depth of knowledge and wisdom (or skill) that illustrates just how much human beings had achieved,

1. Erez Ben-Yosef et al., "A New Chronological Framework for Iron Age Copper Production at Timna (Israel)," *BASOR* 367 (2012): 33.

2. See Edward L. Greenstein, "The Poem on Wisdom in Job 28 in Its Conceptual and Literary Contexts," in *Job 28: Cognition in Context*, ed. Ellen van Wolde, Biblical Interpretation 64 (Leiden: Brill, 2003), 261–63.

3. The name of Enki's temple, the Sumerian being translated woodenly as "the house the watery Deep."

4. "Enki and Ninmaḫ," trans. Jacob Klein (*COS* 1.159:516).

even millennia before the present. The point this is used to then make is that, despite the quite astonishing wisdom of human beings, there has remained, still remains, and always shall remain wisdom that eludes us that only God has access to.

Another piece of ancient Near Eastern literature also brings light to our understanding of verse 11. Traditionally this verse was translated along the lines of the CSB, which reads, "he dams up the streams from flowing so that he may bring to light what is hidden." The idea here is that humans can even dam rivers to reveal the treasures that lie beneath. The Hebrew text, however, is less clear. It might be more woodenly translated as, "He binds from the weeping of the river." Some scholars have appealed to language used in the Ugaritic "The Baʿlu Myth," which makes reference to the source of the two rivers as being the dwelling place of the high god El or ʾIlu:

> So off she goes
>   to ʾIlu at the source of the double river,
>   midst the upspringings of the deeps.
> She penetrates ʾIlu's abode,
>   enters the dwelling of the King, father of Šunama;
> At ʾIlu's feet she bows and falls,
>   does homage and honors him.[5]

Here the account of ʾAṯiratu's (the Ugaritic name for Asherah) visit to ʾIlu (the Ugaritic name for El, the high god of the Ugaritic pantheon) who dwells at the source of the two rivers (the Tigris and Euphrates). That source, like the source of many rivers, was also thought to be hidden, and in this poem human ingenuity even serves to find this mysterious hidden place.[6]

From this initial reference that touches on hidden places, the poem moves to even more remote and mysterious places, in particular "the deep" of Job 28:14. This mention of the deep references the primeval waters from which God brought forth the land (see Gen 1:2), itself a reference to the broader cosmology of the ancient Near East. Even this place that lies well beyond the reach of human ingenuity of any time does not contain this most valuable of all commodities: wisdom.

---

5. "The Baʿlu Myth," *COS* 1.86:259; cf. Walton, *Job*, 286.

6. A small emendation to the text in Job 28:11 is also made in which the Hebrew *khbsh*, "to bind," is instead read as *khbs*, "to search." See Clines, *Job 21–37*, 900, 914.

EXPLAIN the Story

Many readers find Job 28 to be something of a puzzle. Throughout the book, each time a character speaks, their words are explicitly introduced by the narrator. The most recent example before this chapter is found in 27:1 in the words "And Job continued his discourse." That would imply that the poem we have in chapter 28 is spoken by Job. Yet, most scholars agree that these words do not belong to Job. Indeed, embedded within this poem is a summary of the primary message of the book of Job: human beings do not know all the answers, and some things are known only to God, something Job only fully realizes after Yahweh speaks to him in chapters 38–41.[7] There are other reasons to support the denial of Job as the speaker. First, God is referred to using the terms *'elohim* ("God," v. 23) and *'adonay* ("Lord," v. 28 [note: not Lord as in Yahweh]), terms Job does not use anywhere in his speeches. Moreover, the words Job uses throughout the book to refer to God do not appear in chapter 28. Second, the poem presents a starkly different tone to the words of Job that both precede and follow it.

If not Job's words, then whose words are these? Various suggestions have been proposed. For some, the words are simply an insertion by a later writer who has not taken sufficient care when adding them (or perhaps their original introduction has been lost). David Clines has suggested that the poem has been misplaced and ought to appear among Elihu's words later in the book.[8] And while they do fit better with some of the themes in Elihu's speeches, there is another solution that leaves this poem where it has always been.

The one voice in the book of Job that never has any introduction is the voice of the narrator. We hear his voice in the prologue and when he introduces each character as they speak. We also hear his voice as Elihu appears on the scene. Yet, in none of these instances are his words announced. The narrator's voice is identified as words that refer to the characters in the third person and that clearly do not fit into the speech of any of the characters. When we consider Job 28, it does not explicitly mention any of the characters (except God), but its message does not fit with any of the characters. It refers to

7. See Walton, *Job*, 29–30; M. Cheney, *Dust, Wind and Agony: Character, Speech and Genre in Job*, ConBOT (Stockholm: Almqvist & Wiksell, 1994), 42–45; Wharton, *Job*, 373; Wilson, *Job*, 133; Derek Kidner, *The Wisdom of Proverbs, Job and Ecclesiastes: An Introduction to the Wisdom Literature* (Downers Grove, IL: InterVarsity Press, 1985), 80.

8. Clines, *Job 21–37*, 908–9.

God in the third person, so it is unlikely to be God speaking. It announces that there is some wisdom known only to God, which does not fit with the three friends, whose speeches all presume that they know God's purpose in letting Job suffer. As such, it is best to view these words as the narrator's own voice interrupting the debate and revealing to the audience something of the purpose of the book as a whole.

What is more, the location of this poem within the book is conspicuous. Biblical Hebrew literature is particularly fond of a literary device known as chiasmus, wherein themes or ideas within the piece of literature are repeated, each enveloping other themes with the result that one particular part of the text stands at the center of a pyramid-like structure. The book of Job as a whole can be conceived of as following such a structure (see the diagram above on page 20).

This literary device places a particular focus on the central element. Viewing Job as an example of a literary chiasm draws particular attention to this poem. Furthermore, this makes very good sense, since one major theme of the book as a whole is that human beings do not know all the answers and sometimes events in life unfold for which we cannot offer a simple explanation, where we cannot say that we understand what God is doing in our lives. Job 28 is making that point as well, and so it is fitting that it stands in the center of the book.

The poem itself falls into three parts. The first part (vv. 1–11) highlights the ingenuity of humans in finding that which is hidden, the second (vv. 12–19) notes that despite this ingenuity wisdom remains beyond their reach, and the third (vv. 20–28) remarks that this elusive wisdom can only be found by God, and so the only access humans have to this wisdom is through God.

Human Ingenuity Demonstrated (28:1–11)

The opening stanza (vv. 1–11) is a poetic account of ancient mining practice and so provides no real hint about the ultimate subject of the poem. The resources mined include the important metals silver, gold, iron, copper (which was used to make bronze), and lapis lazuli. These precious metals (vv. 1–2) were used in commerce and for decoration, with iron and bronze being particularly important in warfare and agriculture. "Lapis lazuli" (v. 6) translates the Hebrew word *sappir*, which older versions translated "sapphire" but most likely refers to a deep blue, semi-precious stone that was widely used in the ancient world due to its intense color, availability, and the relative ease with which it could be worked (certainly in comparison with the gemstone sapphire). In the ancient world it was mined in what is now Afghanistan, and so the remote location of its source fits well with the themes of this poem.

The point of the stanza is that these resources are found in hidden places in the earth, far from human civilization in holes cut deep into the earth. Furthermore, for some of these items there is more involved than just digging them out of the earth; they must be smelted and refined, as verses 1–2, 5 note. The changes wrought by fire referred to in verse 5, in the context of mining of metals, are likely to refer to the refining of metal ores, which turns dirt into metal. The transformation is dramatic, and so the implication here is that human mining for these metals results makes dramatic changes to that which lays under the earth.

Verses 7–8 highlight the element of human ingenuity involved in finding these precious materials. Birds of prey are renowned for their acute eyesight, yet they are unable to find these items. That wild animals, which roam the remotest regions and so travel over places humans typically avoid, have not come across these materials further highlights just how hidden they are. Of all animals, humans alone can find and extract these things from the depths of the earth. Human beings stand out from all creatures in their ability to discover things hidden in the earth.

The closing verse of the first stanza, verse 11, makes reference to searching the "sources of the rivers." Older translations rendered this rather differently, but Ugaritic texts have provided some background here clarifying the meaning of the Hebrew. In these Ugaritic texts, the source of the two rivers is a hidden place where the high god El (known as 'Ilu) dwelt. This source was believed to be hidden underground, hence the relevance to the present poem. While this poem is not referring in any way to the Canaanite deity, it is using this idea to make it clear just how far human ingenuity drives us in finding hidden treasure.

Some Wisdom Escapes Human Ingenuity (28:12–19)

The second stanza (verses 12–19) introduces the one precious material that is the ultimate resource: wisdom. After the first stanza's description of the lengths human beings go to in order to find hidden treasures, this stanza opens asking where wisdom is to be found, although the answer to that question is only touched upon before the author returns to it in the third stanza. The initial answer to the query, however, appears odd: "No mortal comprehends its worth." What makes this odd is that it is about wisdom's value, not its location as would be expected. There are grounds, however, for understanding the Hebrew term translated in the NIV as "worth" as actually referring to "place," thus making sense of the verse.[9] Human beings do not know where wisdom

9. Hartley, *Book of Job*, 378–79; Clines, *Job 21–37*, 917.

is to be found, so it certainly cannot be found among the living (v. 13). The next stanza will expand the scope of this search for wisdom and reveal that it cannot be found among the dead either (v. 22).

Not only can wisdom not be found in the human realm, but it is not found anywhere in the sea (v. 14). The "deep" (*tehom*) and the "sea" (*yam*) are essentially synonymous, but the first of these words refers to the primordial depths at the beginning of creation (see Gen 1:2; 7:11) and is only elsewhere used in the book of Job in the speeches of Yahweh near the end of the book. In the ancient world, the depths represented chaotic powers that presented a danger to humans, and for many in the ancient Near East the sea was the realm of the deity Yam. Together the sea (Job 28:14) and the "land of the living" (v. 13) encompass the living world, in contrast to the underworld, which shall be addressed in the final stanza of the poem.

Aside from being impossible to find, wisdom's value is impossible to estimate and beyond anything humans could offer (vv. 15–19). The verses present a catalog of valuable items, including four distinct words for gold (one is repeated) as well as silver, onyx, lapis lazuli, crystal, "jewels of gold," coral, jasper, rubies, and topaz. Gold from Ophir is mentioned elsewhere (1 Kgs 9:28; 10:11; 22:48; 1 Chr 29:4; 2 Chr 8:18; 9:10; Job 22:24; 28:16; Ps 45:9; Isa 13:12) and was prized for its purity and quality, although the location of Ophir remains uncertain. While the precise translation of a number of these precious items also remains uncertain, the emphasis here is on their value for two reasons. First, despite their great value, they cannot be used to acquire wisdom. Second, despite their great value, wisdom is still far more valuable (a point made in other places in relation to precious items, see Prov 8:11; 16:16; Ezek 28:4).

Some Wisdom Belongs to God Alone (28:20–28)

The final stanza (verses 20–27) almost repeats in verse 20 the opening question of verse 12, varying only in asking not where wisdom is to be found but from where it comes. The remainder of the stanza reveals that wisdom is well hidden from all except for God, beginning with the fact that it is hidden from all the living. Even the birds of the sky, who would have the optimal vantage point from which to find the elusive wisdom, cannot find it.

Not only is it hidden from the living, but it is also not to be found in the realm of the dead, or at least there is no more than the merest rumor of where it is to be found. The underworld is a place hidden from the living, and so a good place to hide something from the gaze of humanity, and yet even here there is only a hint as to where wisdom is to be found. "Destruction" in verse 22 is the Hebrew word *'abaddon* (see "Abaddon" in Rev 9:11) and is simply another name for Sheol, the place of the dead (see Job 26:6).

Having established that any search for wisdom by humans is futile, in verses 23–27 the author turns to consider God's relationship with wisdom. Without hesitation, the poet states that God alone knows where to find wisdom. God alone has a vantage point from which he may survey all of creation (v. 24). God actively employs wisdom in dealing with the created world, as vv. 25–26 make clear. Although some commentators treat these verses as referring to creation,[10] and the tense of the verbs in many English translations point in this direction, it makes better sense to understand these comments about the weather (wind, rain, storms) to refer to God's ongoing providential governance of the weather. The point is that God uses wisdom in managing the weather from day to day. He has immediate and direct access to this marvelous resource.

It is in applying wisdom that God, according to verse 27, tested wisdom and proved its value. Unlike human beings (v. 13), he knows where to find it. Unlike human beings (vv. 15–19), he has the capacity to acquire and employ it. The obvious conclusion, then, is that for humans to access wisdom, they need to turn to God.

The final verse (v. 28) provides a fitting conclusion to the hymn. Although some commentators dismiss it as a later addition to the text that undermines the message of all that has gone before—wisdom is hidden and inaccessible to humans—that is to read too much into these final words. The hymn has already asserted that there is some wisdom that God alone has access to (v. 23), and so the conclusion that the only way for people to access that wisdom is through God makes perfect sense.

The closest that any other character has come to referring to the fear of the Lord is found in Job's words of 6:14 (where he refers to "the fear of the Almighty"). Yet the fear of the Lord is a fundamental underpinning of biblical wisdom. The book of Proverbs opens with six verses explaining the purpose of the book—"For gaining wisdom and instruction" (Prov 1:2)—followed by its first instruction establishing the very first step in acquiring wisdom: "The fear of the Lord is the beginning of knowledge" (Prov 1:7; see also 9:10).

What, then, is this "fear of the Lord"? The first hint is the poetic parallel in the last part of Job 28, "to shun evil is understanding." Fearing the Lord and shunning evil go hand in hand, the first inevitably results in the second. "Fear" is often explained as a response of religious awe, standing before God thoroughly amazed at his magnificence. While there is an element of truth in

10. For example, Clines, *Job 21–37*, 920.

this, it is hardly an adequate explanation of the meaning of the expression in the Bible. Biblical "fear" language encompasses a full range of emotions from "awe" to "terror." Encounters between humans and God recorded in the Bible often reflect considerably more than just awe (e.g., Gen 3:10; Exod 20:18–19; Isa 6:5; Rev 1:17; 11:13). It should be no surprise that encountering the Creator of the universe would be an overwhelming experience!

LIVE the Story

The Continuing Value and Scarcity of Wisdom

History reveals the sometimes-unsteady progress of human ingenuity, from a time when tunneling through the hidden depths of the earth in search of ore, precious metals, and gems was the most remarkable achievement to a time when we can communicate across vast distances, travel beyond the confines of the atmosphere, search out distant planets, and delve into the inner workings of atoms. Humans have demonstrated their ingenuity in numerous ways and continue to do so. We have achieved things the ancient writer of Job and his audience could not have imagined. In spite of all the advances we have made, however, true wisdom remains both the most valuable and most elusive prize. We might, in light of all we have learned about the universe in the roughly three millennia since the book of Job was originally written, like to think that we have uncovered the hidden wisdom that was then thought only to be available to God, but it does not take much time to realize that this is not the case. We live in a world suffering from the continued and consistent inability of human beings to care for the creation, a world in which species after species goes extinct, where damage to the planet through pollution and exploitation results in putting our own welfare in danger through short-sighted, selfish hubris. How is any of this wisdom? As the apostle Paul wrote, "Although they claimed to be wise, they became fools" (Rom 1:22).

Wisdom, it is important to understand, is not intelligence. Nor does intelligence guarantee wisdom. Wisdom is the ability to make decisions that allow us to live well and to live rightly. As such, wisdom has a moral dimension that is absent from raw intellect. It is rooted in an understanding of the nature of the creation and our place and purpose in it. As such, it is founded on a recognition of and relationship with the Creator of the universe in which we live. It is, in the words of Proverbs, founded on the fear of Yahweh: a relationship with God that recognizes our place in his universe, our role in his purposes, and our dependence on his wisdom.

Chapter 28 of Job also prompts us to ask what is valuable in our lives. In a world where material gain and possessions dominate so much, it is easy to lose sight of what is truly valuable. For the author of Job and the composer of this poem in chapter 28, the answer is clear: true wisdom is of greater value than any material possessions, even the most precious, can be. Yet even if we realize this and search for wisdom, we can reach only a rather superficial grasp of it. The deepest wisdom remains the domain of God alone, yet in his wisdom he sent his Son into the world, the Christ, "the power of God and the wisdom of God" (1 Cor 1:24). This message is as relevant today as it ever was. We live at a time that often confuses scientific knowledge with wisdom and so invests science and scientists with the task of determining the moral basis for our existence. The major difficulty with this is that raw knowledge is amoral—it can be used for evil as well as good. Just because we can do something does not mean we ought to do it! There is no harm in knowing more about the world in which we live; there can be great harm in abuse of that knowledge. And so, wisdom is needed now more than ever, but wisdom remains as elusive as ever.

The true wisdom that eluded Job and his audience, that eludes the world to this day, is to be found in God's anointed Son, as Paul wrote:

> We do, however, speak a message of wisdom among the mature, but not the wisdom of this age or of the rulers of this age, who are coming to nothing. No, we declare God's wisdom, a mystery that has been hidden and that God destined for our glory before time began. None of the rulers of this age understood it, for if they had, they would not have crucified the Lord of glory. (1 Cor 2:6–8; cf. Eph 3:10; Col 2:2–3)

This connection between wisdom and Jesus is made apparent repeatedly in the New Testament (e.g., 1 Cor 1:24, 30; note especially Matt 12:42 where Jesus claims to be greater than Solomon, where it is specifically Solomon's wisdom that is on view; and perhaps Matt 11:19; Luke 7:35). The hidden wisdom of Job 28, wisdom known only to God, is revealed in Christ. I'm not claiming that repentance and changing our lives to serve Jesus as Lord invariably makes us successful or wise in the eyes of the world. It does, however, bring us into step with the purposes of God in creation and prepares us for the future when the last day dawns.

As wisdom that was available to God alone, it is his alone to reveal. While there is nothing to suggest that we who live after the Messiah's life, death, resurrection, and ascension have access to all of God's wisdom, and so the claims of Job 28 that there is wisdom to which only God has access remain true, we also know now more than did any Old Testament believer. There was hidden wisdom that has now been revealed to us in Jesus. This is why Jesus could say that John the Baptist was, up until his time, the greatest among all who were born of women (Matt 11:11; Luke 7:28) and yet the least in the kingdom of God since that time is even greater than John. It is simply true that we can now point more clearly to the Messiah than any who had preceded him, even John the Baptist. We have access to more of the revealed mystery of God that is the gospel than any of those who lived prior to the ministry of Jesus.[11]

It is here also that wisdom fits into the story of God. In fact, to say it "fits into" the story is probably not the best way to put it, as if wisdom had to be shoehorned into God's plan in some way. Wisdom is ultimately what God employs to design and implement his plan to bring his purposes to their ultimate realization and fulfillment. That is the wisdom that only God knows the way to, the wisdom to which Job 28 refers. Indeed, as we shall discover when God speaks to Job in chapters 38–41, this is the wisdom that the book of Job as a whole teaches us about. While there doubtless remains wisdom that only God has access to, some of that wisdom that was hidden—the critical part that relates to the coming of the Messiah and his place as king of the new creation and our place as his subjects in his kingdom—has been revealed to us in these last days. Wisdom, as it turns out, is the guiding principle of the story of God.

---

11. See D. A. Carson, "Matthew," *Matthew–Mark*, REBC 9, ed. Tremper Longman III and David E. Garland (Grand Rapids: Zondervan, 2010), 307–8.

CHAPTER 20

Job 29–31

Job's Final Speech

LISTEN to the Story

29:1 Job continued his discourse:

2 "How I long for the months gone by,
for the days when God watched over me,
3 when his lamp shone on my head
and by his light I walked through darkness!
4 Oh, for the days when I was in my prime,
when God's intimate friendship blessed my house,
5 when the Almighty was still with me
and my children were around me,
6 when my path was drenched with cream
and the rock poured out for me streams of olive oil.

7 "When I went to the gate of the city
and took my seat in the public square,
8 the young men saw me and stepped aside
and the old men rose to their feet;
9 the chief men refrained from speaking
and covered their mouths with their hands;
10 the voices of the nobles were hushed,
and their tongues stuck to the roof of their mouths.
11 Whoever heard me spoke well of me,
and those who saw me commended me,
12 because I rescued the poor who cried for help,
and the fatherless who had none to assist them.
13 The one who was dying blessed me;
I made the widow's heart sing.

[14]I put on righteousness as my clothing;
justice was my robe and my turban.
[15]I was eyes to the blind
and feet to the lame.
[16]I was a father to the needy;
I took up the case of the stranger.
[17]I broke the fangs of the wicked
and snatched the victims from their teeth.

[18]"I thought, 'I will die in my own house,
my days as numerous as the grains of sand.
[19]My roots will reach to the water,
and the dew will lie all night on my branches.
[20]My glory will not fade;
the bow will be ever new in my hand.'

[21]"People listened to me expectantly,
waiting in silence for my counsel.
[22]After I had spoken, they spoke no more;
my words fell gently on their ears.
[23]They waited for me as for showers
and drank in my words as the spring rain.
[24]When I smiled at them, they scarcely believed it;
the light of my face was precious to them.
[25]I chose the way for them and sat as their chief;
I dwelt as a king among his troops;
I was like one who comforts mourners.

[30:1]"But now they mock me,
men younger than I,
whose fathers I would have disdained
to put with my sheep dogs.
[2]Of what use was the strength of their hands to me,
since their vigor had gone from them?
[3]Haggard from want and hunger,
they roamed the parched land
in desolate wastelands at night.

4In the brush they gathered salt herbs,
and their food was the root of the broom bush.
5They were banished from human society,
shouted at as if they were thieves.
6They were forced to live in the dry stream beds,
among the rocks and in holes in the ground.
7They brayed among the bushes
and huddled in the undergrowth.
8A base and nameless brood,
they were driven out of the land.

9"And now those young men mock me in song;
I have become a byword among them.
10They detest me and keep their distance;
they do not hesitate to spit in my face.
11Now that God has unstrung my bow and afflicted me,
they throw off restraint in my presence.
12On my right the tribe attacks;
they lay snares for my feet,
they build their siege ramps against me.
13They break up my road;
they succeed in destroying me.
'No one can help him,' they say.
14They advance as through a gaping breach;
amid the ruins they come rolling in.
15Terrors overwhelm me;
my dignity is driven away as by the wind,
my safety vanishes like a cloud.

16"And now my life ebbs away;
days of suffering grip me.
17Night pierces my bones;
my gnawing pains never rest.
18In his great power God becomes like clothing to me;
he binds me like the neck of my garment.
19He throws me into the mud,
and I am reduced to dust and ashes.

20"I cry out to you, God, but you do not answer;
I stand up, but you merely look at me.
21You turn on me ruthlessly;
with the might of your hand you attack me.
22You snatch me up and drive me before the wind;
you toss me about in the storm.
23I know you will bring me down to death,
to the place appointed for all the living.

24"Surely no one lays a hand on a broken man
when he cries for help in his distress.
25Have I not wept for those in trouble?
Has not my soul grieved for the poor?
26Yet when I hoped for good, evil came;
when I looked for light, then came darkness.
27The churning inside me never stops;
days of suffering confront me.
28I go about blackened, but not by the sun;
I stand up in the assembly and cry for help.
29I have become a brother of jackals,
a companion of owls.
30My skin grows black and peels;
my body burns with fever.
31My lyre is tuned to mourning,
and my pipe to the sound of wailing.

31:1"I made a covenant with my eyes
not to look lustfully at a young woman.
2For what is our lot from God above,
our heritage from the Almighty on high?
3Is it not ruin for the wicked,
disaster for those who do wrong?
4Does he not see my ways
and count my every step?

5"If I have walked with falsehood
or my foot has hurried after deceit—

6 let God weigh me in honest scales
and he will know that I am blameless—
7 if my steps have turned from the path,
if my heart has been led by my eyes,
or if my hands have been defiled,
8 then may others eat what I have sown,
and may my crops be uprooted.

9 "If my heart has been enticed by a woman,
or if I have lurked at my neighbor's door,
10 then may my wife grind another man's grain,
and may other men sleep with her.
11 For that would have been wicked,
a sin to be judged.
12 It is a fire that burns to Destruction;
it would have uprooted my harvest.

13 "If I have denied justice to any of my servants,
whether male or female,
when they had a grievance against me,
14 what will I do when God confronts me?
What will I answer when called to account?
15 Did not he who made me in the womb make them?
Did not the same one form us both within our mothers?

16 "If I have denied the desires of the poor
or let the eyes of the widow grow weary,
17 if I have kept my bread to myself,
not sharing it with the fatherless—
18 but from my youth I reared them as a father would,
and from my birth I guided the widow—
19 if I have seen anyone perishing for lack of clothing,
or the needy without garments,
20 and their hearts did not bless me
for warming them with the fleece from my sheep,
21 if I have raised my hand against the fatherless,
knowing that I had influence in court,

22then let my arm fall from the shoulder,
let it be broken off at the joint.
23For I dreaded destruction from God,
and for fear of his splendor I could not do such things.

24"If I have put my trust in gold
or said to pure gold, 'You are my security,'
25if I have rejoiced over my great wealth,
the fortune my hands had gained,
26if I have regarded the sun in its radiance
or the moon moving in splendor,
27so that my heart was secretly enticed
and my hand offered them a kiss of homage,
28then these also would be sins to be judged,
for I would have been unfaithful to God on high.

29"If I have rejoiced at my enemy's misfortune
or gloated over the trouble that came to him—
30I have not allowed my mouth to sin
by invoking a curse against their life—
31if those of my household have never said,
'Who has not been filled with Job's meat?'—
32but no stranger had to spend the night in the street,
for my door was always open to the traveler—
33if I have concealed my sin as people do,
by hiding my guilt in my heart
34because I so feared the crowd
and so dreaded the contempt of the clans
that I kept silent and would not go outside—

35("Oh, that I had someone to hear me!
I sign now my defense—let the Almighty answer me;
let my accuser put his indictment in writing.
36Surely I would wear it on my shoulder,
I would put it on like a crown.
37I would give him an account of my every step;
I would present it to him as to a ruler.)—

[38]"if my land cries out against me
and all its furrows are wet with tears,
[39]if I have devoured its yield without payment
or broken the spirit of its tenants,
[40]then let briers come up instead of wheat
and stinkweed instead of barley."

The words of Job are ended.

Listening to the Text in the Story: "The Babylonian Theodicy"; instruction of "Amenemhet"; "Book of the Dead" (Egyptian); "The Kirta Epic"; "The 'Aqhatu Legend" (Ugaritic)

As with so much of the book of Job, these chapters reflect their situation within the ancient Near East in numerous ways. Job's words in Job 30:1 speak of the manner in which Job has been reduced to a figure of scorn and mocking by those who were once well beneath him in their social standing, contrasting his reminiscence of the days when he was held in high esteem in 29:2–25. "The Babylonian Theodicy" offers the same reflection:

> What has it profited me that I knelt before my god?
> It is I who must (now) bow before my inferior!
> The riffraff despise me as much as the rich and proud.[1]

The loss of social stature is used by each of these texts to highlight the downfall of the protagonist as an expression of the injustice to which they feel they have been subjected.

As Job recounts his former glory, he reminds his friends of how he actually behaved toward those in need (in contrast to the claims made earlier by his friends that he exploited the needy; see, for example, Job 22:5–9). This expectation that the powerful should care for the needy is repeated throughout the Old Testament (cf. Exod 22:21; Deut 10:18; 24:17, 19; 26:12–13; Isa 1:17) but can also be found elsewhere in the ancient world. For example, the opening lines of the Egyptian instruction of "Amenemhet" extol his virtue with claims about his treatment of the poor and vulnerable:

1. "The Babylonian Theodicy," *COS* 1.154:494.

> I gave to the beggar, I raised the orphan,
> I gave success to the poor as to the wealthy;[2]

From Ugarit, in "The Kirta Epic," Kirta is accused of failing the vulnerable:

> You let your hands fall slack:
> you do not judge the widow's case,
> you do not make a decision regarding the oppressed.
> . . .
> You let your hands fall slack:
> you do not judge the widow's case,
> you do not make a decision regarding the oppressed
> you do not cast out those who prey upon the poor.
> Before you, you do not feed the orphan,
> behind your back the widow.[3]

Similarly, in "The 'Aqhatu Legend" (also from Ugarit), Dānîʾlu (Danel) is recorded as having acted on behalf of the widow and orphan:

> He judged the widow's case,
> Made decisions regarding the orphan.[4]

Clines also notes that parallels exist between Job's claims here and similar claims in tomb inscriptions from Egypt, such as those found on the tomb of Harkhuf: "I gave bread to the hungry, clothing to the naked; I brought to land him that had no ferry-boat."[5] It is clear that the notion of justice as being manifest in one's treatment of the poor and vulnerable (often illustrated by widows and orphans) was shared throughout the ancient world and that Job's appeal to this would have been universally understood as demonstrating his exemplary righteousness.

Some have also noted parallels between Job 31, where Job protests his innocence, and the Egyptian "Book of the Dead 125," in which the dead person appears before an underworld tribunal of Osiris and forty-two other gods as part of that person's preparation for the weighing of their heart, which itself was the prerequisite for entrance into the afterlife. A portion of that text reads:

2. "Amenemhet," trans. Miriam Lichtheim (*COS* 1.36:67). See lines 6–7.

3. "The Kirta Epic," *COS* 1.102:342 (= *CTA* 16).

4. "The 'Aqhatu Legend," *COS* 1.103:346 (= *CTA* 17).

5. Clines, *Job 21–37*, 987, citing J. G. Griffiths, "The Idea of Posthumous Judgment in Israel and Egypt," in *Fontes atque pontes: Eine Festgabe für H. Brunner*, ed. M. Görg, ÄAT 5 (Wiesbaden: Harrassowitz, 1983), 199–200.

I have not committed wrongdoing against anyone.
I have not mistreated cattle.
I have not done injustice in the place of Truth.
I do not know that which should not be.
I have not done evil.
I have not daily made labors in excess of what should be done for me.
My name has not reached the bark of the Governor (i.e., Re).
I have not debased a god.
I have not deprived an orphan.
I have not done that which the gods abominate.
I have not slandered a servant to his superior.
I have not caused pain.
I have not caused weeping.
I have not killed.
I have not commanded to kill.
I have not made suffering for anyone.[6]

Although this might suggest that Job's speech should also be seen as preparatory for his entry into the underworld,[7] this is unlikely. While the protestations of innocence appear in both texts, the protests in the "Book of the Dead 125" do not depict the entire life of the subject. Among the things presented are assertions that the deceased has "not winked" and "not waded in water." These suggest that the list of activities that the deceased avoided were not necessarily throughout his life but more likely during a period of preparation for this appearance before the gods. Nonetheless, Job's assertions echo these words and do vouch for his innocence in a similar but more thoroughgoing manner.

EXPLAIN the Story

Job's final speech begins with a note about who is speaking. Similar narrative notes usually mark a change in speaker, lending support to the claim that chapter 28 should not be understood to be spoken by Job.[8]

6. "Book of the Dead 125," trans. Robert K. Ritner (*COS* 2.12:60).

7. See, for example, Timothy Jay Johnson, *Now My Eye Sees You: Unveiling an Apocalyptic Job* (Sheffield: Sheffield Phoenix Press, 2013), 141–42.

8. The appearance of the same phrase in Job 27:1 partway through Job's speech, which began in chapter 26, does not form a strong precedent for the counterclaim, as there are indications that the speech by Job there has been corrupted in transmission.

The Blessings of Job's Early Life (29:1–25)

The beginning of Job's first speech after his three friends have stopped engaging with him has Job reflecting on his blessed life before his troubles began. Job's thoughts here reveal something of his perception of his present situation, providing an implicit contrast to his understanding of his present predicament, particularly his understanding of his relationship with God. For example, in verses 3–5 he implies that now God no longer guides his path and is neither his friend nor with him. While it is certainly easy to appreciate how Job has arrived at this conclusion, we ought to be aware that Job's vision is limited and—as Job himself will come to discover—his comprehension of reality is severely distorted by his circumstances and his finitude.

His opening expression, "the months gone by" (v. 2), is an unusual way to refer to his earlier life, but it expresses plainly his one true desire—a return to the way things were. The remainder of this chapter recounts Job's perception of the way things were in some detail. In those days, God watched over him, the idea being that God protected Job. The lamp metaphorically conveys the idea that God blessed Job and guided him through the darkness of the world (cf. Ps 119:105), keeping him safe from danger and protecting his life.

Job was, at that time, in his "prime" (v. 4), the precise meaning of the Hebrew term here (*khorep*) is disputed but from context clearly refers to the time in Job's life when his entire household enjoyed the protection offered by close friendship with God. Part of that included the abundance of blessing represented by "cream" (more correctly, curdled sour milk, see Job 20:17) and "olive oil" (v. 6). The excesses here are not meant to indicate that Job's existence was wasteful but rather to express the abundance of God's blessing in those former days.

Verses 7–10 recall Job's former status within the community, where he was respected and admired by all. The implicit contrast with his present existence is clear and reflected somewhat in the arguments of his friends who, no doubt along with many others, believe that Job's state reflects his sinfulness, and so he is now afforded no respect. The locations Job makes reference to—"the gate of the city" and the town square (NIV "public square")—were the places where town elders gathered and made important decisions pertaining to the governance of the town in both judicial and administrative matters. Archaeological evidence suggests that the square was itself often quite small (for example, Clines notes that the square of Beersheba was only 20m × 10m).[9] That others made way for Job as he took his place and when he spoke highlights his respected status in the town.

9. Clines, *Job 21–37*, 985.

This respect was founded, at least in part, upon Job's treatment of those who were less well off than he (vv. 11–17). Job's aid went out to the poor, the orphan, the dying, widows, the blind, the lame, the needy, and the stranger (cf. Deut 27:18–19). Furthermore, he fought against those who oppressed these vulnerable parties. The phrase "fangs of the wicked" (Job 29:17) portrays the wicked as wild beasts who devour the impoverished and weak.

Another aspect of Job's former existence was his expectation of a long and blessed life (v. 18)—a common hope throughout the Old Testament for those who were faithful and upright (e.g., Prov 9:11; Isa 65:20). His hope that he would die after a long life in his own home is more about him being surrounded by his family rather than making reference to the building in which he would die. He had expected to die peacefully surrounded by his family after a long life.

In addition to this, Job had been confident in his resilience and ability to weather life's storms (Job 29:19–20), an idea he expresses by imagining himself to be a sturdy tree whose roots reached a reliable water source and whose branches caught the nightly dew that fell and was thus able to endure times of drought. This resilience would ensure that he always maintained his honor (NIV "glory") and strength (as represented here by his "bow").

Job's honor and strength were recognized by those around him (vv. 21–25). He was accorded respect, and his advice was sought and heard with anticipation as if it were as life-giving as the spring rain (cf. Deut 32:2). David Clines points out that Job's hopes and recollections here (e.g., that everyone hangs on his words, which are never disputed) appear to be somewhat unrealistic. But these words do serve to express the stark contrast between Job's former and present life.[10]

The Curse of Job's Present Life (30:1–31)

Having given voice to his longing for the days gone past, Job contrasts those pleasant times with his present experience in the first eleven verses of chapter 30. For starters, in verse 1 he finds himself now mocked by men who themselves are worthy of no honor, not merely because they are younger than he but moreso because even their fathers were of so little import in society that Job would formerly not have put them out with his dogs.[11] Dogs were not well regarded in Old Testament times (e.g., 1 Sam 17:43; 2 Sam 3:8; 2 Kgs 8:13) but were nonetheless of some value for protecting the flock (cf. Isa 56:10–11).

10. Clines, *Job 21–37*, 993.

11. The Hebrew word Job uses for "mock" is the same that he used in Job 29:24 when he "smiled" on those in the town square. The connection highlights the contrast he is picturing here.

If even these, the least honorable of men, mock Job, it is clear that he felt so treated by anyone of any higher status in society as well.

The remainder of Job 30:2–8 elaborates on the lowly status of these young men who mock Job with the effect of further highlighting just how far Job has fallen. These mockers were not merely somewhat insignificant young men; they were weak, poor, gaunt with hunger, and homeless. They had been banished as criminals would have been (vv. 5, 8). They were, in short, the scum of the earth.

And yet, even these men were mocking Job "in song" (v. 9; cf. Lam 3:14). He has become a "byword," meaning that merely invoking his name had come to be a way to express disdain or identify someone as an object of ridicule (cf. 1 Kgs 9:7). Much in the way we might speak of someone as a Jezebel or a Judas today, the young men could speak of someone as a Job and, in so doing, impute all the terrible mockery they had poured onto Job upon the subject of that new taunt.

So profound was the disdain of these scum of the earth for Job that they would keep their distance from him, and when they did come close, they would spit in his face (v. 10). This particular expression of disgust at Job is repeated in the treatment of Jesus in the Gospels (e.g., Mark 10:34; 14:65; 15:19).

The section closes in Job 30:12–31 with Job identifying the one he holds accountable for his fall in status and who is ultimately responsible for his mockery by the outcasts of society—God. An unstrung bow (v. 11) is useless and, having lost everything and having been afflicted by God, Job feels himself to be useless. There is an explicit contrast to the hope Job had formerly had as expressed in Job 29:20. Now Job is certainly no longer of any use to the town in whose square he sat or to the widows, orphans, and others he once helped. As God has afflicted him, so then all others feel no restraint from mocking him (30:11).

Verse 12 refers to those who attack Job as being a "tribe" (NIV), but the Hebrew term is difficult (appearing only here in the Old Testament), and so its meaning is not clear. A common translation is "mob, rabble," and it does refer to a group who attacks Job as an enemy by setting traps for him or besieging him (30:12–14).[12] What is not clear is whether these attackers are the same young men Job spoke of in the opening verses of the chapter or are a different group, but the significant point is not so much the identity of the attackers but that they threaten Job. The small detail that they attack Job on his right

12. Clines, *Job 21–37*, 931; Hartley, *Job*, 399–400. Among English translations see GNT, ICB, NASB, NCV for "mob"; CSB, ESV, NCB, NKJV for "rabble."

has been suggested to point to the position an opponent in a law court would stand (e.g., Ps 109:6), but given the violent imagery used, it is more likely that the reference to the right represents Job's stronger side. The image, then, shows Job's opponents as having no fear of Job, not even bothering to direct their attack at his weakest side.

In Job 30:13, Job recounts the attacks as though he were a city. Like a city, these attackers metaphorically besieged him with siege ramps and cut off any means of escape by laying snares and breaking up the roads away. He is effectively isolated, and once his defenses are breached, they will pour in to finish him off (v. 14).

In verse 15 Job moves on from imagining himself as a city under siege to more immediate language about his suffering and imminent death. The "terrors" here may be a reference to demonic forces from the underworld who now form another front in the attacks Job is experiencing (see at 18:14 on the use of this word). These attacks take both Job's physical and emotional well-being from him. Clines explains that the reference to "dignity" here refers not only to his public honor but also his self-worth and sense of importance.[13]

The opening words of verse 16, "and now," repeat a phrase already used in verses 1 and 9, moving Job's thought forward from the preceding section. Job reveals that he feels that the end is upon him—there remains little of his life in the midst of his present suffering. In verse 17 "night," being depicted anthropomorphically as a torturer boring into his bones, brings no relief. His suffering endures uninterrupted.

Verse 18, as it stands in the NIV, makes little sense. It is probable that we should understand the text here as expressing the idea that God (while God is not explicitly mentioned in the Hebrew, it is clear that Job is referring to God here and in the following verses) has grabbed Job by his clothing and then thrown him into the mud (v. 19) as a wrestler or even a mugger might do.[14] Job recognizes that God is the one who is ultimately responsible for his humiliation, and he gives full voice to this accusation in these verses. He has called out to God, but God does not answer (v. 20). Although at one time Job enjoyed God's favor, now God has changed and instead attacks Job, leaving him exposed in a storm that will ultimately end in his death (v. 21–23).

Job closes this portion of his speech in verses 24–31 with reference back

---

13. Clines, *Job 21–37*, 1005.

14. See, for example, Longman, *Job*, 350; Clines, *Job 21–37*, 1006. See "חפש," *HALOT* 341, which proposes that the Hebrew here, which reads *yitkhappes*, should be emended to *yitpos* from the root *tps* meaning "lay hold of, seize." See also the LXX, which reads, "with great force he took hold of my robe" (NETS).

to the beginning of this section. There in verses 18–20 Job had accused God of ignoring his pleas and seizing him by the clothes and throwing him down. Here in verse 24 he highlights the injustice of such behavior. Who would do such a thing? Who would take hold of a broken man who is calling for help and attack him? Yet, from Job's point of view, this is exactly what God has done.

Job ends this part of his speech by returning to an account of his righteous behavior and the injustice of what has happened to him (30:25–31). Like his friends, Job reveals that he believes in the principle of retributive justice. He has done good and ought therefore to be rewarded. His dispute with his friends has not questioned the principle; it has questioned God's justice in failing to implement it appropriately. Thus, despite his good life, evil came upon him (v. 26).

Job's reference to his "churning" innards (v. 27) reflects the psychological impact of his condition—he is plagued by anxiety and stress. His skin is disfigured by the disease with which he has been afflicted (v. 28). He is an outcast who lives with wild animals while he endures this illness (vv. 29–30), and all his life is consumed with mourning (v. 31). This is not what he had expected. This is not what he felt that he deserved. This, for Job, makes no sense, and there is nothing in his theology that has prepared him for the troubles he now endures.

Job Presents a Case for His Innocence (31:1–40)

The bulk of chapter 31 has Job making a strong case for his blamelessness in the face of both the accusations of his friends and the afflictions that God has sent upon him. He protests his innocence in a number of areas:

- he has avoided looking lustfully at a young woman (vv. 1–4)
- he has not deceived anyone (vv. 5–8)
- he has not slept with another man's wife (vv. 9–12)
- he has not denied justice to his servants (vv. 13–15)
- he has met the needs of the poor and widows (vv. 16–23)
- he has not placed his faith in anything other than God (vv. 24–28)
- he has treated his enemies with due respect (vv. 29–30)
- he has shown kindness to strangers (vv. 31–32)
- he has no hidden sin for which he must account (vv. 33–34)
- he has treated his tenants with justice (vv. 38–40)

Job's list is extensive and serves to highlight in specific detail that which we already knew from the prologue and that—as we also know from the prologue—God also knows. Toward the end in a brief aside (vv. 35–37), Job reveals the point of these claims: this is his defense, his testimony to prove his innocence, and thus the injustice of the terrible things that have happened to him. This also tells us clearly that Job still thinks that the world operates according to the principle of retributive justice just as much as his friends do.

Job's opening claim in 31:1 relates to lust directed toward a young unmarried woman who is probably a virgin (the word used here, *bethulah*, often has that meaning, e.g., Gen 24:16; Judg 21:12). What is perhaps surprising here is that the Old Testament does not elsewhere explicitly condemn such behavior—the commandments prohibit coveting another's wife (cf. Exod 20:17; Deut 5:21). Yet, even if the man who is lusting after the young unmarried woman is already married, there is no explicit condemnation since polygyny was permitted—the man could take the young woman as a second wife. What Job does, however, is hold himself to an even higher standard of godliness than was required, to a level implied in Genesis 2:24 and ultimately expressed through Jesus's teaching in the Sermon on the Mount (see Matt 5:27–30).

Then in Job 31:2–4 Job spells out the consequences of failing to meet the standard he has set himself, and that is essentially judgment from God. God, he notes, is watching, and will repay the wicked for their wickedness. This is the very basis of the idea of retributive justice.

Job's second claim relates to honest dealings with others (vv. 5–8). Here he makes his point by effectively swearing an oath, an act that recurs through the remainder of the chapter. If Job proved to be guilty of the behavior described following the initial "if," then the oath calls upon the subsequent penalty to be applied.[15] Some of these oaths here are incomplete—the penalty is missing—but the rhetorical effect is clear: Job is vehemently denying participating in the proscribed behavior. He has not "walked with falsehood" (v. 5), his steps have not "turned from the path" (v. 7), his heart has not been "enticed by a woman" (v. 9), etc.

The phrase "walked with falsehood" in verse 5 refers not to the physical act of walking but is a common metaphor for way of life (see, e.g., Ps 1:1). If it was suspected that Job's life had been characterized by deceiving others, then God should weigh his actions in the scales of justice. If he were to do so, Job is confident that he would be cleared—so confident, in fact, that he would then be happy for the fruit of his labors to be distributed to others (Job 31:6–8).

Job's third claim is a simple denial of adultery—Job has not slept with another man's wife (vv. 9–12). Whereas his opening defense had reflected his

15. See 31:5, 7, 9, 13, 16, 19, 21, 24–26, 29, 31, 33, 38–39.

own high standards, now he explicitly notes his innocence with regard to the law (even though Job, as a non-Israelite living before Moses, would not have had the law of Moses). Job's notion of an appropriate punishment here may leave modern readers somewhat disturbed, for it appears to be directed at Job's wife. If he were to commit adultery, then the punishment would be that his wife would then have sex with multiple other men (noting the plurals of v. 10). This would seem more to be a punishment for Job's wife than for Job.

Perhaps the best understanding of this rather inappropriate outcome is to understand verse 11 as referring not to Job's hypothetical sin of verse 9 but his wife's actions in verse 10. As such, Job is saying that he views the evil of him committing adultery as equal to that of his own wife sleeping with many others. Rather than spelling out a specific punishment he feels to be appropriate for such sin, he presents a situation that any ancient reader would find appalling as a clear illustration of how evil he holds adultery to be. The consequences of such sin are devastating—a destructive fire that burns down to the place of the dead ("Destruction," *ʾabaddon*, in v. 12; see also 26:6; 28:22). Clines notes that "the act of adultery, Job means to say, is not a self-contained or containable incident, but the initiation of a process of annihilation."[16]

That sexual sin features so prominently in Job's claims points to its powerful allure even in the ancient world. It is certainly not difficult in the modern world to appreciate the significance of this power, as many modern societies revel in open expressions of sexuality that run counter to the standards God expresses in his word.

Job's next defense is that he has treated his servants with justice (31:13–15). At the heart of this is Job's recognition that he is no different to them—they too were created by God, the implication being that God regards them no differently to Job. Again, Job's standard of behavior exceeds the standards of his contemporary culture and even some of the standards of the modern world, where some are treated as lesser than others.

It is true that the Mosaic law provided some rights to servants or slaves (see, for example, Exod 21:2–11, 20–21, 26–27; Lev 25:39–55), yet once again Job presents himself as exceeding the righteousness of his contemporaries and so makes it clear that he is not deserving of the suffering he is experiencing.

Job next turns his attention to his treatment of the poor, the widow, and the orphan in Job 31:16–23. These three groups are mentioned together elsewhere in Isaiah 10:2 as the victims of the wicked who will ultimately face justice for

16. Clines, *Job 21–37*, 1019.

their wickedness. They represent the most vulnerable in the ancient world, and so Job affirms his just treatment and compassion toward them.

The desires of the poor (v. 16) would refer to the things they need to survive. The mention of eyes that grow weary could refer to fading eyesight associated with age or disease (e.g., Lev 26:16), but it can also refer to the idea that one's eyes fade as a result of endlessly looking for something but never finding it (e.g., Deut 28:32; Pss 69:3; 119:82; Lam 2:11). Here it is this latter sense that results in the eyes of the widows failing, that is, when they look for help but do not ever see it. Job has not allowed this to happen. Indeed, he has done the opposite: for as long as he can remember (the phrase "from my youth" of v. 18 is hyperbole for this same idea) he has fathered the fatherless, clothed the naked, and guided the widow.

Job reveals that at least part of his motivation to care for the vulnerable was his fear of God and the judgment that would befall him. Job's motives here reflect the great fear he expressed back in 3:25, where he revealed that he had always feared coming under God's judgment. While this is reminiscent in some ways of the opening challenge where the Satan had claimed that Job would curse God if he withdrew the blessings he had showered upon him (1:9–11), there is a subtle distinction here. The important points to note are that Job has not cursed God and that we know that Job is not suffering as a punishment for some sin he had committed.

In 31:24–28 Job highlights his single-minded devotion to God. Material wealth—gold and riches—are not his source of confidence. We might say, from a New Testament perspective, that his treasure is not his wealth and gold but is his treasure stored in heaven (see Matt 6:19–24). His god is not money, nor does he worship created things (Job 31:26–27). Both the sun and the moon were regarded as deities in many ancient Near Eastern cultures, and Job's reference to a "kiss of homage" (v. 27) suggests an act of devotion to these deities, a religious act in which Job did not participate. Despite this, Job could recognize both the sun and the moon as splendid objects while acknowledging that they were no more than heavenly objects created by the one true God, in whom he did place his trust and devotion.

Job's upright nature extends to his treatment of enemies, once again reflecting the extent of his blamelessness (vv. 29–30). Throughout this chapter, the "if" verses introduce a behavior that Job finds unacceptable and ardently disavows. It is thus clear that Job does not rejoice at his enemy's misfortune, and he certainly does not bring about their death (the implication of cursing their life).

Furthermore, Job's kindness extends not just to his enemies but also to strangers, those with whom he has no real connection (vv. 31–32). Job here attests to the hospitality he shows others. So generous has he been, he notes, that members of his household would potentially pose the rhetorical (and perhaps humorous) question indicating that one would be hard pressed to find anyone whom Job had not fed. No traveler would ever have been found in the streets near Job's home at a loss for somewhere to stay, because Job's home was always open to those who needed it.

In verses 33–34 Job turns to addressing sin in his life. This is a necessary response to the accusations of his friends, who had repeatedly claimed that there must have been some hidden sin that had prompted God to afflict him. Job insists that there is no such hidden sin; he has concealed nothing.

Scholars differ over whether "people" in verse 33 is a reference to Adam, the first man of Genesis 2 (see the NIV footnote for Job 31:33). The difficulty lies in the fact that the Hebrew *'adam*, serves as both the name of the first man Adam and, most commonly, as the generic word for humanity or "people." So, Job could be referencing Adam's behavior in seeking to conceal his sin in Genesis 3, or it could point to the general human propensity to hide our sin from others. Job certainly makes many references to creation, and so it would not be out of place to refer to Adam. In the end, however, it matters little who Job points to as hiding sin. It is the very idea of concealing sin, doubtless something everyone can relate to, that he is using to make his point.

Job's review of his righteousness is interrupted in Job 31:35–37 as he now wishes that he had access to a document from his accuser that would detail the charges made against him. Job had previously mentioned such a document (13:26). Scholars debate why these verses appear here, interrupting the series of points Job makes, a series that resumes and concludes in 31:38–40. Since the suggestions are all hypothetical and unprovable, and since the meaning is ultimately unchanged, there is little merit in expending much time discussing the point. The way the text stands, we have Job expressing a longing to finally face God and to hear his response.

Job in verse 35 uses the legal metaphor he has adopted elsewhere. He has signed his defense (NIV "I sign now"). The Hebrew here woodenly reads "here is my *tav*"; *tav* is a word meaning "mark, sign"[17] and is also used as the name of the final letter of the Hebrew alphabet. In the paleo-Hebrew alphabet the *tav* was a cross shaped something like an English X and likely here refers to Job having made his mark at the end of his recorded legal defense (rather than suggesting he simply marked it with a cross).[18] Job is declaring that he has finally come to

17. See "תָו," in *DCH* 8:597.
18. See "תָו," in *DCH* 8:597.

the end of his case and has signed off on the document; he has nothing more to add. The narrator reinforces this point once more at the end of verse 40.

Job declares that he now awaits his God's response. Furthermore, he is so confident in his defense that he is prepared to put any response on public display by wearing it on his shoulder or like a crown. He is willing to be subject to scrutiny so intense that his every step would be under surveillance. Indeed, Job now feels so confident that he says he would approach God not as a simple man but as though he were a ruler![19] This tells us that he has grown in his confidence in his own rightness from the earlier speeches where he felt approaching God was futile (e.g., 9:14–20).

Job's last full speech (except for his brief responses to Yahweh in the middle and at the end of the divine speeches) concludes by returning to more of Job's collected evidence of his own righteousness in verses 38–40. This time, the subject is his land. Initially, the land itself is personified as Job affirms his innocence by suggesting that if he had done anything against the land, then he would willingly accept the consequences—that the produce of the land would be nothing more than thorns and weeds (the NIV's "stinkweed" reflects the Hebrew word *ba'shah*, which is connected to a verb *b'sh*, meaning "to stink, to turn rancid").[20]

Precisely what Job's possible crime against his land would be is not entirely clear. It may be some form of environmental vandalism, which is an idea that is not as anachronistic as it might first appear. The law included a Sabbath rest for the land (Exod 23:10–11; Lev 25:2–7), and it could be such an idea that lies behind the text here. Alternatively, it might be that the crime against the land is parallel to that described in verse 39, which raises the possibility that Job could have defrauded workers on his land.

At this point, "the words of Job are ended" (v. 40).

LIVE the Story

The Impact of Suffering

Job's final speech essentially presents his closing arguments. He recalls his former status and contrasts it with his present situation—mocked by those

19. The NIV translates this as though God is the ruler and so Job approaches God as he would a ruler. While the Hebrew is syntactically ambiguous—allowing for both readings—the Hebrew term *nagid* is not elsewhere used in reference (even metaphorically) for God, and so it is best to understand Job here to be expressing his confidence in his own righteousness as he approaches God. See Clines, *Job 21–37*, 1035–36; Hartley, *Job*, 425; ESV; KJV; LSB; NASB.

20. See "באשׁ," in *HALOT* 107.

who once respected him and who themselves should be socially far beneath him and afflicted by God. He then proceeds to argue that despite all this he is blameless. He has remained faithful to his wife, such that he has even avoided looking lustfully at other women (Job 31:1, 9; cf. Matt 5:28). He is willing to have his life scrutinized by God and is confident that if this is done, he will emerge justified. Indeed, after reading Job's account of his life, it is difficult not to agree with Yahweh's boast about him in the opening chapters of the book, and because the two accounts correspond so completely, it is indeed appropriate to believe Job's claims about his life. He has lived a blameless and upright life and, compared to anyone else alive (either in his day or since), it really seems to be true to say that "there is no one on earth like him; he is blameless and upright, a man who fears God and shuns evil" (Job 1:8).

To some extent this all puts Job in a rather unique position, for none of us could ever claim to be as upright as Job. We would even rightly be suspicious of anyone making such claims for themselves. At this point Job is more like the Lord Jesus than he is like us—he suffers but is innocent. As noted earlier in the commentary, I am not making the claim that Job is sinless—what we know is that he is scrupulous in ensuring that his sin is dealt with in the manner that God had set down in times before the coming of the Messiah. This we learned in the opening chapter, where Job's concern over sin and offering sacrifices in order to deal with it was made clear. Nonetheless, here was a man unlike any other in his piety, devotion to God, and integrity.

Yet, Job does not stand unaffected by his suffering; he cannot view it in a clinically detached manner. It has had a profound impact on him, as he makes clear in 30:15: "Terrors overwhelm me; my dignity is driven away as by the wind, my safety vanishes like a cloud." Following his reflections on the past in the opening words of this speech, we see the impact Job's suffering is having on him: his inner world has been torn apart by the pain and isolation he has experienced over the time since his present experiences first struck him. If he emerges from his predicament, he is going to need to heal and recover from the scars that this suffering will inevitably leave on him. Job is, after all, human. He, no less than any of us, will be shaped by what has been happening to him. While the book of Job will not dwell on this reality, its author is not ignorant of it, and we also should not overlook this in the lives of those around us who are suffering and in our own lives when we suffer.

Some of us, particularly those of us in pastoral ministry, will encounter people who have lived through profound suffering and loss much as Job had. There is a great temptation to rush in and offer solutions or explanations, and doubtless there is a place for these. But they do not account for the emotional toll, the grief, or the time needed for the healing of the scars that are the result of suffering of all forms. There is no quick or simple fix for such scars in the lives of others—or in our life, for that matter. When supporting others, we need first to show deep empathy, love them, and not rush to offer advice or practical support and expect that this will somehow resolve the sufferer's pain.

When we suffer ourselves, we need to face up honestly to the effects suffering has on us in the same way that Job does here, and we need to be willing to both ask for and accept the help of others—others who hopefully offer more beneficial assistance than did Job's friends. One danger for us is to fail to acknowledge the true magnitude of our grief and loss, or the physical or emotional pain we are actually in. Certainly, some cultures are better at this than others, but suffering, pain, and loss all will leave scars on us that cannot helpfully be suppressed and will not quickly evaporate. Expect healing to take time.

Was the Satan Right?

Reflecting on Job's argument, and indeed on the arguments from his friends, it is worth asking whether there was not something to the Satan's claims in the opening chapters of the book. Job is very clearly unhappy about his lot. He expects more and believes justice has been abrogated. Both he and his friends believe that right behavior ought to result in blessings from God. The Satan, in the prologue, claimed that Job's piety was self-motivated; it was Job's strategy to ensure he could secure good from God. And throughout the book to this point, we have heard Job's complaints that his upright life was now not reaping blessings from God. Similarly, Job's friends argue that he would be restored to a blessed life were he to repent of some hypothetical sin that had led to his downfall, since God rewards the faithful with good.

Presented thus, it might be tempting to think that the Satan was right after all: Job expected to be rewarded by God for his devotion. Such a conclusion, however, is premature. Job and his friends did indeed share a theological understanding that maintained that pious living, doing the right thing, and adhering to God's commands would lead to automatic blessing from God and that doing the wrong thing would result in disciplinary action from God. Their theology was wrong, and those who would later persist in believing and teaching this theological position—at least in the simplistic form adopted by Job and his friends—were and are wrong as well. But is it sinful to have wrong theology? The answer to that question is not so clear, and it is a far larger question than can be addressed in brief reflection on Job's words here. Suffice it to say that not all wrong theology is sinful, but in some instances the way we implement and the way we put into practice that theology can be sinful, and even if not downright sinful, it can still be profoundly unwise and damaging. Job might have misunderstood the nature of God's dealings with his people in a sinful world where very little is as straightforward as our thinking or theology sometimes can be, but the way his misunderstanding about God's retributive justice worked out into his life did not play out the way the Satan had expected. Job did not curse God to his face. Rather, he struggled to understand while maintaining his integrity. Despite all his emotional and mental struggles with all that had happened and was happening to him, he did not abandon his faith because he could not understand what God was doing. Even though he felt that God had turned away from him, he did not turn away from God. His wrong theology at this point did not lead to sinful behavior.

A small caveat is worth noting at this point. While the book of Job goes to great lengths to demonstrate that the theological views of retributive justice held by Job and his friends were wrong, there is a danger in taking this too far and coming out from the book with a view that it has swung the pendulum of understanding too far in the other direction. It would be wrong to conclude, in the face of the book's invalidation of the notion of retributive justice, that there is no ultimate blessing or punishment to be meted out, or that there is no justice at all. Job and his friends operate entirely within the framework of this life, that is, life on this side of death or the return of the Lord Jesus. When we step back and take a broader view that encompasses not just this life but that which is to come after death, we are assured by the entire New Testament that retributive justice is, at the point of the final judgment and eternal blessing or punishment, a reality. What we cannot say—where this theology leads us astray—is that the promised blessings are all manifest in the present age or that by performing certain actions now we can secure blessings in the here and now, whether financial, medical, or other. That is the egregious lie of prosperity teaching, a teaching far too prevalent in parts of modern Christianity.

At this point at least, the book of Job should leave us dissatisfied and wanting more. The issues it raises are not fully resolved in its pages, for despite the fact that at the end of the book Job will find himself blessed and living well, that happy ending does not negate all that he has suffered through and all that he has lost. It does not finally answer the questions the book raises about justice in the world, about how the wicked so often prosper and the righteous so often suffer. Nor are we given any explanation for all of Job's suffering, despite the initial impression given in the prologue that the Satan's wager with Yahweh was the cause. That does not account for Job's ongoing suffering after the wager with the Satan has been won at the end of chapter 2. We, like Job, now find ourselves in the dark about the full reason for Job's continued suffering. We can side with the friends and think we have a complete explanation for Job, but to do so fails to listen closely to the wisdom of God as it is revealed through the book of Job. That wisdom tells us that there is more to know, more to understand about Job's suffering than either simple retributive justice or the wager between the Satan and Yahweh in the prologue can explain.

The story of Job is unsettling, and rightly so. It has no final answer to the problems of suffering and evil in the world; it merely highlights them and will offer in its remaining pages a way for faithful people to accept that the problems are not incompatible with faith in a loving all-powerful God. It will not negate the desire to know more or to understand more. Indeed, it should raise our expectations that God is not finished with Job and that there is more to come. And more does come, as the unfinished business of the book of Job longs to find its answers in the future king, God's Messiah. God will have more to say to us on the questions raised by the tale of Job: he will speak through the Word made flesh in whom we shall encounter God who himself is innocent and suffers much as Job did, but whose teachings and suffering will provide many of the answers that Job sought.

There are a number of additional lessons to draw from this. To start, we can be very judgmental, particularly toward those whose theology differs from our own. This does not just apply to the aspect of our theology related to retributive justice, as addressed in the book of Job, but also to many other areas. Differences over our understanding of the future—premillennial, amillennial, or postmillennial interpretations—are a good example. Do we judge others who differ from us in these matters so harshly that we consider them and their positions to be sinful? Now, I am not saying that all doctrine should be weighed equally; there are lines to be crossed and positions to be avoided. Not all theological beliefs should be so flexibly held, and the history of the church is peppered with examples where differences in theology reflected fundamental and critical beliefs that had such serious consequences that they would result in drawing people away from the true and living God. But for every such difference there are many that amount to minor disagreements that we, as sinful and proud human beings, tend to blow way out of proportion.

The End of Job's Words

At the end of Job's final speech, we are left with a clear picture of Job's case and where he stands. He is blameless and has done nothing to deserve the suffering and loss that he has faced at God's hand. Despite the sustained efforts of his friends, he has maintained his integrity and has not conceded to their bullying.

He has stood his ground and will not budge. Left at this point, the reader may be tempted to doubt God's justice in the matter of Job's life. Job is upright. He is unlike anyone else, and God himself has affirmed this fact! Where does that leave us? Is God unjust? Has God made a mistake? Is God capricious or arbitrary in his dealings with people? These certainly seem possible at this point, and whatever the case, there are questions to be answered, and it is likely that only God could answer these questions.

But we are not going to hear from God just yet. First there will appear a rather mysterious fourth friend, Elihu, to whom we now turn.

CHAPTER 21

Job 32–33

Elihu

LISTEN to the Story

32:1 So these three men stopped answering Job, because he was righteous
in his own eyes. 2 But Elihu son of Barakel the Buzite, of the family of Ram,
became very angry with Job for justifying himself rather than God. 3 He
was also angry with the three friends, because they had found no way to
refute Job, and yet had condemned him. 4 Now Elihu had waited before
speaking to Job because they were older than he. 5 But when he saw that
the three men had nothing more to say, his anger was aroused.
6 So Elihu son of Barakel the Buzite said:

"I am young in years,
  and you are old;
that is why I was fearful,
  not daring to tell you what I know.
7 I thought, 'Age should speak;
  advanced years should teach wisdom.'
8 But it is the spirit in a person,
  the breath of the Almighty, that gives them understanding.
9 It is not only the old who are wise,
  not only the aged who understand what is right.

10 "Therefore I say: Listen to me;
  I too will tell you what I know.
11 I waited while you spoke,
  I listened to your reasoning;
while you were searching for words,
  12 I gave you my full attention.
But not one of you has proved Job wrong;

none of you has answered his arguments.
13Do not say, 'We have found wisdom;
let God, not a man, refute him.'
14But Job has not marshaled his words against me,
and I will not answer him with your arguments.

15"They are dismayed and have no more to say;
words have failed them.
16Must I wait, now that they are silent,
now that they stand there with no reply?
17I too will have my say;
I too will tell what I know.
18For I am full of words,
and the spirit within me compels me;
19inside I am like bottled-up wine,
like new wineskins ready to burst.
20I must speak and find relief;
I must open my lips and reply.
21I will show no partiality,
nor will I flatter anyone;
22for if I were skilled in flattery,
my Maker would soon take me away.

33:1"But now, Job, listen to my words;
pay attention to everything I say.
2I am about to open my mouth;
my words are on the tip of my tongue.
3My words come from an upright heart;
my lips sincerely speak what I know.
4The Spirit of God has made me;
the breath of the Almighty gives me life.
5Answer me then, if you can;
stand up and argue your case before me.
6I am the same as you in God's sight;
I too am a piece of clay.
7No fear of me should alarm you,
nor should my hand be heavy on you.

8 "But you have said in my hearing—
I heard the very words—
9 'I am pure, I have done no wrong;
I am clean and free from sin.
10 Yet God has found fault with me;
he considers me his enemy.
11 He fastens my feet in shackles;
he keeps close watch on all my paths.'

12 "But I tell you, in this you are not right,
for God is greater than any mortal.
13 Why do you complain to him
that he responds to no one's words?
14 For God does speak—now one way, now another—
though no one perceives it.
15 In a dream, in a vision of the night,
when deep sleep falls on people
as they slumber in their beds,
16 he may speak in their ears
and terrify them with warnings,
17 to turn them from wrongdoing
and keep them from pride,
18 to preserve them from the pit,
their lives from perishing by the sword.

19 "Or someone may be chastened on a bed of pain
with constant distress in their bones,
20 so that their body finds food repulsive
and their soul loathes the choicest meal.
21 Their flesh wastes away to nothing,
and their bones, once hidden, now stick out.
22 They draw near to the pit,
and their life to the messengers of death.
23 Yet if there is an angel at their side,
a messenger, one out of a thousand,
sent to tell them how to be upright,
24 and he is gracious to that person and says to God,

'Spare them from going down to the pit;
I have found a ransom for them—
25let their flesh be renewed like a child's;
let them be restored as in the days of their youth'—
26then that person can pray to God and find favor with him,
they will see God's face and shout for joy;
he will restore them to full well-being.
27And they will go to others and say,
'I have sinned, I have perverted what is right,
but I did not get what I deserved.
28God has delivered me from going down to the pit,
and I shall live to enjoy the light of life.'

29"God does all these things to a person—
twice, even three times—
30to turn them back from the pit,
that the light of life may shine on them.

31"Pay attention, Job, and listen to me;
be silent, and I will speak.
32If you have anything to say, answer me;
speak up, for I want to vindicate you.
33But if not, then listen to me;
be silent, and I will teach you wisdom."

Listening to the Text in the Story: "The Poem of the Righteous Sufferer" (Babylonian; also known as "The Babylonian Job" or "Ludlul Bēl Nēmeqi")

For the first time since chapter 2, a new character appears in the story of Job, a younger man named Elihu. His introduction contains more detail than that of any of the other characters: we are told his name, his father's name, his broader family connections, and his geographical provenance. This unprecedented level of detail likely aims to make up for the late introduction of this character and to set him apart from the other participants in Job's drama.

Just like all the other events in the book of Job, Elihu's words reflect aspects of the ancient Near Eastern milieu in which they originated. Elihu, for example, refers to dreams as a means by which God can communicate

(Job 33:15–18). In the Babylonian text "The Poem of the Righteous Sufferer" (also known as the "Babylonian Job" or "Ludlul Bēl Nēmeqi"), the sufferer receives a message related to his restoration through a dream. The early portion of tablet iii is damaged, but later we read:

> A second time [I saw a dream].
> In the dream I saw [at night],
> A remarkable purifier [ ],
> Holding in his hand a tamarisk rod of purification,
> "Laluralimma, resident of Nippur,
> Has sent me to cleanse you."
> He was carrying water, he po[ured it] over me,
> He pronounced the resuscitating incantation, he massaged [my] bo[dy].
> A third time I saw a dream.
> In my dream I saw at night:
> A remarkable young woman of shining countenance,
> Clothed like a person(?), being li[ke] a god,
> A queen among peoples [ ],
> She entered upon me and [sat down] . . . [ ]
> She ordered my deliverance [ ]
> "Fear not!" she said, I [will]
> Whatever one sees(?) of a dream [ ]."
> She ordered my deliverance, "Most wre[tched] indeed is he,
> Whoever he might be, the one who saw the vision at night."
> In the dream (was) Ur-Nindinugga, a Babylonian(?)
> A bearded young man wearing a tiara,
> He was an exorcist, carrying a tablet,
> "Marduk has sent me!
> To Shubshi-meshre-Shakkan I have brought a sw[athe],
> From his pure hands I have brought a sw[athe]."
> He has entru[sted] me into the hands of my ministrant.
> [In] waking hours he sent a message,
> He reve[aled] his favorable sign to my people.
> I was awake in my sickness, a (healing) serpent slithered by.
> My illness was quickly over, [my fetters] were broken.
> After my lord's heart had quiet[ed],
> (And) the feelings of merciful Marduk were ap[peased],
> [And he had] accepted my prayers [ ] . . .[1]

1. "The Poem of the Righteous Sufferer," *COS* 1.153:490.

Here information is divulged to the sufferer in a dream that will ultimately lead to his release from suffering.

The connections to the ancient world do not end there. Elihu's words in Job 33:18 may also refer to a river that must be crossed to gain entry into the underworld described as "the pit" (*shakhat*), the equivalent of Sheol. The Hebrew text is difficult here, but many modern scholars and some translations (against the NIV "perishing by the sword") prefer the meaning of crossing this river (cf. "from crossing the river" in the NIV footnote). If this is the case, the reference to "the pit" would seem to be to a body of water like the one Gilgamesh must cross to reach the immortalized hero of the flood, Utnapishtim.[2]

Job 33:22 then makes reference to "messengers of death" in parallel with "the pit." The Hebrew term *memitim* (NIV "messengers"), is found nowhere else in the Bible in this form and closely reflects the Akkadian term *mush-miruti*.[3] Hartley notes that these *memitim* may be angelic beings tasked with transporting the deceased into the underworld.[4] If this is the case, then Elihu is here using them as a means to highlight just how close to death the sufferer may come before their ultimate rescue, an apt description of where Job finds himself at this point in the story.

EXPLAIN the Story

Job's Fourth Friend Introduced (32:1–5)

Job's fourth friend, Elihu, unexpectedly appears from nowhere, and after he has spoken, he disappears from the book and is not mentioned again even in the conclusion to the book. As such, some have suggested that he is a later addition to the story. Some think him a precocious upstart who speaks a lot but says little, essentially repeating the arguments of the other friends. Some suggest he serves as comic relief for the book. The truth, however, is that Elihu makes an important and unique contribution to the message of Job, as shall become apparent as we work through his words.[5]

Whatever we might think of what Elihu has to say, it is beyond dispute that Elihu is a windbag—only Job has more to say in this book. Elihu says more than any of the other friends and more than Yahweh will say later in

2. "Gilgamesh," trans. Bejamin R. Foster (*COS* 1.132:458–60).
3. Clines, *Job 21–37*, 734.
4. Hartley, *Book of Job*, 444.
5. For a full discussion of Elihu's role and other views, see Shields, "Was Elihu Right?"

the book. Yet, this functions as misdirection. His words may not be as elegant as those of his older companions, but he does say some things that are new and important.

Structurally, Elihu stands between Job and Yahweh, who will appear following the end of Elihu's speech. Without the speech from Elihu, there is a danger that Yahweh would appear to be responding not freely but because Job had demanded he do so. Having Elihu speak between them preserves God's independence.

The lack of any further response to Job by his older three friends is explained here by the narrator as due to Job being "righteous in his own eyes" (v. 1). What is not quite so clear is why this should now stop them from arguing, given that it has been Job's consistent position from the start (cf. 12:4). And while it might sound like a negative assessment, from what we have been told in the prologue we should realize that Job may well be right to see himself as righteous. Both the narrator and God have noted that Job was blameless and upright, so it has been the friends who have been mistaken up to this point. As such, the narrator is here most likely indicating that the older three friends had finally concluded that Job's belief in his own righteousness was so intractable as to make further response pointless. The negativity in the assessment was theirs and not the narrator's or God's.

The very first words used to introduce Job's youngest friend in the Hebrew text of Job are "very angry." In fact, the expression "very angry" appears three times in the narrator's introduction of Elihu to the story (32:2–5). The phrase is quite common in the Bible, most often as a description of God's response to sin (e.g., Judg 2:14, 20; 2 Sam 6:7; 2 Kgs 13:3). The issue we are faced with as we first encounter Elihu, however, is whether his anger is justified or even proportional. The answer to that can only be determined by hearing what he has to say.

Elihu, unlike the older three friends, is given more extensive background: "Elihu son of Barakel the Buzite, of the family of Ram." Ash notes that this is one clue that we ought to take Elihu seriously, whereas Hartley notes that this is a reflection of his youth.[6] Both ideas are probably present. What is clear from these names is that Elihu, unlike all the other participants in the debate, is more directly associated with Abraham's descendants (remembering that the tale is set in patriarchal times, it would be anachronistic to suggest that Elihu was an Israelite). The names of Elihu and his ancestors are straightforward Hebrew theophoric names: Elihu means "he is my God" and is shared with

6. Ash, *Job*, 328; Hartley, *Book of Job*, 429.

others in the Old Testament (see 1 Sam 1:1; 16:6; 1 Chr 12:21; 26:7) while his father's name, Barakel, means "God has blessed."

While Hartley understands "Buz" to be a reference to Elihu's tribe, it reads more like a reference to the place he lives. In Genesis 22:21 Buz is the name of a cousin of Abraham. More helpfully, Buz appears as a place name in Jeremiah alongside Dedan and Tema (see Jer 25:23; 49:7–8). Dedan and Tema are in the northern part of the Arabian Peninsula, suggesting that Buz would also be in that general area and may be the location known as Bâzu in Akkadian texts.[7] In the later passages in Jeremiah, Dedan is also associated with Edom, a connection that fits well with the geography of the book of Job. Elihu's family name, "Ram," is also a Hebrew term meaning "high, exalted" (compare with the early form of Abraham's name, Abram, "exalted father").

That his arrival was not mentioned in the prologue suggests that he may have arrived later than the other three friends. The remainder of the narrator's introduction to Elihu offers an explanation for his previous silence and his motivation for speaking up now. His silence was due to his respect for his elders, a point Elihu will make as he begins to speak. His motive for speaking now is his anger at the friends' failure to answer Job while still condemning him, together with his anger at Job for choosing to justify himself in a manner that diminished the justice of God.

Elihu's Disappointment with His Older Friends (32:6–9)

Elihu begins in verses 6–9 with an explanation of his silence to this point. He describes Job's other friends using a rare word, but it has been used in parallel with "grey-haired" back in Job 15:10. As such, Job's friends (and most likely Job too) are at least in their late 40s. Elihu has deferred to their age in allowing them to speak, describing himself as "fearful" to speak. His reluctance is based on the convention that with age comes wisdom (v. 7; cf. 12:12), but perhaps as a result of hearing some of their words, Elihu has come to realize that wisdom is not the exclusive domain of the aged. True wisdom, he asserts, comes from God, and so he is as qualified as anyone to state his case.

Some have suggested that Elihu is a prophetic figure in the book of Job, largely because of his comment here that "it is the spirit in a person, the breath

7. James A. Thompson, *Jeremiah*, NICOT (Grand Rapids: Eerdmans, 1980), 518, 720. Thompson notes that "the oasis of Dedan lay in northwest Arabia, to the southeast of Edom, and may have been part of Edom." References to Bâzu are found on "Esarhaddon's Thompson Prism" (*COS* 4.39:173, 177) and also locate it in what is today northwest Saudi Arabia.

of the Almighty, that gives them understanding" (v. 8).[8] This does not stand close scrutiny. Elihu's reference to the "breath of the Almighty" means little more than that wisdom and understanding are available to all people. Elihu is simply arguing that true wisdom is not the exclusive purview of the aged and that despite his relative youth (we do not know exactly how old any of the characters are), he can make a meaningful contribution to the discussion. Later, in 33:4, Elihu will use similar language to say no more than that he is alive. Furthermore, elsewhere where the words "Spirit" (*ruakh*) and "breath" (*neshamah*) appear together they do not refer to prophetic revelation (see Gen 7:22; Isa 42:5).[9]

Elihu's claim here is simply that he is equally qualified to speak to the issues raised by Job's predicament and that he ought to be heard, particularly now that the friends have failed to silence Job with their arguments.

Elihu Asserts the Importance of What He Will Say (32:10–33:7)

By and large the remainder of the opening chapter of Elihu's speech is taken up with his verbose justification for finally speaking and his disparaging assessment of the friends' speeches, all the while talking himself up. The friends have failed (vv. 12–13, 15–16). As such, this entire chapter is more addressed to the friends than it is to Job, so despite asserting the urgency and importance of his words (vv. 17–22), he spends an inordinate amount of time not getting to the point. At one level this is a reflection of his youth and inexperience, and the skill of the poet who composed these words in reflecting that aspect of Elihu's character in his speeches.

Elihu's final explanation of his need to speak is that he is so filled with things to say that he will burst if he is not given the opportunity to speak. The reference to wineskins connects to the fermentation of the wine they hold that, if not vented, will result in such pressure building up in them that they explode (32:18–20). Thus, Elihu must give vent to the words he has built up inside. The analogy is also apt in suggesting that Elihu's words may not flow out in elegant and well-prepared rhetoric but rather gush out under pressure. Yet, that is no reason to claim that there is nothing meaningful in what he will have to say.

Just when we think Elihu might be about to say something substantive at

---

8. See Ash, *Job*, 331–36; William P. Brown, *Character in Crisis: A Fresh Approach to the Wisdom Literature of the Old Testament* (Grand Rapids: Eerdmans, 1996), 85.

9. See Martin A. Shields, "You Can't Get a Sage to Do a Prophet's Job: Overcoming Wisdom's Deficiency in the Book of Job," in *Riddles and Revelations: Explorations into the Relationship Between Wisdom and Prophecy in the Hebrew Bible*, ed. Mark J. Boda, Russell L. Meek, and William R. Osborne, LHBOTS 634 (London: T&T Clark, 2018), 185–89.

the beginning of chapter 33, he again tells us (or, more specifically, Job) that he has something important to say (vv. 1–7). Ultimately, the impression given by this long-winded introduction to the actual arguments he will present is that he is nervous, uncertain of the reception he will get. As such, he spends a long time justifying himself, trying to convince the others that he is worth listening to.

Having said that, Elihu is the only of the friends to address Job by name (v. 1; see also Job 33:31; 37:14). For all Elihu's bluster and youth, his interaction with Job is already more immediate and personal.

Elihu Defends God Against Job's Claims (33:8–33)

Elihu frames his first response to Job in verses 8–11 by making reference to Job's own words. In spite of Elihu's opening words in verse 8, he does not provide a verbatim quote of Job's words. Rather, he provides a fairly accurate summary of Job's speeches. Job has claimed (correctly, as stated by the narrator and God in the prologue) that he is blameless (e.g., 9:21; 10:7; 23:11–12). Job has said that he believes that God considers him to be his enemy (13:24). He has accused God of putting his feet in shackles and scrutinizing his paths (13:27). So Elihu's complaint about Job's claims about God is valid. And Job's claims about God were wrong, as we know from the prologue. Job, like his older friends, was so bound by the theological straitjacket that belief in retributive justice creates that he could only wind up accusing God of actions that were wrong.

Elihu's response to Job's claims is to defend God (33:12–18). Even Job's complaint that God does not respond (30:20) is, in Elihu's opinion, incorrect. Elihu tells Job that God could, should he so choose (the verb form Elihu uses here makes it clear that he is not suggesting that he is certain about God speaking to Job in this way; he is simply raising the possibility), communicate in numerous ways (v. 14), for which he provides two examples.

The first example of divine communication cited by Elihu is "in a dream, in a vision of the night" (v. 15). The language is reminiscent of that used by Eliphaz in 4:13, where he had claimed to have had a revelatory dream. Dreams are frequently cited as a means by which God communicates with people (e.g., Gen 20:3; Num 12:6; 1 Kgs 3:5), and the reference in Job 33:15 to "a vision of the night" suggests that the dreams that Elihu speaks of here are not necessarily verbal but visual. The purpose of such dreams may be to save the recipient from doing something sinful which will ultimately lead them to disaster (i.e., winding up in the "pit" [*shakhat*], which is equivalent to Sheol, so pointing to a violent premature death by the sword, see v. 18).[10]

---

10. For more detail, see Shields, "Was Elihu Right?"

The second part of verse 18 is difficult, as can be seen in the NIV's footnote that offers the alternative "from crossing the river." The Hebrew term *shelakh*, understood either as "sword" or "river," is not the common term (occurring only twice in the Hebrew Bible, here and Job 36:12) for either item in Hebrew (cf. *khereb*, "sword" [e.g., Gen 34:25], and *nahar*, "river" [e.g., 2 Kgs 5:12]). Job does reflect some ideas from the ancient Near East, and thus here the "river" would likely refer to the body of water one must cross to gain entry into the underworld in Mesopotamian mythology.[11] In the end, the point is clear. For Elihu, the purpose of the message, the "vision of the night," is to avoid an untimely death.

The second example of divine communication the Elihu suggests comes through suffering itself. Job 33:19–22 describes suffering so severe and so persistent that the person is brought to the brink of death, emaciated and in constant pain. The source of this suffering is alluded to in the opening description—the passive verb "be chastened" (v. 22) suggests that the pain itself is punishment for some prior action, as is made clear in verse 27 and is ultimately inflicted by God.

The "messengers of death" in verse 22 are woodenly rendered as "the ones who cause death." This, too, may be a reference to ideas from Mesopotamia where a similar term refers to demonic messengers.[12] The point of the verse is clear: the sufferer is perilously close to death before the situation is turned around in verse 23 through the intervention of another angelic being.

The idea of one in a thousand was earlier used by Job to express the hopelessness of his situation before God (9:3). Here, however, Elihu uses the extreme odds to express hope. It only takes one out of one thousand potential mediators to speak up on one's behalf for God to act. The implication is that there are many ready to step into this role and thus that the chances of success are good. Job had already hoped that there would be a mediator to represent him in the divine court (16:19–21), and here Elihu takes up the idea. This angel, first of all, reveals to the sufferer the nature of their offence—what it is that they have done that has brought upon them this suffering. In verse 23 the "angel" (*mal'ak*, a word that just means "messenger"), also called a "messenger" in the second line of the verse (Hebrew *melits*, a "go-between" in various capacities[13]), which could be a human intermediary, such as a prophet. But verse 24 makes it clear that "messenger" has a heavenly role of the angel.

In verse 24 this angelic mediator appeals in the heavenly court for the

11. See Longman, *Job*, 388.

12. See Clines, *Job 21–37*, 734.

13. "מֵלִיץ," *HALOT* 590.

sufferer's restoration, at least partly on the grounds that the angel has found a ransom for the sufferer. "Ransom" (v. 25) refers to a payment made to release someone. In the modern world we usually think a ransom as a form of extortion for someone taken captive, but in the Old Testament ransom usually refers to a payment made to release someone from a just punishment (e.g., Exod 21:30; 30:12). The ransom here is a payment that atones for the sin of the sufferer. It is not the sufferer's suffering that constitutes the ransom, since it is an offering of the angelic mediator that takes place in order to bring an end to that suffering. Precisely what the ransom would be is not made clear. From our place in history, we can look back at the suggestion of Elihu that the ransom is paid by a third party on behalf of the sufferer and see it reflected in the work of Jesus, whose death served as a ransom for we who were unable to pay the debt owed to release us from the punishment of death (Matt 20:28; Mark 10:45; 1 Tim 2:6).

The other aspect of the payment of a ransom by a mediator—where there is a legitimate penalty to be paid—is that the cost is not borne by the sufferer but by the mediator. Elihu's hypothetical sufferer acknowledges this too when he states that "I did not get what I deserved" (v. 27). The ransom payment results in God's demands for justice being fulfilled, and so the sufferer is spared the death that they deserved (v. 28).

While this second scenario presented by Elihu depicts a situation in which sin is the ultimate cause of the suffering, he does not believe that Job is guilty of such a sin. For one, no angelic mediator has appeared to Job to reveal the nature of his supposed sin. More clearly, in 36:21 he will warn Job against turning to sin, a warning that implies that he had not yet turned to sin and more closely reflects the first of Elihu's proposed explanations for suffering (33:12–18). Furthermore, the scenarios Elihu presents here are phrased as possibilities rather than certainties (this is made clear by the Hebrew verbal forms used).[14] As such, we ought not to see these as an analysis of Job's particular situation but as a range of possibilities. Job might hear from God in a dream (cf. vv. 15–18), Job might be experiencing suffering as a result of sin (cf. vv. 19–22), and it may be that Job ought to understand the suffering he is experiencing as a call to repent, or perhaps it is designed to prevent him from falling into sin in the future (cf. vv. 23–28). Unlike Job's other friends, Elihu is careful here to refrain from pronouncing specific judgment on Job's circumstances.

Elihu wraps up his discussion of the ways in which God uses suffering

14. See Shields, "Was Elihu Right?," 163.

to communicate in verses 29–30 by letting Job know that God is persistent. God will do these things repeatedly in order to save someone. Elihu argues that God does not want his people to perish but will strive to preserve their lives (see 2 Pet 3:9).

In the last verses of Job 33, where Elihu sounds as though he may be finished, he concludes his first speech by making it clear that he has more to say. If Job remains silent, then Elihu plans to continue, but he does invite Job to have his say or otherwise to let him finish. Elihu claims here to desire Job's vindication, although in the subsequent speeches he will focus largely on affirming God's justice, which Job has called into question. Yet this desire expressed by Elihu has already been reflected in his suggestion that suffering may not be a result of sin, and so he may be hoping that Job would chime in and express his acceptance of this idea. At the very least, Elihu has highlighted the possibility that Job is right about his innocence and God is just in his judgments.

LIVE the Story

The Danger of Stereotyping People

"You can't judge a book by its cover," so the old saying goes. Yet we all do judge books—and many other things around us—by the superficial external appearance that is presented to us. If someone is poorly clothed or groomed, if they attend a particular church or are part of a particular denomination, if they are a member of a specific ethnic group (even if we would never admit to classifying someone thus), if they are old and seemingly slow or, as is the case with Elihu, if someone is young and does not speak in quite the way that we do, then we all too easily pass judgment on them without giving them a fair hearing. We apply labels to people, categorizing them so that we can simply lump them together with a stereotype that we have built up, and then we dismiss them. We proclaim that people from *that* church have a wrong understanding of the Bible, or *their* doctrine is too liberal or too conservative. In the end it all comes down to, "They are different from us."

Such judgments or prejudices (as in times we pre-judge someone) prevent us from hearing people, and no matter whether someone is wrong about some things, rarely is someone wrong about everything. If we do not listen, we isolate ourselves in a protective bubble where our own false beliefs and assumptions are never challenged. It is, ultimately, the reason to listen carefully to those you disagree with or who hold different opinions, to hear those you are tempted to dismiss out of hand. Into just such a situation comes Elihu, Job's young friend, who speaks up against the prejudice of others (even if that prejudice is not real but only perceived by Elihu himself). He warns us that if we are tempted to write him off just because we think only the elders are wise, then think again. True wisdom comes from God, and so it is not the exclusive purview of the aged.

The narrator, and Elihu himself, give us reasons to prejudge Elihu. He is young and he is angry. When we hear him speak, he is different from Job's other friends, and he takes an awfully long time to get around to saying anything of actual substance. But are these reasons to write him off, to ignore what he does say? No. For one thing, his verbosity and repetition throughout the opening part of his speech may simply reflect his uncertainty about how he will be received, and so his rhetorical style may be quite innocent and not at all an indication that what he does have to say is not worth hearing. So, we ought to listen to what Elihu has to say. Only then will we be in a position to decide whether he has anything of value to add to the conversations that have taken place to this point.

This is a simple lesson that strikes at the heart of our pride, and that lesson is this: sometimes we learn something from the most unexpected of places, if only we are willing to hear it. Job has three older friends who, according to conventional wisdom, would be considered to be the wise men, the ones we ought to pay heed to, the ones who would be most likely to impart wisdom and knowledge that would shed light on Job's situation, and ones whose advice would ultimately lead him out of his awful situation and restore him. But they do not. Instead, it is the younger friend, the one who on the surface appears to be the one we can safely ignore, who has something of value to add to the conversation. Sometimes the truth comes from the most unexpected of places.

"You Can't Always Get What You Want"

Way back in 1969 the British band The Rolling Stones sang the song "You Can't Always Get What You Want." The lyrics continue with the message that if you keep trying, you will get what you need. If we do avoid the initial temptation to dismiss Elihu, we might notice that when he eventually gets around to saying something meaningful in this speech, he could be paraphrased as saying something similar to The Rolling Stones: "you don't always get what you deserve . . . you get what you need!" It is difficult to dispute the fact that Job has gotten neither what he wants nor what he deserves. We know that not just from Job's words, but from the words of the narrator and of God himself in the prologue. Job is not suffering because he has some specific sin for which he has not made atonement. He has nothing for which he must repent and seek forgiveness. His suffering is not a punishment for some hidden sin, as his older three friends have claimed. No, the one thing we can be certain of at this point is that they were indeed wrong about the reasons for his suffering.

What comes as a surprise is that Elihu—this younger, somewhat brash, and rather verbose friend—introduces something new into the discussion. He offers another possible rationale for Job's suffering. Elihu suggests that Job's suffering might possibly be occurring because it might ultimately prevent him from straying from true devotion to and worship of Yahweh at some point in the future. Elihu explains that God can communicate with his people in many ways, and one of those ways may be through suffering. We might paraphrase his words in 33:14–22 thusly: "God can choose to speak in many ways—through dreams or even through suffering." Yet, showing wisdom beyond his years (if we can be forgiven for saying such a thing after Elihu's opening claims about wisdom and the aged), Elihu never claims that he knows for certain God is working through Job's suffering to prevent some future sin. This is just a possibility, but the possibility does offer an explanation for suffering that is *not* the result of a past sin in Job's life. Perhaps his suffering has been God's way of communicating with him, and perhaps that suffering will ultimately turn out as the critical and necessary means to keep Job on track at some point later in his life. Perhaps.

Why is it important to the message of the book that Elihu introduces this possibility if it does not turn out to be a valid explanation of Job's suffering? The answer is straightforward: among those whose thinking on suffering is dominated by the idea that it reflects the outworkings of God's retributive justice, it helps to show that this idea does not exhaust all of the possible explanations for suffering that fit with their understanding of God and how he works in the world. If retribution were the only possible explanation, then Job's older three friends would have to have been right in their insistence that Job had sinned and needed to repent and plead for forgiveness. That it is not the only possible explanation—and Elihu does not claim that he has exhausted all possible alternate explanations in offering this suggestion—leaves the door open for the possibility that Job is right in his claims but God is also just in his actions.

The other important factor here is that Elihu does not insist that this explanation for suffering is definitive, that this is *the* explanation for Job's suffering. As we reach the end of the book of Job, we will find that there is no comprehensive explanation for all that happened to Job. We have even seen that the explanation offered in the opening chapters of the book was only partial and that there was more to Job's suffering than we were told. In a book designed to teach that sometimes people suffer and never know with any certainty why they suffer, it makes perfect sense to maintain some amount of mystery about Job's suffering. Job never understands it, and explaining it all to us would undermine this important message.

Elihu's Mediator

In this speech Elihu also speaks about the possibility of an angelic mediator (33:23–24) who would both deliver a message to the sufferer ("sent to tell them how to be upright," v. 23) and also plead with God on the sufferer's behalf ("Spare them from going down to the pit; I have found a ransom for them," v. 24). Job, we remember, has already been described as "upright" (1:1, 8; 2:3), and so we should realize that Elihu's words here are not immediately relevant to Job. At this point we need to remember two more things. First, Elihu does not know—any more than the other three friends or Job himself—why Job is suffering as he is. Second, Elihu is not dismissing the idea of retributive justice completely; all he has done is add that the sort of preemptive action he has suggested as an explanation for suffering in Job 33:14–18 is one possible explanation, not the only one. No one in the book of Job—not even God—will claim that retributive justice is *never* an explanation for suffering. That would be to take the message of the book too far. The remainder of the Bible makes clear that God does hold us accountable for our actions and that there will be a final judgment where justice will be meted out on all. Retributive justice is an undeniable aspect of creation and a necessary result of a just Creator. The book of Job rather counsels against simplistic judgments we might make about suffering that reduce all suffering in the present to a necessary consequence of divine justice.

Yet, while Elihu's reference to a heavenly mediator does not immediately apply to Job in the story, its relevance to all of us becomes apparent as the story of God unfolds in the pages of the Bible. It will become clear that we are all in need of such an intermediary, for the price that must be paid as ransom for our offence against God is one that we cannot pay ourselves. Even Job, who is described in the prologue as upright (1:1, 8; cf. 33:23 which presents this as the goal of the mediation provided by Elihu's intercessor), needed such an intermediary. What Elihu does not know about Job is that his case had already been made for him; a mediator had already stepped in. His sins had been dealt with, and so at this point in Job's story the particular problem of him needing to be made upright and blameless had already been resolved. That was the function of the elaborate sacrificial system of the Old Testament: to provide a means by which sin could be dealt with. What we come to discover in the New Testament is that those sacrifices functioned as a means for God's people to express their faith and through that faith find forgiveness and be made blameless through the ultimate sacrifice of the Messiah.

And so, God, knowing of our predicament and out of love for us, found an intermediary who would be able to pay the ransom. That intermediary, who was able to both walk the earth and let us know the cause of our predicament (Job 33:23) and also present that ransom in the heavenly places (Job 33:24), is Jesus. His death served as a ransom for us, as we are unable to pay the debt owed to release us from the punishment of death (Matt 20:28; Mark 10:45; 1 Tim 2:6). Job, unbeknownst to him, was made blameless not through his own good works or his scrupulous observance of cultic sacrifices, but by the sacrifice that would be made at a time still in the distant future for Job. God would through his forbearance hold over the punishment for the sins of those who lived before the time of Christ in order to demonstrate his justice in Christ, as Paul says in Romans:

> God presented Christ as a sacrifice of atonement, through the shedding of his blood—to be received by faith. He did this to demonstrate his righteousness, because in his forbearance he had left the sins committed beforehand unpunished—he did it to demonstrate his righteousness at the present time, so as to be just and the one who justifies those who have faith in Jesus. (Rom 3:25–26)

Job's blamelessness, as well as ours, is an achievement of the sacrificial death of Jesus. That Job was recognized as blameless by God in the prologue is a result of Job's faith and God's forbearance. These together resulted in Job's right standing before God, and they ensure that the Job we encounter in the opening chapters of the book has indeed been made blameless and is indeed not suffering as a penalty for undisclosed sin. So Elihu was right about Job's need for a mediator. Where he was wrong was in suggesting that Job's present predicament required that mediator to step in.

CHAPTER 22

Job 34–37

Elihu Continues

LISTEN to the Story

34:1 Then Elihu said:

2 "Hear my words, you wise men;
listen to me, you men of learning.
3 For the ear tests words
as the tongue tastes food.
4 Let us discern for ourselves what is right;
let us learn together what is good.

5 "Job says, 'I am innocent,
but God denies me justice.
6 Although I am right,
I am considered a liar;
although I am guiltless,
his arrow inflicts an incurable wound.'
7 Is there anyone like Job,
who drinks scorn like water?
8 He keeps company with evildoers;
he associates with the wicked.
9 For he says, 'There is no profit
in trying to please God.'

10 "So listen to me, you men of understanding.
Far be it from God to do evil,
from the Almighty to do wrong.
11 He repays everyone for what they have done;
he brings on them what their conduct deserves.

12It is unthinkable that God would do wrong,
that the Almighty would pervert justice.
13Who appointed him over the earth?
Who put him in charge of the whole world?
14If it were his intention
and he withdrew his spirit and breath,
15all humanity would perish together
and mankind would return to the dust.

16"If you have understanding, hear this;
listen to what I say.
17Can someone who hates justice govern?
Will you condemn the just and mighty One?
18Is he not the One who says to kings, 'You are worthless,'
and to nobles, 'You are wicked,'
19who shows no partiality to princes
and does not favor the rich over the poor,
for they are all the work of his hands?
20They die in an instant, in the middle of the night;
the people are shaken and they pass away;
the mighty are removed without human hand.

21"His eyes are on the ways of mortals;
he sees their every step.
22There is no deep shadow, no utter darkness,
where evildoers can hide.
23God has no need to examine people further,
that they should come before him for judgment.
24Without inquiry he shatters the mighty
and sets up others in their place.
25Because he takes note of their deeds,
he overthrows them in the night and they are crushed.
26He punishes them for their wickedness
where everyone can see them,
27because they turned from following him
and had no regard for any of his ways.
28They caused the cry of the poor to come before him,

so that he heard the cry of the needy.
29But if he remains silent, who can condemn him?
If he hides his face, who can see him?
Yet he is over individual and nation alike,
30to keep the godless from ruling,
from laying snares for the people.

31"Suppose someone says to God,
'I am guilty but will offend no more.
32Teach me what I cannot see;
if I have done wrong, I will not do so again.'
33Should God then reward you on your terms,
when you refuse to repent?
You must decide, not I;
so tell me what you know.

34"Men of understanding declare,
wise men who hear me say to me,
35'Job speaks without knowledge;
his words lack insight.'
36Oh, that Job might be tested to the utmost
for answering like a wicked man!
37To his sin he adds rebellion;
scornfully he claps his hands among us
and multiplies his words against God."

35:1Then Elihu said:

2"Do you think this is just?
You say, 'I am in the right, not God.'
3Yet you ask him, 'What profit is it to me,
and what do I gain by not sinning?'

4"I would like to reply to you
and to your friends with you.
5Look up at the heavens and see;
gaze at the clouds so high above you.

6If you sin, how does that affect him?
If your sins are many, what does that do to him?
7If you are righteous, what do you give to him,
or what does he receive from your hand?
8Your wickedness only affects humans like yourself,
and your righteousness only other people.

9"People cry out under a load of oppression;
they plead for relief from the arm of the powerful.
10But no one says, 'Where is God my Maker,
who gives songs in the night,
11who teaches us more than he teaches the beasts of the earth
and makes us wiser than the birds in the sky?'
12He does not answer when people cry out
because of the arrogance of the wicked.
13Indeed, God does not listen to their empty plea;
the Almighty pays no attention to it.
14How much less, then, will he listen
when you say that you do not see him,
that your case is before him
and you must wait for him,
15and further, that his anger never punishes
and he does not take the least notice of wickedness.
16So Job opens his mouth with empty talk;
without knowledge he multiplies words."

36:1Elihu continued:

2"Bear with me a little longer and I will show you
that there is more to be said in God's behalf.
3I get my knowledge from afar;
I will ascribe justice to my Maker.
4Be assured that my words are not false;
one who has perfect knowledge is with you.

5"God is mighty, but despises no one;
he is mighty, and firm in his purpose.

6He does not keep the wicked alive
but gives the afflicted their rights.
7He does not take his eyes off the righteous;
he enthrones them with kings
and exalts them forever.
8But if people are bound in chains,
held fast by cords of affliction,
9he tells them what they have done—
that they have sinned arrogantly.
10He makes them listen to correction
and commands them to repent of their evil.
11If they obey and serve him,
they will spend the rest of their days in prosperity
and their years in contentment.
12But if they do not listen,
they will perish by the sword
and die without knowledge.

13"The godless in heart harbor resentment;
even when he fetters them, they do not cry for help.
14They die in their youth,
among male prostitutes of the shrines.
15But those who suffer he delivers in their suffering;
he speaks to them in their affliction.

16"He is wooing you from the jaws of distress
to a spacious place free from restriction,
to the comfort of your table laden with choice food.
17But now you are laden with the judgment due the wicked;
judgment and justice have taken hold of you.
18Be careful that no one entices you by riches;
do not let a large bribe turn you aside.
19Would your wealth or even all your mighty efforts
sustain you so you would not be in distress?
20Do not long for the night,
to drag people away from their homes.
21Beware of turning to evil,

which you seem to prefer to affliction.

22“God is exalted in his power.
Who is a teacher like him?
23Who has prescribed his ways for him,
or said to him, ‘You have done wrong’?
24Remember to extol his work,
which people have praised in song.
25All humanity has seen it;
mortals gaze on it from afar.
26How great is God—beyond our understanding!
The number of his years is past finding out.

27“He draws up the drops of water,
which distill as rain to the streams;
28the clouds pour down their moisture
and abundant showers fall on mankind.
29Who can understand how he spreads out the clouds,
how he thunders from his pavilion?
30See how he scatters his lightning about him,
bathing the depths of the sea.
31This is the way he governs the nations
and provides food in abundance.
32He fills his hands with lightning
and commands it to strike its mark.
33His thunder announces the coming storm;
even the cattle make known its approach.

37:1“At this my heart pounds
and leaps from its place.
2Listen! Listen to the roar of his voice,
to the rumbling that comes from his mouth.
3He unleashes his lightning beneath the whole heaven
and sends it to the ends of the earth.
4After that comes the sound of his roar;
he thunders with his majestic voice.
When his voice resounds,

he holds nothing back.
5God's voice thunders in marvelous ways;
he does great things beyond our understanding.
6He says to the snow, 'Fall on the earth,'
and to the rain shower, 'Be a mighty downpour.'
7So that everyone he has made may know his work,
he stops all people from their labor.
8The animals take cover;
they remain in their dens.
9The tempest comes out from its chamber,
the cold from the driving winds.
10The breath of God produces ice,
and the broad waters become frozen.
11He loads the clouds with moisture;
he scatters his lightning through them.
12At his direction they swirl around
over the face of the whole earth
to do whatever he commands them.
13He brings the clouds to punish people,
or to water his earth and show his love.

14"Listen to this, Job;
stop and consider God's wonders.
15Do you know how God controls the clouds
and makes his lightning flash?
16Do you know how the clouds hang poised,
those wonders of him who has perfect knowledge?
17You who swelter in your clothes
when the land lies hushed under the south wind,
18can you join him in spreading out the skies,
hard as a mirror of cast bronze?
19"Tell us what we should say to him;
we cannot draw up our case because of our darkness.
20Should he be told that I want to speak?
Would anyone ask to be swallowed up?
21Now no one can look at the sun,
bright as it is in the skies

after the wind has swept them clean.
[22]Out of the north he comes in golden splendor;
God comes in awesome majesty.
[23]The Almighty is beyond our reach and exalted in power;
in his justice and great righteousness, he does not oppress.
[24]Therefore, people revere him,
for does he not have regard for all the wise in heart?"

Listening to the Text in the Story: "The Baʿlu Myth" (Ugaritic); "Atra-ḫasis"

Although these four chapters are interrupted by the narrator in Job 36:1 with the simple words, "Elihu continued," the content of his message throughout is dominated by the theme of the justice of God, and so it makes sense to treat the remainder of Elihu's words as a single unit.

Once again, we find the text contains many echoes of its ancient background, some of which are foreign to us and, without some understanding of them, may lead us to misunderstand the meaning of the text. One particular focus of these words of Elihu is the association between God and storms, an association that will allow for a smooth segue to the appearance of Yahweh in the following chapter through the arrival of a storm. At one point in chapter 36, Elihu offers what appears to be a description of the water cycle well before it was understood scientifically, seemingly speaking of water evaporating and turning into rain high in the atmosphere and then pouring back down on the earth. The NIV reads:

[27]"He draws up the drops of water,
which distill as rain to the streams;
[28]the clouds pour down their moisture
and abundant showers fall on mankind.

The language, however, is difficult, and it would be unwise to read too much modern science into this. The term translated "draws up" here is not used with this meaning elsewhere; the term usually has the meaning "trim, diminish" (e.g., Job 15:4), in which case it could just as easily mean that God breaks down drops into smaller droplets to create the "mist" (*ʾed*, which the NIV translates "streams")—a word only elsewhere found in Genesis 2:6 and understood by some commentators to refer to the heavenly stream that, in ancient cosmological terms, flowed above. So, while there are some vague indications elsewhere of some awareness of the rudiments of the water cycle (e.g., Eccl 1:7; Amos 9:6), the ambiguities in the Hebrew simply will not allow us to extract too much detail from these words.[1]

Chapter 37 contains further associations between the storm and Yahweh, even aligning the thunder of the storm with his voice. This idea is found elsewhere in the Bible (e.g., at Mount Sinai, see the discussion in the next chapter, or in Ps 29). The idea of a deity's voice sounding like thunder is also found in other places. One example is found in the description of Baʿal's voice:

> (So) he opens up a window in the house,
> a latticed window in the palace.
> Baʿlu (himself) opens up the rift in the clouds,
> Baʿlu emits his holy voice,
> Baʿlu makes the thunder roll over and over again.
> His [holy] voice [causes] the earth [to tremble],
> [at his thunder] the mountains shake with fear.[2]

In the ancient Near East storms were generally associated with a storm god such as Baʿal in Canaanite thinking or Iškur/Adad in Mesopotamia. Akkadian texts speak of Adad in such a way as to make clear his manifestation as or in storms. For example, in the "Atra-ḫusis" (or "Atraḫasis") epic, we read:

> The outlook of the weather changed,
> Adad began to roar in the clouds.
> The god they heard, his clamor.
> He brought pitch to seal his door.
> By the time he had bolted his door,
> Adad was roaring in the clouds.
> The winds were furious as he set forth,
> He cut the mooring rope and released the boat.[3]

---

1. Tremper Longman, for example, translates v. 27 as, "He holds in check drops of rain. He filters rain for his stream, which the skies pour forth and drop abundantly on humanity." See Longman, *Job*, 403–4. One problem with this translation is that the Hebrew translated "he filters" here is a plural verb, and so it more readily takes the antecedent plural, "drops of rain," as its subject. A review of other scholars' translations reveals quite a diverse array of readings which, at the very least, ought to make us reluctant to be too dogmatic about the specifics of the text. The ancient Greek translation of Job has God numbering the raindrops in v. 27, so yet another understanding of these words.

2. In this translation, the Ugaritic of Baʿal is transliterated with Baʿlu. See "The Baʿlu Myth," *COS* 1.86:262.

3. "Atra-ḫusis," trans. Benjamin R. Foster (*COS* 1.130:452); see ii 48–55.

Despite similarities, there is an important distinction between this passage from Atra-hasis and Job 37, noted by Longman, who helpfully observes that "faithful Israelites (and Elihu) rightly recognized that the storm was under the control of the one and only God, Yahweh."[4] Elihu points to the storm that is presumably visible in the distance as he speaks as a demonstration of God's power over all things, not as his specific area of control like the storm gods of the ancient world.

As is true elsewhere in Job, references to aspects of the cosmos reflect the ancient cosmology that would have made sense to the ancient audience. Had the text introduced concepts from modern cosmology, it would only have served to confuse the ancient reader. Thus, when referring to the skies in Job 37:18, Elihu's words reflect the idea that there was a solid barrier in the sky (Elihu uses the verb form of the noun in Gen 1:6–7, which older translations called the "firmament"). This barrier stretched above the atmosphere to hold up the waters above and the higher heavens. Once again, we have to understand that concepts that appear strange to us and cannot be reconciled to modern thought were used in order to communicate effectively with an ancient audience that thought and spoke in these terms, but use of such ideas was not an endorsement of their scientific accuracy.

EXPLAIN the Story

Elihu's Call to Hear (34:1–4)

Elihu launches into his second speech by challenging his companions to hear his words and recognize his wisdom. This speech opens with Elihu addressing the friends about Job rather than addressing Job directly. Only at verse 16 does Elihu tentatively speak as though he were expecting Job to be listening to his words. Here instead he asks his audience ("you wise men" v. 2, probably the three friends, excluding Job, in light of the way Elihu speaks about Job in the third person) to share with him in judging whether he or Job is right in what they say. Elihu is confident that he is in the right, just as the friends were confident of their rightness.

Elihu Continues to Respond to Job (34:5–9)

Elihu does not quite quote Job verbatim in verses 5–9, and some of the ideas he attributes to Job—particularly in verse 6—are difficult to find clearly expressed

4. Longman, *Job*, 405.

in Job's words. Elihu notes that Job has claimed to be "innocent" (the Hebrew verb is frequently rendered "be righteous" and should be understood to be the claim that he is in the right; see 9:15) and to have been denied justice by God (see 27:2). The Hebrew of 34:6 is quite difficult, but Job's only other use of the term "lie" (*kzb*) has been in 6:28, where he promised not to lie. Nonetheless, Elihu's claim about Job lying does reflect the perspective of the friends who, presumably, believe that his protestations of innocence cannot be true given his suffering, which they see as evidence of sin. Finally, Job has definitely spoken of the arrows of the Almighty (6:4).

Elihu in 34:7–9 responds to this summary of Job's claims. At first reading it may appear that Elihu is claiming that Job has endured scorn, given that drinking something is to take something into oneself. In light of the context, however, it is clear that Elihu is suggesting that scorning others sustains Job in the same way water does the thirsty man. Job, he says, prefers to keep company with the wicked. Although we might be tempted to dismiss Elihu's observation, for we know that Job has not kept company with the wicked, what he means here is that Job's behavior is in keeping with that of the wicked when he asserts that there is no benefit in seeking to please God (the connection between verses 7–8 and 9 is made clear by the explanatory "for" at the beginning of verse 9).

This assessment of Job's thinking does, to some extent, reflect Job's comments in 9:22–24; 21:7–13, where he questions God's justice in allowing the wicked to prosper while ignoring the needs of the innocent—a point also reflected in God's question to Job in 40:8. Job, however, never went quite as far as Elihu claims here, and so the summary treats Job a little unfairly. Nonetheless, Elihu's argument from this point on is largely founded on defending the justice of God in the face of Job's attacks upon it. And it is going to be clear, by the ferocity of Elihu's argument, that this is the crux of the issue. Whatever is happening to Job, whatever the cause of his suffering, the one thing Elihu will not accept is that God is unjust.

Elihu Affirms the Righteousness of God (34:10–30)

Elihu continues to address all of the friends in 34:10–12, describing them as "men of understanding." The Hebrew here is woodenly "men of heart," reflecting the ancient notion that the heart was the center of human intellect. He raises his primary concern: God cannot do wrong. Job has implied that God's justice is flawed, but Elihu will not allow such a claim to stand unchallenged.

Elihu's argument here that God does punish the wicked (v. 11) could be used to argue that Elihu's understanding of the world does not differ from that of his three friends and so falls under the same condemnation as their words do when Yahweh responds to them in chapter 42. However, a couple of observations indicate that such a conclusion is premature. First, Elihu's emphasis is strongly on defending God's righteousness—hence the final verse:

> It is unthinkable that God would do wrong,
> that the Almighty would pervert justice. (34:12)

Second, it would be incorrect to argue that God never applies retributive justice—that God never punishes sin. The problem addressed in Job is slightly different, namely, that specific suffering can be identified as a direct consequence of a particular sin. The consistent testimony of the Bible, including the book of Job, is that God does punish sin. However, Scripture is just as consistent in insisting that God also provides a way to have such punishment dealt with via sacrifice, and we know that Job was scrupulous in carrying out sacrifices (1:5). Ultimately, we know that those sacrifices inherently achieved nothing but anticipated Jesus's ultimate sacrifice for sins on the cross for, "in his forbearance he had left the sins committed beforehand unpunished" (Rom 3:25). The Old Testament sacrifices were didactic and served as an expression of faith in God's justice and his promises in that they allowed the supplicant to have his or her sins dealt with. The upshot of this is that the prologue's insistence that Job was blameless and upright does not mean that Job was without sin, but it does mean that any sin had been dealt with, and so Job was not due any punishment for those sins.

In short, Elihu is right to state that justice demands that God will hold people accountable for their actions, that they will be punished where it is deserved. What he does not say, however, is that this is the only cause of suffering, and indeed he has earlier suggested that there are other possible causes of suffering that are not expressions of immediate divine judgment on sin.

Elihu's primary assertion, however, is apparent here through repetition of the one idea: God cannot do evil (v. 10), he does not do wrong (v. 10, 12), and he would not pervert justice (v. 12). Whatever one may say, whatever questions one may ask, this truth is immutable: God does not act unjustly. He is just in all his ways.

In verses 13–15 Elihu argues, by asking rhetorical questions, that God is the ultimate ruler of all creation; he answers to no one. The questions of verse 13 clearly expect the answer "No one"—God is the final authority, and all life depends on him to continue to exist. Although this much is clear in these verses, what is less clear is exactly how they relate to Elihu's argument about the justice of God. The answer comes in the following section, where Elihu makes the connection between sovereignty and justice clear.

Elihu switches to addressing his words specifically to Job, as made clear by the switch from plural to singular imperatives in verse 16. He begins by again posing his argument in the form of a rhetorical question, although it is a question that initially appears to be quite naive: "Can someone who hates justice govern?" Most of us would immediately answer, "Yes," for there are too many examples throughout history of just such a situation. Yet Elihu's argument depends on the answer being "No."

As often is the case, looking closer make sense of these words. Elihu's employment of the term translated "govern" in v. 17 uses the Hebrew root *khbsh* which elsewhere refers to binding up (e.g., Lev 8:13; Isa 30:26; Ezek 24:17; Job 5:18). Its use here indicates that Elihu's emphasis is on governing by administering justice or binding up injustice. The sense here then is that the true administration of justice (i.e., "governing") can only be done by one who loves justice. It conveys the nature of Elihu's question better to render it as: "Can the one who hates justice administer justice?" To this question the answer is clearly "No."[5]

Elihu proceeds to describe the attribute of God that demonstrates his qualifications to judge: he is impartial, unimpressed by wealth or status, seeing all as equally his creatures (v. 18–19). These powerful worldly rulers are taken from this life in an instant by God ("without human hand," v. 20), and so in this God's just judgment is enacted.

In verses 21–30 Elihu expands the scope of God's just governance from the wealthy and powerful to all people (although the focus remains on the powerful, vv. 24–30). God's omniscient sovereignty results in swift justice, for there is no need for further detective work to build a case against the accused—God knows all their deeds (v. 24). David Clines notes that Elihu here may be responding to Job's complaint about the lack of regular court hearings held by God to facilitate the administration of justice (see 24:1).[6]

Job 34:25–28 make it clear that the powerful are still very much in Elihu's view, for the fact that they have turned from God results in the poor crying out to God for rescue (v. 28). Elihu is not so naive to argue that all of God's actions whereby he implements his justice are readily visible to mortal onlookers. Rather, he insists that God is at work behind the scenes, quietly working in

5. Another possible way to interpret this question is that the "one who hates justice" is a reference to Job who has condemned as guilty "the just and mighty One." The point is, then, that Job is not qualified to administer justice, but God is.

6. Clines, *Job 21–37*, 779.

the world to discharge his justice. There is an explicit contrast here between God's ability to see humans even in their most hidden moments and God's inability to be seen by people when he does not want to be seen. The point Elihu makes here is that God works his righteous justice out in the world even when humans are unaware that he is doing it. The result is that, even when God appears to be silent, he is working behind the scenes, quietly, to dispense justice such that unjust rulers who through their wickedness lay snares for people are removed from power. "Snares" are traps used for hunting, and so these rulers are depicted as hunting their own people. In such circumstances it is clear that God's justice needs to be dispensed, and Elihu makes it clear that even when it cannot be seen, God is passing judgment on the wicked.

Rethinking Job's Situation in the Light of God's Righteousness (34:31–37)

Elihu continues to argue by means of questions in verses 31–33. He paints a picture of someone who is suffering and who is unaware of the reason for their suffering. Again, the Hebrew is rather opaque at this point and may be translated, "I have endured but I will not sin." There is no explicit admission of wrongdoing, only of having experienced some form of suffering. Despite the incognito nature of Elihu's words, the description quite precisely fits Job. Elihu's hypothetical sufferer, however, now responds to his suffering by asking, if he has indeed done anything wrong, that God would reveal it to him so that he will not do it again. This, too, reflects Job's words as found in 6:24, although there he had implored his friends to reveal his sin to him, not God.

Job 34:33 is particularly difficult. The gist seems to be that Elihu is asking Job whether he should be the one to determine what he receives from God (which he has implicitly done by deeming that his suffering is inappropriate). The Hebrew of the second clause reads simply "when you reject" without any clear indication of what is rejected (the NIV renders "refuse" and supplies "to repent" to complete the thought). Perhaps the best understanding is that Elihu is noting that Job has rejected God insofar as he has rejected God's righteousness (which Elihu here seeks to defend). He then places the onus on Job, telling him that he should give an account of himself; it is not Elihu's place to do so. In short, Elihu challenges Job to rethink his claims without calling into question God's righteousness.

Why should Job rethink his challenges? Elihu expands on this by reporting what he has been told about Job by "wise men" (probably not the three friends given Elihu's description of how he heard these words in verse 34). While the NIV and other translations limit the quoted words to verse 35, it is better to understand that all of verses 35–37 are the words of the wise men quoted by Elihu.[7] His point is that he has been told quite harsh things about Job. He knows that Job has made claims that question God's justice, but he himself has argued vociferously that there are no grounds upon which God's justice can be questioned. Elihu would like to hear Job's response to his suffering reconsidered in light of this unassailable fact. In Elihu's mind, the quoted words of the wise men who have spoken to Elihu serve to emphasize the need for Job to make a more reasoned reappraisal of his argument.

Who Is Righteous: God or Job? (35:1–16)

In 35:1–8 Elihu begins questioning Job's understanding of justice, for it is clear to Elihu and others (see the preceding verses) that Job's reasoning implies that he is in the right, that is, he has a better notion of what is just than does God. In verse 3 he claims to quote Job as having asked what the point of refraining from sin is if there is no beneficial outcome from such restraint, which could be a summary of the sentiment of some of Job's thinking (e.g., 7:19–20; 9:22–31) but is actually closer to the words Job had ascribed to the prosperous wicked (21:7–15).

Elihu's answer to this is addressed to Job and the friends, whom he sees as having failed to have answered Job adequately (cf. 32:3). At first blush it may appear that Elihu is downplaying the significance of sin in the sight of God, but that would be premature. His point, instead, is that the transcendence of God, who is higher than the heavens, does not benefit or suffer from the consequences of human sin. Our sin, argues Elihu, does not influence God in any way; he remains impartial, impassive, and transcendent. In the end, the only ones who suffer or benefit from one person's sin are other people. Eliphaz had made a similar point earlier in the book (see 22:3).

Elihu's argument answers the question he put in Job's mouth in 35:3. While it is not possible to influence God by our behavior, there is an advantage in not sinning, and that relates to the impact that has on other people. Elihu does overstate the case here, for from the outset of the story of Job we have known that God is interested in the blamelessness of human beings, for that formed the very basis of the whole story of Job. Elihu does, however, explain more completely what he is saying in the next section.

Elihu expands on God's response to human behavior in the remainder of the chapter. He posits a couple of reasons why God may not appear to respond to those under oppression. First, in their suffering they do not call out to God

7. See Clines, *Job 21–37*, 784.

(vv. 10–11). It makes sense that a sufferer can become so focused on their suffering that they lose any focus on God and so do not call out to him in prayer, but we have heard Job repeatedly calling on God to explain himself. Job's problem has not been that he did not call out to God.

So, what if the oppressed do cry out but still receive nothing from God? This scenario is presented by Elihu in verses 12–14. In such circumstances, he notes, their downfall is indeed their wickedness. Just because one is oppressed does not make one virtuous, upright, or blameless. Sometimes the oppression can itself be the outworking of justice. It is important to note, however, that this is not the situation for Job. Indeed, neither was Elihu's first option, for Job has continually addressed himself to God, imploring him to instruct him and explain the suffering he is enduring.

Elihu applies this logic to Job in verses 14–15. Job, says Elihu, claims not to see God, and this does reflect Job's assertion that God is not answering him (e.g., 23:8–9). But why has God not answered Job? Elihu's answer is that if God does not answer those who do not look to him for answers (vv. 10–11), how much more will he not respond to one who calls him unjust (i.e., who claims he is ignoring the case Job has presented [v. 14] and who claims God does not enact justice in the world, [v. 15.])? Someone who spouts such ignorant claims about God should not expect to hear God.

This, then, is Elihu's argument. Job's failure to apprehend God's justice, his willingness to question it or even to deny it, warrants no response. It is a position of profound ignorance (v. 16).

Defending God's Justice and Righteousness (Again) (36:1–15)

Elihu begins his final speech in chapter 36 with a new introduction (vv. 2–4) that some feel again has him claiming prophetic insight for his words (see 32:7–9). Once again, however, that is to read more into Elihu's words here than they will support. The characteristic feature of all of Elihu's words thus far has been that they seek to defend the righteousness of God (as he makes clear in the first half of 36:3: "I will ascribe justice to my Maker"), and that is set to continue here—"There is more to be said in God's behalf."

Elihu claims his knowledge comes from far off, and some have seen in this a claim that it comes from God. That, however, is unlikely. While we do not know precisely where this story is set, we do know that it is not in Israel. If we are correct that it is set in patriarchal times, then there is no Israel to speak of anyway. Job and his three older friends do not have Hebrew names, but Elihu does (see 1 Sam 1:1; 1 Chr 12:20; 26:7; 27:18). In light of this, his claim that his knowledge has come from far off likely does not equate to "from God" but instead should be understood geographically—Elihu himself has traveled from afar and brought this knowledge with him. Indeed, we might infer that he has traveled farther than the others and so his later arrival was unheralded.[8]

The other aspect that may suggest that Elihu is making prophetic claims for his speech is the assertions of verse 4 that he has "perfect knowledge." The word translated "perfect" here (*tamim*) is elsewhere used to describe, for example, an unblemished animal for sacrifice (e.g., Exod 12:5). The word is used in Job only three times (Job 12:4; 36:4; 37:16) and is used in the latter passage to refer to Yahweh's knowledge—the only other passage in the Bible where the word is used adjectivally of knowledge. On the surface this certainly makes Elihu seem pretentious and arrogant.

However, this may also be overreading Elihu's meaning here. The Aramaic cognate term *tamim* often simply means "honest,"[9] a meaning that fits the parallelism of the first half of the verse as the opposite meaning of "false." The noun from the same root is used of Job in Job 2:3, 9 in reference to his integrity, which also fits well with the use by Elihu here. In short, Elihu is likely claiming no more than that he speaks honestly, with integrity, and his words ought to be heeded.[10]

In 36:5 Elihu moves again to defend the justice and righteousness of God by focusing on how that justice plays out in the lives of the wicked (vv. 6a, 13–14) which he distinguishes from the lives of the righteous (v. 6b–7), including those of them who have fallen into error (vv. 8–12). Should these people find themselves suffering in various ways, Elihu announces that God will tell them what they have done wrong and call them to repent.

At this point Elihu appears to be expounding traditional retributive justice in much the same way as Job's older three friends had consistently throughout their speeches. It should be noted that there is no problem, as far as the book of Job is concerned, with this idea. The problem raised in the book of Job is that suffering is not inevitably the result of sin, not that it never arises as a form of divine discipline for sin. While Elihu here asserts that God will reveal to the righteous person who has stumbled what their transgression is so that they may then repent, the fact that he has not so spoken to Job puts him in a different category. At this point we ought to remember Elihu's other thoughts

8. See Shields, "You Can't Get a Sage to Do a Prophet's Job," for more discussion.

9. See "תָּמִים," *HALOT* 1749–50.

10. See Clines, *Job 21–37*, 854–55. An alternative understanding would be to see the phrase "perfect in knowledge" as a reference to God, and so here Elihu claims a prophetic role, conveying God's words to Job.

on causes of suffering back in chapter 33. Here, however, Elihu's argument is more traditional: God disciplines sinful people and calls them to repent.

He returns, beginning in 36:13, to those who are interminably wicked, describing them as "godless in heart" (woodenly, "defiled of heart"), including those who will not respond with repentance to the discipline they receive from God (vv. 13–14). Such people, Elihu claims, die among male shrine prostitutes. As Clines points out, it is not plausible to imagine that Elihu could realistically have maintained that all of the godless die in such circumstances![11] What is more likely here is that Elihu is employing this terminology to point to the ignominious and shameful end of the godless rather than that we should read these words so specifically as to be spelling out the precise circumstance of death for every such godless person.

In the end, Elihu returns to the disciplinary nature of suffering (v. 15), recalling the idea that the suffering itself is a means by which God speaks to the sufferer (see 33:19).

God Is Warning Job Not to Sin (36:16–21)

Elihu turns explicitly to address Job in verses 16–21 as indicated in the move from third-person speech to second-person singular in verse 16. Elihu plays with the words he uses. The Hebrew word translated "distress" in verse 16 literally means "narrow," which Elihu then contrasts with "wide" (NIV "spacious") in the next line. Otherwise, this verse is quite difficult and frequently misunderstood. For instance, while "mouth of distress" (a more wooden rendering than the NIV's "jaws of distress") may sound as though it refers to Job's current predicament, a better understanding is that it refers to an opening beyond which lies distress.[12] What Elihu likely means here is that God has, in the past, kept Job away from distress, placing him in a safe place where he was well provided for (hence the abundance of food on his table).

Now, however, Job endures suffering that would normally be reserved for the wicked (v. 18). What is surprising here is that Elihu does not then proceed to document Job's sins for which he is being punished but instead warns him not to succumb to the temptation to fall into sin! He warns him against being tempted by the offer of riches (although it is not at all clear that such a temptation was anywhere on the horizon for Job in his present condition). Such wealth, says Elihu in verse 19, will not resolve Job's suffering. He then warns him not to think he can hide from his suffering in the darkness

11. Clines, *Job 21–37*, 861.

12. See the use of "mouth of" to refer to the opening edge of something in Gen 29:8 (a well opening); Jer 48:28 (a cave opening); Prov 8:3 (a gate entrance of a city).

of night (v. 20)—likely a reminder of the description of the wicked from Job himself back in 24:13–17. These warnings are rounded out with a more expansive admonition to avoid the temptation to turn to evil in the midst of his present travail (34:21).[13]

These words, the last from Elihu addressed directly to Job about his situation, are a warning not to sin during the time he is suffering. Put together with Elihu's understanding of the possible significances of suffering in the life of the believer recounted in chapter 33, we have a call to Job to retain his integrity during his suffering. Add to this the strong emphasis in Elihu's speeches on the justice and righteousness of God, and we have the case that Elihu is encouraging Job to persist but also to acknowledge that God is always right. The remainder of Elihu's words return to the theme of the character of God.

The Greatness of God (36:22–37:24)

The remainder of chapter 36, together with most of the next chapter, has Elihu tell (or perhaps remind would be more accurate) Job about the greatness of God (note the continued use of the singular verb form; the command "remember" in v. 24 is singular in Hebrew, whereas in English commands are ambiguous in terms of number). At one level he speaks of this in order to reinforce his claims about God's justice and righteousness. No one is like God, existing far above all others not only in power but also as a teacher. The connection, as Clines eloquently states, is that "every demonstration of the power of God is itself instruction, every aspect of his ways in creation . . . is itself pedagogy."[14]

Elihu tells Job to praise God's handiwork (v. 24) in the way people have long done, for everyone has seen what God has done (see, for example, Rom 1:20). Yet even though all humans are witnesses of God's works, we view them from afar, for God is far above us, beyond us in understanding in every way imaginable (Job 36:25–26). This idea dominates the remainder of Elihu's words through to their conclusion (the chapter break is poorly placed to highlight this).

The concluding section to the words of Elihu (vv. 27–33) very much anticipates the arrival of Yahweh and his words in chapter 38. He turns to consider the water cycle, storms, and God's governance of the natural world—all themes that will appear in Yahweh's speeches. This builds to a crescendo

13. It is worth noting that Clines observes of vv. 13–21 that "these verses . . . have been among the most difficult and controverted in the book" (*Job 21–37*, 864). We, as readers, ought thus to display an amount of humility in pressing one particular understanding above others.

14. Clines, *Job 21–37*, 865.

as Elihu views the approaching storm in 37:14–24, a storm that heralds the arrival of God to address Job.[15]

Here Elihu begins with a proposition, established with a rhetorical question, about the greatness of God and the fact that he is eternal (Job 36:26). There are similar references to God's age elsewhere in the Bible—most obvious is the title "Ancient of Days" (Dan 7:9, 13, 22). The significance of this for Elihu is unlikely to be simply that God is great because he is old, but that because of his uncountable age he has immeasurable knowledge and wisdom.

Following this, in Job 36:27–33 Elihu identifies some of the magnificent activity of God in governing the weather. There is a risk in reading too much modern knowledge about the water cycle into Elihu's words when his words may not be so specific (see above under Listen to the Story for more detail). Walton, for example, warns that "We do not have a clear idea of what *grʿ* means, and *zqq*, with its connection to refining and filtering, most logically concerns how salt water in the cosmic seas (perhaps those above and below?) becomes fresh water in rain."[16]

Nonetheless, the emphasis of Elihu's words is simply that God controls the weather and through it governs the nations and provides for all people. This control of the weather extends to the target of individual bolts of lightning (v. 32, NIV "strike its mark," perhaps giving rise to the popular notion that being struck by lightning is a punishment from God).

The Hebrew text of verse 33 is difficult whichever translation option is chosen (note the NIV footnote for this verse). If taken as a reference to animals, we shall meet them again in verse 8 of the next chapter, so a sudden mention of cattle may not be as inappropriate as some seem to think. On the other hand, the connection with God's providence and judgment in the preceding verses suggests that the NIV's footnote on v. 7b ("he fills all people with fear by his power") is probably the better reading. The verse thus ends by expanding on the significance of God coming in thunder by describing that as "the passion of his anger against iniquity."[17]

The dramatic personal response that Elihu relates in 37:1–13 suggests that he is referring and responding to the approach of an actual storm, one we know brings God to speak to Job (see 38:1). Elihu uses this to express

15. See Robert Alter, *The Art of Biblical Poetry* (New York: Basic Books, 2011), 113–14.

16. Walton, *Job*, 366. Walton also notes that, "Some are inclined to see Elihu as offering a scientifically sophisticated understanding of the water cycle, including evaporation and condensation. This idea would anticipate its scientific confirmation by millennia and one might wonder why, if that was what Elihu was understanding, that the scientific knowledge did not develop much earlier."

17. Clines, *Job 21–37*, 873.

further the magnificence and power of God. There is nowhere that escapes him (37:3), and following the lightning comes the thunder of his voice. All of this, according to Elihu, should remind us that we are largely ignorant of God's works (v. 5b), a point that anticipates the impact of Yahweh's words to follow.

Beyond thunder and lightning, in verse 6 Elihu moves to God's sovereign control of rain and snow. The reference to "rain shower" in the NIV translates the Hebrew phrase "rain of rain" (*geshem matar*), the meaning of which is not certain, but rather than being a reference to a "rain shower," it may be a reference to torrential rain (think "song of songs" [*shir hashirim*], which identifies the song as being the best of all songs, though this expression uses the same noun in both places, the second being plural). So here the rain being referenced is exceptional rain. And it is this torrential rain (NIV "mighty downpour" [*geshem miteroth 'uzzo*, woodenly "rain of rains of might"]) that God is here said to send on the land.

The impact of this extreme weather sent by God (as, according to Elihu's argument, all weather is under God's control; it is just that the extreme weather demonstrates God's power and wisdom more effectively) is felt by people and animals (vv. 7–8). These verses do contain another difficulty in v. 7b, which woodenly reads, "on every human hand he sets a seal." The meaning of this could either be, following the NIV, that God prevents human hands from working by sending severe weather, or (taking the sealing positively) as a reminder of ownership such that "the snow and rain remind people of God's work."[18] That the seal is on the hand of every person is a difficulty for the latter understanding, and the NIV's rendering should be retained, particularly in light of verse 8 where Elihu explains that the same severe weather drives animals to take cover.

The view of the world (or cosmology) of Job's day was very different to our own. Even though we are here dealing with poetry, the imagery used reveals something of their understanding of the world around them. This is apparent at the beginning of verse 9 (cf. 38:22) where the weather is stored in various heavenly storerooms (see also Ps 135:7; Jer 10:13). When God releases the tempest, a violent windy storm, it chills the land and ice forms (Job 37:10). God even orchestrates the movements of the clouds themselves, for he is in control of all and the weather obeys its Creator (v. 11). Furthermore, the weather is sent by God for specific purposes (vv. 12–13)—for punishment, providence, or mercy.

As God approaches, Elihu's words anticipate the words God will speak to

18. Longman, *Job*, 406.

Job. In this final section of his speeches (vv. 14–24) he again mentions Job by name, an attempt to drive home the personal implications of his words for Job. This is no disinterested account of nature. Elihu's words are for Job, and Elihu wants him to know it. Having spoken at some length about various weather phenomena, he moves to question Job about his knowledge of these things. The questions are clearly rhetorical, just as God's questions will be in the coming chapters. Job does not know the answers (nor, of course, does Elihu). He does not know how God controls the clouds or makes lightning flash. He does not know how the clouds hang in the heavens (vv. 15–16).

In verse 17 Elihu offers a reminder of Job's powerlessness—not only can he not control the winds, all he can do is sweat as he faces the south wind, which brings heat into the land (v. 17). Then Elihu asks whether this man who cannot even keep cool in hot weather can do any of the great works that God has done. Verse 18 uses language reminiscent of the description of creation in Genesis 1:7, reflecting the ancient idea that the sky was a solid canopy placed there as if God had beaten it out of molten metal. Again, it is important to remember that the book of Job is not aiming to teach a particular cosmology; rather it is using the cosmology of its original audience in order to effectively communicate something of the nature of God.

What is Job to do in the face of God's power, wisdom, and majesty—attributes he has failed to adequately comprehend? For Elihu the appropriate response is clear: there is nothing to be said, no case can be made (v. 19) because, to translate colloquially but in a way that catches the flavor well, "we are in the dark about too many things." Our knowledge is too limited, a fact that again anticipates the point of Yahweh's words to follow.

To further illustrate his argument, Elihu points to the sun in verse 21. It is so bright, so intense, that it is not possible to stare at it. And if that is the case for the sun, how much more is it true of the awesome splendor that radiates from God (v. 22)? The "golden splendor" that appears in the north at this point cannot be a sunset (which does not happen in the north unless things are very confused) but more likely represents a glow heralding the arrival of God. There are other places in the Bible where God is said to come out of the north, usually with some symbolic significance (e.g., Ezek 1:4, which depicts God remaining with the exiles despite their being in exile in Babylon; cf. Isa 14:13). Here Elihu notes that the golden splendor he sees appears in the place from which one would expect God to make an appearance.

God, as far as Elihu is concerned, is beyond the reach of any person (v. 23). The entire last portion of Elihu's final speech has largely made this point: God is beyond us in his knowledge, wisdom, power, righteousness, and justice.

He judges, punishes, rewards, shows mercy, and provides for his creation. The appropriate response to this is to "revere" God (v. 24a)—the repeated exhortation of the wisdom literature of the Bible (the same word as in Prov 1:7, "the fear of the LORD is the beginning of knowledge"). This "fear" is not terror but respectful submission to the wisdom of the Creator of the universe.

The very final words of Elihu, v. 24b, are unclear. Why should God not regard the wise of heart? Scholars have offered numerous suggestions on how to make these words better fit the context. In light of Elihu's argument, he is likely saying that being wise does not afford one any greater insight into the ways of God that Elihu had referred to, nor does it afford one the right to an audience with God. Job, together with all the wise, should remember his place and fear God.

LIVE the Story

The Justice of God

Despite Elihu's consideration of the purposes of suffering in his first speech—where he proposes that suffering could be a form of preemptive discipline in addition to the traditional belief that it was retributive justice in action, and so raising the possibility that Job may not have been the egregious sinner that the older friends have assumed—he nonetheless does think that Job has erred in at least one clear way: Job has spoken of God in such a way that he has impugned his justice. Elihu's response is to defend God's justice and righteousness, and so he begins with the words, "far be it from God to do evil" (34:10), a sentiment repeated as he proceeds, "it is unthinkable that God would do wrong" (v. 12).

Indeed, much of Elihu's remaining words are motivated by the idea that God's justice is inviolable and unquestionable. He is emphatic that, whatever else is said and whatever the reason for Job's suffering, the one thing that cannot—that must not—be called into question is the fact that God always does what is right. Over and over he makes this point, defending it from different angles. He considers God's justice as a qualification and requirement as the one who governs (a term that inherently incorporates the notion of dispensing justice) and that such a role inherently requires that the sovereign is both just and able to dispense justice (vv. 16–20). Furthermore, God is impartial and cannot be bribed or manipulated—there is simply no one alive, not even the most powerful, who can sway God's judgments.

God's justice, notes Elihu, is informed by his omniscience—he knows all (v. 24) and hence there is no protracted legal process required to reach a verdict. The prosecution need not build a case over months or even years before a judge and jury are able then to reach a verdict. God has the evidence; he has it instantly; his decisions are informed by perfectly accurate knowledge. In vv. 25–30 Elihu goes on to note that God's justice is at work whether we are aware of it or not.

This all flies in the face of Job's claim that God has not acted rightly in his dealings with him. In this, Elihu is right and Job is wrong, but in this also we are presented with the fundamental paradox of the story of Job: on the one hand, if one begins with the assumption that all suffering is a manifestation of divine retributive justice, then Job's suffering is unjust (as Job has argued repeatedly); on the other hand, God is just (as the reader should already know and which Elihu vociferously asserts). How can these two truths be reconciled? Elihu has offered a clue in chapter 33, but for the final answer we await the ultimate appearance of God in the closing chapters of the book—and that is all that lies before us at this point.

Paul in Romans also tackles questions of God's justice, again insisting that God acts justly. There we read, for example, "But if our unrighteousness brings out God's righteousness more clearly, what shall we say? That God is unjust in bringing his wrath on us? . . . Certainly not!" (Rom 3:5–6; cf. Rom 9:14). As Paul deals with various objections, his argument always concludes by demonstrating the righteousness (and so necessarily the justice) of God. If Old Testament sacrifices could not truly deal with our sin and so all the sins of Old Testament believers had not been dealt with, where was God's justice to be seen? Paul tells us it was seen at the cross. There God ultimately dispensed the justice that was necessary to deal with the sins that had been committed beforehand (Rom 3:25–26). And while the sin of Old Testament believers was dealt with long after it had been committed, the sin of modern believers was dealt with long before it was committed. The cross event—the death, resurrection, and ascension of the Messiah—was the central point in history that worked to both demonstrate God's righteousness and justice and to atone for the sins of all of God's people.

Elihu, from his place in the story of God, did not comprehend all of this. His confidence in God's justice was founded only in faith, the trust that the Creator of all could do no wrong, a belief that informed his understanding of the events that had unfolded in the life of Job. Job's other friends shared a similar set of convictions but were too narrow in their application, concluding that the only logical manifestation of God's justice was to see Job's suffering as the outworking of a guilty judgment by God. Where they had called for Job's repentance for sins committed, Elihu suggested Job's suffering might not be the punishment for sin but may have some other purpose (33:14–18), and that Job must now be careful not to fall into sin in the midst of his suffering (36:16–21).

John Walton notes that Yahweh, when he comes to speak in the next chapters, "does not defend his justice and does not posit justice alone as the foundation of his policies."[19] While the observation is valid—Yahweh does not defend his justice and, in fact, all he will do is ask questions of Job and, through Job, of us—it is not valid to conclude that justice is *not* foundational to Yahweh's interactions with his creation. For one, he never denies that he is just, but more significantly, we noted that the use of the divine name for God (i.e., Yahweh) in the prologue, and its use again as he comes to speak in the next section, functions to point beyond the confines of the book of Job alone to the broader faith of Israel, indeed to the broader story of God. In using God's name, the author of the book reminds us that we already know this God, and we already know that the point Elihu makes about God's justice and righteousness is well established. In Exodus, for example, we hear Yahweh speak,

> And he passed in front of Moses, proclaiming, "The Lord, the Lord, the compassionate and gracious God, slow to anger, abounding in love and faithfulness, maintaining love to thousands, and forgiving wickedness, rebellion and sin. Yet he does not leave the guilty unpunished; he punishes the children and their children for the sin of the parents to the third and fourth generation." (Exod 34:6–7)

Having quoted these words, it is necessary to add a brief note about how true justice can be done if children are punished for the sins of their parents, as mentioned in Exodus 34:7. The answer can be found earlier in Exodus 20:5, where the commandments include the words, "I, the Lord your God, am a jealous God, punishing the children for the sin of the parents to the third and fourth generation *of those who hate me*" (italics added). Here those generations of children who share the parents' punishment are included in the description as "those who hate me." Walter Kaiser explains this well:

> Children who repeat the sins of their fathers evidence it by personally hating God; hence they too are punished like their fathers. Moses makes it plain in Deuteronomy 24:16: "Fathers shall not be put to death for their children, nor children put to death for their fathers; each is to die for his

19. Walton, *Job*, 362.

> own sin." The effects of disobedience last for some time, but the effects of loving God are far more extensive—"To a thousand [generations]"[20]

There are many examples throughout the Old Testament where children and grandchildren follow the path set by their parents and grandparents (particularly among the kings of the nation). In a culture where multiple generations lived in the same household it is, perhaps, not so surprising that this would occur. In these cases, justice would demand that each subsequent generation that persists in sin should be judged for that sin.

It is clear from these words (and many others about Yahweh in the Old Testament) that God will dispense justice and not let the guilty escape their punishment. He does not leave the guilty unpunished, and it is this we already know and have been assured of as we began our journey through the book of Job, for the explicit identification of God as Yahweh has been made just so we might be able to make this connection. This God, the God of Abraham, Isaac, and Jacob as well as the God of Job, is a just God.

This does, however, leave us with a problem. Our inability to meet God's standards (which are reflected in the Old Testament law) should lead us to realize we are all deserving of judgment. The book of Job does not directly address this problem. For that we must look beyond this account of innocent, underserved suffering to the account of vicarious innocent suffering first described in Isaiah, where the suffering servant is said to be pierced for our transgressions (Isa 53:5; cf. Matt 8:17; Luke 22:37; Acts 8:33; 1 Pet 2:22–25). Here we find one described by Yahweh as "my servant" (Isa 52:13) whose suffering stands in line with the sacrifices offered in the tabernacle and temple. Yet again, as with the account of innocent suffering in Job, the suffering of the servant leaves us with questions. It leaves us looking for answers that were yet to be given.

The big questions raised in both Job's suffering and the suffering of the servant are, at their heart, about how such suffering can be fair. How can the suffering of the innocent be fair? How can vicarious suffering of an innocent person be fair? Are not these failures of justice? That would certainly appear to be the inescapable conclusion.

Yet, the story is not complete at this point. The book of Job does not answer the question directly. Rather, it points to our epistemological finitude: we do not know everything and we are incapable of knowing everything.

20. Walter C. Kaiser Jr., "Exodus," in *Genesis–Leviticus*, REBC 1, ed. Tremper Longman III and David E. Garland (Grand Rapids: Zondervan, 2010), 481.

As such we should be wary of jumping to conclusions based on the data we have when that data is incomplete, and we also need to learn that our belief in the extent of our own knowledge is exaggerated. It is possible to be convinced of the certainty of our knowledge simply because we are unaware of the limits and information that lies outside of our experience. The example of science in the late nineteenth and early twentieth centuries (see the Live the Story section for Job 40:6–41:34 below) is instructive. Being unaware of the limits of our own knowledge results in a misapprehension about the veracity of our conclusions. We can convince ourselves that we are right and that we have all the data when actually we are wrong because we do not have all the data.

This brings us to the New Testament, the place where the limits of Job's knowledge (and the knowledge of his friends) are made more apparent (it was already apparent from the absence of answers and the impression of injustice that we are left with in the Old Testament). Similarly, the limited nature of the depiction of the suffering servant's vicarious suffering is addressed, most specifically by Paul who notes that the true work of atonement symbolized in the Old Testament sacrificial system finds its true expression in the sacrifice of God's Messiah Jesus. The absence of some answers in Job and Isaiah is not an indication that there are no answers or that the wrong answers promulgated by Job's friends are right. They are indications that the original audiences for these works must trust in the revealed nature of Yahweh until all that has been planned has come to pass.

We may now look back on the suffering of God's Servant Messiah and appreciate more fully the complex nature of the atonement and the manner in which God worked to deal with human treachery, to show mercy, and to uphold justice. Yet, to conclude that our knowledge and understanding is now complete would be just as tragic a mistake as it was when Job's audience first heard his story. We all continue to face events and circumstances in our lives and in the lives of others that leave us with questions we cannot answer. We need to remember that we do not know everything. And sometimes we may think we have an answer when in reality our answer is premature and fails to see how limited our understanding really is. We ought to be reminded of these limits as we read Job, indeed as we read the entire Old Testament. As we learn more about God and his purposes, so too we should learn not to reach hasty conclusions but to see always the limits of our understanding.

Elihu and Compassion

As Elihu closes his speeches he points to the coming storm, and from that storm we shall hear God speak in the next chapter. Before turning to God's words, however, it is worth reflecting a little further on Elihu's words. Has he responded to Job appropriately, or has he, like the other three friends, been too quick to overlook Job's plight, eager to defend God but neglecting to show Job the compassion and kindness he sorely needs? Would such a concern have been one that would have occurred to the original audience, or is it simply an imposition of modern sensibilities on the ancient story? If it were something of relevance only to the modern reader, then it would be inappropriate to judge Elihu or Job's other friends based on this criterion.

Yet, there have been indications that compassion and the comfort it would have offered Job are very much a concern of the text. Job has criticized his older friends for their lack of compassion (e.g., Job 16:2), and the narrator announces the arrival of the older three friends by describing their reason for making the journey to visit Job with the words, "they set out from their homes and met together by agreement to go and sympathize with him and comfort him" (2:11). We shall also see that the resolution of Job's story comes when he finally is comforted (42:6, 11).[21] It is clear that comfort, consolation, compassion, and kindness are very much issues of concern to both Job and his friends.

Job's older friends arrive with the stated intention of comforting Job but do not achieve this end. Elihu's arrival is heralded by no such statement, and we might legitimately consider his words to be insensitive and lacking grace, but of all the friends he is the only one to allow that Job's claims about his own integrity and innocence could actually be true. He allows God more freedom than either Job or the older friends, the latter of whose thinking is constrained by the conviction that God is bound by the demands of retributive justice.

This distinction is significant. Where we are faced with people in difficult circumstances, we need to remember that we do not know everything—only God knows that, and so only God is in a position to judge. Furthermore, some amount of comfort will be afforded simply by not dismissing the sufferer's claims. Job's older friends did this to Job and were wrong to do so. Even if there are times when it turns out we would be right to do so, those generally do not arise out of our omniscient knowledge of the circumstances but from some amount of inference and assumption.

Moreover, much the same applies when we suffer. We do not know everything, and as Job thought about his own suffering and struggled to reconcile his experience with his understanding of God, he reached conclusions about God that were incorrect, namely, that God was his enemy, or that God had made

21. See Job 42:6 and the note there in this commentary.

a mistake. Elihu would have none of this, and neither should we. Whether it is our own suffering or that of others, the one thing we can be sure of is that whatever God is doing through it, he has not made a mistake. As Paul faced the "thorn in my flesh" (2 Cor 12:7), which he described as "a messenger of Satan," he also realized that this thorn was inflicted upon him "in order to keep me from becoming conceited," and that was certainly not Satan's purpose; that was God's purpose. When we suffer, or when those around us suffer, we need to be aware that, most of the time, the purpose behind the suffering, the reason God has allowed us to suffer, may not be made clear to us, and there is no guarantee that we will know why it happened even much later with the benefit of hindsight.

What is valuable, however, is to remember the epistemic humility we see, surprisingly, in Elihu's words. He is the only speaker to allow that Job's suffering—and suffering in general—may come about for some reason other than some sin on the part of the sufferer. The lesson is simple: the reason for suffering—ours or that of others—may not be obvious. Accepting this truth is itself a step toward finding comfort and consolation, particularly when it offers an escape from condemnation and guilt when those are not appropriate. Good theology and sound exegesis offer comfort to the afflicted and hope to the hopeless.

CHAPTER 23

Job 38:1–40:5

Yahweh's First Speech (and Job's Response)

LISTEN to the Story

38:1 Then the LORD spoke to Job out of the storm. He said:

2 "Who is this that obscures my plans
with words without knowledge?
3 Brace yourself like a man;
I will question you,
and you shall answer me.

4 "Where were you when I laid the earth's foundation?
Tell me, if you understand.
5 Who marked off its dimensions? Surely you know!
Who stretched a measuring line across it?
6 On what were its footings set,
or who laid its cornerstone—
7 while the morning stars sang together
and all the angels shouted for joy?

8 "Who shut up the sea behind doors
when it burst forth from the womb,
9 when I made the clouds its garment
and wrapped it in thick darkness,
10 when I fixed limits for it
and set its doors and bars in place,
11 when I said, 'This far you may come and no farther;
here is where your proud waves halt'?

12 "Have you ever given orders to the morning,

or shown the dawn its place,
13 that it might take the earth by the edges
and shake the wicked out of it?
14 The earth takes shape like clay under a seal;
its features stand out like those of a garment.
15 The wicked are denied their light,
and their upraised arm is broken.

16 "Have you journeyed to the springs of the sea
or walked in the recesses of the deep?
17 Have the gates of death been shown to you?
Have you seen the gates of the deepest darkness?
18 Have you comprehended the vast expanses of the earth?
Tell me, if you know all this.

19 "What is the way to the abode of light?
And where does darkness reside?
20 Can you take them to their places?
Do you know the paths to their dwellings?
21 Surely you know, for you were already born!
You have lived so many years!

22 "Have you entered the storehouses of the snow
or seen the storehouses of the hail,
23 which I reserve for times of trouble,
for days of war and battle?
24 What is the way to the place where the lightning is
dispersed,
or the place where the east winds are scattered over
the earth?
25 Who cuts a channel for the torrents of rain,
and a path for the thunderstorm,
26 to water a land where no one lives,
an uninhabited desert,
27 to satisfy a desolate wasteland
and make it sprout with grass?
28 Does the rain have a father?

Who fathers the drops of dew?
29 From whose womb comes the ice?
Who gives birth to the frost from the heavens
30 when the waters become hard as stone,
when the surface of the deep is frozen?

31 "Can you bind the chains of the Pleiades?
Can you loosen Orion's belt?
32 Can you bring forth the constellations in their seasons
or lead out the Bear with its cubs?
33 Do you know the laws of the heavens?
Can you set up God's dominion over the earth?

34 "Can you raise your voice to the clouds
and cover yourself with a flood of water?
35 Do you send the lightning bolts on their way?
Do they report to you, 'Here we are'?
36 Who gives the ibis wisdom
or gives the rooster understanding?
37 Who has the wisdom to count the clouds?
Who can tip over the water jars of the heavens
38 when the dust becomes hard
and the clods of earth stick together?

39 "Do you hunt the prey for the lioness
and satisfy the hunger of the lions
40 when they crouch in their dens
or lie in wait in a thicket?
41 Who provides food for the raven
when its young cry out to God
and wander about for lack of food?

39:1 "Do you know when the mountain goats give birth?
Do you watch when the doe bears her fawn?
2 Do you count the months till they bear?
Do you know the time they give birth?
3 They crouch down and bring forth their young;

their labor pains are ended.
4Their young thrive and grow strong in the wilds;
they leave and do not return.

5"Who let the wild donkey go free?
Who untied its ropes?
6I gave it the wasteland as its home,
the salt flats as its habitat.
7It laughs at the commotion in the town;
it does not hear a driver's shout.
8It ranges the hills for its pasture
and searches for any green thing.

9"Will the wild ox consent to serve you?
Will it stay by your manger at night?
10Can you hold it to the furrow with a harness?
Will it till the valleys behind you?
11Will you rely on it for its great strength?
Will you leave your heavy work to it?
12Can you trust it to haul in your grain
and bring it to your threshing floor?

13"The wings of the ostrich flap joyfully,
though they cannot compare
with the wings and feathers of the stork.
14She lays her eggs on the ground
and lets them warm in the sand,
15unmindful that a foot may crush them,
that some wild animal may trample them.
16She treats her young harshly, as if they were not hers;
she cares not that her labor was in vain,
17for God did not endow her with wisdom
or give her a share of good sense.
18Yet when she spreads her feathers to run,
she laughs at horse and rider.

19"Do you give the horse its strength

or clothe its neck with a flowing mane?
20Do you make it leap like a locust,
striking terror with its proud snorting?
21It paws fiercely, rejoicing in its strength,
and charges into the fray.
22It laughs at fear, afraid of nothing;
it does not shy away from the sword.
23The quiver rattles against its side,
along with the flashing spear and lance.
24In frenzied excitement it eats up the ground;
it cannot stand still when the trumpet sounds.
25At the blast of the trumpet it snorts, 'Aha!'
It catches the scent of battle from afar,
the shout of commanders and the battle cry.

26"Does the hawk take flight by your wisdom
and spread its wings toward the south?
27Does the eagle soar at your command
and build its nest on high?
28It dwells on a cliff and stays there at night;
a rocky crag is its stronghold.
29From there it looks for food;
its eyes detect it from afar.
30Its young ones feast on blood,
and where the slain are, there it is."

40:1The LORD said to Job:

2"Will the one who contends with the Almighty correct him?
Let him who accuses God answer him!"

3Then Job answered the LORD:

4"I am unworthy—how can I reply to you?
I put my hand over my mouth.
5I spoke once, but I have no answer—
twice, but I will say no more."

Listening to the Text in the Story: "The Exaltation of Inanna" (Sumerian); "Gilgamesh" (Mesopotamian)

Job's encounter with God comes here, toward the end of the book, to provide a final answer to Job's questions. As we shall see, while the answer Job receives ultimately silences and satisfies him, it also fails to answer directly the questions he did have. God's "answer" here is neither what Job nor what we expected.

Encounters with God, such as that recorded here, are not uncommon throughout the Bible, and a number of parallels exist in ancient Near Eastern depictions of the appearances of various gods. There, such encounters are recorded and often use language and symbolism similar to that found in the Bible. As far back as the twenty-fourth century BC the Sumerian goddess Inanna (later identified with the Akkadian Ishtar) was presented as a deity who appeared in a storm.[1] There we read:

> [28]In the guise of a charging storm
> you charge.
> [29]With a roaring storm
> you roar.
> [30]With thunder
> you continually thunder.
> [31]With all the evil winds
> you snort.[2]

Many of these accounts from the ancient Near East are related to military actions on the part of the nation associated with the text. Thomas Mann notes that

> In the Mesopotamian texts . . . motifs of divine presence—often related to the storm deity—were used in conjunction with critical historical events,

1. See Jeffrey Jay Niehaus, *God at Sinai: Covenant and Theophany in the Bible and Ancient Near East* (Grand Rapids: Zondervan Academic, 1995), 125–26, referencing work by William W. Hallo and J. J. A. van Dijk. They date the original hymn to the time of Sargon I (2329–2274 BC).

2. "The Exaltation of Inanna," *COS* 1.160:519. See Thomas W. Mann, *Divine Presence and Guidance in the Israelite Traditions: The Typology of Exaltation* (Baltimore: Johns Hopkins University Press, 1977), 31.

> often reflecting the exaltation of a particular deity, and the glorification of that deity's royal devotee.[3]

Later Mann clarifies further:

> Moreover, the particular literary expression of divine presence was often that of the vanguard motif, which portrayed the god(s) as being involved in historical battles resulting in the political supremacy of the human ruler and devotee.[4]

In the Bible there are a number of times that God is said to appear in the midst of a storm. The most prominent is the encounter between Israel (and specifically Moses) and God at Sinai. In Exodus 19:16–18 we read of thunder, lightning, and a thick cloud engulfing the summit of the mountain.

Prophetic accounts of God's appearance amid a storm are generally related to judgment, although given the prevalence of judgment in prophetic discourse it would be inappropriate to infer that all storm theophanies related to judgment, a point that will become particularly apparent in this example in Job. As far as prophetic storm theophanies go, Jeremiah 23:19, for example, reads:

> See, the storm of the LORD
> will burst out in wrath,
> a whirlwind swirling down
> on the heads of the wicked.

Similarly, Jeremiah 30:23–24 reads:

> See, the storm of the LORD
> will burst out in wrath,
> a driving wind swirling down
> on the heads of the wicked.
> The fierce anger of the LORD will not turn back
> until he fully accomplishes
> the purposes of his heart.
> In days to come
> you will understand this.[5]

3. Mann, *Divine Presence and Guidance*, 96.
4. Mann, *Divine Presence and Guidance*, 234.
5. See similar examples of storm theophanies and judgment in Ezek 1:4; Nah 1.

Of the biblical storm theophanies, Zechariah 9:14–17 most closely resembles the ancient Near Eastern versions where the deity leads his protégé into victorious battle. Elsewhere in the prophetic books of the Old Testament, God's appearance in the storm typically portends judgment on his own rebellious people.

In the lead up to God's appearance to Job in this chapter, Elihu has made us aware of the approaching storm and used storm language to describe God speaking (cf. Job 37:2–5 and v. 9, where the word *supah* [NIV "tempest"] is used to refer to the storm).

So finally, here in chapter 38, Yahweh comes to speak to Job from a "whirlwind" (Hebrew *se'arah* [first letter ס], "high wind,"[6] NIV "whirlwind"—both in the theophanies of the Lord in 38:1 and 40:6). An echo of this word is found only once elsewhere in Job in 9:17, "storm" (Hebrew word spelled slightly different from the former word in most manuscripts *śe'ara* [first letter שׂ]), where Job complains that "[Yahweh] would crush me with a storm and multiply my wounds for no reason." In the context of 9:17, Job had complained that any confrontation with Yahweh would be pointless and only wind up causing him more trouble. The introduction to Job's encounter with Yahweh here reminds us of Job's expectation.

This background would have raised expectations in the minds of those who first encountered the story of Job. The common notion from the ancient Near Eastern literature, which has a deity arriving in a storm to lead his people into triumphal battle, is clearly inapplicable in the context of Job. The notion that God may have arrived in judgment, as found in the Old Testament prophets, could well seem an appropriate turn in the story of Job at this point. Furthermore, the opening words from Yahweh make it clear that he is not entirely happy with Job's thinking up to this point. So, the reader begins expecting Job to be chastised and judged. Will God now announce that perhaps the Satan had been right all along? As it turns out, things take a very different turn from what we might have expected with the arrival of God in the storm. Instead of judgment, perhaps the best category for what we are about to encounter is "wisdom theophany" (see further discussion in the next section).

Another significant background that lies behind much of what we read in these chapters is the ancient cosmology that ancient readers presupposed as they would have heard the words of Yahweh's speeches in the following chapters.[7] While the ideas seem foreign to modern readers, it is essential to reiterate that

6. "סְעָרָה," *HALOT* 762.

7. See the discussion under Listen to the Story for chapter 22 as well as Clines, "One or Two Things," 238–342.

the book of Job does not set out to correct its audience's cosmology—had it done this it would have turned Job into a science textbook and its point about wisdom and suffering would have been lost. Instead, it uses language and ideas that the audience was comfortable with to help make a point to them by speaking to them in terms they understood. As modern readers we need to appreciate this methodology and not judge the outcome on the accuracy of its cosmology.

Yahweh's opening questions in chapter 38 take the form of a journey through creation, of one traveling around viewing the sights, and Clines notes that such a journey was recorded of Gilgamesh, the Mesopotamian king and demigod.[8] Unlike Gilgamesh, however, Job has not even come close to completing such a journey, and so Yahweh's sequence of questions here serve only to highlight the inadequacy of Job's knowledge of the universe and so the presumption in his questioning of its operation.

Finally, the personal intervention of Yahweh in the story serves to counter the fact that Eliphaz had begun his discussion with Job by claiming that his response was based on a spiritual revelation (Job 4:12–21). Further such prophetic insight would have only presented competing claims with the same level of authority. God's personal intervention clearly trumps the false claims of Eliphaz and is here the ultimate word in the tale of Job. One clear way to identify a false prophet is when God appears to you personally and contradicts that false prophet's message!

EXPLAIN the Story

Yahweh Appears in the Storm (38:1–3)

A number of scholars understand Yahweh's speeches to be raw demonstrations of power designed to humiliate Job and make it quite clear that this is Yahweh's world and he may do in it whatever he please, that he is neither accountable to anyone nor subject to anyone's will.[9] This understanding, however, largely misses the point of the words of Yahweh here in Job. While it is certainly true that Yahweh is powerful and unchallenged, the stream of rhetorical questions that forms the substance of these speeches is not designed to demonstrate Yahweh's power—Job was all too aware of that without needing to be reminded. Instead, the focus of the series of questions lies in contrasting

8. David J. A. Clines, *Job 38–42*, WBC 18B (Nashville: Nelson, 2011), 1106, and see Carol A. Newsom, "The Book of Job," *NIB* (Nashville: Abingdon, 1996), 4:603.

9. See Stuart Weeks, *An Introduction to the Study of Wisdom Literature*, T&T Clark Approaches to Biblical Studies (Edinburgh: T&T Clark, 2010).

Yahweh's wisdom with Job's. This is made clear in verse 2 where Yahweh begins speaking by highlighting the ignorance of Job, not his powerlessness. Furthermore, the subject of most of the questions in these speeches—aspects of the natural world to the point where some scholars have described these chapters as Yahweh's taking Job on a tour of the universe—is a subject that was of particular concern to the ancient sages. This is apparent in the descriptions of Solomon's wisdom in 1 Kings 4:33: "[Solomon] spoke about plant life, from the cedar of Lebanon to the hyssop that grows out of walls. He also spoke about animals and birds, reptiles and fish."

The objection could be raised that this view fails to account for the questions that do not seem to relate to wisdom and do seem to relate to power, such as Job 38:31–33. Yet this difficulty arises primarily because of the difference between modern and ancient concepts of wisdom. Wisdom in the Old Testament is more than the adept use of intellectual reasoning, although this is certainly part of it. Rather, it incorporates all manner of skills, including building (see Exod 35:30–36:1), tailoring (Exod 28:3), and perhaps even acting (2 Sam 14:1–3). Read against this background, the diverse subjects of the questions in Yahweh's speeches become means to demonstrate the breadth of Yahweh's wisdom and highlight just how meager is Job's wisdom.

Structurally, Robert Alter helpfully notes that the final poem of the book, Job 38–39, begins with an initial challenge to Job (38:2–3) followed by major sections focusing on cosmogony (38:4–21), meteorology (38:22–38), and zoology (38:39–39:30).[10]

As chapter 38 opens, Yahweh speaks to Job from a storm. Alex Luc has noted that "storms are the most astonishing, most destructive, and most feared of all weather phenomena."[11] That God speaks from a storm again highlights his sovereign control over all creation. Elihu has used storm language to describe God speaking in the previous chapter (37:2–9), giving the impression that he and the others could see the coming storm that has now arrived. Furthermore, the association between the appearance of God in a storm and God's speaking is found throughout the Old Testament (e.g., Exod 19; 2 Kgs 2:1; Ps 18:12; Ezek 1; Jer 10:13; 51:16; Nah 1:3). That God is referred to here by his name Yahweh is also significant—it had not been used by any of Job's friends, appearing after Job 2 only once on the lips of Job himself in 12:9 (which is itself an allusion to Isa 41:20). That the friends do not use God's name suggests a lack of familiarity with him that forms a subtle comment on

10. Alter, *Art of Biblical Poetry*, 116.

11. Alex Luc, "Storm and the Message of Job," *JSOT* 25 (2000): 111.

their own wisdom and understanding. The narrator's use of God's name here, however, draws us back to the events of the prologue, where we had last heard Yahweh speak, and it reminds us that we are about to hear from the true God whom we readers know from the remainder of the Bible.

God's words in Job 38:2–3 clearly provide a somewhat negative evaluation of Job's preceding words—Job has obscured God's plan (woodenly, "darkens counsel"). Although Job is not mentioned by name, it is clear that he is the target of God's words by the use of the singular rather than plural terms. God has not yet turned his attention to Job's friends—their turn will come in chapter 42. Furthermore, Job later admits that he is the one who has obscured God's plan (42:3) when he acknowledges that he has said more than he should have in light of an objective assessment of his true wisdom. Job will well and truly learn this after listening to God's words to him!

The expression "gird your loins" (38:3; 40:7) is thought by some to be an activity associated with wrestling in the ancient world.[12] While this may be the case, it is unlikely that it was foremost in the mind of ancient Israelites when they encountered this expression. As David Clines points out, elsewhere it is used in "the strenuous work of fighting (2 Sam 20:8; 1 Kgs 2:5; Isa 5:27) . . . in preparation for running (1 Kgs 18:46) or for traveling (Exod 12:11; 2 Kgs 4:29)."[13] Yahweh is here telling Job to prepare to explain himself.

The tacit implication of Job's challenge to Yahweh throughout his speeches had been that he knew better than God and that God had somehow failed to treat him properly. God ends his self-introduction in verse 3 playing on this implication, setting up the general thrust of what follows. If Job knows better, surely he can teach God a thing or two by answering God's questions so that Job's wisdom can be clearly demonstrated.

What Does Job Know of the Cosmos? (38:4–38)

The sequence of questions addressed to Job in verses 4–7 moves through aspects of creation: the foundations of the earth, confining the sea, rolling out the dawn followed by the realm of day and night, and the weather.

---

12. So according to Meredith G. Kline, "Trial By Ordeal," in *Through Christ's Word: A Festschrift for Dr. Philip E. Hughes*, ed. W. Robert Godfrey and Jesse L. Boyd (Phillipsburg, NJ: P&R, 1985), 88–93; Cyrus H. Gordon, "Belt-Wrestling in the Bible World," *HUCA* 23.1 (1950): 131–36. Hartley, *Book of Job*, 492n7, says regarding Gordon's article, "C. Gordon considers this passage an allusion to the ordeal of belt wrestling in which two contestants girded with a belt wrestled to resolve a dispute ('Belt Wrestling in the Bible World,' *HUCA* 23 [1950–51] 131–36; cf. 9:3). Some (e.g., Fohrer) accept this custom as background for the language of v. 3, but others (e.g., H. L. Ginsberg, 'Interpreting Ugaritic Texts,' *JAOS* 70 [1950]: 158; Gordis) vigorously reject it."

13. Clines, *Job 38–42*, 1096.

The first questions Job is asked by God relate to the creation of the world. The questions asked of Job describe creation itself as a building project undertaken by God (similar language is used elsewhere, e.g., Ps 104:5; Isa 48:13; Zech 12:1), replete with foundations, measurements, footings, and a cornerstone.

The rhetorical questions in Job 38:4–7 are ones Job can answer with ease. The point is not here to pose questions Job cannot answer but rather questions for which the answer highlights Job's lack of qualification in calling into question the way that God deals with the universe.

There is no break between the preceding questions and the set of questions found in verses 8–11. The Hebrew of verse 8 does not even include the pronoun "who" that is found in the NIV and other modern translations; it is simply carried over from Job 38:6b.

God continues to question Job about creation, turning to the sea. In the ancient world the sea was often thought of as a dark, foreboding, and dangerous place. Other ancient Near Eastern cultures deified the sea, associating it with the god Yam (cf. the Hebrew word for sea, *yam*). By contrast, however, the sea is here emphatically part of Yahweh's dominion. The imagery reflects ideas found in the creation account of Genesis 1, where the waters were separated, contained, and controlled by God alone.

God initially speaks about the sea using the metaphor of birth, describing it as a newborn coming forth from the womb (some suggest the "doors" of v. 8 refer to the opening of the birth canal). The NIV's "wrapped it in thick darkness" presents an image of swaddling the newborn sea with thick darkness (imagery that probably reflects a heavy mist). The imagery does not so much convey maternal concern for the sea on Yahweh's part so much as his control, a notion confirmed by verses 10–11, which explicitly recount the imposition of strict boundaries on the sea. The foreboding, dangerous sea is, from God's perspective, merely a baby he has delivered, clothed, and constrained.

Yahweh turns, in verses 12–15, to question Job about the dawn that arrives at God's command and, with light that banishes the darkness, exposes and expels the evil that is done under the cover of night (see Job 24:13–17). The question as to whether Job has "ever" commanded the morning (38:12) highlights the fact that, although the event takes place daily, Job has not once in all the days of his life so commanded the dawn.

In verses 13–14 the dawn is described as taking hold of the corners of the earth (or "land," an alternate way to understand the Hebrew word *'erets*) as if it were a dirty rug and shaking out the darkness and its associated evil, the advancing light then revealing the texture and features of the land, as it does when shone on a carved relief or a patterned garment.

Verse 15 returns to the wicked people referred to in verse 13 by affirming their allegiance to darkness and God's light as their undoing, robbing them of the cloak under which they perform their acts of violence (represented by the image of an upraised arm that is broken, see 31:22; Jer 48:25; Ezek 30:21–22; etc.).

The introduction of the wicked in these verses is a little surprising, given that the realm of human beings is not elsewhere addressed directly in Yahweh's speech, but may be prompted in light of Job's complaint about God's apparent lack of justice in his own circumstances. By contrast, God here insists that each day evil is exposed and expunged and that Job has not even once himself initiated such renewal.

Verses 16–30 focus not on questions of whether Job has performed various tasks but instead on whether Job knows the way to various cosmic locales. In this sense it is somewhat reminiscent of the poem of Job 28, which highlighted the hiddenness of wisdom. Here, however, Job is asked if he knows the way to the source of the sea (v. 16; cf. Gen 7:11), the abode of the dead (v. 17), the vast expanses of the land (v. 18), the homes of dark and light (v. 19–20), the storehouses of the snow and hail (v. 22–23), the lightning (v. 24a), wind (v. 24b), heavy rains (v. 25a), and thunder (v. 25b).

While poetic, this array of expressions nonetheless reflects the cosmology of the ancient world, and so they are not as purely metaphorical as the modern reader might be inclined to think. The expression "springs of the sea" (v. 16) refers to the source of waters thought to exist deep under the seas (see Prov 8:24), which leads us to the entrance to the underworld and the place of the dead ("gates of death," v. 17, elsewhere named Sheol).

A number of scholars suggest that when verse 18 refers to "the vast expanses of the earth," it is better understood as a further reference to the underworld.[14] While the word here is the normal Hebrew term for "land" or "earth," it is used elsewhere in reference to the land of Sheol (e.g., Job 10:21–22; Jonah 2:6 [v. 7 in Hebrew]). Given that the "abode of light" (Job 38:19) and the place where darkness resides were also understood to be beyond the human realm, this seems to be a reasonable understanding of the reference. More than not even visiting the gateway to the underworld, Job has failed to then survey its vast expanse!

The "abode of light" and the place where darkness resides (v. 19) would also appear to be references to a place below the earth, for in ancient cosmology the sun would travel through the underworld each night preparing to return to

14. Clines, *Job 38–42*, 1059; Andersen, *Job*, 298; Hartley, *Book of Job*, 500.

the heavens (or skies) the next morning. Behind all these expressions lies the identity of God as creator (e.g., Gen 1:3–4, where light and dark are created and separated), and so all of them serve to highlight the difference between the knowledge and wisdom of God and Job.

From the underworld, the journey moves to the heavens in verse 22. The association of the various weather phenomena recounted here—snow, hail, wind—with heavenly storehouses is found throughout the Old Testament and other ancient literature (e.g., Deut 28:12; Jer 10:13; Ps 135:7). Again, this appears to be more than merely figurative language but rather a reflection of the belief that God held these in store in places in the heavens ready to be used when needed.

The later verses in this portion of Yahweh's speech (Job 38:24–30) turn specifically to rain as it falls across the earth and, in particular, in uninhabited places specifically beyond those with which Job has any familiarity. Throughout the entire speech we are led through places Job has never visited, of which Job's knowledge is sorely limited. And that is the point for Job to realize: there is far more of which Job is ignorant than he could possibly have imagined before this encounter with the Creator of all!

In the midst of this barrage of questions, verse 21 contains a sarcastic comment about Job's wisdom affirming that such knowledge only comes with vast age and experience. The verse ultimately highlights one significant difference between Job and Yahweh—Yahweh stood before any of these were established and was witness to and initiator of their creation. As such he does know their way and Job cannot. As with Yahweh's speech in its entirety, this section highlights Job's failure to comprehend his own ignorance before pressing charges of injustice against God.

Verses 31–33 turn to asking Job whether he is capable of manipulating the cosmos in various ways. While some of the precise astronomical details of these verses are uncertain (see below), the fundamental point being made is clear: Job has neither the knowledge nor the power to understand or accomplish these things; only God has this knowledge and power.

What can we say of the details? Three of the constellations mentioned—the Pleiades, Orion, and the Bear—have appeared earlier in Job 9:9. The Pleiades (the Hebrew name is *kimah*) is a star cluster visible in the northern hemisphere consisting of six stars usually visible to the naked eye (curiously for some car owners, but not really of any relevance, in Japanese this constellation is named Subaru). Many of the constellations we see in the sky consist of stars which are only visually close to one another, some stars are far more distant from us than others. The Pleiades, however, are all part of a localized cluster of stars located about 425 light years from us.[15] The individual member stars are particularly bright and so have been well known since ancient times.

One significance of the constellations mentioned in these speeches lies in their relationship to the seasons and their associated weather patterns (see Gen 1:14; Job 38:32). From Israel, the Pleiades are visible from October to the beginning of April and so mark the period of the wet season, an association that provides a suitable segue to the subsequent discussion of rain and lightning. The constellation identified in English translations as the belt of Orion is in Hebrew named *kesil*, meaning "fool." The "belt" consists of three bright stars now named Alnitak, Alnilam, and Mintaka which, while they appear close in the night sky, are separated by hundreds of light years.[16]

The fourth constellation, the Bear, has the Hebrew name *ʿayish* (which may be related to a Semitic word meaning "lion"; see the footnote in the NIV identifying this with Leo). Scholars are uncertain over the precise identification, with a few suggesting this could refer to Aldebaran, the bright star that forms the eye of Taurus the bull.[17] Whatever the correct identification, it was clearly understood to represent a living creature, as it is followed by its cubs (woodenly, "its sons").

The astute reader will note that I have skipped over the reference of the NIV to the first half of verse 32. Here the reference for the Hebrew term translated "the constellations" (*mazzarot*) is uncertain (this is the only time the word appears in the Hebrew Bible). One ancient suggestion is that it is a reference to Venus (Latin translations identified it as *lucifer*, meaning "light bearer,"[18] also serving as the Latin name of Venus). Other suggestions include the zodiacal circle, Arcturus, Sirius, and more. In the end we cannot be sure precisely what the reference here is.

As noted above, the point of these verses is clear and spelled out by the question in 38:33. The second half of this verse is a little tricky—the word translated "dominion" in the NIV is another word that appears nowhere else in Biblical Hebrew. There are a number of suggested meanings: "authority" (based on a similar Hebrew noun meaning "official") or "writing" (as in writing in the sky, based on similar words in Arabic and Akkadian). Attached to this

---

15. Ronald Stoyan, *Atlas of the Messier Objects: Highlights of the Deep Sky* (Cambridge: Cambridge University Press, 2008), 187.

16. Clines, *Job 38–42*, 1113–14, states that Orion's belt is loosened from early July onward, but that does not correspond with any of the information I can find that notes that Orion is principally visible in the night sky during the northern winter, from around November to March. This would seem to undermine Clines's argument about it heralding summer.

17. See Clines, *Job 1–20*, 231; Clines, *Job 38–42*, 1114; Hartley, *Book of Job*, 173.

18. See "lūcĭfer," *Lewis and Short's Latin Dictionary* 1080.

word in the Hebrew is a singular pronoun ("his" or "its") but what that refers to is also not immediately obvious. Some suggest a reference to the heavens, but we would then expect this to be a plural pronoun. The NIV opts for God, and so renders this as "God's dominion," an understanding that represents the least difficult understanding of the Hebrew. God asks Job if he understands the laws that govern the operation of the heavens or if he has the authority to tie the operation of the heavens to the seasons on earth that they govern.

As with each of God's questions, Job neither knows how the universe operates nor has the ability (or wisdom) to make it function.

While modern readers may differentiate between the focus of verses 31–33 on stars and that of verses 34–35 on torrential rain and lightning, for the ancient audience these all lay in the realm of the heavens, and so the distinction was not so significant. Verse 34 has God ask Job whether he has the ability to command the clouds to pour out rain—of course he does not. Verse 35 then depicts God probing Job about whether he is able to control the lightning, asking not merely whether Job can initiate the lightning but also whether the lightning bolts then obediently respond, as a subject of a king might, by answering, "Here we are!"

The precise meaning of verse 36 is difficult to ascertain, as a quick comparison of English translations reveals. The difficulty lies in the words the NIV (and many other translations) translates as "ibis" and "rooster." For the first of these words, a variety of translations have been suggested, including "inward parts, heart" (CSB, ESV, NASB, NET), "clouds" (RSV), and more.[19] The NIV is probably correct to have understood the term to refer to the ibis, a bird that was associated with wisdom in ancient Egypt and, more particularly, with the annual flooding of the Nile.[20]

Similarly, the term translated "rooster" is difficult, and a number of suggestions have also been made for it. Nonetheless, the NIV's "rooster" is again probably the best understanding. As with the ibis, in the ancient world the rooster was believed to possess the ability to anticipate rain and flood. This is described in verse 36 as "wisdom" and "understanding" and so fits well with the immediate context, which has just referred to rains and lightning, and next verse 37 poses further questions about clouds and rain.

The theme of rain continues in verses 37–38 with Job being questioned about whether he can count the clouds—and not count the clouds on a sunny day but when it rains with sufficient vigor to result in the dust of the earth

19. Clines, *Job 38–42*, 1065, provides an extensive list of at least ten different suggestions for the meaning of the Hebrew word *tukhom*.

20. Clines, *Job 38–42*, 1116.

sticking together in clumps (as the temporal "when" of verse 38 makes clear). The reference to wisdom in the verse also makes it clear that the task is not merely one of enumerating the clouds but one of ensuring the number of clouds is correct and suitable.

In addition to counting the clouds, Job is asked whether he can tip over the "water jars of the heavens" (v. 37b), a metaphorical description of the stores of water in the heavens. This is a task that involves not only power but also, more particularly in this context, wisdom. The result of the rains—that the dust of the earth forms clumps—suggests that the question relates to getting the amount of rain right, not merely providing the rain. Whether this is precisely the implication or not, the gist of these questions is to continue to highlight to Job the limits of his knowledge and wisdom.

What Does Job Know of Wild Animals? (38:39–39:30)

The remainder of Yahweh's first speech in 38:39–39:30 moves from the heavens to ask questions about various animals—lions, ravens, mountain goats, donkeys, wild oxen, the ostrich, horses, and finally hawks. These clearly contrast with the cosmic scale of the opening series of questions, turning to matters with which we might initially expect Job have had more familiarity. Yet all of these animals are wild—with the exception of the horse—and so exist outside the realm of human dominion. This further highlights the extent of Job's ignorance and just how presumptuous he has been in calling Yahweh's justice and rule into question.

Yahweh asks Job if he is the one who provides for the lion or raven (vv. 39–41). The two animals are probably chosen to represent the broad spectrum of the animal kingdom from the powerful, frightening lion all the way to the small and relatively delicate bird. Choosing the two extremes is a way to illustratively encompass all animals from A to Z. Yahweh provides for all creatures in his wisdom. Can Job claim as much?

The "lions" (*kephir*, v. 39b), for whom the "lioness" (*labi'*) is hunting prey, are possibly young lions or lion cubs rather than mature adults (the linguistic evidence is somewhat equivocal, but such a reading makes good sense of the verse and is reflected in a number of English versions including the ESV, KJV, and NLT).

These questions about the animal kingdom are not merely related to whether Job has the capability to make such provision but also highlight his lack of wisdom (in the ancient sense of skill or ability) in yet another aspect of life. The implication of the questions is that Yahweh can and does provide for these creatures. And so again his wisdom surpasses Job's.

The next animal is the mountain goat (or ibex), described in 39:1–4 as a reclusive animal typically found in rugged rocky regions unsuitable for human occupation. Consequently, it is a clear example of an animal that is not easily studied by humans and with which Job cannot be expected to have a great deal of experience. Yahweh questions Job about his knowledge of the husbandry of these animals—knowledge that implies dedicated and close observation and concern for the animals. This makes clear God's concern for the ibex, even though they have virtually no impact on Job's world.

The "wild donkey" (*pere'*, vv. 5–8) is probably to be identified with the onager, a member of the horse family unsuitable for domestication. Once again, it is an animal noted for avoiding human settlements (cf. Gen 16:12 [*pere'*]; Dan 5:21 [Aramaic *'arad*]) and its untamed existence. Again, Yahweh shows that his sovereign governance of creation extends to places no human had much cared to venture, particularly in the ancient world.

God next turns to the wild ox (Job 39:9–12), most likely a reference to an extinct (since 1627) ancestor of modern cattle known as aurochs (the early Greek and Latin translations of the Old Testament understood the word to refer to the rhinoceros), noted elsewhere for their large dangerous horns (e.g., Num 23:22; 24:8; Deut 33:17).[21] Once again, this animal is identified as one without value or connection to humans, one that remains wild and untamable. Despite this, Yahweh is responsible for this creature.

The stanza of the speech relating to "the ostrich" (Job 39:13–18) is expressed somewhat differently to the surrounding material, for it lacks any questions at all. Rather, it observes that the ostrich is a rather perplexing creature, one whose very existence readily demonstrates Job's relative lack of wisdom. A bird that cannot fly in spite of the exuberant flapping of its wings, a bird that demonstrates an almost casual disregard for the welfare of its eggs and young, a bird that epitomizes the lack of wisdom in so many aspects of its existence. Most of these statements about the ostrich reflect ancient beliefs about the bird, beliefs that are not entirely accurate. David Clines notes, for instance, that ostriches do protect their eggs and that their eggs are strong enough that an adult human can stand on one without breaking it.[22] The words here are, however, not intended to provide a scientifically precise description of the behavior of the bird but to appeal to popular ancient understanding in order to draw out the point that, in spite of the accepted beliefs about the absurdity of the ostrich, it nonetheless outpaces even the fastest horse, rather like how

21. Clines, *Job 38–42*, 1123.
22. Clines, *Job 38–42*, 1126.

the roadrunner in the cartoons always outdoes the coyote (remembering that we are not talking about modern race horses that are bred for their speed). Even this apparently foolish bird nonetheless possesses this skill—that is a type of wisdom in the ancient sense.

The point made from the ostrich is that God has imparted wisdom to all manner of creatures but that their wisdom is limited. For the ostrich its wisdom is limited to its ability to run at speed without apparent effort, laughing off the approach of the fastest of horses. Creatures have some wisdom, but God has all wisdom.

Yahweh moves no to question Job about "the horse" (vv. 19–25). This may seem to be a surprising choice of an animal in light of the wild, untamed nature of all the other creatures under discussion. However, the inclusion of such a familiar animal highlights the extent of Job's (and, by extension, the reader's) lack of wisdom in relation to even the most familiar of creatures.

The domestication of the horse, a process that seems to have taken place between about 3500 and 2000 BC, was the foundation of a major technological advance in agriculture, transport, and perhaps most significantly, warfare.[23] These verses focus on the place of the horse in warfare (note the references to how the horse "charges into the fray" (v. 21b) and "does not shy away from the sword" (v. 22b). It is depicted as fearless and powerful, eager for battle and formidable in any circumstance. This connection between horses and battle is made elsewhere in the Bible (e.g., Joel 2:4; Nah 3:2). Here is a creature whose strength and ways are astonishing to behold and, despite having been domesticated by human beings, God is the source of its power and might. This again highlights the superiority of God's wisdom over Job's, for Job lacks the wisdom to create and invigorate such a mighty creature, while God is the one who used his wisdom to create it.

The final animals referenced in Yahweh's first speech (Job 39:26–30) are unclean birds of prey (see Lev 11:13–19; Deut 14:11–18), specifically the hawk (*nets*) and the eagle (Hebrew *nesher*, which could refer to either the eagle or the vulture). Job is not an Israelite and so, perhaps, we should not expect the category of uncleanness to have any bearing on his understanding, for the original Hebrew audience the choice of unclean birds would likely not have

23. There is considerable debate about the timing of the domestication of the horse, although most cited dates predate the time when the book of Job would have been written. There is some evidence, based on dental wear in horse teeth attributed to the presence of a bit used in a riding harness, that riding of horses may have begun as early as six thousand years ago. For more discussion see David Anthony, Dimitri Y. Telegin, and Dorcas Brown, "The Origin of Horseback Riding," *Scientific American* 265.6 (1991): 94–101. It ought to be noted, however, that debate continues and there is no consensus on the date.

escaped their attention, particularly when in verse 30 their association with the bodies of the dead is highlighted. This choice, then, would perhaps best be understood as creatures whose interaction with the human realm is indirect and of less import than clean birds. Yet, while for Job these birds are of little immediate significance and are of little interest to him, Yahweh knows these birds and their ways.

The first question—"Does the hawk take flight by your wisdom and spread its wings toward the south?" (Job 39:26)—is asking more than just whether Job understands the migration of hawks. It is probably also asking Job if it is his understanding that leads the hawk to migrate. This is clear from the parallel in verse 27, where Yahweh asks if eagles or vultures choose the location of their nests as a result of Job's instruction. The answer is clearly "No," and the implication is that it is through Yahweh's wisdom that the hawk is taught to migrate and the eagle is directed to nest. The remainder of the stanza highlights the benefits of the nesting habits of the eagle/vulture.

So once again Job's wisdom and understanding of the universe is shown to be inadequate. The point has been made over and over by Yahweh, through different illustrations and via different questions, but the repetition serves to drive this one point home: Yahweh's wisdom exceeds Job's, and the universe—most of which exists outside Job's notice—operates only through that divine wisdom. To Job he says, "You are not just ignorant and lacking wisdom in a couple of things, but in many things."

Job's First Response (40:1–5)

The midpoint in Yahweh's speeches is marked by an interruption in the opening verses of chapter 40 by the narrator who, by so interrupting, draws attention to the subsequent question even though Yahweh continues to speak. The interruption highlights the import of these next words, which explicitly demand a response from Job. Job is depicted as one who has initiated a legal case against God. The word "contend" in verse 2 in the NIV translates the Hebrew *riḇ*, which is often used and translated in various ways in a forensic sense (e.g., Exod 23:2; Prov 25:8; Isa 3:13; and see Job 9:3; 31:35). God has presented his case, and now it is Job's turn to respond.

While Yahweh's response to Job did not seem to answer Job's immediate questions about the justification for his suffering, Job's answer to Yahweh in 40:3–5 is equally unsatisfying, for Job's response is merely to focus on the fact that he is not worthy to respond. The word "unworthy" translates a Hebrew term that elsewhere presents a recognition of one's insignificance, of how small one is (e.g., Gen 16:4–5, "despise"; 2 Sam 6:22, "become . . . undignified").

Although Job recognizes his insignificance in comparison to God, his response makes clear that he has not yet come to appreciate fully the force of God's argument. So, God continues until Job finally does get the point at the end of the next speech. At that point in Job 42:2–6, Job finally understands that God does not wish him merely to appreciate that he is small but also to recognize that, in the face of a vastly complex universe, he lacks the wisdom and knowledge to see how everything fits together. Furthermore, it is clear that God's aim here is not to drive Job to silence, or else he would have stopped his questioning. Rather, God wants Job finally to understand that some questions are too complex and the human mind is too limited (both his and ours) to comprehend fully.

LIVE the Story

The Right Answer for the Wrong Question

At last God has come to speak to Job. Job has been waiting for this moment, for the time when God would arrive on the scene. Job had demanded that God answer him, that God give an account of the way he had exercised his rule over Job's life. Why did Yahweh target him? Why has he suffered so? We might well ask similar questions about aspects of our own lives, and as we look to God for answers in his word, we are left without a specific answer. Why have we suffered? Why have we experienced loss? Why are we alone? Why has God not answered us when we sought him? Job had aired his questions and has endured answers from his friends, but now finally he gets to hear from God.

In many ways God's appearance fits with many of his other appearances (or theophanies) throughout the Bible. While these encounters usually present God's judgment on his people, this theophany is different. And while we (and Job) might be expecting God to answer Job's questions and to give an account of his justice and his rule over the universe (and more specifically over Job's life), this is not what we hear from God. Instead, God asks Job questions about how the universe works. These are questions about Job's knowledge, his wisdom, and his understanding of the world in which he lives. These are things that the sages ostensibly claimed to comprehend. Just as Solomon in his wisdom was said to have written extensively about the natural world (see 1 Kgs 4:33), so too these questions in Job focus on the natural world. Yet, rather than highlighting Job's wisdom, these questions reveal his ignorance and lack of wisdom.

The lack of an answer from God may initially seem to be disappointing.

While it could be argued that Job would have benefited from an explanation for his suffering, it would not have helped any other reader of the tale. We are not Job, a point the prologue makes in detail by telling us that "there is no one on earth like him; he is blameless and upright, a man who fears God and shuns evil" (Job 1:8; 2:3). There is no reason to think that any suffering we encounter in our lives could be explained in the same way that Job's suffering would have been explained to him. Some do suffer the consequences of their sinful actions, sometimes God does discipline his children, and sometimes people suffer for contending for their faith and, by so doing, follow in the steps of the Lord Jesus. There is no one reason for suffering in this world, even if the root cause was that sin damaged all creation and its relationship to the Creator. Without prophetic revelation it is often impossible to discern accurately the reason for any individual's suffering. And, if we are honest about our own lives, it is hard to believe that we could measure up to Job as he is described in the opening chapters of the book. And so, we would have to doubt the applicability of any explanation for Job's suffering to our own lives.

On the other hand, we should not doubt that we, like Job, are ignorant about many aspects of how God, in his wisdom, governs the universe. Although we may, through the knowledge humankind has gained over the past few millennia, be able to answer some of the questions that Job could not, if we believe that we therefore have all the answers, that we understand everything about God's management of the world, then we need to realize that we are mistaken. Such hubris was the mistake not only of Job but also the one that led to the downfall of his three friends.

The opening words of chapter 38 make clear to us that, despite our inability to perceive it, God does have a plan. This is a really important piece of information that is vital for understanding the book of Job and its relationship to the remainder of the Bible. There is a plan. Creation has a purpose that is integral to its design, and while it may often be invisible to mortals like Job, his friends, and people today, creation remains on track to fulfill that plan. Now this is not to say that all suffering is purposeful in a way that we might be able to look back on our times of suffering and see and understand that there was some important purpose in our lives or in the lives of others that explains the suffering. To make such an assertion is the flip side of claiming that suffering is always proof of personal sin. But there is a plan, so what we can know is that suffering is not accidental or something that arises because of God's ignorance or oversight. No, it is only to say that we do not have insight into the purpose of every instance of suffering. We cannot always know if there is an explicit purpose or if that suffering fits into God's plan in some other way. God's words to Job (and through him to us) are a reminder that the plan remains intact despite Job's ignorant assertions.

And although it may feel harsh to call Job ignorant, that is ultimately what he is, and he will ultimately admit this in the opening words of chapter 42. His assumption that he ought to be able to grasp the way God works in a sufficiently comprehensive way to be able to boil it down to the simplistic ideas inherent in the notion of retributive justice reflects his failure to understand the true complexity of the universe. The overall plan of God, the story of God, is revealed in the Bible. But the details, the minutiae of each individual's life, are far beyond the scope of that body of special revelation. If every event in every person's life were explained in full, then the volume of information would be so vast that we would not be able to absorb it. Indeed, even the amount of information necessary for one person to understand all that had been allowed to happen to them in a single lifetime would be more than they could take in during the course of that lifetime. Thus, we ought to begin from such a position and accept that things will happen to us, as they happened to Job, that we shall not understand. There is certainly no guarantee in the Bible that we will understand how it is that all things work together for the good of those who believe, at least in any detailed way that explains everything we experience in our lives.

While there are no specific answers for Job, there are a number of lessons to be learned from God's words here. First, God is in control. As David Clines writes, "there is no chaos in the universal structure; everything that exists evidences forethought, planning, and wisdom."[24] Second, God understands and rules the universe at all levels, from the stars (38:31–33) and the oceans (vv. 8–11), right down to the time that mountain goats give birth (39:1–4). Third, the extent of Job's ignorance and lack of wisdom is immense. God's questions clearly demonstrate this point to Job. Furthermore, while Job is (understandably) focused on his own situation, Yahweh does not directly address it at all, instead highlighting to Job the breadth of his own purview. This is not to suggest that Yahweh is making light of Job's situation but rather that he is putting it in perspective. In the New Testament the apostle Paul clearly had learned this lesson, for he considered his own sufferings to be inconsequential compared to the backdrop of the all-encompassing work of God through Christ to reconcile all things to himself (Rom 8:18–21).

Despite Job's ignorance, his lack of wisdom—a lack that we share with Job—, we do have one very important advantage over him. Any encounter

24. Clines, *Job 38–42*, 1089.

with God in the Old Testament cannot but remind us of the encounter with God in the New Testament that supersedes these events. For there we find God who comes to us in human form, as John explains: "the one and only Son, who is himself God and is in closest relationship with the Father, has made him known" (John 1:18). And from Jesus we learn of a mystery that Job could only dream of knowing—the mystery of the good news itself (see Matt 13:11; Rom 16:25–26). And while we know more about why it is that we may suffer (see, for example, John 9:2–3; Rom 5:1–5; Col 1:24; 2 Tim 3:12), our knowledge is not complete. Reassuringly, though, we learn from God's speech in the next chapters of Job that neither silence nor unquestioning submission is a necessary or even an appropriate response. Job's final realization will come in Job 42, where he will understand the full implications of the limits of his knowledge.

CHAPTER 24

Job 40:6–41:34

Yahweh's Second Speech

LISTEN to the Story

40:6 Then the LORD spoke to Job out of the storm:

7 "Brace yourself like a man;
I will question you,
and you shall answer me.

8 "Would you discredit my justice?
Would you condemn me to justify yourself?
9 Do you have an arm like God's,
and can your voice thunder like his?
10 Then adorn yourself with glory and splendor,
and clothe yourself in honor and majesty.
11 Unleash the fury of your wrath,
look at all who are proud and bring them low,
12 look at all who are proud and humble them,
crush the wicked where they stand.
13 Bury them all in the dust together;
shroud their faces in the grave.
14 Then I myself will admit to you
that your own right hand can save you.

15 "Look at Behemoth,
which I made along with you
and which feeds on grass like an ox.
16 What strength it has in its loins,
what power in the muscles of its belly!
17 Its tail sways like a cedar;

the sinews of its thighs are close-knit.
18 Its bones are tubes of bronze,
its limbs like rods of iron.
19 It ranks first among the works of God,
yet its Maker can approach it with his sword.
20 The hills bring it their produce,
and all the wild animals play nearby.
21 Under the lotus plants it lies,
hidden among the reeds in the marsh.
22 The lotuses conceal it in their shadow;
the poplars by the stream surround it.
23 A raging river does not alarm it;
it is secure, though the Jordan should surge against its mouth.
24 Can anyone capture it by the eyes,
or trap it and pierce its nose?

41:1 "Can you pull in Leviathan with a fishhook
or tie down its tongue with a rope?
2 Can you put a cord through its nose
or pierce its jaw with a hook?
3 Will it keep begging you for mercy?
Will it speak to you with gentle words?
4 Will it make an agreement with you
for you to take it as your slave for life?
5 Can you make a pet of it like a bird
or put it on a leash for the young women in your house?
6 Will traders barter for it?
Will they divide it up among the merchants?
7 Can you fill its hide with harpoons
or its head with fishing spears?
8 If you lay a hand on it,
you will remember the struggle and never do it again!
9 Any hope of subduing it is false;
the mere sight of it is overpowering.
10 No one is fierce enough to rouse it.
Who then is able to stand against me?
11 Who has a claim against me that I must pay?

Everything under heaven belongs to me.

12"I will not fail to speak of Leviathan's limbs,
its strength and its graceful form.
13Who can strip off its outer coat?
Who can penetrate its double coat of armor?
14Who dares open the doors of its mouth,
ringed about with fearsome teeth?
15Its back has rows of shields
tightly sealed together;
16each is so close to the next
that no air can pass between.
17They are joined fast to one another;
they cling together and cannot be parted.
18Its snorting throws out flashes of light;
its eyes are like the rays of dawn.
19Flames stream from its mouth;
sparks of fire shoot out.
20Smoke pours from its nostrils
as from a boiling pot over burning reeds.
21Its breath sets coals ablaze,
and flames dart from its mouth.
22Strength resides in its neck;
dismay goes before it.
23The folds of its flesh are tightly joined;
they are firm and immovable.
24Its chest is hard as rock,
hard as a lower millstone.
25When it rises up, the mighty are terrified;
they retreat before its thrashing.
26The sword that reaches it has no effect,
nor does the spear or the dart or the javelin.
27Iron it treats like straw
and bronze like rotten wood.
28Arrows do not make it flee;
slingstones are like chaff to it.
29A club seems to it but a piece of straw;

it laughs at the rattling of the lance.
[30]Its undersides are jagged potsherds,
leaving a trail in the mud like a threshing sledge.
[31]It makes the depths churn like a boiling caldron
and stirs up the sea like a pot of ointment.
[32]It leaves a glistening wake behind it;
one would think the deep had white hair.
[33]Nothing on earth is its equal—
a creature without fear.
[34]It looks down on all that are haughty;
it is king over all that are proud."

Listening to the Text in the Story: "The Contendings of Horus and Seth for the Rule" (Egyptian); "The Ba'lu Myth" (Ugaritic)

Yahweh's second speech to Job moves beyond the array of wild animals to Behemoth and Leviathan. These two creatures are less familiar to modern readers (although see the discussion below on the identity of Behemoth) and occupy more time in Yahweh's speech to Job than any of the other animals. Leviathan, in particular, is of some significance across multiple cultures of the ancient Near East, and that background material helps us to better appreciate the way that Job and his friends would have understood the points Yahweh makes about this creature.

The first of these two creatures, however, is Behemoth. The common understanding that this refers to the hippopotamus is probably correct, but the connection should not be left at that, as it fails to appreciate the apprehension of the hippo in the ancient world. Hippos were primarily inhabitants of northern Africa and were thus familiar and significant in Egyptian thought. Specifically, they have some association with the Egyptian god Seth, and some of that can be seen, for example, in the Egyptian text, "The Contendings of Horus and Seth."

In this tale, Seth suggests a competition to Horus. It involves their transforming themselves into hippos and competing to remain submerged for a period of time:

> Thereupon Seth said to Horus, "Come, let's both transform ourselves into hippopotamuses and submerge in / the deep waters in the midst of the

sea. Now as for the one who shall emerge within the span of three whole months, the office shall not be awarded him." Then they both submerged.[1]

Later in the story Seth again transforms himself into a hippopotamus. The creatures were renowned for their strength and power, but beyond this is their association in Egyptian literature with the god Seth, who himself was also associated with storms. Here in Job, a similar conjunction of elements—God, storm, and hippopotamus—occurs, albeit without the identification of any of the elements with one another. The Egyptian background here primarily highlights the more foreign nature of the hippopotamus when compared to the animals of Yahweh's first speech as well as its threatening nature.

Moving to the second creature, Leviathan, we find a richer background in the ancient world. For example, tablet V of the Ugaritic "The Baʿlu Myth" includes two references to Leviathan (referred to in the translation as Lôtan):

Môtu's Reply to Baʿlu (viii 48—*CTA* 5 i 8)
[Message of Môtu, son of ʾIlu,

word of the beloved warrior of ʾIlu:
My throat is the throat of the lion in the wasteland,
and the gullet of the 'snorter' in the sea;
And it craves the pool (as do) the wild bulls,
(craves) springs as (do) the herds of deer;
And, indeed, indeed,
my throat consumes heaps (of things),
yes indeed, I eat by double handfuls;
And my seven portions are in a bowl,
and they mix (into my) cup a (whole) river.
So invite me, Baʿlu, along with my brothers,
have me over, Haddu, along with my kin,
And eat bread with my brothers,
drink wine with my kin!

---

1. "The Contendings of Horus and Seth," in *The Literature of Ancient Egypt: An Anthology of Stories, Instructions, Stelae, Autobiographies, and Poetry*, ed. William Kelly Simpson, 3rd ed. (New Haven: Yale University Press, 2003), 97. This work is also known as "Horus and Seth" in Miriam Lichtheim, *Ancient Egyptian Literature*, 3 vols. (Berkeley: University of California Press, 1973–1980), 2:214–23, and as "The Contest of Horus and Seth for the Rule," trans. John A. Wilson (*ANET*, 14–17).

Have you forgotten, Baʿlu, that I can pierce you through?
. . .]
When you smite Lôtan, the fleeing serpent,
finish off the twisting serpent,
the close-coiling one with seven heads,
The heavens wither and go slack
like the folds (?) of your tunic.
(Then) I, with groans, am devoured,
(like) a piece of dung I die.
(So) you must (for your part) descend into the throat of Môtu,
son of ʾIlu,
into the watery depths of the beloved warrior of ʾIlu.

Môtu's Message is Delivered to Baʿlu (i 9–?)

The gods do not hesitate;
they head off
for Baʿlu on the heights of Ṣapānu.
Gupanu-wa-Ugaœru report:
Message of Môtu, son of ʾIlu,
word of the beloved warrior of ʾIlu:
My throat is the throat of the lion in the wasteland,
and the gullet of the 'snorter' in the sea;
And it craves the pool (as do) the wild bulls,
(craves) springs as (do) the herds of deer;
And, indeed, indeed,
my throat consumes heaps (of things),
yes indeed, I eat by double handfuls;
And my seven portions are in a bowl,
and they mix (into my) cup a (whole) river.
So invite me, Baʿlu, along with my brothers,
have me over, Haddu, along with my kin,
And eat bread with my brothers,
drink wine with my kin!
Have you forgotten, Baʿlu, that I can pierce you through?
[. . .]
When you smite [Lôtan, the] fleeing [serpent],
finish off [the twisting serpent],
the close-coiling one [with seven heads],

[The heavens] wither [and go slack
like the folds (?) of] your [tunic].
[(Then) I, with groans, am devoured,
(like) a piece of dung I die.
(So) you must (for your part) descend the throat of Môtu, son of ʾIlu,
into the watery depths of the beloved warrior of ʾIlu].[2]

This portion of the Ugaritic "The Baʿlu Myth" is one of the more difficult portions marred with some lacunae, but according to Dennis Pardee the basic plot here is that

> when Baʿlu defeats Lôtan, Môtu dies also as a consequence, dies by being devoured. . . . It is not stated why he dies. But then the message concludes by stating that Baʿlu must also die. The most logical explanation of this cause-and-effect sequence is to see Lôtan and his reptilian allies as the kinsmen of Môtu to which reference has already been made. If Baʿlu attacks them, Môtu must, as their kinsman, take up their cause.[3]

Leviathan also makes an appearance in a couple of other places in the Bible. In Isaiah 27:1 we read,

In that day,

the Lord will punish with his sword—
his fierce, great and powerful sword—
Leviathan the gliding serpent,
Leviathan the coiling serpent;
he will slay the monster of the sea.

Here Leviathan is described as a snake-like (or serpent-like) creature dwelling in the sea and, as in Job, Isaiah affirms Yahweh's power over this creature. More compelling is Psalm 74:12–14, which also speaks of Yahweh's power over Leviathan, a sea monster with multiple heads:

But God is my King from long ago;
he brings salvation on the earth.

---

2. "The Baʿlu Myth," *COS* 1.86:264–66.
3. "The Baʿlu Myth," *COS* 1.86:264n201.

> It was you who split open the sea by your power;
> you broke the heads of the monster in the waters.
> It was you who crushed the heads of Leviathan
> and gave it as food to the creatures of the desert.

Here it is quite clear that although Leviathan is imagined as reptilian, it is clearly not a natural creature such as a crocodile, as some scholars claim,[4] for it has multiple heads. (Furthermore, the reference to "the sea" in this psalm should probably be understood as a reference to the Canaanite deity Yam, such that the psalmist is asserting God's sovereignty over the gods of the nations.)

Whatever the details, it is clear that Leviathan (Lôtan in "The Baʿlu Myth") is a powerful supernatural creature. The parallels between this passage in "The Baʿlu Myth" and Isaiah 27:1 (in particular) are striking, but it strengthens the case that Leviathan in Job is a not merely a crocodile as some have argued. Furthermore, Leviathan-like water monsters with multiple heads are found elsewhere in the ancient world, perhaps the best known of which is the Hydra of Greek and Roman mythology. The idea of a supernatural sea monster like Leviathan was evidently a reasonable belief in the ancient world, and so its appearance in Job need not be explained away as an example of hyperbolic poetry.

While most of these ancient tales of Leviathan—particularly those from outside of the Bible—are foreign to modern readers of Job, they nevertheless form an important background to understanding the significance of much of God's final speech. Thus far God's interaction with Job has highlighted the "known unknowns," that is, parts of creation with which Job at least has some passing familiarity. Now God introduces the "unknown unknowns," revealing to Job (and us) that there are important and powerful parts of creation of which he is almost entirely ignorant.

Leviathan has gone on to inspire the naming of the an extinct genus of sperm whale (*Livyatan melvillei*), which was one of the largest sea predators ever to have lived (the second part of the scientific name comes from the author of the book *Moby-Dick*, Herman Melville). It would be a mistake to think that this creature (or any similar) provides a background to the references in the book of Job.

---

4. E.g. Clines, *Job 1–20*, xlvi, but see the helpful discussion by Mark Sneed, "Is Biblical Studies Stuck in Antiquarianism? The Case of Behemoth and Leviathan," *JBRec* 10.2 (2023): 221–44.

EXPLAIN the Story

Does Job Have the Power of Yahweh? (40:6–14)

Yahweh's second speech begins in Job 40:6–7 in the same way the first had: the announcement by the narrator that Yahweh is responding to Job and the first words calling on Job to prepare to answer Yahweh. The repetition functions to highlight the fact that Job's intervening response has done nothing to amend his allegation of injustice that he had leveled at Yahweh throughout his debate with his friends. Job has not understood what he has been told, responding with silence rather than comprehension, and so God chooses to continue.

Before returning to aspects of his creation, Yahweh points to the "elephant in the room" in verses 8–14: Job's persistent insistence of his own innocence has come at the expense of God's justice. Job's fundamental presuppositions about divine justice do not differ from those of his friends—God punishes the wicked and rewards the faithful. Job has not questioned this belief but rather has suggested that God's justice is flawed, or at least in his case. Job correctly holds to his unshakeable conviction that he has done nothing to warrant the suffering he has experienced (and we know this because God himself made it clear in chapters 1 and 2). The problem, however, is that Job's theology allows him to conceive of no other implication from this than that God's justice is flawed. In verse 8 God makes it clear that this implication has not escaped his notice.

Underlying Job's logic, however, is a presumption about his own wisdom and power that has gone largely unquestioned . . . until now. This issue was raised implicitly in God's first speech, but now God raises it explicitly. Through a somewhat sarcastic series of instructions in verses 10–14, God calls on Job to demonstrate his wisdom and power as well as his qualifications for raising such accusations of God. If Job had not understood the implications of God's questions in his first speech, they are made clear here before turning to consider two final (and remarkable) creatures.

Consider Behemoth (40:15–24)

Whereas in his first speech Yahweh had questioned Job about ten different animals, in the second speech only two are mentioned—Behemoth (ten verses in 40:15–24) and Leviathan (thirty-four verses in 41:1–34[40:25–41:26 in the Hebrew]). Questions remain over whether these are somewhat colorful descriptions of actual animals (usually identified as the hippopotamus and the crocodile) or mythical creatures of some sort. Reading some of the descriptions, particularly of Behemoth, certainly makes it sound as though these are natural creatures—Behemoth "feeds on grass like an ox" (40:15) and "lies under plants, hidden among the reeds in the marsh" (v. 21). Furthermore, the elements that sound unnatural could easily be no more than examples of poetic imagery.[5]

An important point to note, however, is that while we might today sharply differentiate between naturally occurring animals and supernatural or divine creatures, in the ancient world such a distinction was not so clear. Some animals, for example, were either strongly associated with gods or believed to represent them in some way (see Exod 32:4). So, while almost all English translations simply transliterate the Hebrew terms and so imply something other than a naturally occurring animal, the distinction is easily overstated.

Perhaps the more important issue is why Yahweh chooses to focus on and spend more time discussing these two creatures than on the animals mentioned previously. The best answer to this question is that these creatures present a significant contrast to those previously discussed. Whereas Job as a sage could be expected to know something about all the creatures mentioned previously, Behemoth and Leviathan represent more mysterious, dangerous, unfamiliar, and probably somewhat supernatural creatures. Choosing these two marvelous creatures magnifies the points made in the first speech and drives home to Job the inadequacy of his wisdom and understanding of the universe. Here are two creatures that lie completely outside Job's experience. Beyond the world with which Job is familiar, there is a vast world with which he is completely unfamiliar. In this realm he has nothing to offer—no wisdom to present and no answer to give. In this realm, his ignorance and lack of wisdom is unassailable. Faced with these questions Job cannot but finally concede that his ignorance must ultimately negate any basis he has for questioning Yahweh's governance of the universe and, within it, his own life.

The first of the two creatures specifically mentioned in Yahweh's second speech is Behemoth (Job 40:15–24), which is simply a transliteration of the Hebrew word instead of a translation. Grammatically, the word is an intensive plural form of the Hebrew word *behemah*, which refers elsewhere to cattle or large animals in general (e.g., Gen 1:24). Furthermore, although most scholars argue that the Behemoth and Leviathan are both either regular animals or supernatural/mythical creatures, there is no particularly compelling reason to argue that we might not have one of each—the (natural) hippopotamus and the (supernatural) Leviathan. As noted above, the distinction we impose

5. So, for example, Andersen, *Job*, 310; Clines, *Job 38–42*, 1183–86.

between natural and supernatural creatures may itself have been foreign to the original audience of the book of Job. Justification for reading this passage in this way is readily apparent in the text itself in that far more time is spent on Leviathan than Behemoth, and the description of Behemoth places it in a far more natural setting than that of the Leviathan (refer to the details discussed below).

A couple of points could count against understanding Behemoth to be a hippopotamus. First, hippos are primarily found in Africa (including Egypt), but their presence in Job's locale is uncertain. Clines cites some research that suggests they may have lived around Palestine, and this would also fit the author's purpose to introduce creatures with which Job (and the reader) would have had less familiarity.[6] Second, the description of Behemoth's tail as swaying like a cedar (40:17) presents a difficulty. The tail of a hippo is not particularly long or impressive to look at as one might expect from this description. This is hardly conclusive evidence that the author is not referring to the hippo—the point of comparison may be the stiffness of the tail, its strength, or, as some have suggested, the entire phrase may be a euphemism referring to the animal's penis.[7] All in all, there is no conclusive evidence that Behemoth is not referring to the hippo.

Aside from these considerations, there is much to commend the identification of Behemoth with the hippo. It is an herbivore (v. 15), it is immensely strong (vv. 16, 18), it hides among the reeds in the marshes overshadowed by trees (vv. 21–22), and it is unperturbed by rushing water in the Jordan (v. 23).

The concluding verse of the account of Behemoth highlights the difficulty in capturing this creature and so again highlights the power and danger it presents.[8] Certainly it was beyond Job's capacity to capture one, as Yahweh makes clear here. The Hebrew of the verse itself is not particularly clear—there is no formal indication that this is a question at all, and the text more woodenly reads something like, "he may take it by its eyes, he may pierce [its] nose with pins" (cf. KJV). Given that hippos were both hunted and captured in ancient Egypt, the verse is perhaps better understood not as an unmarked question but as a statement highlighting the difficulty in capturing the beast rather than the impossibility of doing so.[9]

The point of this account of the hippo/Behemoth is made in the final verse

6. See Clines, *Job 38–42*, 1143, 1185.

7. See, e.g., Clines, *Job 38–42*, 1187.

8. As Clines notes, "The text does not say that it is impossible to capture a hippopotamus but alludes to the magnitude of the task" (Clines, *Job 38–42*, 1189; see also Hartley, *Book of Job*, 526.).

9. See Michael V. Fox, "Behemoth and Leviathan," *Bib* 93.2 (2012): 263.

of the section—Yahweh has turned his attention to a creature on the periphery of Job's existence, a creature whose attributes border on the supernatural, a creature of famed power and stealth. Yet, God created this creature (just as he created Job; see 40:15) and is intimately familiar with it and rules over it. The point of the previous speech is emphasized: Job's wisdom falls far short of Yahweh's.

Consider Leviathan (41:1–34)

Leviathan, the final creature presented to Job for consideration, is given the most detailed and longest description of all in the Yahweh's speeches (41:1–34).[10] Most scholars who identify Behemoth as the hippopotamus go on to identify Leviathan with the crocodile, and this identification is not without some grounds. Leviathan is said to have strong limbs (v. 12), a coat of armor (vv. 13, 15–17) that extends to its belly (v. 30), fearsome teeth (v. 14), and a strong neck (v. 22). It leaves a trail in the mud (v. 30) and churns the water (vv. 31–32).

Yet there are also significant problems with understanding it to be any natural animal, and so some scholars argue that this is a supernatural being. The description in Job 41 alone is replete with claims that are either more hyperbolic than those describing any of the preceding creatures or else must describe something supernatural. There is no hope of subduing Leviathan (v. 9), flames and smoke come from its mouth to ignite coals (vv. 19–21), and it is impervious to iron and bronze weapons (vv. 26–27). Even allowing for poetic hyperbole, a natural reading feels to be something of a stretch in the face of such a description. At least here in my native Australia, crocodiles can be caught and secured by human beings (but please do not try this at home or at church) without too much dependence upon modern technology. Even in the ancient world, this was not unknown—"Amenemhet" has Amenemhet recount: "I subdued lions, I captured crocodiles."[11] Yet, Job 41:1–2 makes it clear that Leviathan cannot be subdued or captured by people. Even the basic elements of the description are problematic for equating Leviathan with a crocodile (see comments on Job 41:1–2 below).

Furthermore, the original audience of the book of Job would already have been familiar with Leviathan, a creature mentioned elsewhere in the Old Testament (Job 3:8; Pss 74:14; 104:26; Isa 27:1). In these passages we learn

---

10. In this commentary I follow English numbering, but other works may follow Hebrew verse numbering, which differs for this chapter of Job. In Hebrew the numbering for the Leviathan section is Job 40:25–41:26.

11. "Amenemhut," trans. Miriam Lichtheim (*COS* 1.36:67).

that this creature has multiple heads (Ps 74:14), a feature that is also apparent in the Ugaritic "The Baʿlu Myth" (see above). In Psalm 104:26 it lives in the deep of the sea, which cannot apply to a crocodile. In Isaiah 27:1, repeated from Live the Story above, we read,

In that day,

> the LORD will punish with his sword—
>   his fierce, great and powerful sword—
> Leviathan the gliding serpent,
>   Leviathan the coiling serpent;
> he will slay the monster of the sea.

Here Leviathan is depicted as a "monster of the sea" (or "dragon" [ESV]; Hebrew *tannin*) that represents chaos and evil. For the original audience of the book of Job, this is what the mention of Leviathan conjured up. Here is a powerful, supernatural enemy of Yahweh who is, nonetheless, powerless before him. Job, too, is expected to know the power and threat Leviathan poses, and this speech is designed to awaken him to the realization that the God he has confronted should not be domesticated and his wisdom should not be underestimated, two things Job and his friends have definitely been guilty of to this point.

For Eric Ortlund this identification of Leviathan as a supernatural evil creature prompts the conclusion that Yahweh is implying that Job's suffering has come about from just such a source.[12] While this is an enticing reading—tying the conclusion to Yahweh's speeches with the events of the prologue—there is simply nothing explicit in the book that allows for such a connection. Furthermore, the suggestion that the reference to a supernatural chaos creature here is offered to provide Job with some explanation for his suffering undermines the point of the book itself.

We have seen that the point being raised by Yahweh relates to Job's knowledge, and Yahweh's questions have built to a crescendo, ultimately arriving at the point where Job's knowledge of Leviathan is tested and his complete lack of understanding of the complexities of both creation and the divine plan are made most apparent. That this is the effect of these chapters on Job will become apparent in his final words in the book at the opening of chapter 42,

12. Eric Ortlund, "The Identity of Leviathan and the Meaning of the Book of Job," *TJ* 2/34 (2013): 17–30.

where he admits that he spoke of things too difficult for him and that he did not understand.

Nonetheless, the main point of this part of this speech does not ultimately depend on whether Leviathan is natural or supernatural. The point is that this creature is beyond the realm of human control, and yet it is subject to Yahweh's sovereign rule. In the midst of the description of Leviathan are these words:

> No one is fierce enough to rouse it.
> Who then is able to stand against me?
> Who has a claim against me that I must pay?
> Everything under heaven belongs to me. (41:10–11)

Yahweh interjects in the middle of the chapter to highlight precisely what the description of Leviathan—and those of all the preceding creatures—is meant to relate to Job. Some scholars[13] and a few Bible translations (GNT; LEB; NET; NRSVue) are so surprised by the sudden change of topic from Leviathan to Yahweh that they suggest that there has been a corruption of the pronouns and that these verses should refer to Leviathan, asking "who can stand before it?" (NRSVue). There is no textual evidence to support this change, nor is there any real need to make this change, for the Hebrew makes sense as it stands. It highlights the point that if no one can face Leviathan, how much more must it be true that no one can face Yahweh. No one can present a charge against Yahweh, for everything in creation is his, and his wisdom and power surpasses all. In the face of ever more powerful creatures—all of whom are lesser than Yahweh and subject to his power—Job is finally forced to see the true folly of his claims. He has sought to bring a legal case against God without even the slightest comprehension of just how ill-prepared he really was and just how meager was his understanding of the true wisdom and power of the Creator.

The first verses relating to Leviathan (vv. 1–2) refer to methods used to capture or control other animals. The use of a fishhook is largely self-explanatory, but so absurd is the notion of employing it in order to catch this creature that it forms the basis of this first rhetorical question. Clines notes that the ancient Greek historian Herodotus does describe the process for catching a crocodile with a hook and, as mentioned in the second half of the verse, that in the

13. See, for example, Longman, *Job*, 442; Clines, *Job 38–42*, 1161; Pope, *Job*, 335–37; Robert Gordis, *The Book of Job: Commentary, New Translation, and Special Notes* (New York: Jewish Theological Seminary of America, 1978).

ancient world crocodiles were believed to have no tongue. Both points further enhance the case that sees Leviathan as a supernatural creature.[14]

The references to rope in the center of the chiasm of these verses (A fishhook—B cord—B′ rope—A′ hook) appear to be about controlling the creature rather than capturing it, although the two ideas are probably connected (once captured it would need to be controlled).

To emphasize further the absurdity of the notion of capturing Leviathan, Yahweh pushes the image further in verse 3: Having captured this creature, would it then continuously plead for mercy from you, speaking with gentle words? The language here is reminiscent of Proverbs 15:1a, "a gentle answer turns away wrath," evoking the idea that Leviathan would be pleading with Job in words designed to placate him. The question is asked because it conjures a ridiculous image while simultaneously implying that Leviathan would speak to Yahweh in such a way. Job is being reminded that he is not God and has neither control over creation nor even a semblance of understanding of it.

The image continues into verse 4, where the Lord asks whether the subdued Leviathan would then seek to secure its safety by entering into a covenant with Job, making it his slave forever (the NIV's "for life" translates the Hebrew *ʿolam*, usually translated "forever"; also rendered "for life" in Deut 15:17; 1 Sam 27:12), presenting an image of a defeated foe so overawed by its opponent that it is willing to concede any hope of freedom simply to secure its life. Once again, the absurdity of the idea that Job could ever be in such a position carries with it the implication that this is precisely the place Yahweh occupies.

Job is next asked whether he could play with this captured, subdued creature as he might with a bird (Job 41:5). To put things in perspective, Psalm 104:26 uses the same verb "frolic" (*sakhaq*) with reference to Leviathan. While most English translations understand that psalm to be referring to Leviathan playing in the sea, the Hebrew could be understood to read, "Leviathan whom you formed to play with," depicting Leviathan as Yahweh's plaything. If that is the case, the contrast between Job and Yahweh implied by Job 41:5 is enhanced by the psalm's explicit expression of Yahweh's power over even the most unruly elements of creation. This terrifying Leviathan is like a "pet," a plaything for Yahweh.

The author moves from the idea of Leviathan as plaything to a source of food in verses 6–7. This notion is immediately absurd—it is already clear that this creature cannot be captured, so it will hardly be possible to turn it

14. Clines, *Job 38–42*, 1192.

into a meal. There are no recipe books from the ancient world that include slow-cooked Leviathan, and for good reason!

In verses 8–9 the questions give way to instructions (via imperative verbs) describing how a person would respond to an encounter with Leviathan. Yahweh is telling Job in verse 8, "Lay a hand on him and remember the battle" (there is no Hebrew word behind the "if" in the NIV). The implication is that there could be no peaceful encounter with this creature; any encounter would invariably take the form of a battle. And Job would lose so badly that he would never do it again.

In verse 9[15] Yahweh speaks plainly, stating that any hope one has of a different outcome of an encounter with Leviathan is false. The second line in Hebrew is again expressed as a question: "Is the person who encounters Leviathan not brought down even at the sight of it?" Any hope to capture, defeat, or tame Leviathan is absurd and delusional. And yet to Yahweh, Leviathan is a mere plaything.

The reference to rousing Leviathan in verse 10 recalls Job's own words in 3:8 where the same verb (*'ur*) is used. The NIV's "no one is fierce enough to rouse it" doesn't fit well with Job's reference to those who would seek to rouse Leviathan in 3:8. However, the Hebrew here is difficult and perhaps the simplest solution is to treat this as a rhetorical question: "Is it not fierce when it is roused?" (cf. NET).

The second line in 41:10 then presupposes that Job has now acknowledged the power of Leviathan despite it being a mere plaything for Yahweh. If people cower before Leviathan, how much more should one be in awe before Yahweh? The idea of God's surpassing greatness continues through to the conclusion of this section of the speech in verse 11.

The first line of verse 11 takes the form of a rhetorical question to which the answer is clearly "No." The Hebrew seems to address Job's situation quite directly, the question basically asking, "How can someone who fully comprehends my wisdom offer an argument that I will find satisfying?" Job, who would never have dreamed of confronting Leviathan, has confronted Yahweh, even if it took some time for him to reach that point. These poetic words from Yahweh about Leviathan have served to make it quite clear to Job that he had done so without adequately understanding whom he was addressing. And while it may initially appear that the difference is a matter of power—Yahweh is incomparably more powerful than Job—the implication of Yahweh's words

15. Here the Hebrew versification differs from the English and begins at 41:1.

up to this point is clearly that the difference is primarily one of wisdom. Yahweh is incomparably wiser than Job.

The remainder of chapter 41, from verse 12 to the end, marks a shift in tone. Gone are the rhetorical questions, which are replaced by an extended description of Leviathan, much of it in military terminology relating to defensive armor and offensive fire. The questions have served to highlight for Job the vast difference between him and God by drawing his attention to Leviathan, who is far more powerful than Job and yet far less powerful than Yahweh (as has already been established in the preceding verses). These remaining verses serve to remind Job of everything about Leviathan that he may have overlooked, ensuring that he does not underestimate the scope of the challenge he has laid before Yahweh.

The first aspect of Leviathan described is the armor that encompasses its body. The language used reflects the sort of armor that would have been familiar to the audience when the story was written to help ensure they both understood and could relate to these words.

The Hebrew word translated in the NIV as "coat of armor" (*resen*) refers to a "bridle, rein,"[16] a device used to control an animal. That, however, makes little sense here, and the earliest translators (and most who have followed) understood the Hebrew word to be *siryon* meaning "coat of mail [i.e., armor],"[17] the confusion presumably arising at some point when the consonants of the Hebrew text were transposed. The fact that Leviathan bears a double coat enforces the notion that it is impenetrable beyond that which anyone would have normally expected in battle.

Verses 14–17 build on this image of Leviathan as the ultimate warrior. That his teeth are terrifying recalls the response in other places to the arrival of a military foe against whom no hope is to be found (cf. Exod 23:27; Deut 32:25; Josh 2:9). The mouth of Leviathan is not its Achilles's heel—it is too well protected to be considered a point of vulnerability. Its back is covered with impenetrable shields so that not even air (the Hebrew word is *ruakh*, "spirit, breath") can pass through, let alone any weapon. Leviathan is the ideal warrior, perfect in every way for waging war, and consequently it is terrifying to all who would encounter it. There is only one exception to this rule and that is, as has been made clear earlier in the chapter, Yahweh.

Job 41:18–21 move from Leviathan's defenses to its offensive capabilities. This creature possesses an arsenal of fire such that any who oppose it would be

16. "רֶסֶן I," *HALOT* 1249.
17. "סִרְיוֹן," *HALOT* 769.

consumed. Light pours from its eyes, fire from its mouth, and smoke from its nostrils. Fire was used in warfare (e.g., Jer 49:2; Joel 2:5) but seems more often to be a weapon employed by God. Here, then, is Leviathan, who embodied this superhuman power to the peril of all who would approach it.[18]

The description returns to Leviathan's defenses in Job 41:22–24. The neck is, at least in other creatures, a point of control and potential weakness. It is where an animal or a human is yoked and where people in battle can be restrained (cf. Josh 10:24), and as such it is usually a point of vulnerability. But not so for Leviathan—its neck is a source of strength. The second line of Job 41:22 is difficult, with the word "dismay" translating a Hebrew word that appears nowhere else. The early Greek translator understood it to mean "destruction, annihilation," which certainly fits the context here, but this is not certain. The idea appears to be that in the face of Leviathan all opposition falls.

Verse 23 refers to the flesh of the creature. The point is essentially the same as elsewhere, and taken together these all indicate that there are no vulnerabilities to be exploited in Leviathan. This idea is reinforced by verse 24. The NIV captures the meaning well in rendering the Hebrew word for "heart" here as "chest," for the translation "heart" would mislead the English reader to think the creature is stubborn (as "hard-hearted" means elsewhere). Here the word for "hard" (*yatsuq*) is not one of those usually used in the common expression of stubbornness.[19] This word is elsewhere used to refer to cast iron. "Heart" in Hebrew (*leb*) can also refer to more than the physical organ, and so "chest" fits the context well. The overall image is again one of invulnerability.

Such invulnerability has clear implications for any who would choose to attack this creature as explained in verses 25–29. "The mighty" who are terrified here are described in Hebrew using *'elim*, the plural form of the word *'el*, "god." This could be a reference to the gods of the nations who are, from time to time, described as being afraid of something in ancient Near Eastern literature. It could otherwise refer to some other supernatural beings (e.g., 1 Sam 28:13; *'elohim* is mostly used to refer to the one true God), or it could be used as a superlative to describe the greatest human warriors on the earth, as it is understood by the majority of English translations (cf. Gen 23:6; Ps 82:6, both *'elohim*). Whichever way it is taken, the implication is

---

18. "The Great Cairo Hymn of Praise to Amun-Re," *COS* 1.25:38, speaks of the enemies of the deity falling to flame. Typically, it seems to be an offensive weapon of deities more than of human armies.

19. Three roots commonly used are *kbd* (e.g., Exod 8:15), *khzq* (e.g., Exod 4:21), *qshh* (e.g., Deut 2:30).

that the bravest, strongest warrior—whether natural or supernatural—is no match for Leviathan.

Verses 26–29 describe the futility of attacking Leviathan with weapons—the sword, spear, dart, javelin, arrows, slingstones, clubs, and lances. The iron and bronze of verse 27 are references to the materials used to make the weapons listed, materials that were "cutting edge" (pun intended) at the time Job was written. No human weapon worries Leviathan in the least, so it is no wonder the bravest warriors are terrified of it. Yet, behind this lies the fundamental truth that Leviathan is but a plaything for Yahweh, and so if Job fears Leviathan, then he ought to remember that he is dealing with one far greater still when bringing his case before God.

Verses 30–32 describe what happens when Leviathan moves about: the sharp protrusions on its underside mark the mud as would a threshing sledge. David Clines describes a threshing sledge:

> A threshing sledge was a flat heavy wooden board, bent upward at the front and with projecting stones or pieces of iron fixed into its under side; as it was dragged over the threshing floor, weighed down with stones or workers, it tore the husks from the grain and cut the straw into chaff.[20]

Leviathan is dangerous from all angles, even from below!

From moving on land to moving through the deep water, the description here suggests Leviathan moves unimpeded at speed, stirring up the waters as though they were boiling. The second half of verse 31 parallels this idea with a pot of ointment. This probably refers to the manner in which ointment was prepared, cooked up in a pot of its own.

Verse 32 continues this depiction of Leviathan through a description of its wake. "Glistening" translates a Hebrew word meaning "shine" (e.g., Ps 31:16) or "give light" (e.g., Gen 1:15). The idea is somewhat reminiscent of the wake of a large ship as it churns up the waters and the foaming sea in its trail is illuminated in the dark.

The description of Leviathan, and Yahweh's speech, come to an end with a summary of the standing of this creature in Job 41:33–34. It is unequaled on earth, fearless, and above every other creature. In particular, it stands over the proudest and highest people, fearing none.

Putting Leviathan in perspective as he has done, Yahweh has also put himself into perspective in Job's mind. The result of this sustained examination of

20. Clines, *Job 38–42*, 1199.

this extraordinary creature is not merely to enhance Job's appreciation of this creature but to remind Job of God's own transcendence. As far above Job as Leviathan is, God himself is even farther above Leviathan. Job's awareness of the gap between himself and God is made clear.

LIVE the Story

Expanding Our Vision of God

By the end of the nineteenth century, many physicists felt that they had a good grasp on the workings of the universe and that those final minor parts that had still eluded explanation would soon yield their secrets. The Enlightenment had, at least scientifically, almost reached its conclusion where human thought had mastered all. Yet, like someone pulling on a loose thread on a knitted jumper, digging into those apparently minor unknowns brought the entire scientific edifice undone. With the arrival of Einstein's theories of relativity and the quantum physics of Bohr, Schrödinger, Heisenberg, and others, the supposedly certain scientific knowledge that had accumulated to that point in time was suddenly revealed to be wrong. From afar, the older ways of thinking that had been up to that point treated as unshakeable truth looked correct. But when scrutinized carefully, what had appeared to be small discrepancies proved to be a sign that the theories could not truthfully explain the universe they sought to describe. Scientists learned a humiliating lesson about hubris, one we would do well not to forget.

When Job found himself facing God in chapter 38, he was suffering the misapprehension that he had a fairly solid grasp on the way the universe operated (a misapprehension shared by his older three friends). Yet, somewhat like many late nineteenth-century scientists, the reality was that Job's perspective was too limited. While Job wanted to understand the reasons for his suffering, what he needed was to have his understanding of the universe broadened from the limited, human perspective he inhabited to the all-encompassing, sovereign view of the universe that only God has.

Yahweh's speeches to Job lead him (and us) through one of those small cracks in his worldview, in his understanding of the universe in which he lives. Job had been comfortable with what he knew about the world in which he lived. He felt he had sufficient enough grasp of the way that God dealt with and operated the world that he could build his case on that knowledge. His confidence in his claims to be right and to have been wronged by God were built on his certainty in his understanding. The same, of course, was true for Job's older three friends. It was true to the point that they were apparently oblivious even to the possibility that their understanding was fundamentally flawed.

But then Yahweh arrived and opened up a world beyond the comfortable limits with which Job and his friends had lived. He suggested, through the persistent barrage of questions that repeatedly demonstrated just how little they really knew, that their worldview was too limited and too narrow for them to understand truly the complexities that Yahweh had to apply his wisdom to from moment to moment in governing the universe. We might summarize the rhetorical effect of Yahweh's speeches to Job, his friends, and to us, by reference to the words that Shakespeare has Hamlet say to Horatio:

> There are more things in heaven and earth, Horatio,
> Than are dreamt of in your philosophy. (*Hamlet*, act 1, scene 5, lines 166–67)[21]

The wisdom and knowledge of Job and his friends inevitably falls far short of that required to truly comprehend the scope of God's sovereign administration of the universe.

The danger for us is exactly the same as that of Job and his friends. It might even be exacerbated by our place in history. We live at a time when the fundamental forces of the universe are understood far more accurately than when Job lived. We can do things and explain things that Job could not even have dreamt about. We can even answer quite a few of the questions that Yahweh posed to Job. Does this mean that we are now in a position to make valid judgments on God's behavior in a way that Job tried to but failed? When bad things happen to good people today, are we now so much more enlightened than Job and his friends were that we can have a far surer basis for thinking that God has failed us, or may really not be paying attention? The temptation is real, and for many who are rightly deeply troubled by the suffering they see in the world today, or for those who believe that science has dispensed with the need for a Creator, confidence in our collective knowledge and wisdom as a species has been enough for them to thus judge God. Implicit in rejection of God is, after all, a fundamental judgment made by each person that their understanding is sufficient to reach that conclusion.

Yahweh's speeches function to undermine the confidence that Job and his friends had in their knowledge and wisdom. His questions should do the same

21. John Livingston Lowes (ed.), *Shakespeare's Hamlet* (New York: Henry Holt and Company, 1914), 35.

for us today although doubtless, were the story of Job written to a modern audience, many of the questions posed would be different, updated to address us more directly. In the same way that the questions posed to Job worked in such a way that he readily understood the questions but knew very clearly that he did not know the answer. It is relatively easy to pose questions so complex that it is not even clear what is being asked, but to better challenge the self-confidence of Job and his friends (and of us) it is important to understand the question in order to highlight our ignorance.

The climax of God's speech comes with questions and observations about the supernatural sea creature known as Leviathan. We know from elsewhere that this creature is an enemy of God, an untamed creature of chaos and evil whose abode is the sea (which is itself frequently a symbol of chaos and darkness in the Bible). In spite of this, Leviathan is entirely under Yahweh's control; it poses no threat to him. Evil and chaos are not given free rein in Yahweh's universe, just as the calamities that befell Job at the beginning of the book did not take place without Yahweh's approval.

At the very least this makes it clear that Job was right to seek an answer from God rather than, for example, the Satan. The buck, as they say, stops with God, for nothing happens in God's creation that falls outside of his control. This is not a dualistic universe wherein good and evil come about from an ongoing battle between Yahweh and the Satan and his forces. The forces of evil, represented in Yahweh's speech by Leviathan, do not have free rein. They are no match for Yahweh; they cannot act outside of God's sovereign control and will. Yet, when these forces may act seeking evil, the Bible elsewhere makes clear that Yahweh is at work in the very same events for good. As Paul prayed earnestly for the removal of his "thorn in [the] flesh," which he also described as "a messenger of Satan," he realized that it was given to him "in order to keep [him] from becoming conceited" (2 Cor 12:7–9). Joseph's brothers committed an evil act when they sold him into Egyptian slavery, and yet, as Joseph recognized, God was at work in their evil deed for good (Gen 50:20).

The ultimate example of this comes with the death of Jesus. The actions of Herod Antipas, Pontius Pilate, various gentiles, and Jews in conspiring to crucify Jesus was itself evil, yet they were doing what God "had decided beforehand should happen" for the good of all (Acts 4:27–28). Certainly, the intention of the Jewish and Roman authorities in crucifying Jesus was not to engineer the salvation of all, but that was God's purposes from the beginning. Furthermore, the Bible consistently presents this tension between God's sovereign control of the universe and human freedom to choose without sacrificing the agency of either. For many this tension poses a problem, and for some this is an insurmountable problem. We see that in John 6, where Jesus affirms divine agency in salvation—"No one can come to me unless the Father who sent me draws them, and I will raise them up at the last day" (John 6:44; cf. v. 65)—and yet the response of many listening was to turn away—"From this time many of his disciples turned back and no longer followed him" (John 6:66).

Can we reconcile this apparent contradiction? Many attempts have been made that invariably wind up affirming one side to the detriment of the other and, in so doing, lose sight of the balance inherent in the Bible's teaching on the subject. Stressing divine sovereignty at the expense of human choice (and therefore responsibility) results in a mechanistic universe where no creature has moral agency. Stressing human freedom at the expense of divine sovereignty results in a view of God who is himself contingent and subject to the whims of our wills. Neither view is supported by the Bible.

Rather, to maintain a biblical position means maintaining the tension inherent in the Bible's presentation. And what Yahweh's words to Job in Job 38–41 should teach us is that there are some things for which we are not going to be able to offer an adequate explanation. Some things are too complex and impenetrable for such finite, limited creatures as we are. After all, the entirety of our intellect can be contained within the space provided by our skulls, amounting to quite a bit less than two liters. Is it reasonable to expect a comprehensive understanding of the entire universe—let alone its Creator—to be available to us? That is the point Yahweh is making to Job and to us. At the heart of our salvation and at the heart of God's sovereign control over the creation is this mystery that allows God agency over everything and yet doesn't rob us of our own agency. The message of Yahweh to Job and to us is far more far reaching than simply saying that we may not always understand the reasons for suffering. It encompasses all of God's interactions with his creation.

And for this reason, this is not license for us to do evil! If God works through evil, how much more will he work through our good works that he has, after all, also prepared for those living as citizens of his kingdom with Jesus as Lord (Eph 2:8–10)? What we should take away is this simple truth: evil does not have ultimate control of the world or the universe, no matter how dire things appear (and they were certainly dire for Job). No, despite the terrible events around us, God is working out his good purposes. Whatever the reasons for Job's suffering—and by this stage we know that Job is not getting a clear answer on the reasons for his suffering—, we should by this point understand that despite how limited our understanding of the universe is, our confidence in God's ultimate goodness remains steady. We have seen, again and again, how apparent evil is used for good, such that we can reliably look forward to the end of the story of God.

CHAPTER 25

Job 42:1–6

Job's Response to Yahweh

LISTEN to the Story

[1]Then Job replied to the LORD:

[2]"I know that you can do all things;
no purpose of yours can be thwarted.
[3]You asked, 'Who is this that obscures my plans without knowledge?'
Surely I spoke of things I did not understand,
things too wonderful for me to know.
[4]"You said, 'Listen now, and I will speak;
I will question you,
and you shall answer me.'
[5]My ears had heard of you
but now my eyes have seen you.
[6]Therefore I despise myself
and repent in dust and ashes."

Listening to the Text in the Story: The annals of "Tiglath-Pileser I," king of Assyria

Encounters between gods and humans are recorded in a number of texts from the ancient Near East. In some texts a human response is recorded, although the situation is complex. The Neo-Assyrian ruler Tiglath-Pileser I recounted, for example, the reaction of a military opponent to the appearance of the god Ashur, noting that "terror and fear of the splendor of Ashur, my Lord, overwhelmed [the enemy]."[1] This is not atypical among such texts in

1. Jeffrey Niehaus, "Joshua and Ancient Near Eastern Warfare," *JETS* 31.1 (1988): 42–43; cf. "Tiglath-Pileser I," trans. D. D. Luckenbill (*ANET*, 277, 281–282, 286–287, 289, 294); "Cylinder

its focus on the reaction of an enemy to the divine presence. Complicating matters further is the divine status accorded the monarch in much ancient Near Eastern thought, such that in some texts the splendor (or glory) of the king overwhelms the enemy in much the same was as that of the gods. As such, any record of the king being humbled by an encounter with a god would seem inappropriate. By contrast, in the Bible, any encounter by any person—common, royal, or even prophet—results in that person being overwhelmed.

EXPLAIN the Story

Job's Concession of Ignorance and Job's Comfort (42:1–6)

Job's final words contain a number of difficulties that deserve some detailed discussion if we are to arrive at a satisfactory understanding of the significance of the book as a whole.

Job's response to Yahweh's appearance in the preceding chapters is to recognize both God's omnipotence and omniscience—that God can do anything and knows everything. But more significant are the consequences of this for Job, who has not been able to answer any of the questions posed by Yahweh in the preceding chapters. Job realizes his own ignorance. While Job was counted as among the wisest of his time, only now does he finally see just how inadequate his knowledge of the world really is. And Job readily admits this now: "Surely I spoke of things I did not understand" (v. 3). Job realizes that his insistent claims about injustice arose out of ignorance rather than knowledge.

In verse 3, Job quotes God's question from Job 38:2. This is the one question Job is ready to answer. The NIV's reference to "my plans" (i.e., God's plans) refers to God's plan or design for his creation. Job had called into question the way that God dealt with his creation, believing that he knew far more than he has now come to realize that he did.

The idea of Job's ignorance is reinforced in his subsequent words. He admits to speaking of things he did not know. The last line of verse 3 can be translated in a couple of ways, but the NIV's "*too wonderful* for me to know" can also be translated as "things *too difficult* for me to know" (the same translation is used, for example, in the NIV Deut 17:8: "if cases come before your courts that are *too difficult* for you to judge"). This better fits with Job's newfound awareness

Inscription of Tiglath-Pileser I," in *The Annals of the Kings of Assyria*, ed. E. A. Wallis Budge and L. W. King (London: British Museum, 1902), 1:42; "Shalmaneser III," trans. K. Lawson Younger Jr. (*COS* 2.113:261, 274, 276, 290, 292); "Esarhaddon's Thompson Prism (Nineveh A)," trans. Victor Avigdor Hurowitz (*COS* 4.39:175).

of just how little he really knows about God's workings in his universe. It is not just something he finds difficult to learn, such as a foreign language that we find difficult to master but, given time and effort, eventually acquire. No, it is not just difficult; it is "too difficult," that is, it is impossible for Job to know these things, and he has, at last, understood and realized the point.

While many people understand Job to be repenting later in verse 6 (see below), if there is any repentance made in Job's response, it occurs here in verse 3. It is here that Job acknowledges that he has spoken without understanding, and so he has said things that he really should not have. The fact that he does not utter the word "repent" here avoids any chance of the reader inferring that Job had actually done something that warranted his suffering or counted as sinful, but his acknowledgment here is an expression of a limited form of repentance for some of the things he had said and thought from chapter 3 onward.

For a second time in his response Job paraphrases Yahweh's words (vv. 4–5; see 38:3 and Elihu's words in 33:31) as a way to introduce his final response in the next verses. This is the only place in the Bible where the Hebrew phrase found here is translated "heard of you" as opposed to "heard you," and while the context seems to demand it, it may be that Job's reference to hearing God is a reference to his experience in Job 38–39 that left him almost speechless (cf. Job 40:4–5) but that, as the need for another speech from Yahweh demonstrated, did not bring Job to the point of understanding. Elsewhere in the Old Testament, hearing and seeing often go together to represent a more complete understanding of a matter (e.g., 2 Kgs 20:5; Isa 18:3; 37:17; 38:5), suggesting that Job is not claiming that he knew nothing of God before this encounter but rather that in light of this encounter he has come to understand far more than he did before. "But now" Job has seen Yahweh—perhaps not literally unless he is referring to the whole experience of the theophany but rather meaning that he now more fully understands (see, e.g., Job 9:11; Prov 7:7 where "seeing" and "understanding" are used in parallel). Job describes the transformation of his understanding as a result of his encounter with God, despite the fact that God did not answer any of his questions.

The meaning of verse 6 also poses a few difficulties that need to be addressed. The first clause, "therefore I despise myself," is complicated because "myself" is supplied in NIV, whereas the Hebrew lacks an object for the verb translated "despise," which elsewhere means "refuse, reject." As such, most English versions suggest that Job is himself the object of the verb. But this is far from certain and seems largely to be influenced by the reading of the second clause. If Job is rejecting his previous statements about and to God, then it would fit with him repenting in the second clause of the verse. However, given the subsequent approval of Job's words by God in verse 7 and the preferred understanding of the remainder of this verse outlined below, that seems improbable.

The best understanding of the clause understands Job here to be withdrawing his complaint against Yahweh.[2] This resolves one of the major issues in the book by letting us know that Job has finally found some resolution to his complaints against God. While he has not been given any specific answer, he has had his eyes opened to see just how vast and complex the universe he lives in is, and how ultimately simplistic was his expectation that he ought to be able to comprehend the way that God governs creation.

The second clause in verse 6 then completes the resolution of Job's situation in the book. Although many Bible translations record Job's repentance here, it raises quite a few questions. In Job 42:7 God will indicate that Job did not speak incorrectly about God, and in the opening chapters we have been assured that Job did nothing of which he needed to repent. If he here repents, does that not vindicate his friends' arguments? Furthermore, the friends' words prompt the need for sacrifices to be made, but no sacrifices are required of Job for his own actions. The question has surprised and confused many readers of Job. However, the Hebrew word here typically translated "repent" (*nkhm*) can also mean "to comfort, console,"[3] and indeed it has this meaning every other time it appears in Job (see 2:11; 7:13; 16:2; 21:34; 29:25; 42:11). Looking at these passages we see that "comfort" is something of a theme in the book and a concern of Job's.[4] Job looks to be comforted through his troubles, and so it makes good sense to find that, in the end, he finds comfort from his newfound awareness of the complexity of the universe and the inadequacy of the simplistic application of retributive justice. He now knows that a person can suffer, and that suffering is not necessarily indicative of some specific sin that would have prompted it. Furthermore, that Job is here said to find comfort following Yahweh's words to him further highlights the failure of his friends as comforters, for in all their many words Job was not comforted.[5]

What of the "dust and ashes" in 42:6? These words are often understood to be a reference to either Job's mortality, which is how they are used in Gen 18:27, or else to repentance, although "dust and ashes" are not elsewhere

2. See Clines, *Job 38–42*, 1218–23.

3. As opposed to the verb *shwb*, "turn, return, repent," see "שׁוב," *HALOT* 1429–30, esp. under qal, §§1–2.

4. So, Clines noted that "one way of viewing Job's deepest longing is as a need for 'comfort'"; see Clines, *Job 1–20*, 190.

5. For a more detailed discussion of the Hebrew text, see Martin A. Shields, "The Ignorance of Job," *ABR* 68 (2020): 28–39; Clines, *Job 38–42*, 1218, 1220–21.

associated with this act. However, they are also associated with mourning (e.g., Ezek 27:30). Understood thus, Job here announces that he has finally found comfort over the tragedies that unfolded in the opening chapters of the book. Further support for this understanding of these words is found in the use of these key words in those chapters where Job's friends arrive to comfort him (Job 2:11). At that time, from a distance they see him sitting in ashes (2:8) and in response they throw dust over their heads (2:12). This closing reference to dust and ashes thus recalls again the opening of the story, helping bring closure to the story and reinforcing that Job has now found a resolution to his situation that he finds acceptable, even if not comfortable.

LIVE the Story

Encountering God

The final chapter of the book of Job recounts Job's response to his encounter with God. The invariable outcome of such encounters throughout the Bible always results in the human witness expressing a full awareness of their comparative status. The Creator, unsurprisingly, overwhelms the creature. Encountering God in this way is something so outside the normal realm of experience that there is nothing that prepares us for the event.

Perhaps the ultimate biblical example of this is the encounter with Yahweh experienced by the prophet Isaiah (Isa 6). Isaiah, who had already spent five chapters delivering prophecies, encountered Yahweh and immediately felt his life to be in danger. Directly encountering God's glory through such a theophany is always so far outside of our experience that there is simply no way to be fully prepared for it. Even if we might try and argue that Jesus has prepared us for such an encounter by coming and living among us, the New Testament still records encounters between humans and the risen Messiah in terms that make it clear that the people involved were not prepared (e.g., Matt 17:1–8 // Mark 9:2–7; Rev 1:17).[6]

So it is that Job's encounter with God, together with God's words to Job spoken during that encounter, have transformed Job's understanding—a transformation that is evident in his response here. Job was never given an answer by God. He never found out why he suffered and lost so much. Yet, despite this we see him now satisfied—we might say he has closure. Before this point we have seen his faith in the justice and goodness of God shaken by his

6. See also George Savran, "Theophany as Type Scene," *Prooftexts* 23.2 (2003): 130–31.

circumstances, leading him to question God and the wisdom that God applied as he worked in the lives of his people. What has changed has not been a revelation of the reasons for his suffering but a revelation of the complexity of the universe as well as the manner in which it is governed by God and the finitude of human understanding.

For Job this was enough to make it clear that his expectations built on the assumption that the circumstances of one's life somehow reflect an immediate judgment on one's behavior, such that the good are rewarded and the bad are punished, were misplaced. God had revealed to Job the complexity of the universe by simply and repeatedly highlighting the extent of Job's ignorance about the world around him. It became clear to Job that he really did not know as much as he had thought he did. This was a clear case where, through learning more, Job realized he knew less than he previously thought he did. His eyes were opened to the extent of his knowledge and the extent of his ignorance. When Job came to realize, after being faced with God's unanswerable questions, how little he understood, he came to understand that his view of justice was just as small as his view of the universe. It was this realization that allowed him to maintain his faith in God's goodness, justice, and faithfulness.

This should speak to us as well. Job's story makes faith in the real world possible. Like Job, we experience things in our world and in our own lives that we cannot understand and that we find difficult to reconcile with a loving, just God. There are times when we wonder what God could possibly be doing, when we might be tempted to wonder if God does not care, or has forgotten about us, or is angry at us for no clear reason. Or we are told by others that our faith is too weak, our works are insufficient, or we just need to do more and try harder to please God. And such explanations may be fine in instances where we can see clear reasons for the problems that befall us. But what of occasions when there is no clear reason, such as when we are left with an instinctive feeling of injustice or when the trite explanations of others simply do not stack up with the realities that we (or others) are facing?

It is at such times that the book of Job should speak to us. In the midst of the inexplicable injustices of life, Job reminds us that we live in a complex universe that God governs from its beginning to its end, and his purposes span time and space. We, like Job, see only our miniscule part in this vast scheme and fail to appreciate the whole. Job had his eyes opened by his encounter with God and finally realized that his worldview was too small.

Once we understand this part of Job's story, we are freed to believe. This perspective helps us to see that our messed-up lives in this messed-up world are not incompatible with God's purposes, and they do not indicate that God has let us down, forgotten us, or is somehow dissatisfied with us. Beyond all this, we are far, far better off than Job, for we are better off than any Old Testament saint. We are better off even than John the Baptist—the last prophet of the old covenant and one who lived to see the arrival of the Messiah (Matt 11:11). For we can look back on the time that our Messiah walked the earth, died, and rose again, and having done so, we see the fullness of God among us, showing us God's true character. So, we know from Job that God's universe is incomprehensibly complex, and we know from Jesus that God has gone to the greatest of lengths so that we may know of his love for us, of his justice in dealing with sin, of his faithfulness, and of his wisdom. When we face suffering or do not understand what God is doing in the world, we have both the lesson of Job and the example of Jesus. Let us not forget, however, that despite this far more extensive knowledge and insight into God's purposes, we are still subject to limits. Although the desire to understand the reason for the things that happen to us will likely never depart, Job sets our expectations at a realistic level. There is no guarantee that God will explain to us everything that happens in our lives or in the lives of those around us. There is not even a guarantee that we would understand such an explanation if it were given! We are told that God loves us, that he wants what is best for us, and yet bad things do inevitably happen to us. Job faced this quandary, unable to account for his losses and suffering. Job felt, for a long time, that they reflected a failure on God's part, and we may feel the same thing.

This is what the story of Job brings to our own faith. We may not be like Job—blameless and upright—but those attributes of Job serve primarily to assure us that the suffering he faces does not arise as a result of the just desserts for some sinful action on his part. Job suffers, but it is not out of punishment. Neither he nor we fully understand why, yet in the end his faith in God remains, and he learns to accept that God has not made a mistake because he gains a new appreciation of his own finitude. When we face the reality that we cannot fully understand all that is happening to us—much less control it—we realize that trusting in our own understanding is ultimately placing faith in a house of cards. Instead, we have the option of trusting the God who has demonstrated his love for us by sending his Son into the world to reveal himself to us and to rescue us. Just as the person rescued from a desert island by a helicopter need not understand the mechanisms by which the helicopter operates to be rescued by it, we need not—and perhaps cannot—completely understand the works of God in bringing us through this life in this fallen world to the end where we may enjoy eternal life with him, a life without sin, suffering, death, or pain.

CHAPTER 26

Job 42:7–17

Job's Restoration

LISTEN to the Story

[7]After the LORD had said these things to Job, he said to Eliphaz the Temanite, "I am angry with you and your two friends, because you have not spoken the truth about me, as my servant Job has. [8]So now take seven bulls and seven rams and go to my servant Job and sacrifice a burnt offering for yourselves. My servant Job will pray for you, and I will accept his prayer and not deal with you according to your folly. You have not spoken the truth about me, as my servant Job has." [9]So Eliphaz the Temanite, Bildad the Shuhite and Zophar the Naamathite did what the LORD told them; and the LORD accepted Job's prayer.

[10]After Job had prayed for his friends, the LORD restored his fortunes and gave him twice as much as he had before. [11]All his brothers and sisters and everyone who had known him before came and ate with him in his house. They comforted and consoled him over all the trouble the LORD had brought on him, and each one gave him a piece of silver and a gold ring.

[12]The LORD blessed the latter part of Job's life more than the former part. He had fourteen thousand sheep, six thousand camels, a thousand yoke of oxen and a thousand donkeys. [13]And he also had seven sons and three daughters. [14]The first daughter he named Jemimah, the second Keziah and the third Keren-Happuch. [15]Nowhere in all the land were there found women as beautiful as Job's daughters, and their father granted them an inheritance along with their brothers.

[16]After this, Job lived a hundred and forty years; he saw his children and their children to the fourth generation. [17]And so Job died, an old man and full of years.

Listening to the Text in the Story: "The Code of Hammurabi" (Mesopotamian); "The Inheritance of a Brother and a Sister" (Alalakh); LXX expansions on Job 42:16–17

The LXX (i.e., the Septuagint, the Greek version of the Old Testament) expands somewhat on the conclusion to Job revealing something of how Job's ending was understood by some of its earliest interpreters and readers. The final verses of Job (written "Iob" in this translation of the Greek text) in the LXX read:[1]

> [16a]Now Iob lived after his calamity one hundred and seventy years, [16b]and all the years he lived were two hundred and forty-eight years. [[16]※and Iob saw his sons ※and the sons of his sons, a fourth generation, [17]※and Iob died, old and full of days.] [17aα]And it is written that he will rise again with those the Lord raises up. [17bα]This man is interpreted from the Syriac book as living in the land of Ausitis, on the borders of Idumea and Arabia, and previously his name was Iobab; [17cα]now he took an Arabian wife and fathered a son, whose name was Ennon, and he in turn had as father Zare, a son of the sons of Esau, and as mother Bosorra, so that he was the fifth from Abraam. [17dα]And these are the kings who reigned in Edom, which country he too ruled: first Balak the son of Beor, and the name of his city was Dennaba, and after Balak, Iobab, who is called Iob, and after him Hasom, who was a leader from the Thaimanite country, and after him Hadad son of Barad, who cut down Madiam in the plain of Moab, and the name of his city was Geththaim. [17ea]Now the friends who came to him were: Eliphaz, of the sons of Esau, king of the Thaimanites, Baldad, the tyrant of the Sauchites, Sophar, the king of the Minites. (NETS)

Some of the details included in the LXX of chapter 42 appear to be an attempt to link Job into the mainstream of biblical history (so the reference to him previously being named Iobab; see Gen 10:29; 36:33–34). The only other facet of these additions is the clear reference to the resurrection and Job's participation in it, a reference that dates these additional details to a period considerably later than the original composition of the Hebrew text of Job.

One other surprising aspect to the story—at least surprising in the ancient world—is that Job's daughters are assigned an inheritance along with his sons. It was the normal practice that only sons would receive an inheritance because when a daughter married, she generally came into her husband's family. The consequence of this would be that any land she held title to would essentially be entailed away from the father's family. While this may not sound like a big

1. The sections marked ※ come from the second-century AD Jewish revisor Theodotion.

deal, it was in the ancient world where this could jeopardize the future wealth of the father's family.

Despite this, there are instances in the ancient world where daughters did inherit, and not just those times when there were no sons in the family. One example can be found in an Old Babylonian text from Alalakh, "The Inheritance of a Brother and a Sister."[2] The text records a legal dispute between a brother and sister over their inheritance, which was brought before the king as a judge. The sister, Bittatti, claimed an equal share in the father's estate, whereas her brother Abbael argued that she ought to receive no share. The king's decision is recorded as follows:

> 19 The king replied as follows:
> 21 Let Abbael choose and take
> 20 from the estate the property that he wants.
> 22 The property that he rejects, Bittatti
> 23 shall take.
> 24 Thus the king replied.

Following this decision, the estate is divvied up and Bittatti does receive a share.

In "The Laws of Hammurabi," there is allowance for a wife to be given part of the estate, after which she may grant it to one of her children, and there's no clear prohibition against that being to a daughter:

> §150 If a man awards to his wife a field, orchard, house, or movable property, and makes out a sealed document for her, after her husband's death her children will not bring a claim against her; the mother shall give her estate to whichever of her children she loves, but she will not give it to an outsider.[3]

What is relevant here, however, is the concessional nature of the grant—it would still be unusual and hence a sign of special favor to the wife or daughter, as it appears to be with Job's daughters. Others of Hammurabi's laws explicitly allow for a daughter to receive a share of his estate under certain circumstances, making it clear that such inheritance was not unheard of in ancient Mesopotamia.[4] Indeed, under some circumstances—such as the failure

2. "The Inheritance of a Brother and a Sister" (Alalakh), trans. Richard S. Hess (*COS* 3.129:283).
3. "The Laws of Hammurabi," *COS* 2.131:345.
4. See laws 178–184, (*COS* 2.131:347).

of the father to provide a dowry for a daughter—inheritance of a share of the estate was mandated.

Zafrira Ben-Barak goes so far as to claim that the evidence suggests that "in Elam, it seems, a daughter legally enjoyed equal rights with sons in matters of inheritance."[5] The evidence does suggest, however, that this was the exception to the rule across the region in general, and the fact that it is noteworthy to the writer of Job here highlights the exceptional nature of the matter in ancient Israel.

EXPLAIN the Story

Restoration of Job's Friends and the Restoration of Job (42:7–17)

"You have not spoken the truth about me, as my servant Job has" (v. 7). These words of God could come as a surprise to some readers, for as Norman Snaith once noted, "the three friends have been thoroughly orthodox. . . . There are times when [Job] has gone near to accusing God of unjust and irresponsible behavior as any man can well go."[6]

God's assessment of Job's speech about him is thus, to say the least, surprising. After all, Job has not always spoken kind words of his Creator, he has only just admitted to his own ignorance, and God has explicitly accused him of obscuring the divine plan through his ignorance (38:2; 42:3). Thomas Krüger has highlighted the problem: "Was Job right when he said that God 'destroys the blameless and the guilty' and mocks the plight of the innocent 'when suddenly a scourge brings death' (9:22–23)? Is it true that God does not take action against evil and does not care about the victims of injustice (21; 24)? Has God 'disarmed and humbled' Job, 'regarded him as clay,' and made him 'like dust and ashes' (30:11, 19) without cause?"[7]

In addition to this, at the beginning of Yahweh's speeches Job was described as "one who obscures my plans with words without knowledge" (38:2). All this prompts the question of whether Yahweh's assessment of Job's words can at all be reconciled with what Job had actually said. This apparent discrepancy, however, should prompt us to pause and consider some relevant matters before leaping to conclusions.

---

5. Zafrira Ben-Barak, "Inheritance by Daughters in the Ancient Near East," *JSS* 25.1 (1980): 32.

6. Norman H. Snaith, *The Book of Job: Its Origin and Purpose* (London: SCM Press, 1968), 4.

7. Thomas Krüger, "Job Spoke the Truth About God (Job 42:7–8)," in *"When the Morning Stars Sang": Essays in Honor of Choon Leong Seow on the Occasion of His Sixty-Fifth Birthday*, ed. Scott C. Jones and Christine Roy Yoder, BZAW 500 (Berlin: de Gruyter, 2018), 71.

The first point to notice is that the words of Job described as truthful are only those "about" (woodenly translated, "to me") God. Second, the Hebrew term translated "the truth" here refers to what has been established as true.[8] That is, Yahweh is likely not simply offering blanket approval of everything that Job had said at any time in the preceding chapters.

While Job does indeed say such things about God, at other times he makes essentially the opposite claims. If all of Job's words about God are to be taken as true, then God is fundamentally and logically contradictory. While such a notion has a certain amount of appeal to modern readers who often revel in such paradoxes, reading the ancient text in that manner is fundamentally anachronistic. Inconsistencies in Job's thoughts, especially in light of his realization in 42:1–6 that his understanding is so inherently limited, ought not to be understood as a true representation of the character of God.

It is possible that God's words here refer to the words Job has just spoken in conversation with Yahweh in verses 1–6 (as opposed to earlier when Job's words were rhetorically addressed to God but went without response from God). Krüger objects that verses 7–8 seems to refer only to God's speech of the preceding chapters and ignores verses 1–6, and so it seems unlikely that it refers to those words. Yet, such an objection is overly pedantic.

It has also been suggested that it would be better to read these words as "you have not spoken the truth *to me* as my servant Job has."[9] The Hebrew certainly allows this reading, and Job has addressed God on a number of occasions, most recently in the immediately preceding verses. On the other hand, Job's friends have never addressed God directly, so God's objection here may seem rather odd. Yet, it would certainly be true, if they had never addressed God, to say that they had not spoken the truth to God as Job had just done.

Furthermore, objecting to God's assessment of Job's words as truthful fails to read the intention of these words. God is not so much interested in the words spoken but their meaning—and so what is approved of is that Job's expression of his newfound understanding of the manner in which God oversees the universe, including the lives of women and men, has come to incorporate

8. See Clines, *Job 38–42*, 1227, who notes "lit. 'the established (thing)' . . . used elsewhere in the sense of 'the truth' at Ps 5:9 (10); Deut 13:14 (15), and 'what is proper' at Exod 8:26; at Gen 41:32 it means 'fixed' . . . , at Ps 57:7 (8) of the heart being 'steadfast'—as well as 'established' in more obvious contexts, e.g., of David's throne (2 Sam 7:16). Here it is translated 'the thing that is right' (KJV), 'what is right' (RSV, NIV), 'truthfully' (JB), 'correctly' (NJB), 'truth' (NJPS), 'as you ought' (NEB)."

9. For example, see Manfred Oeming, "Ihr Habt nicht recht von mir geredet wie mein Knecht Hiob: Gottes Schlusswort als Schüssel zur Interpretation des Hiobbuches und als kritische Anfrage an die modern Theologie," *EvT* 60 (2000): 103–16.

the lesson God had set out to teach in his speeches. Job's friends—excluding Elihu—had not understood this lesson. The premise of their understanding lay in their presumption that God operated according to their strict application of retributive justice. Their understanding failed to appreciate the breadth and complexity of the universe and so left them misunderstanding God's ways.

Perhaps the best understanding, then, is to see in God's words here a commendation of Job's prior conversation with him in the opening verses of this chapter. Further, if Job is commended for the truth of his observation that God's ways are inscrutable, that fits with the overall message of the book of Job itself: the hidden things belong to Yahweh. The failure of the friends to reach the same conclusion, as reflected in their continual appeal to the idea of retributive justice, is reflected here in God's judgment upon them. Yet, hope is not lost for them, as the following verses make clear.

In light of their failure to speak the truth about Yahweh, his anger against them warrants some action. In verses 8–9 God makes it clear to Eliphaz what action is necessary to propitiate his anger: the sacrifice of seven bulls and seven rams. As David Clines points out, this is a relatively high price—elsewhere a similar count of animals appear as sacrifices for what seem to be far more significant situations, such as at the installation of the ark of the covenant (cf. 1 Chr 15:26).[10] What we should not miss, however, is that the number seven is used here and probably appears to make the point that the complete number of sacrifices was necessary.

What is also noteworthy is that the sacrifices themselves are not all that God requires here. In fact, God makes it clear that it is actually Job's intercessory prayer on behalf of his friends that will be the key to their forgiveness. The sacrifices themselves do place a cost on the forgiveness of the friends, for the bulls and rams would have been of considerable value, and it is a cost that they must bear. But there remains more, and that is Job's prayer. Such prayer reflects the notion found elsewhere in the Bible that mediation sometimes forms an integral part in the restoration of one's relationship with God. Moses, for one, mediates for various people (or all the people) on a number of occasions (e.g., Exod 32:11–14; Num 21:7; Deut 9:20).

Job had himself hoped to find a mediator to help him (e.g., Job 9:33–35; 16:19–21). The story of God consistently presents us with the need for a mediator when we face God, someone who can speak when we cannot. Job had hoped for one when he thought his problem was that God was his enemy. Now he has come to learn that God was not his enemy. Instead, Job's friends

10. See Clines, *Job 38–42*, 1232.

now need a mediator, and Job will fulfill that role for them. Ultimately, however, the perfect mediator would come when God himself walked among us in the person of Jesus.

The remainder of Job's story, recounted in 42:10–17, spans many years but only a few verses. There is nothing particularly difficult to understand in these words: he is restored with double the wealth he had previously and with more children, and he lives a long life. Long life is, throughout the Old Testament, a sign of God's blessing and favor (e.g., Gen 25:8; 35:29; 2 Chr 24:15).

Job's extended family arrive and bring him gifts—a piece of silver and a gold ring. At the time the story of Job is set, there was no money, and so quantities of silver, gold, or other precious materials served in its place. Furthermore, the amount they give him here would hardly have been sufficient to restore his fortunes, and so they are likely symbolic of his restoration.

The numbers of Job's livestock here are exactly double those he had in the prologue (see Job 1:3). The numbers, once again, are likely here in part because of the symbolism associated with them. That the values seven and ten that formed the basis for the numbers in the prologue are here doubled points not only to an affirmation of the blessing that Job enjoyed then but also to the generosity of Yahweh, as he essentially doubles Job's blessing—a point made clear in verse 12, where the rationale for Job's new wealth is specifically stated to be attributed to Yahweh's blessing.[11]

The number of Job's children, unlike his livestock, is not doubled. While there could be no replacing the children Job lost in the prologue (and the number here does remind us of those children he had lost), to be left without children in the ancient world would have been considered a sign that one was under a curse or bearing God's displeasure. To ensure that we are not left with such an impression, it is made clear that Job is left no worse off, at least in terms of progeny to carry on his line, than he was before. This is made clear by the explicit reference to the distribution of his estate in verse 15 in a highly unusual way. Not only did his sons inherit a portion of Job's estate but his daughters did as well. This was far from the norm in ancient Israel and throughout much of the ancient Near East (see the comments under Listen to the Story above). Job was no Scrooge; he was generous beyond expectation even when distributing his estate.

In addition to demonstrating Job's generosity to his daughters, there are

11. See Hartley, *Book of Job*, 540. Some suggest that the doubling of Job's wealth was Yahweh's way of compensating Job for all of his trouble. The difficulty with such a view is that it presumes to know more than we do about why Job suffered, and it runs counter to the explicit explanation provided in the text in verse 12.

a couple of other notable points to make about his children. The prologue focused on the sons—it was they who celebrated with (possibly birthday) feasts in their homes and, while the daughters were included in the festivities, they did not get their own feasts. Here in the final verses of the book, however, the focus falls firmly on Job's daughters: they are named while the sons are not, and they share the inheritance. This marks a clear contrast with the depiction of Job's children in the prologue. What is not entirely clear is the significance of this distinction. So, for example, while we are told the daughters' names, we are not told the significance of those names. Names in the Bible frequently reveal something of the character of the person bearing that name, and while scholars suggest various significances for the names of Job's daughters here, there is no clear consensus.

The names are Jemimah (from the Aramaic for "turtledove"), Keziah (the name of an aromatic spice), and Keren-Happuch (probably referring to a small container of black eye makeup).[12] The note in the next verse suggests that, if anything, the names reflect their beauty, and the connection can be readily seen. "Dove" is used of the beloved in the Song of Songs (although that is a different Hebrew word, the point remains true), sometimes in parallel with the expression "my flawless one" (e.g., Song 5:2; 6:9), but always emphasizing the beauty of the beloved. With the name Keziah it should be noted that spices were not just used in cooking but also in perfumes (e.g., Ps 45:8; Prov 7:17). So again the term is associated in some way with beauty. Finally, for Keren-Happuch, makeup would serve to highlight the beauty of the person wearing it.

For some the contrast in Job's treatment of his daughters between the prologue and epilogue reflects his recognition that the patriarchal culture of his time did not treat women well. For some it grows out of all that Job had endured: the loss of his original children, his own suffering, and his ill health—all of which prompt a new appreciation for the precious children he now has. Still others point to some ancient Near Eastern epics wherein daughters are highlighted as a reflection of the blessing that has befallen the father and his consequent generosity and wealth. In reality it may be that there is some truth in all of these points. Through his suffering and loss Job has become more acutely aware of the value of all of his children—daughters and sons—and of ensuring their wellbeing into the future out of the newfound wealth that God has lavished upon him.

Finally, we are told that Job lived a long life. The reference to 140 years

12. Clines, *Job 38–42*, 1238.

is also a noteworthy number, for it is twice seventy (see Ps 90:10) and so incorporates the values we saw in the prologue that lent symbolic weight to his wealth (i.e., seven and ten) and then, in line with his wealth in these verses, doubles them. It is likely that this, too, highlights the extent of Yahweh's blessing of Job. It is also noteworthy that we are not told of the full length of Job's life; the text highlights the duration "after this," as though Job's life had begun anew with his restoration.

LIVE the Story

Does the End of Job's Story Spoil the Message of the Book?

For some readers, the happy ending to the book of Job is thought to undermine the entire point of the book. If the initial wager between God and the Satan has, at its heart, the idea that it is possible for a human to be devoted to God and to worship him without that devotion being at its heart an act of self-interest, then the happy ending is seen as sending the message that if you persevere through the hard times then ultimately God will reward you. There will indeed be light at the end of the tunnel. Clines, for example, writes that "what the book has been doing its best to demolish, the doctrine of retribution, is on its last page triumphantly affirmed."[13]

Such a view, however, misreads the book and its message. The wager between God and the Satan in the prologue to the book is not about proving that God is mean or nasty or unloving. It shows that Job's devotion to God was not entirely motivated by self-interest and that it would persist without all of the blessings that he had enjoyed. What is more, as noted in the commentary in the opening chapters, God's faith in Job was vindicated when, after losing everything, Job maintained his faith and did not reject God. The wager had been won; God had been proved right.

It is also a misunderstanding of the book of Job to think that, in undermining the simplistic application of the idea of retributive justice, it was dispensing with any and all notions of justice. It claims too much for the message of the book of Job to suggest that just because we cannot interpret every instance of individual suffering as a sign of God's judgment on that person that God never punishes wickedness. Similarly, it is inappropriate to interpret all good fortune in someone's life as a sign of divine approval. The truth lies in the middle of

13. David J. A. Clines, "Deconstructing the Book of Job," in *What Does Eve Do to Help? And Other Readerly Questions to the Old Testament*, JSOTSup 94 (Sheffield: Sheffield Academic, 1990), 113.

these two positions, halfway down the slippery slope from one extreme to the other. God is just and justice demands appropriate reward and punishment, so in the end we must see that justice is done or else the book of Job would have proven rather more than its author set out to prove.

That is not to say that the happy ending of the book of Job does not raise a problem. The problem, however, is not that it undermines the fundamental claim of the author but rather that it took so long to arrive. If the book has not set out to paint God as mean and nasty, why did Job have to wait so long for restoration after the wager had been won? Why did he continue to suffer if God truly is a God of love, who cares for his creatures, who protects his servants and wants the best for them? This is the real question raised by the long-delayed restoration of Job.

The answer to this question is one of the "riddles of the wise" (see Prov 1:6). The wisdom literature that is found in the Bible, and particularly in Job and Ecclesiastes, should be read with an eye on the realization that the sages' teachings were often couched in riddles where the whole picture could only be revealed through careful unraveling of those riddles through the lens of the fear of God. This is precisely the message of Proverbs 1:6–7, where the writer has made it clear that true understanding of the teachings of the wise is bound up with a true relationship with the Creator:

> [The book of Proverbs is]
> for understanding proverbs and parables,
> the sayings and riddles of the wise.
> The fear of the Lord is the beginning of knowledge,
> but fools despise wisdom and instruction. (Prov 1:6–7)

Any fool can quote a proverb or repeat a wise saying (Prov 26:7), but that does not make him or her wise. No, wisdom is bound up in understanding how that wisdom applies to life. And that understanding is inextricably bound up in a correct relationship with God—what the Bible calls the "fear of the Lord."

What, then, does all this tell us about the happy ending to the book of Job? It tells us that there is more to the story than first meets the eye. If the wager that we as readers are privy to in the prologue to the book was won by the end of the second chapter, then there is something else going on that prompts the next forty chapters. Job's continued suffering, the protracted debates, and all the many questions all point to there being other reasons for Job's continued suffering and the long delay in his restoration. So, what is the reason for that long delay?

We are not told. We never find out.

I know, it is a frustrating answer. But that this is the answer makes perfect sense, if you think about it. If, as I have argued, the primary message of the book of Job is that finite, limited human beings cannot realistically expect to understand the way that God governs a vastly complex universe in order to bring about his purposes, then there are always going to be things that happen in our lives which we cannot understand. This was the case for Job, of course, who is never told why he suffers. But it is also the case for each of us. There is no guarantee to us from God that we will, at the end of our lives, be able to look back and understand exactly what God was doing at each and every point. There are almost certainly going to be difficult times in life where we cannot clearly see what God is doing. We will never understand the full ramifications of everything that happens in our lives, how those things affect us and those around us in a world of billions of people on one planet orbiting one star out of billions in one galaxy out of billions in the universe. God is sovereign over it all, and to think that we should be able to comprehend the manner in which things that happen to us work their way out in such a complex universe would be the ultimate act of self-deception.

If indeed the major lesson of the book of Job is that we should not expect to understand everything, then the rather clever way the author has driven that point home to us, the readers, is by ensuring that we do not know everything.

Where does that leave us? It leaves us with a happy ending and the fear of Yahweh. These two things go hand in hand. The fear of Yahweh drives us to know who God is, and ultimately that points us to Jesus as the full revelation of God. We know that God is love and that God is at work in all things for the good of those who believe (Rom 8:28). And we are also left with a promise of a happy ending. For Job, living at a time when so much remained to be revealed—not least the revelation of the Son of God—the happy ending was expressed in terms of this life: material and familial blessings and long life. We, however, live on the other side of the cross, the central event in all human history, and so have a clearer perspective—we know far more of the story of God. For us, for those who trust God and have been reconciled to him, living with Jesus as Lord, the happy ending we look forward to takes on far more profound expression:

> Then I saw "a new heaven and a new earth," for the first heaven and the first earth had passed away, and there was no longer any sea. I saw the Holy City, the new Jerusalem, coming down out of heaven from God, prepared as a bride beautifully dressed for her husband. And I heard a loud voice

from the throne saying, "Look! God's dwelling place is now among the people, and he will dwell with them. They will be his people, and God himself will be with them and be their God. 'He will wipe every tear from their eyes. There will be no more death' or mourning or crying or pain, for the old order of things has passed away." (Rev 21:1–4)

CHAPTER 27

An Epilogue to the Book of Job

Just as the book of Job is framed by a prologue and epilogue, it seems appropriate to structure this commentary similarly. I began with a brief account of a tragic event. Now that we have come to the end of Job's story, it seems appropriate to ask whether we can take what we have learned from Job and apply it in any way to terrible situations that arise in our lives and in the lives of those around us. What does the book of Job have to say, for example, to my friend Anne, whom I mentioned in the introduction?

There seem to be a number of reasons to think it has little to say at all. Job was, as noted at the beginning of this commentary, rather unlike each of us. He was an incomparable individual in his day, and he is no less incomparable today. Who today could reasonably claim to be such that God would say of them that, "there is no one on earth like [them]; blameless and upright, . . . who [fear] God and [shun] evil" (Job 1:8)? In fact, anyone who made such a claim would likely be considered to be living in a fantasy world. There was, after all, no one on earth like Job—both then and now.

Yet, Job's unique nature serves to assure us that the calamities that befell him were not deserved. And if Job could suffer as he did "for no reason," then the rationale for our own suffering can only be less certain. If Job suffered for some reason other than his own personal sin, then we can be assured that our own suffering cannot be said, with any certainty, to be the result of some heinous personal sin that has been hidden away in our lives.

This is not to deny that in this life we may suffer consequences of our sin. But that was never in dispute; Job and all his friends agreed on that point. The problem arises when there is no specific sin and yet we suffer. It is here that Job's life story makes faith possible through the darkest moments of this life. When we find ourselves in those dark places, we find ourselves standing alongside Job. It is then that we understand not just intellectually but viscerally the inexpressible pain that Job faced. He lost everything. He desperately wanted to know why. At times we, too, will want an explanation, to understand how it is that God could let bad things happen to us or to those around us. Then we, like Job, will be faced with the choice to trust God or to curse God.

Job did the right thing. He sought an answer from God. And eventually

God did appear and speak to him. We might be tempted to object to any parallel between our situation and Job's at this point, noting that God has not appeared to us in the way that he did to Job. While there is some truth to this, it is at this point that we ought to remind ourselves of exactly what God said to Job. He spoke to Job at length but never explained Job's suffering. Not a hint about why he lost everything. No mention of a wager with the Satan, no revelation of any other reasons. Nothing.

Perhaps even more surprising—at least initially—was that Job was satisfied with the nonanswer he got from God. For rather than providing a specific answer to Job's unique, individual situation, the words God spoke—or more specifically, the questions God asked—teach a point that is relevant not just to Job but to us all. Not only did God remind Job that he had a very limited understanding of the universe, but he also expanded Job's appreciation of just how limited his perspective was and how little he really grasped of the complexities and vastness of all creation. Job finally understood the hubris inherent in the idea that he could possibly comprehend all that could feasibly be implicated in contributing to the circumstances he endured—both in his past and in the future. He could not have appreciated the impact of his suffering in the days, months, or years ahead of him on either himself or others. Job came to appreciate more fully the limits of his own understanding and, in the light of this, came to accept the wisdom of God even when—or especially when—he could not make sense of it.

The lesson Job learned should be something we learn as well, for it applies to each of us. We may have more knowledge at our disposal, but we will never have the capacity to understand the universe the way God does. At some point we have to decide to trust in God's goodness, and we have more reason to do so than Job did. For we now know the extent of God's love for us: "For he did not spare his own Son, but gave him up for us all. How will he not also, along with him, graciously give us all things?" (Rom 8:32).

Scripture and Extrabiblical Literature Index

Old Testament

Genesis

Exodus

Psalms

Proverbs

Jeremiah

Lamentations

Ezekiel

Daniel

Hosea

Joel

Amos

Obadiah

Jonah

Nahum

Habakkuk

Zephaniah

Haggai

Zechariah

New Testament

Matthew

Mark

Luke

John

Acts

1 John

Revelation

Ancient Near Eastern Texts

Deuterocanonical Books

Sirach

Pseudepigrapha

Greco-Roman and Early Christian Writings

Subject Index

Author Index